Mama's Curse

Mama's Curse

T.M. Morris

Dedication

I dedicate this book to my mother, Reverend Carmen Rose May (Mama), for she is responsible for my life, and my strength comes from her. Mama set the stage for how I responded to life's struggles and rewards. She provided me with a sense of family like no other, and because of her I am the woman, mother and wife that I am. Secondly, and most importantly, I dedicate this book to my husband Percy J. Morris Jr. and my two daughters, Brittany Alese, and Natalia "Tai" Sheree Edwards. They are and have always been my biggest supporters and caretakers, and have allowed me to nurture them and grow from every experience that we shared. Lastly, I welcome into my life a beautiful loving spirit, my Son-In-Law Michael Francis Edwards the son I never had. I love you all with all of my heart and soul.

Table of Contents

Disclaimer

PLEASE NOTE: THIS MEMOIR IS a compilation of my mother's recollection of events; my recollection of events; conversations with my mother, grandmother, my husband and daughters; my cousin Wilkerson Johnson Jr.; my experiences and perceptions since my birth in my personal life, and professional life in law enforcement. I have related them to the best of my knowledge. Some identities have been changed.

Foreword

I NEVER MET MY MOTHER. She, alongside my father, raised my sister and me.
I know her, but I never *met* her. I never met the Woman. I never met the
friend, the daughter, the wife, the little girl, the human being, and the survivor. I never truly knew her... until now. When my mother handed me the
manuscript, that our family now recognizes as the "first draft," with each
page, I began to peel back the layers of a woman I thought I had known all
my life. Within these pages reads a life connected by hundreds of thousands,
if not millions, of others across the globe. Each voice lends itself to the next,
in order to tell the story that is universally ours. It is often quoted that if we
don't learn from history, then we are bound to repeat it. Those historical types
of generational curses have plagued mankind since the dawn of time. It is
up to us to look at our lives and attempt to understand, attempt to learn, so
that each curse can be lifted and so that we can receive the blessing that was
promised to us long ago by Christ, Himself: Life, freedom, and most of all,
Love. Regardless of your religious or spiritual propensities, one thing that is
abundantly clear is we all have a purpose. In some way we are responsible to
reach out and love someone, a family member or a stranger because you never
know what anyone is going through. Our experiences shape us and in turn,
determine the quality of the experiences we have on the road to our destiny.
The strength, humility, Faith, vulnerability, and Love that it took to pen this
memoir is inspiring. If I can become a fraction of the woman that I now know
my mother to be today, I will have lived a truly fulfilling and successful life.
I thank God for my mother for telling this story, her story, because it is also

mine. If nothing else, this piece will serve as a starting point for the recorded history of my family. The lack of celebrity attached is perhaps the most important. We are not all rich and famous, nor are we public figures, whose lives are lived on the television screen in front of millions of viewers during prime time on weekdays; or dissected in the blogs of obnoxiously meddlesome twenty-something year olds attempting to make a name for themselves. But the value of the life that is described in this book is equally as, if not more, important because it speaks to the masses of the common folk. Those blue and white collar workers, who would otherwise be left invisible, unseen and unheard, are highlighted here; they are celebrated here for living the everyday life, neither fast paced nor slow; they are celebrated for their flaws and not-so-glamorous lifestyles. They are encouraged here to be vulnerable, open, and comfortable with themselves and reassured that they are strong and beautiful and that they matter. So, to my mother, the loyal friend, the faithful daughter, the scared little girl, the glorious human being, and the most beautiful survivor, thank you for telling your story. Thank you for telling ours.

Love, Brittany

Preface

◦──~○

STUDIES HAVE SHOWN THAT APPROXIMATELY 1 in 8 women in the United States will develop invasive breast cancer over the course of her lifetime. According to BreastCancer.org, in 2016, an estimated 246,660 new cases of aggressive forms of breast cancer were expected to be diagnosed in that same population, along with 61,000 new cases of non-aggressive types. It has also been shown that a woman's risk of breast cancer just about doubles if she has a first-degree relative such as a mother, sister, or daughter, who has been diagnosed with breast cancer. Ironically though, less than 15% of women who get breast cancer have a family member diagnosed with it and they inherit the condition as a sort of family heirloom; and about 85% of breast cancers occur in women who have absolutely no family history of the disease. As the daughter of a woman diagnosed with and overcome by breast cancer, and a survivor of the same ominous disease, I felt it was imperative that my daughters, their friends, my friends, and those women I don't know, be enlightened by my experiences. Many of life's tribulations tend to have a silver lining woven into their tapestries and serve to better the individuals who face them. I often wonder if I was one of the 15% of women who are diagnosed with breast cancer as a result of genetics or if I was an unfortunate member of the 85% of women who just happened to get it. You may not know me personally, but I truly believe that my story, my life, is also yours. This is not a book about breast cancer and the effects of radiation and chemotherapy; but it is about seeing life from a fresh perspective in order to close old dysfunctional doors and to open new, exciting possibilities for living a more fulfilling and unburdened life.

Introduction

I AM NO ONE. BUT I am everyone. I'm not a celebrity or public figure like Oprah or First Lady Michelle Obama, but I am you. I'm your mother, your sister, your best friend, your co-worker, your boss, the woman in line in front of you at the store, or perhaps the woman begging for change on the corner in front of *that* store. I am *everyone*. While the details of my story may differ greatly from yours, the essence of it rings universal. As the saying goes, "It takes a village to raise a child," I say it takes a village to survive life. As a wife to a loving husband and a mother to two incredible daughters, I have experienced the best gifts that life has to offer. Conversely, as a breast cancer survivor and law enforcement veteran for one of the most infamous police departments in the world, I've also seen humanity at its worst, both within the ranks and in the community. In my official capacity, I have witnessed and experienced some of life's most tragic events unfold, including generational curses such as gang violence, teenaged pregnancy, welfare and drug abuse, domestic and family violence, as well as the effects of untreated mental illness. When my 33-year career began to wind down in 2013, I had a lot of time to think about those generational curses and their respective societal impacts; and about how I was not so different from the poor souls I had vowed to protect and serve. I also thought of the possibility of being wrought with my own generational curse in terms of my family's breast cancer history, among other things. Was my bout with breast cancer a coincidental happening or circumstance? Or was I simply a casualty of my Mama's generational curse? Regardless of the answer, I know that as a result of my journey, I was changed for the better. So, here, I venture into the contemplative and historical journey to connect the dots of my life, and that of my family, in order to shed light and bring clarity to many of society's plagues, and what possible good can come from them. My story's no different than yours in all of the ways that matter. One thing I have learned for sure is that, cursed or not, none of us are alone.

"Weakened"

*"I'm weakened by chemicals strong enough to cause depletion of a virus
that can drain an entire species. Women...childbearing, nurturing by
nature, God-fearing, feminine seeds; a counterpart of man, Adam's Eve.
This disease plagues the very thing no one yet can see: the future. The future
to me may only and always be a dream but as a woman and mother, I'll
suffer all conditions and educate my daughter on early detection, infections
of lymph nodes, and cancer's inception. I'm weakened, sometimes being
brought to my knees because strength is a luxury that we all can't afford.
Hair falling from head to the floor, follicles once so full exist no more. I'm
weakened, but not broken, I'm hopeful but not hopeless. I'll speak the
unspoken silence of this potent violent plight, so I won't wait for mid-life
for a crisis to strike I'll fight this battle night after night until it's won and
if not by me, by someone. We take advantage of our lives until they are
compromised. I advise we shouldn't be afraid even though the odds may
seem stiff, because I believe that, if not all, some of us can beat this."*

-Tai French, *Phoenix*

CHAPTER 1

"The Appointment"

It was early in January 2006, and my husband, PJ, and I had come to terms with taking our Los Angeles home off the market. It was up for sale for a few months and we were only going to be able to hold the reservation on our new home until January 12th, when it would be released to another prospective buyer. It was a booming housing market just as it had been in the early 1990's, so contingent buyers, like us, were dropped like hot potatoes if they weren't ready to proceed in a timely manner. The homes in the new community were beautiful and sat on half acre lots, which was plenty of space for a lot of possibilities. We hired one of the top realtors in the area, who also lived in our gated-community. She had sold and re-sold many of the homes in the area, so we figured she was *the* one to sell ours. PJ and I agreed that if it was meant to be, our house would sell and we would move into the beautiful new home; and if it weren't meant to be, then we would accept that it wasn't meant for us to move.

On the Saturday prior to the January 12th deadline, our realtor scheduled what was supposed to be our last open house at 3pm that afternoon. PJ and I decided to catch a matinee so we scurried around trying to get out of the house before the potential buyers starting arriving. At about 1:30 PM we were leaving through the garage when we saw a man and a woman getting out of a newer model Mercedes Benz that was parked at the curb in front of our house. The woman walked towards the house and was inspecting the property.

"Can I help you? The open house starts at 3," I said in a polite tone as I set my purse on the back seat of my car. The man walked towards me and identified himself as the woman's real estate agent. PJ and I looked at each other and nodded in a silent agreement. "You're a little early, but do you want to come in and look around now?"

At that point we weren't standing on formality because by 6:01 that evening, if we didn't have a serious offer, our house was coming off the market. The realtor looked at his client and she expressed her happiness about going in early to see the property. I'm sure that me allowing them in early was against some real estate protocol, but oh well; we wanted to sell the house so we let them come in. PJ and I sat in the downstairs den as the realtor and his client walked about the interior. They had only seen the bottom half when the woman turned towards us.

"I like it. I want it."

PJ and I looked at each other and silently mouthed to each other *Shut the front door!* Well we said something like that. *Was this divine intervention or what?*

"Don't you want to at least see the upstairs?" I asked. We were hoping for a serious prospect and not just a "looky-loo," and the woman seemed seriously interested but we wanted to seal the deal. The woman eventually went upstairs, and liked upstairs even better than the downstairs.

"I want it just the way it is, furniture and all," she said.

"Uh, no, ma'am. The furniture isn't for sale," I responded.

The woman decided not to attempt to bargain with me and continued looking around the downstairs while her realtor feverishly tried to contact our realtor. Within minutes, our Agent pulled up to the house to meet with the prospective buyer. PJ and I thought about not going to the movie since we had an interested party but we kept our plans so that the realtor could move forward with the actual open house just in case the pending deal fell through. By the time we arrived at the movie, got our popcorn, and took our seats, both of our cell phones started ringing off the hook. It was our realtor desperately trying to reach us.

"Well, it looks like we have a buyer," she said excitedly. "She's a professional golfer, *and* she left a $20,000 cash deposit. She's got a pre-approved loan letter from Wells Fargo Bank, and has requested a 15-day escrow." Our realtor sounded so proud, you would have thought we were selling our house to Tiger Woods.

That woman was not playing, *and* she was serious about buying my furni-ture too. PJ and I were as excited as our realtor so we didn't stay to finish the movie. We returned home and met with our Agent and got the ball rolling.

"Ok, Ms. Tia, you need to go through the house and make a list of all the furniture that you are willing to let the buyer purchase with the house," the realtor advised. "And will you please let her have the drapes in the dining room? I don't know why you are trying so desperately to keep them."

"I got plans for those drapes in my new house." I responded playfully.

The drapes weren't custom made so I agreed to leave them hanging. Some of my furniture pieces I refused to part with regardless of how much the lady wanted to pay for them. Ultimately we came to an agreement as to what was included in the sale and we moved on. PJ and I couldn't wait to notify the new home community that our house had sold. The completion date of the new house was supposed to be in mid February 2006, which was about six weeks away, so there was no way we could commit to a short 15-day escrow. We agreed to a 30-day escrow instead, in order to time it just right to coincide with closing on our new property, however, when the clos-ing date arrived, we were notified that the gas meter at our new home would not be installed for yet *another* two weeks, which meant that we were essen-tially homeless for that period of time. It was a good thing our daughters, Brittany and Natalia, were away at college, so we didn't have to worry about their lives being interrupted. We put our belongings in storage and lived at the Hilton Hotel near downtown Los Angeles for that two-week period. It was like being on a really nice winter vacation except we were still working. Those two weeks flew by and when we got the nod we called the Moving & Storage Company, and scheduled delivery of our belongings to our new home. It was like a double move because we had to pay for the initial move into storage and then an additional $2500 for them to move our things from the storage facility to the new house.

PJ and I settled into the new house pretty quickly. We shopped for new furniture to go along with the few items we brought from the old house to fill every room in the new house. I loved brand new starts and the new house was a perfect new beginning. PJ and I both worked for the infamous Los Angeles

Police Department. I was a Lieutenant assigned to Internal Affairs Division and PJ was a Homicide Detective Coordinator working at Northeast Station in the Eagle Rock area of Los Angeles. Our new home was 58 miles from my office in Burbank, and 66 miles from PJ's office. The only thing that made our new commutes tolerable was that we each had company cars with free gas, which was a real perk. PJ and I joined the Police Department in 1981 and met in January 1982, when we were assigned as rookie officers at North Hollywood Division. PJ was a recent transplant from Atlanta, Georgia before he decided to join the department whereas I had been in California since I was 14 years old from Detroit, Michigan. My mother, or Mama as I called her, didn't want me to become a cop because she was afraid for my safety. I wanted nothing more than to be a big time police investigator so I convinced Mama that I would be ok. After much discussion, Mama agreed with my decision when she saw I was pretty adamant. Mama always encouraged me to be self-sufficient, and a job in law enforcement definitely afforded me the opportunity to do so. The bonus was that I found a good husband in the process.

"Baby, always have your own; don't depend on a man to take care of you; get your education because no one can take that away from you; a pretty face is a dime a dozen and beauty fades, so be smart and independent," she would say. I listened to all of Mama's admonitions time after time and I really took them to heart. One thing I loved about Mama was that no matter how many failed relationships she had, she never male bashed. Instead, she focused on me valuing myself.

In spite of Mama's fears, I survived the mean streets of Los Angeles and promoted up through the ranks, and out of the field. At this time in my career I was a 25-year veteran heading up a criminal unit investigating crooked cops. Although I was scheduled to be on 9-hour shifts in order to meet the demands of my workload, on most days I went in at 5 AM and ended my shift at 7 or 8 PM, which made for 12-14 hour shifts. The inherent stress of my job was taking a toll on my physical and mental being and I was working extra hard. My Assistant Officer-in-Charge position was vacant for a few months so the increased workload is what made my days longer and fuller than normal. I was literally burning the candle at both ends. It didn't help that my body was out of whack because I was forced into early menopause a few years earlier when I underwent a full hysterectomy due to a huge fibroid tumor, which had taken over a big portion of my abdomen. That sucker needed to come out.

It was the start of the spring semester for Brittany and Natalia at their respective universities. Brittany was at San Jose State University on a full basketball scholarship, and we were so thankful for the *full ride* because PJ and I had not saved up for college for the girls even though our expectation was that they would both go to college. We figured we would just pay when the time came. Brittany was a junior, and happy that this chapter in her life would soon be coming to an end. During her sophomore year, she went through a homesick meltdown phase and wanted to leave San Jose for another school closer to home in Southern California. I didn't want her to be unhappy, but she had already turned down a great opportunity to play ball at Cornell University, an Ivy League school in Ithaca, New York because she wanted to be closer to home, which is why she accepted the offer to play ball at San Jose. Being at San Jose made it convenient for us to attend her home games, which we did; and she could come home often during the off-season, which she did. Upon becoming aware of Brittany's meltdown, PJ and I told her that she needed to follow through with her commitment to play ball at San Jose.

"But mom, I don't like it up here," she complained. "I just want to come home and go to school down there."

"Ok then," I replied. "If you want to come home and go to a local university then you are going to have to do what *you* need to do to get into another school. You made a commitment, Brittany, and you need to honor that commitment."

I had already met my responsibility as a parent by assisting Brittany and Natalia with applying to various colleges. I completed the long tedious Free Application for Federal Student Aid (FAFSA) forms and paid all the requisite application fees, so I was done for the time being. I had a large enough task of dealing with the crazies at work, and most of them were my bosses and members of the Senior Command Staff. After much consideration, Brittany decided to stay at San Jose State and make the best of her remaining college experience. Natalia attended school locally at Cal State University Northridge and she was good with her decision. She had high hopes of getting into their film school because one of her life's goals was to be a movie director. PJ and I were paying Natalia's tuition, and all other incidental expenses, which included campus housing, and a cute little Volkswagen Jetta that we bought her. She could have easily stayed at home versus live on campus, but I read that students who lived on campus were more likely to graduate than those who commuted. We lived an hour away from the university, which made for a horrible commute, especially for someone as impatient as Natalia, and we needed her to finish school in 4 years so commuting was not an option.

PJ and I loved being empty nesters. We missed our girls not being home but they knew they were always welcome to move back home after college as long as they were productive members of society. We had a very small family in Southern California. I had two brothers, Stefon and Edris; Stefon was a year older than I was, and Edris a year younger. The three of us had a very close relationship growing up, but as young adults we had become estranged. Their entire adult lives involved trouble with the law due to alcohol and drug abuse, as well as domestic violence incidences. I loved them dearly, but dealing with them on a consistent basis risked my livelihood, so I had to maintain my distance. On the other hand, Cheryl-Ann, PJ's older sister, lived with their father in San Dimas, California, along with her husband, Rodney. Cheryl-Ann was a legal aide and Rodney was a self proclaimed *Spiritual Advisor*. While they did not lead a criminal lifestyle, our relationship with them ebbed and flowed over the years, and at times came to a screeching halt due to irreconcilable differences.

When we moved from the San Fernando Valley in 2006, after selling our home, Edris was living with some crazy woman somewhere in Long Beach, California, and I had not heard from Stefon since 1997. Over the years I had told my brothers I would never bail them out of jail, nor would I feed into their respective drug and alcohol habits by giving them money. I would, however, feed them if they were hungry and in fact, the last time I saw Stefon in 1997, Brittany and I took him some food. At that time he was living with a woman in a suburb called Studio City close to Hollywood, California. Stefon met us in the subterranean garage of the apartment complex wearing some funky looking sweats and a pair of those black thin-soled cloth, slip on shoes that gang members and jailbirds wear. Stefon looked unkempt as he was very thin and needed a hair cut badly. In the past, Stefon was very meticulous with his style of dress. He reminded me of my father in that he loved tailored suits and nice starched collared dress shirts. So his appearance confirmed for me that he was still on drugs and not doing well in general. After some small talk and some shifty eye glances he worked up the nerve to ask me for money, *allegedly* for cigarettes.

"No, Stefon, I will not give you any money," I said, "but I will *take* you to get some cigarettes." I was so annoyed.

"Oh come on T," Stefon pleaded. "Just give me the money and I'll walk to the store later."

Stefon was very cunning, but I was no fool. I didn't want to buy him cigarettes, and I sure wasn't giving him money so he could feed his *real* habit. I stood firm and did not give him any cash, but I caved and took him to buy cigarettes against my better judgment. Stefon was lucky that I was dealing with him because I was a cop and I was not supposed to be in his company at all considering that he was a convicted felon. But, he *was* my brother and I couldn't stand the thought of him being hungry, which was the only reason I went to see him. After seeing Stefon in that state, I was done placating because he was still into the same old thing. He knew I was hip to him so it would be a while before I heard from Stefon again.

Work was wearing on my nerves and the 58-mile commute from Burbank to the Mojave Desert, where I lived, significantly added to my ongoing fatigue. For most of my adult life, my weight fluctuated due to issues with my under active thyroid gland and, following my hysterectomy, I gained weight mostly in my mid section because I was cast into full menopause. I could not get rid of my gut so PJ and I tried dieting to help *me* drop a few pounds. I was tired of wearing my temporary, post surgery wardrobe, which had ballooned to a size 12 to accommodate my larger girth. I was depressed about not being able to fit into my smaller size 8 clothes and I was not about to start over with a new wardrobe when all I needed to do was lose some inches from my waistline. We started out really good eating small portions, which included fruits, veggies, and lean meats. After a couple of months into our weight loss program, I was still eating well, but I had added regular doses of Cold Stone ice cream to my low calorie menu. I was eating ice cream almost daily, but I continued losing weight considerably in spite of my binging. The consistent weight loss under that circumstance was unusual and a little bit concerning. PJ was the first to voice his opinion as he was perplexed by my substantial weight loss when he had reached a plateau.

"You must be on crack because you are losing so much weight." PJ jokingly quipped looking at me sideways.

"I know," I laughed. "I hope I'm not sick."

I was fitting back into my size 6/8 suits comfortably and feeling good about it. I had literally dropped 25-30 pounds within a few months without trying too hard. The strange thing was that while I was getting smaller, my breasts remained ample, especially the left one, which was actually engorged, so there was something seriously wrong with that picture. The summer of 2006 snuck up on me like nobody's business. Cheryl-Ann and Rodney had relocated to Atlanta, Georgia, and bought a beautiful estate in a wealthy suburb, where they lived amongst the rich and famous. Natalia and Brittany had come home from college because they had to move out of their respective dorms when the school year ended that May. When Brittany came home that was her first time seeing the new house whereas Natalia was home on a regular basis on the weekends throughout the school year since she was living locally. Natalia was not happy with dorm life and fortunately for her, for the next school year we moved her into an apartment that we sublet from a friend of ours in Encino, California, close to where the famous Jackson family once lived. We planned an early vacation that summer around the Memorial Day holiday as we were going to visit PJ's family, including Cheryl-Ann and Rodney in Atlanta. It was fun going to Georgia because PJ had plenty of cousins our age, and they all had children Brittany and Natalia's ages so it was always a great time. Cheryl-Ann had sent PJ pictures of the outside of the house and we thought it had beautiful curb appeal. Brittany had traveled to Atlanta the year before and visited with Cheryl-Ann and Rodney when they first moved so she had already seen their mini mansion. Cheryl-Ann and Rodney boasted about living in the same community as Creflo Dollar, an American televangelist pastor, as well as other less known doctors and lawyers. Common black folks like Cheryl-Ann and Rodney were suspect when they moved into the elite neighborhood because the stay-at-home *Stepford Wives* clocked their comings and goings and wanted to know what *they* did for a living. Well at that time, when Cheryl-Ann and Rodney moved in they didn't work anywhere. They were living off of the money they rode into town with, the proceeds from selling Dad's house, for as long as they could. If the neighbors knew that Cheryl-Ann and Rodney did absolutely nothing for a living, they probably would have started a petition to have them evicted. Cheryl-Ann had very expensive taste so of course I could not wait to see the house. I bought airline tickets for the entire family, and even bought a ticket for Mark, Brittany's boyfriend who was a starving student also home for the summer from San Jose State. Mark and Brittany were in a serious relationship so we invited him to join us in Atlanta so he could meet some of our family. We were scheduled to fly out on the Saturday leading to Memorial Day weekend and after making the travel plans, I realized that my annual mammogram was scheduled for the same week that we were going to be gone, so, before leaving, I called my doctor's office at Facey Medical Center and changed my appointment. The next available appointment was five months later in September. I was feeling fine so I wasn't concerned about delaying the appointment for a few months.

Just as I anticipated, we had a wonderful week in Atlanta and returned home safely. Mark went on home to San Diego where he was from, and we all settled in at home for the remainder of the summer. Things were looking up at work following my return from my short vacation because I interviewed and selected a new Assistant Officer in Charge to assist me in running the office. Jay was a male detective, who came highly recommended by his bosses at his previous assignment, and his employment record, or *personnel package*, as we referred to it on the department, was stellar. It was a promotion for Jay and he was ecstatic about the 11% pay increase he was about to receive. Jay was tall and handsome and he played semi-professional basketball for the department so the men in the unit liked him and the women loved him. The girls in the office referred to him as *eye candy*. Of course *my* eye candy was at home, so I wasn't swooning over Jay, but he was a sweetheart. Over time, he and I developed a big- sister- little- brother relationship and our partnership worked well. I was happy that the guys in the office liked and respected Jay because their camaraderie was great for the work environment.

I spent the rest of the summer hanging out with PJ and the girls in my spare time. We celebrated Brittany's 21st birthday before she returned to school that fall. She actually went back early to help with hosting new and prospective female athletes, which she loved to do. I was about to turn 48 in October, and was looking forward to the first holiday season in the new house. After the girls returned to school it was business as usual for PJ and me. The start of the school year always involved paying tuition, buying books and parking passes for Natalia, and determining which basketball games we would attend in support of Brittany's college team. I had the usual work drama, dealing with my miniature, big mouthed boss, who was as hateful as the day was long, as well as whining employees who didn't appreciate a woman in the workplace guiding and directing them. That was the story of my life for the 16 years that I was in supervisory roles on the male dominated department. Brittany was back at school for about a week when I received a text message from her. I had barely learned how to text on my old flip phone but somehow, I worked it out.

Mom, I think something is going on with Coach because we haven't seen her, the text read. Apparently, the women's Head Basketball Coach, Janice Richard had not yet shown up for pre-season meetings or practices causing the team to speculate about her absence. My return text read: *Do you think she got fired?* I wasn't being facetious. I really thought maybe she was let go since her contract was up for renewal. I mean she hadn't had the best seasons in the recent past either.

No mom...I don't think she was fired. I could feel the inflection in Brittany's text and imagined her face tuned up as if to say, *Mom stop trippin' coach did not get fired.*

Brittany had a love/hate relationship with Coach Richard because the woman pushed her, and was hard on her from day one; nevertheless Brittany admired and supported her coach because Brittany understood that Coach Richard wanted nothing but the best for her. After days of wondering what was going on with Coach, she called a meeting and announced to the team that she had been diagnosed with Stage III Breast Cancer. The girls on the team were all stunned, but Brittany was devastated. That was the last thing any of them expected to hear but it sure explained her absence in a big way. Brittany called to tell me the news and cried incessantly as she shared with me the details of coach's medical situation. I was surprised at first that Brittany took it so hard, but then I realized it was because she had a close connection with breast cancer at an early age. Brittany lost her grandmother, my Mama, who died from breast cancer, so I'm sure Coach Richard's meeting brought back those memories.

I was happy to finally have some help at work but I was still working too hard for a non-slave. In addition to reviewing and triaging criminal cases all day, I also managed 17 sworn and civilian employees, attended unnecessary meetings at headquarters, and sometimes sat in for my hateful little boss when she needed to be out of the office. I loved working, and the busyness was right up my alley because I hated idle time whether at home or work. What I didn't realize was that my body was not getting adequate rest, and I was eating too infrequently. It didn't help matters that we had recently moved, and on my days off I painted rooms, hung pictures, and steadied the ladder for PJ to hang ceiling fans and big wall clocks. I was busy running around so much that I figured the extra activity was the reason for my extreme weight loss.

Several weeks had passed after learning of coach's diagnosis, and she was on my mind heavily because I had my own mammogram coming up in a couple weeks. As my appointment neared, Natalia called me very excited about an upcoming audition she had in Orange County, about an hour's drive from our house. Her audition was on the same day as my appointment and Natalia was afraid she would not be able to find the place, so she asked me if I would please go with her.

"No, honey I can't." I told her over the phone. "I have a mammogram appointment at 2:00 on that same day."

"Mommy, *pleeeeease* come with me." Natalia wasn't hearing me. She begged and pleaded. "Can't you reschedule your appointment?"

"No. I really need to go to *this* appointment. It's already been rescheduled once so I *need* to go." Natalia finally stopped begging when she realized that I was standing firm.

On the afternoon of my appointment it was hot as heck outside but it was just another day at the Medical Center where I had been having mammograms for years, or as I referred to them, my *breast tug of wars*. Even though it was cool inside on that fall afternoon, I was experiencing major hot flashes, and perspiring like crazy. I couldn't wear any deodorant or powder before the test so I was dying. I arrived a little early for my appointment so I sat in the waiting room watching people. I observed young pregnant women come and go with their significant others or, in some cases, with their mothers. There were also quite a few older women either alone or with their spouses; then there was me, just watching everybody. We were all sitting there waiting to be called in for our respective appointments when suddenly the intake nurse interrupted my people watching session.

"Morris. Tia Morris," she yelled from near the front desk.

I gathered my purse and sweater and got up to follow the nurse down the hallway. I had followed this routine so many times I was sort of on auto-pilot. I entered the sterile examination room where a trained mammography technician was waiting for me with a waist length faded hospital gown in hand. She recited her memorized instructions for me to disrobe from the waist up as she exited the cold room to allow me some privacy. I knew the drill. When the technician returned, she requested that I address an envelope to myself, in which the Medical Center would place my test results, and mail them to me a couple of weeks later. The technician also handed me a pink breast cancer survivor wristband. *How nice,* I thought to myself. *I will wear this.* For years, I had participated in the annual *Revlon Run/Walk for Breast Cancer* in Los Angeles, so I thought the wristband was just one more memento I had to show my undying support for the cause. My breasts had increased in size over the years and they were tender at that moment. My left breast was still engorged, but it was always larger than my right one, so I wasn't too alarmed by its inflation. I was not looking forward to the impending tug of war that I was about to have with the technician. After some minor instruction as to how the procedure would go, and the warning about the apparatus being cold, she had me lean into the machine as she tugged and pulled at my breasts one at a time. The machine was cold against my flesh and the twisting, turning, flattening, and squishing of my breasts was uncomfortable as usual, but I knew it had to be done, so I had to *man up,* so to speak. She continued until she had my breasts flattened and stretched to the max, and had captured all of the images she needed from the left, right, top, and bottom of each breast. I was glad it was cold in there because I was rather moist under my arms and downright funky by the end of the day. I didn't really stink, but I was really close. After snapping all the images she needed, I was asked to wait until the technician had a chance to view the film and make sure that the images were appropriately captured. Following the entire procedure, the technician asked me to stand by while she made one last check of all the film, so I sat there and waited with my arms folded for what seemed like an eternity. Upon her return to the room, unlike on previous occasions, she asked me a series of follow up questions.

"Mrs. Morris," she began, "did you have a mammogram in 2005?"

"Yes." I responded indignantly with a roll of my eyes because I was ready to go home and shower. "I have had one every year since I was 25 years old."

That was my standard response whenever any of my doctors asked about my mammogram history. I wanted anyone who asked to know that I was serious about this Breast Cancer business, and because of my strong family history there was not one year, since I turned 25 that I didn't have a mammogram, or so I thought. I stood there with my arms folded across my chest clenching my hospital gown. The technician left the room again, but this time she allowed me to get dressed. When she returned a few minutes later, she continued with her polite interrogation. As I sat there listening to her, I wondered, *where is she going with this line of questioning? No one ever asked me post mammogram questions before. What's her problem?*

"Well, our records indicate that you did not have a mammogram in 2005," she continued. "Your last one was in October of 2004." She was starting to get on my nerves by pressing the issue.

"Ok. Look, now, I know I had one in 2005, because there is no way I would have missed my appointment," I replied. "What is the problem? I know I had one and I had it here at this facility, so you all must have forgotten to document that visit."

Facey Medical, like other medical facilities across the country, was starting to computerize all of their files, so I chalked the confusion up to an employee failing to properly transfer the information into my new computerized file. I had gone to three different Facey locations in the previous years for my annual mammograms, so I thought maybe they just hadn't merged their files.

"Maybe my last appointment was at one of your other facilities." I offered. "I really can't remember for sure, but I *know* I had a mammogram in 2005."

The technician called the other facilities while I waited anxiously. She scurried around for about 20 minutes trying to verify the existence of my 2005 results to no avail. *Did they err, or was it* my *mistake?* She was sure their records were accurate and believed they had not failed to transfer any of my medical information into their new system. I never knew them to be so persistent about a previous mammogram, so it was unsettling. After searching high and low, the technician had one more idea.

"Can you please check with the Billing Office on your way out?" she asked. "If they didn't bill you for the mammogram in 2005, then it's quite possible that you didn't have one that year."

I got dressed and went on a mission to prove the technician wrong. Before I left the facility I marched my butt right over to the Billing Office. I stood by at the window, biting my bottom lip, as the woman in the Billing Office researched her computer. She recapped all of the visits they billed me for previously and, to my surprise, there was no such bill for my 2005 mammogram. *How could I have let that happen? Oh well, they got new pictures from today, as well as the ones from two years ago, so what's the big deal?* I was a little on edge when I left the medical facility, but mostly I was confused. I was trying to figure out what happened in 2005 that caused me to totally miss my mammogram. I was extremely busy at work, but I didn't think I would have forgotten my most important appointment of the year. Two weeks had passed since my troubling mammogram experience and my nerves had settled until I arrived home from work one evening. I walked into my room, kicked off my shoes, and placed my handbag and brief case on the cedar chest at the foot of my bed. PJ was in the bathroom washing his face as he had just gotten home as well. I had barely exhaled after unbuttoning my pants when the phone rang. I picked up on the first ring.

"Hello?"

"So, your doctor says you have breast cancer," said the recorded voice on the other end of the line. My heart dropped as I clenched the phone tighter to my ear.

"Oh my God!" I blurted out as the message continued.

"What?" PJ asked as he peered around the corner from the bathroom door.

I held up my hand motioning for him to wait as I continued to listen intently to the recording in its entirety. After a few moments, I recognized the voice on the phone to be that of Ms. Shirley Jones, the actress from the 1970's hit TV show, *The Partridge Family*, which I loved. When the message ended, I turned to PJ.

"This recording is saying that I have not had a mammogram since 2004 when I *just* had one a couple of weeks ago," I explained. "It startled me because it opened with, 'So your doctor says you have breast cancer.'"

As I repeated the message to PJ, it dawned on me that it was October, Breast Cancer Awareness Month, so when my heart stopped racing I realized that the call was simply a public service announcement from Facey using Ms. Jones as their campaign ambassador, and the message was designed to remind Facey's patients of the importance of Breast Cancer Screening. I was still waiting for the results of my mammogram, so the timing of the call really alarmed me. I had a previous scare following my 2004 mammogram, when my doctor requested that I return for a follow-up so he could have additional views taken of my *left* breast because he saw a suspicious shadow on the film. The results of the follow-up test that year were *normal*.

I had passed the magical age of 42, the age at which Mama was diagnosed with breast cancer. Here I was about to turn 48, and even though I felt fine, my strong family history of breast cancer was in the forefront of my mind always. Mama, her two sisters, and her first cousin all had varying stages of the disease, at different ages, so I remained diligent and cognizant of my heightened risk of developing breast cancer. At that time in my life I felt as if I might have escaped my family's dreaded curse. As a realist though, I knew I could still very well get breast cancer so I prepared myself mentally and financially, just in case. PJ was in tune with me on the issue so he had purchased a supplemental cancer insurance policy from the Los Angeles City Employee

Benefit Association to complement the policy I had already purchased from AFLAC. *God forbid we should ever have to use either of them.* I thought. Shortly after I received the troubling message from Ms. Shirley Jones, my mammography results arrived in the mail. To my dismay, the notice indicated that I needed to return to the medical facility for additional views of my *left* breast. That explained the technician's interrogation at my appointment. She must have known something was wrong. The next day, after receiving the notice in the mail, when PJ and I returned home from work he checked our phone messages. He activated the speakerphone feature on the machine and to my surprise; there was a message from my doctor.

Hello, this message is for Tia Morris. This is Doctor Nielsen. Please call me at your earliest convenience to discuss your mammography results.

I had been going to Dr. Nielsen since 1987; he was a very kind man and skilled physician. After over 20 years of doctors' visits, it seemed as if we were growing old together. I had seen him transition from a very young, boyishly handsome, curly haired intern into a salt and pepper, sleek hair style wearing, experienced, and well respected doctor. I was lucky to be one of his patients because he really cared about people. Dr. Nielsen knew I was a police officer and that I was very active, physically fit, and in good overall health. He was generally concerned about my family history of breast cancer, and knew that Mama had already died from the dreadful disease, which validated his concern. Dr. Nielsen *never* called me because there was never a reason so I was nervous listening to the message. PJ looked at me and I looked at him. Then, the *whys* and *what ifs* started. *What if he's calling to tell me that I have Cancer? Why would he tell me to call at my* earliest convenience? *This has to be a dream,* and *a bad dream at that. If I had cancer, of course he wouldn't have left a message on my answering machine; and he would have sounded more urgent, right? Like,"Mrs. Morris, you need to come into the office right away,"* or *"Mrs. Morris, call me as soon as possible to discuss your results.* Dr. Nielsen seemed so calm that I thought I might be overreacting. *What does he know? Why was this year's mammogram experience so different than the previous years?* It was too late in the evening for me to call him back so I just kept asking PJ a million *what if* questions until I fell asleep.

I woke up the next morning at about 4:30, my usual time and prepared myself for L.A.'s infamous morning rush hour traffic. I had armed myself with the number to Dr. Nielsen's office and planned to call him when they opened at 8am. I arrived at my office at a quarter past five and as soon as I sat down at my desk the phone rang. The caller ID monitor flashed the name of the caller: *Dr. Nielsen.* I sat at my desk staring at the phone as I firmly gripped the receiver and picked up. I was biting my lip as Dr. Nielsen began to speak.

"Boy, you are hard to catch up with," he said in his all too kind and caring demeanor.

"Well, Doctor, I *just* got your message yesterday evening." I had butterflies in my stomach. "I was going to call after your office opened at 8. You must have bad news if you are trying so desperately to get a hold of me."

"Well...no," he replied. "It's just that your mammogram film shows an abnormality."

I was hoping that Nielsen would assure me I had *nothing* to worry about but that was not the case. Unable to contain myself, I interrupted him. I didn't really care about my manners because it was all about me at that moment.

"Please don't tell me...it's my left breast, right?"

"Yes," he paused, "it is, so, we need to get you in here for additional views."

"I knew it!" I blurted out, suddenly feeling the adrenaline start to speed up my heart rate.

"Please call my office and schedule an appointment right away."

Damn it! Damn It! Damn It! It's always my left breast, I thought to myself. *Left* was always an issue with me. I'm left- handed, but I didn't use my left hand for much because I did almost *everything* with my right hand. As a child, my 5th grade teacher tried her best to get me to write with my right hand, but I never fully converted. *What was her problem?* Old people back in the day thought that something was wrong with left-handed people. My left leg was bigger than my right, which made it difficult for me to find boots to fit over my bigger calf; my left foot was bigger than my right, which caused some pairs of shoes to slip off of my smaller foot, so *why would my left breast be any different?* The fact that my left breast was slightly bigger than my right breast was not really an issue, but the fact that it might be *diseased* was a huge deal.

I called Facey immediately and they set my follow-up appointment for Friday, October the 13th. *Really?* I thought, *Friday the 13th?* Although I was not superstitious, that date didn't sit well with me under the circumstances. I reflected back on the day of my initial mammogram when the technician searched feverishly for my 2005 results. She had seen something suspicious on the film, which triggered her search for my previous year's results, but, of course, she was not at liberty to share any results with me. During the week leading up to the ominous Friday the 13th, I was trying to mentally prepare for my new medical mystery adventure. As a result, I took to the Internet to see what abnormal mammography results looked like. I stumbled upon several websites and every step I took online led me to another site, and another, and another, but I ended up on BreastCancer.org. By the time I finished looking at all of the breast cancer images, various types of mastectomies, photos of disfigured women, and reconstructed breasts, I was dizzy. I read about the various options for treating breast cancer and wondered if I would be one of the 15% of women who were diagnosed with cancer in their lifetime, or if I would be one of the 85% of women, who had a benign tumor or some other fibrocystic breast condition. I had dense breasts, which made it harder to detect lumps and tumors so that added to my fear. My hope was that the suspicious area was fatty tissue that had banded together, or perhaps a benign cyst or growth. On the day of my follow-up appointment, my co-workers and I had a prescheduled 1PM meeting in the Deputy Chief of Police's office to discuss the adjudication of pending personnel complaint investigations. I arrived early and before the meeting started, I politely asked the Chief if I could present my cases first because I needed to make it to a doctor's appointment across town by 2 o'clock. She agreed, and upon completion of my presentation, she excused me. As I turned to leave she made eye contact with me.

"Good luck at your doctor's appointment." She said as if she sensed that something was wrong.

I was comforted by the thought. *Did she sense my tension? Could she see the worried look in my eyes? Or was it just an innocuous comment that had no underlying message or meaning at all?* I wasn't sure. I arrived at Facey on time and did my best to relax and act normal. The same technician from my initial appointment greeted me with my original mammogram film in hand. She seemed more focused this time as if she was on a specific mission. *What's she thinking?* I wondered. I didn't like the feeling I had in the pit of my stomach as I entered the cold room again. I tried to remain positive and hoped for a false alarm again. The technician placed my original images on the lighted wall fixture and examined them closely, as if she was plotting her next move in a game of Chess. I stood next to her and peered at the images of my breast from the side profile view. There, on the film, was a highlighted area on the upper left portion of my left breast. *Is that the object of the doctor's concern? Does it have the characteristics of a malignant tumor like what I saw during my online research?* I noted the highlighted area looked different than the surrounding tissue. *Are the borders of the highlighted area smooth, indicating a cyst? Or are they jagged, or star-like, reflecting a more suspicious, abnormal growth?* I was confused. The technician tugged and pulled at my left breast as she attempted to make it as flat as a pancake. It was like déjà vu only this time it was so quiet in the room you could hear a rat piss on cotton. My breathing was shallow and started to sound more like a stifled whimper; and the machine felt colder and harder than I ever remembered. After the tug of war rematch, the technician asked me to remain undressed until she had a chance to review the film. One of the ties had been ripped off of the gown I was wearing, so I folded my arms across my chest to keep it closed. I sat there with my legs crossed at the knee. I was restless. It seemed like an eternity for her to return. It was so cold in the room that I embraced myself in an attempt to stay warm. The technician finally returned and told me I could get dressed and leave. *Is she avoiding eye contact with me? Maybe I'm just paranoid. It is Friday the 13th after all.* I spent that weekend trying to take my mind off of my mammogram drama by preparing for my upcoming birthday celebration. I had finished my invitations and mailed them on my way into work that following Monday. When I got to work that morning I received *another* call from Dr. Nielsen.

"Mrs. Morris…" he started in a pleasant voice. I had the biggest lump in my throat as I tried not to interrupt him again, but I couldn't help it.

"Oh Lord," I interjected "what now?"

"I got your mammography results from the follow-up," he replied, "and it still looks suspicious."

"What?"

"It appears to be level 4," he continued, "but of course we can't be sure if it's malignant until we do a biopsy." I was sitting at my desk, and for once in my life, I was speechless. I was never speechless unless I had some food in my mouth.

"What do you mean *level 4*?" I asked struggling to find the words.

"That is the level of suspicion as to whether the mass is malignant," the doctor replied.

Back when Mama was diagnosed with breast cancer, her doctor told me about the five suspicion levels, and about the stages of the progression and degree of the disease, but I suddenly drew a blank when Dr. Nielsen was breaking the news to me about myself.

"I'm going to refer you to a surgeon, Dr. Richter, who will schedule you for a biopsy soon." Dr. Nielsen advised. "He is very skilled at what he does and I trust him explicitly. He'll take good care of you." I sensed a genuine compassionate aura emanating from the other end of the phone.

"Ok, Doctor. Thanks." I responded in a ghastly tone.

As the phone call ended, I sat there at my desk zoned out as if I was in the midst of a bad dream. *Dr. Richter will take good care of me? What's that supposed to mean?* If the surgeon couldn't make the situation go away, then as far as I was concerned, he could not take *good* care of me.

CHAPTER 2

"The Biopsy"

I CALLED DOCTOR RICHTER'S OFFICE right away and they scheduled my appointment for Wednesday, October 25th at 3:30pm. That was my birthday. *What a coincidence.* I was scheduled to attend an annual Women's Conference on that day as well. It was an all day work event held at the Hilton Hotel in Universal City, just north of Hollywood, California. I looked forward to attending the conference because I knew I would see people I had not seen in a long time, and there were always outstanding topics explored about important women's issues. I arrived at the conference at 7:30 that morning knowing I had to leave by 2:30 in order to make it to my doctor's appointment. One of the guest speakers that day was a Detective named Trish, who had battled breast cancer about seven years prior while in her 30's. I listened intently as Trish shared her story. She talked about how she took 11 months off work, and how during her time off she cared for her sister, who was also fighting breast cancer. Trish was very candid about her treatment and recovery process. The audience laughed at her delightful story about how she danced the night away during a vacation in Mexico, and how after the music waned she discovered that her wig, which she wore to hide the most prominent effect of chemotherapy, hair loss, had twisted just as much as her hips. Trish didn't look like she had been through such an ordeal. She was a gracious but strong beauty with a spicy zest for life. I sat there thinking about how I was going to have to sneak out of the room during the remaining presentations in order to make it to my appointment but the presenters ended just in time for me to make an inconspicuous escape. Before leaving, however, I made it a point to find Trish and tell her how much I enjoyed her story. I also told her briefly about my situation; perhaps I was hoping for some words of encouragement from someone who understood my predicament and she did not disappoint. She gave me hope because I had witnessed her journey and when I looked at her I saw a survivor.

When I arrived at Dr. Richter's office, I was anxious, to say the least. The doctor conducted a quick manual examination of my breast as soon as he entered the room, and without hesitation he delivered the news.

"I can't feel your mass with my hands, Mrs. Morris," he said. "But mammogram images appear to show that you might have a malignant mass. So, I'd like to do an excisional biopsy with a needle-guided wire, followed by a lumpectomy."

The news pierced me like a dagger. It was direct, and it poured out of Richter's mouth like water from a breached dam.

"If the biopsy does indeed reveal a malignancy, then I will perform a sentinel node biopsy to check for spread of the disease into your lymphatic system."

I could barely catch my breath as he continued, "I know how unnerving it is to hear this type of news so I don't want you to have to wait for the results of the biopsy, and then have to return for the lumpectomy. So, I'm prepared to do everything, the biopsy and lumpectomy during the same visit."

By the time Richter finished explaining *everything,* my brain cells were fried. I was stunned. I had told PJ not to come with me since it was supposed to be just a quick follow up visit, but in hindsight I wished he had been there. Dr. Richter handed me a book entitled *Breast Cancer-Treatment Guidelines for Patients,* and directed me to the page where it discussed the procedure he had just described, as well as information about the stages of cancer. The book also explained Adjuvant and Neo-adjuvant treatments for the various *types* of tumors. I walked flatfooted to the nurses' station and scheduled my biopsy appointment. The young woman standing behind the counter was already waiting for me.

"Mrs. Morris, the next available appointment we have is Monday November 27th," she said in a sweet sympathetic tone.

"Oh wow." I chuckled. "That's my wedding anniversary…but thanks," I replied. I had *not* planned on spending my 24th wedding anniversary on an operating table, but obviously the appointment was more important than anything else.

"Ok Mrs. Morris," the young nurse continued as she typed my information into the computer in front of her. "You are all set. Please be here at 8am sharp on the 27th and plan on being here for a few hours." *A few hours? Oh goodness.* I thought. "You will need a driver as you will be administered a general anesthesia for your procedure. Do you have any questions?"

Of course I had questions. I had a million questions, but they were stuck in my throat.

"No, thank you. I will see you then."

On my seemingly long walk out of the office and into the parking lot, it was pretty clear to me that I was officially diagnosed with Breast Cancer. As soon as I reached the car I called PJ and told him the dreadful news. He was very comforting and vowed to help me deal with it no matter what the prognosis. I assured him that I was fine, but actually I was devastated; I was just too stunned to cry. Over the next couple of days PJ and I talked about my situation and the *what-ifs* started all over again. The biggest consideration at that point was whether or not I should tell Brittany and Natalia about the upcoming biopsy. I was worried most about Brittany because of her reaction to her coach's recent diagnosis just a few months before, coupled with her vivid memories of Mama's bout with the disease. Brittany and Natalia had witnessed Mama's declining health and they knew their Mimi had cancer. The girls were grown at this point, but they were still *my* babies so I didn't want them to worry about me. Brittany was a miniature version of me so she worried about *everything* just like I did.

"Are you seriously considering *not* telling the girls?" PJ asked. "What if something happens to you during surgery and they have no clue what's going on? That's not fair. They are grown and can handle it, so you need to tell them." PJ was firm but not harsh.

"I just don't want them to worry needlessly," I said. "If it's benign then they will have worried for nothing but you are right they would be upset finding out after the fact." I sat in silence and pondered over it a bit.

"Ok, I will tell them in person after my party since they will both be home." *Who am I really protecting: them or me?* I asked myself. I really did not want to talk about what was going on with me to anyone because I was afraid.

A lot had happened in the weeks leading up to my birthday with all of the doctor's visits and my biopsy. Somehow, I managed to temporarily escape the looming thoughts of my health crisis as I went on with my birthday party plans. I was so excited about my party you would have sworn I had never had a birthday party before. For all that I knew this could have been my last birthday, but I sure hoped not. My party was planned for Saturday, October 28th, three days after my follow-up appointment with Dr. Richter. I had invited my closest girlfriends many of whom showed up. I lived about an hour from most of them, so I cooked and baked everything so they didn't have to bring anything. I worked with most of my girlfriends in one capacity or another over the previous 25-year period, while on the police department, and I shared a different bond with each of them. I really wasn't in the mood for a party anymore and even thought about cancelling it, but that wasn't going to change anything, and besides I needed a good distraction. The day of the party was a beautiful sunny crisp Saturday. Several of the ladies complained about the long drive, and others just sucked it up and came in the house looking for food and drinks. They were all very different, but I loved each of them just the same.

Josie, was a stoic no nonsense woman. We had been friends for about 25 years and worked together for nine of them. I was Josie's boss during the years we worked together in a Traffic Collision detective assignment, but we were friends nonetheless, and we got along very well. Most importantly, we had mutual respect for one another. I trusted Josie because she had proven that she had my back, and I had hers, but it took several years and many bad experiences on the department for us to get to that level of trust and friendship. The men who worked for us could not get past two women being in charge so, we banded together out of necessity and fought battles that in turn strengthened our bond. We were happiest when we were able to go out in the field together and do what we loved: investigate. Josie and I also loved to shop and we *always* found time on our extended lunch breaks to catch a sale or two at Talbots or Macy's, which were both close to our office in downtown Los Angeles. I loved Josie's work ethic and her strength as a woman and mother; *and* she was a fearless expert investigator. We shared stories with each other about some of our wayward, trifling family members, and about troublemaking officers on the job; and we shared delightful stories about our kids' successes during their school years. Josie raised a beautiful daughter, Andridia, who went on to get her PhD from the University of Tennessee. My friendship with Josie remained strong for years, long after we stopped working together.

Alasea (Lace) and I went to junior and senior high school together. We had lost touch during our college years when she attended Long Beach State and I attended Cal State LA. In 1982, Alasea and I were reacquainted after she joined the police department. She was a statuesque beauty, who I nicknamed "The Countess" because she was so regal in the way she spoke and she always carried herself like a queen. Alasea came to work for me in 1996, when she joined Josie and me, at Central Traffic Detectives, where Lace and Josie were two of my four supervisors. Unlike me, she was soft spoken, and didn't really curse; but she could tell a person off without raising her voice, and that was an effective style of leadership for *her*. Although we embraced our sisterhood on and off duty, our respect for one another, and professionalism was the foundation on which we built a positive working relationship that prevailed against all odds, in the turbulent times we faced in that particular unit we worked in.

Bretha was a Police Service Representative, which was another term for an LAPD Dispatcher. Bretha was new on the job when we met in 1982. I thought she was by far one of the sweetest people I had ever met in my life. She was so kind and naïve that I thought she lied about growing up in Compton. Bretha married a police officer, and PJ and I remained good friends with them as a couple for many years until their divorce, after which time she and I remained close. Bretha and I each had two siblings, who we loved dearly but all of our siblings had similar wayward issues. We often compared stories about how *their* issues affected *us*. Bretha's mom died from a brain tumor in

1991, and a year later Mama died from metastatic breast cancer. I was moral support for her when both of her parents passed away and she was there for me when it was my turn to bury Mama. So, we had a bond I didn't share with any of my other friends.

Dede was Alasea's close friend when we met, but as time went on Dede and I became great friends as well. She was also an LAPD dispatcher and a close friend of Bretha's. Dede and I talked often at work, shared stories about our children, and discussed the latest events going on at First AME Church where we were both members. I called Dede "The Diva" because she was very attractive, *very* petite, and her hair and nails were always well manicured. I loved talking to her because she was hilarious. What I loved most was she was very spiritual, and an encouraging friend. She was an extraordinary event planner and was well known for her fabulous soirees. Dede *loved* Las Vegas, where she was a high roller, and earned plenty of complimentary "stays" in exclusive suites at the best resorts on the Strip. Everything she did she prayed about, even in Vegas.

Stephany and I met on the police department but our friendship became more prevalent off duty because we were neighbors in the San Fernando Valley. She was one of my craziest friends. She was loud, fun, and quite the social butterfly. She was involved in every social organization known to man, including *Jack and Jill*, *Links*, and her sorority, the esteemed AKAs, *Alpha Kappa Alpha Sorority, Incorporated*. Stephanie knew every councilman in the City of Los Angeles, especially in the Valley where she worked closely with community members as part of her police duties. She was also a horse enthusiast; I mean a real black cowgirl. Oh yeah, did I mention that she was an AKA? She would never let you forget that. When she talked about the AKA's it was kind of like Star Jones talking about her wedding on *The View*. Our friendship centered on our children who were close in age. We often laughed about the time we needed a cheap babysitting option for the summer so we stood on line from 4am to 8am on a cold spring morning, outside of a local recreation center in order to secure a spot for our children, in a Summer Camp program, with very limited space available. Needless to say Stephany kept me entertained for the four hours we stood on line. We talked and laughed the entire time. We ended up locking down spots for our kids and that summer proved to be fun for them and us.

Carol and I met in 1994, while working the same division. She was tall with gorgeous skin and hair, and she had a figure to die for. I loved Carol's strength and her sincerity. She was no joke when it came to raising her only child, a son. I admired that, especially because I saw how Mama was not so successful raising my brothers. I raised two girls but I had PJ, so it was easy for me. One thing Carol and I had in common was that we both loved to shop at discount stores. We compared stories about the deals we found at *TJ Maxx and Big Lots*. We knew where every TJ Maxx store in the Southern Cal area was located and we visited many of them often. So naturally Carol was a woman after my own heart. Carol was always a dear friend and supported me, and my girls a great deal. She was always available to help me with my social events throughout the years, and was a wonderful mother hen when Brittany bought her first Condominium in the same building Carol lived in.

Rachel and I met at about the same time that I met Carol. She worked for me as a Traffic investigator. She was an astute and tireless worker and very intelligent. Rachel looked just like the beautiful Actress, Sheryl Lee Ralph. She had beautiful brown skin, deep dimples, and an hourglass figure just like Ms. Ralph. Rachel was my kid sister. She looked up to me and sought my advice on personal and professional matters. I enjoyed hearing the stories about her Section 8 tenants who lived on Welfare in her rental properties in Compton, California. Josie and I mentored Rachel and tried our best to shield her from her male peers who went after her as hard as they came for us.

Stephanie B. was a young officer, who was also like a little sister to me. She worked for me in 2003, when I was a Watch Commander in Downtown Los Angeles. She had no problem calling out officers who weren't paying attention to me in roll call, or those who were being disruptive during my roll call presentations. Her peers hated that she called me by my first name as opposed to my sworn title, "Lieutenant." They sensed that she had an unfair advantage over them because of our friendship, which wasn't the case at all. Stephanie's peers often teased her and called her my *niece* because they thought she could have her way in the workplace. Well they were wrong.

Although we were friends, we maintained a professional relationship at work. Stephanie was always the first to lend a helping hand when I needed help planning events at work and at home. Josie and I mentored Stephanie and she always expressed her gratitude for us helping her make Detective, which she really did on her own, we just supported her.

Valerie was a dental hygienist, who I met in 1981, when PJ and I were dating and I accompanied PJ to a dental appointment where Val worked. Valerie was very beautiful. She had skin like velvet, high cheekbones, and a raspy voice like Demi Moore. She grew up in the San Fernando Valley, and came from a large close-knit family. Over the years we became like real sisters and she even lived with PJ and I for a short while after we were married, before she settled down and started a family of her own. Valerie loved PJ and me equally, and was known as "Auntie Val-wee" to my girls. Valerie knew Mama and was there for me when Mama died just as I was there for her when her mother died a few years later.

Evangelyn, or "Van," was one of my very best girlfriends. She and I became friends in the early 80's when she worked Homicide with PJ. A decade later, she and I were assigned to Internal Affairs division working together as supervising investigators, which is when we became closer. Van was a very attractive athletic woman, who the men *loved*. She ran track during the early years of her career, and as a result, she garnered and maintain friendships with higher-ranking officers, who coached the various department sports teams. These alliances were thought to be a valuable asset during Van's career because the right people liked her and mentored her. Evangelyn was lucky to have these connections but she was smart and capable of thriving on her own, which she did. I loved Van's spirit of giving back. Van was a huge advocate for the underprivileged, and belonged to community organizations, such as the *Boys and Girls Club of America*; and she was instrumental in spearheading several leadership organizations on and off the department. Van apologized for not being able to attend my birthday party that year but it was mainly because she was sorry she missed all of the good food. She wasn't fooling me.

My girlfriends and I ate, drank, gossiped, and shared family stories for the better part of the day at my party. I enjoyed myself immensely, but my medical situation stood in the way of my ability to completely relax. I smiled on the outside but I was sad and alone in my head. When I looked around the room at my girlfriends I thought to myself, *I am the one in eight women, in this room, who will be diagnosed with Breast Cancer in her lifetime as the statistics suggested.* I tried my best not to let on that anything was wrong. The party ended late in the evening as the women left one by one, or in pairs if they carpooled. PJ was still out and about as the party wrapped up so Brittany, Natalia, and I was at home alone once the ladies left. We were sitting at the dining room table talking when I became annoyed about a disagreement the girls were having across the table. I was tired of hearing them go back and forth so I chimed in abruptly.

"I'm not dealing with that. I've got my own issues."

Shocked at my outburst and by the vagueness of my response, the girls looked at me and Brittany responded to my comment.

"Mom," she said, "what's wrong?"

"Nothing," I said as I looked down and away when she noted my absent stare.

"No, mom," she wasn't buying my elusiveness so she continued to question me. "You said you've got your own issues to deal with. What issues are you dealing with? Is there something wrong with you?" Brittany was very intuitive when it came to me; she always knew when something was going on with me. I remained silent and continued to look down.

"Mom!"

"Whoa, Brittany calm down." Natalia scolded with a growing concern.

"No!" Brittany fired back at Natalia then turned back to me. "Mom, what are you not telling us? What's wrong with you?"

All of a sudden, Brittany started to cry. I continued looking down because I didn't know what to say. Well, I knew *what* to say but I didn't know *how* to say it. My silence urged Natalia to pick up where Brittany had left off in the interrogation.

"Mom, what's going on?" She asked. "Is there something wrong?"

"Look, I have to have a biopsy." I finally said quietly, as I slowly lifted my head.

"A biopsy? For what, Ma?" Brittany asked through her silenced tears as she pulled her chair closer to mine.

"They found a lump." I said in a low, soft voice. I couldn't hide my angst any longer.

"No…no…no…no," Brittany started to become emotional again. "What? A lump? What? Like a cancer kind of lump? What kind of lump, Mom?"

Brittany was frantic. She quickly backed her chair away from the table as if putting distance between her and the table paralleled removing herself from the possibility of something being wrong with me.

"They don't know," I replied timidly.

I knew *they*, the doctors, knew, but I didn't have the courage to tell my girls what the medical professionals suspected. I got up from the table and went to sit on the open staircase in the foyer and Natalia followed right behind me and grabbed my hand as I sat down on the steps.

"Mom, everything is going to be fine. I don't feel like this is a doomed situation. Come here, Brittany."

Natalia held out her hand for Brittany, who hurriedly moved to the stairs to join us. Although Brittany was the oldest, Natalia always managed to calm her anxieties, as if they had switched birth orders with Natalia taking on the role of big sister. Brittany reached out to grab Natalia's hand and mine, as we sat there on the steps.

"Now," Natalia began, "bow your heads." I smiled to myself as she prayed for me, and our family.

"Look, girls," I said after we said Amen. "I didn't want to tell you guys until after my biopsy results because I didn't want you to worry needlessly if the tumor is benign."

"Mom you can't keep stuff like that from us," Brittany scolded. "What if something happened while you were in surgery? That would have been the first time we would've known you were even *in* surgery and that's not fair."

"Girl, nothing in life is fair," I retorted feeling more like her mother again, "but you're right, and daddy agrees with you. I just don't ever want to be a burden."

"Mom you aren't a burden," Natalia said wiping tears from her face. "You're our mother."

By then we were all crying.

"So, you just keep this kind of stuff to yourself?" Brittany asked. "That's not good for you or any of us. This is scary, Mommy. You are not alone here."

I looked up and smiled when she called me *mommy* because as old as they were, they were still my babies and I would always be their *Mommy*.

"I know," I said while wiping the tears from my face with the back of my hand like a two year old. "I love you guys."

"We love you too, Mommy," Natalia replied. "Everything is going to be ok."

"I feel that too, Natalia. We're going to be fine." Brittany said with a budding smile.

I felt as if a weight was lifted from my chest as I sat there holding hands with my girls for what seemed like 30 minutes. I knew, then, that everything was going to be okay; because I believed there was power in prayer.

As mid November 2006 approached, I started to get a bit antsy about the biopsy procedure. I spent hours online, again, reading about biopsies and the wide variety of cancer treatments. I read that some women had so many biopsies that they developed the "Whittle Away Effect" because by the time they underwent a few biopsy procedures, they may as well have had a mastectomy since their breasts would have literally been *whittled* away. That scared me so much that I decided to call and talk to my friend Bretha about my medical crisis.

"Tia, don't worry, you will be fine," Bretha said. "I just had a biopsy and my results came back negative for breast cancer. The only problem was it took me two weeks to get my dogonne results."

"Oh no, Bretha," I said. "I can't wait that long. That will be sheer torture. Girl, you must have Kaiser." I laughed, teasing Bretha.

Bretha acknowledged my anxiety and was very sweet as she tried to reassure me that I was going to be ok. After talking with her I was actually hopeful because her results were negative, so I thought maybe, just maybe, mine would be also. Prior to my biopsy, I had to undergo a series of mandatory pre-operative examinations and procedures, including an EKG and blood and urine analyses. Thanksgiving came and went as I mentally prepared for my biopsy on that following Monday, November 27th. PJ and I got up extra early on that Monday morning in anticipation of the 45-minute drive to the medical facility, in heavy traffic. I didn't wear any makeup that morning, and I combed my shoulder length hair back, and tucked it behind my ears. As I combed my hair that morning I thought, *If I have to undergo chemotherapy, I won't be able to tuck my hair behind my ears for a while, because I won't have any hair.* It was my anniversary and it was raining just like it was 24 years before, during the entire week leading up to my wedding day. It was very ironic. I thought we might be late for my appointment due to the crazy traffic but we actually made good time. We pulled up to the Women's Outpatient Diagnostic Medical Center, at Holy Cross Hospital, in Mission Hills, California, at about 8am sharp. PJ dropped me off at the entrance while he went in search of a covered parking spot. I was wearing a sweat suit, sneakers, and a hooded jacket that I pulled over my head to shield me from the rain. I ran towards the door hunched over as I tried to dodge every raindrop. PJ drove further into the covered parking lot as I attempted to enter the facility but the doors were locked. I was slightly annoyed because the nurse told me to be there at 8am *sharp!* So, there I stood, outside in the freaking rain. I pulled out my cellphone and called for PJ to come back and get me. I waited in the car for a little while, complaining like a grumpy old lady until I saw someone finally unlock the door. I got out of the car again but with a major attitude while PJ returned to the parking lot. The rain looked as if it was going to hang around for a while because it was that kind of overcast. Before PJ came inside, I had been called back into the examination room where I changed into my hospital gown. I had left my purse and all other valuables in the car so PJ didn't have to hang on to them. The nurse explained that the biopsy procedure would start at that location, and end across the street at the Surgical Center. I was apprehensive about having my breast cut on but I had no choice. I was afraid to fall asleep and then awaken only to find out that I had cancer. The nurse was explaining the details of the needle-guided wire procedure when PJ walked in. He sat close and comforted me until I was wheeled into a nearby room where the nurse prepped me for the insertion of the wire. PJ then went to a nearby waiting room until that procedure was completed.

"Mrs. Morris, the first part of the procedure is very tedious, and you may become faint or dizzy." I became more and more anxious as she went on. "It's more uncomfortable than painful but it's *very* important that you sit perfectly still, ok? Not to worry though. I will numb the area before the doctor starts to insert the needle." Just as she finished her instruction, Dr. Richter walked into the room.

"Ok. Mrs. Morris, because I can't feel your lump I'm going to use the computerized mammogram images of your breast to help me map a route to its exact location. Then I'm going to use the x-ray pictures from the mammogram to guide a small hallow needle to the tumor, and insert a thin wire through the center of the needle to extract a small sample of tissue." I felt like I was in the front row at a first year medical school lecture. "The sample tissue will be whisked off to the lab and examined under a microscope to determine whether or not cancer is present. If there is cancer, I will perform a lumpectomy and Sentinel Node biopsy to determine the extent of the disease. If, however, there is no presence of cancer, I will stitch you up and send you on your merry way."

"Whew, Ok," I sighed. That was all I could say. It was too much information to digest at that moment. I just wanted it to be over.

Dr. Richter gently, and slowly inserted the needle through the mound of fibrocystic breast tissue until only a small portion of the wire was left dangling outside of my chest. The procedure lasted a long 45 minutes, after which time the tissue sample was sent to the lab. For the second part of the procedure I was wheeled down the street to the Surgical Center. I was draped from head to toe with a mound of hospital blankets. It was still raining outside, so PJ walked close by and covered me as best he could with an umbrella, while the nurse pushed me down the street in an old rickety wheelchair. It was a bumpy ride down the sidewalk of uneven pavement, and I looked crazy wrapped up like a mummy. There was so much anticipation welled up inside of me, because I was within a couple of hours of learning my fate. The nurse pushed my wheelchair up to an unmarked back door and rang the doorbell as if we were guests entering an exclusive resort. The door swung open outwards just barely missing my feet, which were perched on the metal footrests of the wheel chair. The nurse then wheeled me down a long cold hallway and right into the holding room where about 20 hospital beds lined the walls separated by curtains. I was transferred from the wheelchair to one of the beds, reserved just for me. The nurse hooked up an intravenous tube in my arm and prepped me for surgery. The surgical staff was running late so I lay there in the prep room for about two hours exploring the various possible outcomes in my head while PJ stood close to me. I felt Mama's presence as if she was standing right there next to PJ. *Was history repeating itself? First Mama battled cancer; so was it now my turn? Did she pass some twisted proverbial torch to me her only daughter?* I wished Mama was never stricken with this disease, but since she was, I had hoped the family history of Breast Cancer ended with Mama, and that her sacrifice was enough to erase the burden of the cancer plight from the women of my bloodline for generations to come. As fate would have it, our left breasts proved to be problematic for the both of us. I didn't fully understand the gravity of breast cancer when Mama was diagnosed but I would soon be an unofficial expert on the matter. There were too many thoughts in my head to sort out while lying in wait at the surgical center. My wandering thoughts were interrupted when Dr. Richter appeared at my bedside and began explaining the second part of the biopsy procedure *again*. He had already done so in his office when we first met, but at this point, he needed me to sign papers consenting to the procedure. Afterwards, he left the room and went to the Operating Room to await my arrival. A few minutes later the nurse returned to my bedside.

"Mrs. Morris," she said softly, "they are ready for you."

The Anesthesiologist was waiting in the O R when I arrived, to give me a cocktail to put me under. The nurse checked my armband one last time and then stepped aside. The Anesthesiologist went on to explain all of the risks involved with utilizing anesthesia. I confirmed that I understood all the risks and waived the hospital's liability for any possible complications due to the anesthesia.

"Are you allergic to any medication?"

"No, I'm not allergic to anything that I know of."

"Ok great." He said as he injected me with the serum. Within minutes I was feeling *goooood*.

"Ok, Mrs. Morris count backwards from 100 for me."

"Ok…Ninety Nine, Ninety eight, *Niiiiiiiiiinety S..e…v..e…n.*" I was out. I floated away into biopsy land.

CHAPTER 3

"Back In Time"

IT WAS FEBRUARY 28, 1907, when my grandmother, Christine Louise Wesley, was born in Coffeyville, Kansas, a small town located in the southeast corner of Kansas, just north of Tulsa, Oklahoma. The 7.43 square miles of land housed 16,198 citizens with most of the African-Americans living on the east side of the industrial enclave. Coffeyville enjoyed rapid growth from 1890 to 1910, as its population expanded six-fold. From the turn of the 20th century to the 1930s, it was one of the largest glass and brick manufacturing centers in the nation. During that same period, the development of oil production facilitated the founding of several oil field equipment manufacturers, and it attracted more workers and residents. Grandmother grew up on a farm with her parents, and 15 siblings until 1928, when she married Carl Newsome. That same year, she gave birth to her first child, Laberta, and two years later she welcomed her second child, Juanda. Jobs were scarce for black men in Coffeyville during that time, so Carl told grandmother he could find good work about 140 miles away in Wichita, Kansas.

"Chrissy, just give me a few months to find a job, and a small house and I will send for you and the kids," Carl negotiated.

"Alright," Grandmother relented. "I hope you can find work because I need your help taking care of these girls. Things are more expensive in Wichita than they are here in Coffeyville so I sure hope we will be able to afford a house there, Carl."

"Don't you fret about that Chrissy," Carl said. "Let me be the man and you just take care of the chil'ren."

Grandmother reluctantly agreed to the arrangement because Carl was extremely good looking, and quite the lady's man, so she didn't like the idea of being separated from him. Several months went by after Carl set out to look for work in Wichita, and there was no word from him. Grandmother strapped on her walking boots and enlisted the help of one of her older sisters to drive her and her children to Wichita. In those days, all the blacks lived in one area in Wichita, so Grandmother took a photograph of Carl with her and went from door to door in the neighborhood looking for him. Finally, she happened upon a house where the woman recognized Carl, and she pointed Grandmother in the direction of Carl's house. With her young ones in tow, she walked up to that house and knocked on the front door where a beautiful young woman answered.

"Hi, can I help you?"

"Yes ma'am, does Carl Newsome live here?" Grandmother asked without hesitation.

"Yes, he lives here," the woman replied. "Hold on. Carl! Carl!" The woman yelled to get Carl's attention.

"What are you yelling for?" Carl asked as he walked quickly towards the front door. He was shocked when he saw Grandmother and his children standing there on the porch.

"Oh, h-hey Chrissy," Carl said as he stammered and looked back and forth between Grandmother and his new woman. The girls were excited to see their father and tried to run towards him standing in the doorway when Grandmother extended her arms out to her side stopping them in their tracks.

"Hey, what? You good for nothing Negro! I can't believe you left me and the children, and you never called or anything."

"Chrissy…" Carl searched for the right words to say. "Uh I can't believe you went through all this trouble coming to Wichita. Well, now you found me and I'm sorry for not sending for you and the kids."

"Looks like you have started a new life here," grandmother responded solemnly. "I see why you didn't come for the children and me. Girls, go back to the car."

Grandmother was as cool as a cucumber when she slowly turned and followed the girls back to the car. She was heartbroken.

"I wanna stay with my daddy." Aunt Juanda said as she and Aunt Laberta began to cry.

"Baby, I'm sorry, but your father is never coming back home."

Grandmother returned home and started working as a housekeeper for a white family during the day, and she dusted furniture at a store in downtown Coffeyville in the evenings. She had more than a dozen brothers and sisters and all of them lived close by so she had a great support system, especially in her time of need. Within a few months of leaving Carl's behind in Wichita, Grandmother started back dating. After a one-night stand with a man she hardly knew, she became pregnant with twins and on May 10, 1931, Ella and Della were born. During that time it was considered a disgrace to have children out of wedlock so grandmother gave the twins to a friend to rear instead of facing the ridicule. The rumor that circulated around the small town was that Grandmother chose to keep her *light skinned* children, Juanda and Laberta, but she willingly gave the twins away because they were dark complexioned. Unfortunately for them, Aunt Ella and Della were not only dark, but illegitimate as well. Grandmother was living amongst family with Laberta and Juanda for about seven years when she met her second husband, my biological grandfather, Eugene Karps May, at a local church. She clearly had a type of man as Eugene, or "E.K.," as everyone called him, and Carl could have passed for brothers.

E.K. was a soft-spoken, gentle man, who was short in stature, but spoke with authority. He was strong in his faith and proud. E.K., and his 14-year-old daughter from a previous marriage, moved to Coffeyville following the death of his first wife. Grandmother was impressed with his spirituality and was attracted to him immediately. They married in August of 1937, and in June of 1939, my mother, Mama was born. Carmen Rose May was the youngest of Grandmother's five girls. Aunt Laberta and Aunt Juanda were eleven and nine years old respectively at the time, and their new baby sister enamored them. They wanted desperately to name Mama, so Grandmother told them they could pick a nickname for her so they called her, "Chachie." Two years later, in 1941, Grandmother gave birth to her only son, Eugene K. May Jr. and they called him "Sonny." It was shortly after that when the twins came to live with Grandmother, finally meeting their siblings after 12 long years apart. After Uncle Sonny was born, E.K. was stricken with polio, which left him bedridden during all of Mama's childhood. In order to support the family, Grandmother went back to working two jobs. Although sickly, E.K. was a strict disciplinarian and a stickler about all the children using proper English when they spoke. By 1946, Aunt Juanda and Aunt Laberta were teenagers so E.K.'s limited mobility hindered his effectiveness in disciplining the older girls, especially Aunt Juanda. Aunt Laberta was a very soft-spoken, obedient young woman while Aunt Juanda spent most of her teenaged years hanging out in juke joints, smoking cigarettes and drinking alcohol until the wee hours of the morning. By the age of 15 she was completely incorrigible so Grandmother convinced her dad to let her live with him, so off she went to live with Carl's family; his mother and Aunts, in Omaha, Nebraska. Within a few months Juanda was pregnant and later gave birth to a daughter, who she left with the girl's father to raise as she continued partying well into her 20's.

Grandmother, Uncle Sonny, Mama (as a baby and pre-teen) and Aunt Laberta-1950's

In 1947, during a trip to New York City, Aunt Laberta met and married Clarence Hicks, an extremely handsome, fair-skinned man. Clarence was a philanderer, who within a short period of time emotionally destroyed Aunt Laberta's confidence. They both landed good jobs in New York City, but when Clarence got paid on Fridays, Aunt Laberta didn't see him until the following Mondays. He would come home broke, drunk, and smelling like cheap perfume; and Aunt Laberta never wore cheap perfume.

In 1948, Grandfather E.K. died in his sleep; Mama was only nine years old. Grandmother continued to work hard to raise her 6 children. She had always stressed the importance of higher education because she refused to let her children end up like her, with only a 6th grade education, and poor job opportunities. After Grandfather E.K.'s death, Aunt Juanda was still sowing her wild oats, while Aunt Laberta was experiencing married life in the big apple. In spite of their troubles, Clarence and Aunt Laberta tried for three years to have children without any success. Aunt Laberta was hopeful that having children would somehow make their marriage better, but that was not God's plan. A doctor told Aunt Laberta that since she had already tried to conceive for three years to no avail, that children were probably not in her future. Aunt Laberta loved Clarence dearly but she could not take the emotional abuse *and* the turmoil of not being able to have children, so they separated. Clarence's mother was crazy about Aunt Laberta so she begged her to stay and try to work things out with Clarence, but Aunt Laberta refused, and went to live in Chicago, near her sister Della. While in Chicago she often visited with a family friend she called Aunt Clara. Clara knew Aunt Laberta was distraught over her failed marriage, so she told her she wanted to introduce her to someone.

"Laberta," Aunt Clara said. "I hate to see you 'round here pining over a no good man. I know a real nice man that you should go out with. He ain't that handsome, but he is a *good* man."

"Naw," Aunt Laberta responded in her soft Midwestern drawl. "I'm through with men for the time being, Aunt Clara. Please don't try to set me up with anybody."

Clara didn't listen and invited the young man she knew, Wilkerson Johnson, over anyway. Wilkerson showed up dressed in a tailor made suit, crisp white shirt, and silk tie. He may not have been the best looking man, but he definitely had charisma. Thinking that Aunt Laberta would feel more comfortable going out on a date with him in a double dating situation, he invited his sister and her boyfriend to join them for an evening out on the town.

"Well, how was your date?" Aunt Clara asked when Aunt Laberta returned from her night out.

"I could go for him," Aunt Laberta replied in a coy demeanor. "I guess beauty really is in the eye of the beholder. I like him."

After a few dates, Wilkerson was so smitten he told Aunt Laberta that he would pay for her to officially divorce Clarence, whom she had been estranged from for a while. Two years later, on August 19, 1952, Aunt Laberta and Uncle Will were married. On their wedding night, Aunt Laberta confided in Uncle Will.

"You know, Will, I cannot have children," she said almost ashamed.

"That's alright, sweetheart we can adopt if you'd like." Uncle Will's words were comforting.

Nine months later, on May 25 1953, Aunt Laberta gave birth to their first child, a girl.

In 1955, Mama graduated from high school at 16. She was extremely smart, so Grandmother always expected her to go on to college. After graduation, Mama enrolled at Coffeyville Community College. She was very young and very naïve, but she was a fun-loving girl, who made friends easily. One such friendship she struck up was with Paul Higgins Pugh, or as everyone called him, "Chico." Chico was a 24-year-old Cuban immigrant, who was recently discharged from the Army. Chico was a tall, dark, and handsome foreigner, in town visiting a friend when he met Mama. Mama was a plump, shapely, pretty, fair complexioned girl with hazel eyes. Shortly after meeting Chico, Mama became pregnant at 17, and dropped out of college. Grandmother was furious.

"I shoulda known you was going to get yo'self in trouble over there at that college, Carmen," she scolded. "I *knew* you was too young to be around them grown men over there."

"Mother, I'm not pregnant by some college man," Mama replied. "It's Chico's baby."

"*Chico?*" Grandmother exclaimed. "You mean you been sleeping with that man who talk funny and come around here with those fancy suits and shiny shoes looking like some pimp?"

"Mother, he's no pimp," Mama corrected Grandmother. "He is a military man; he just got out of the Army, *and* he is a Tailor. I'm sorry mother. I didn't mean to get pregnant."

"Well that *military man or Tailor,* or whatever he is, better do the right thing because I'm not raising no mo' babies. You just a baby yo'self." Grandmother was visibly angry waving a spatula in her hand as tears welled up in her eyes. "Does he even know how old you are?"

All Mama could do was cry. She couldn't find the right words to explain her actions or comment on her situation at that moment.

Mama and Chico's "shotgun" wedding April 20, 1957

On April 20, 1957, Mama and Chico had a shotgun wedding in Grandmother's wallpapered dining room. Six months later, on October 11, 1957, Mama gave birth to Stefon a beautiful baby boy. Twelve months later, on October 25, 1958, at the age of 19, Mama gave birth to me, and seventeen months later on March 22, 1960, Mama gave birth to my little brother Edris. Mama had three babies in as many years, so it was clear that she was extremely fertile. Although Mama loved my father, she quickly realized that he was just a foreign hustler, who blew into town and repeatedly impregnated her, with no plans for their future. Reluctantly, after having Edris, Mama had her tubes tied to put a halt to her reproduction activity. Chico was not a pimp as Grandmother asserted, however, he was a member of the *Pachuco Gang*, an old school subculture of Mexican- and Latino-Americans associated with "Zoot Suits," street gangs, nightlife, and flamboyant public behavior. In a nutshell, Chico was a street-connected Cuban playboy, who really had no desire for family life. Although he was irresponsible, he wasn't a complete waste of human skin. He was an expert tailor, who made women and men's suits, and he had quite a clientele in Kansas.

In the early 1960s, while Mama was having babies, Uncle Sonny graduated from high school and enlisted in the Army to escape from Coffeyville and see the world. While stationed in California, he met his 14-year-old bride, Barbara, who already had an infant son. Barbara was an army brat and was living on base with her parents when she met Uncle Sonny. She was very promiscuous at an early age so her parents were happy that Uncle Sonny came along and made an honest woman out of her; not to mention, he took her and her child off of their hands. Uncle Sonny and Barbara later had two sons together, and at some point during their marriage, she had an affair, and became pregnant by another man, and had her 4th son. Uncle Sonny raised all of the boys as his own until he and Barbara split up a few years later. I was just a young girl, but I was extremely nosey. I ear hustled a lot, and I heard *all* the gossip when Mama talked to Uncle Sonny and their sisters. I just loved getting into grown folks' business.

Uncle Sonny and Barbara and their boys-1960's

About a month before I was born, Aunt Juanda married General Grant Lee Sullivan whom she met while visiting Aunt Laberta in Chicago. After they wed Uncle Grant and Aunt Juanda moved to the South Side of Chicago in a beautiful brand new tract home, a short distance from where Aunt Laberta and Uncle Will lived. Uncle Grant had six kids by his first wife, but he and Aunt Juanda had no children together. When Edris was born, Aunt Juanda tried to convince Mama to let her adopt Edris. Mama was the proverbial black sheep of the family, and often found herself on the defense when dealing with Grandmother and her siblings. If Grandmother wasn't scolding Mama about her "no good husband" and three kids, then her sisters or other self-righteous family members were doing their best to meddle in one way or another. Everyone felt like they needed to rescue Mama and her *kids*, which was the main reason why Aunt Juanda tried to relieve her of Edris.

"Chachie, you know you don't need no more kids. You are struggling and Chico ain't no good."

"I'm not having anymore kids Juanda, that's why I had my tubes tied." Mama remarked. "Edris is *my* baby and I'm going to keep him. And I'm tired of hearing that 'Chico ain't no good,' because you are no saint, Juanda. You and Grant fight like cats and dogs, so you don't need any kids. If you want a kid so bad go get your daughter from your ex." Mama was upset at Aunt Juanda's *holier than thou* attitude; it was often the source of contention between them.

Also in October of 1958, Grandmother married Wallace "Paw-Paw" McFarland, the only grandfather I knew. He was a sweet man, who cared about us kids and Mama a great deal. I loved Paw-Paw so much and he loved me back.

Grandmother and Paw-Paw and Aunt Juanda and Uncle Grant wed in 1958

Mama was forced to grow up fast after she had us, and when Paw-Paw realized that she was struggling, he convinced Grandmother to help Mama in spite of her *no good* husband. Paw-Paw had a good factory job and proved to be a great partner for Grandmother. He was definitely a wonderful grandfather to all of us children.

Almost everyone in the family loved Chico In spite of his childish and immature ways, because he was good-natured, with boyish charm. For the first five years of my life, we lived between our own home with Chico, and grandmother's house, which was right across the street. After six long hard years of married life, Mama and Chico separated; but because they generally *liked* each other, they remained friends and the amicable split made for a good co-parenting situation. After a while, though, it was apparent that Chico was nothing more than a cheap babysitting option for Mama whenever he wasn't out running the streets. Mama struggled to make ends meet in the small judgmental town of Coffeyville. Things got so bad that when Edris was three years old, after Aunt Juanda's adoption attempt, Uncle Sonny likewise offered to take care of my little brother for a while so Mama could get on her feet. Mama relented because it was clearer to her after breaking up with Chico, that she needed the help, so for two years, Edris lived in California with Uncle Sonny's family while Stefon and I stayed in Coffeyville with Mama. It was the summer of 1964, and if family members and friends weren't trying to take Mama's kids, then they were trying to find her a man, to take care of her and her kids. One of Mama's friends introduced her to a man who was from Wichita; Mr. Gene Vaughn. Gene was a gangly man, who looked just like Kareem Abdul-Jabbar. He was light complexioned and wore black horn rimmed glasses just like Kareem. Gene was a professional man who lived in a very nice home in Wichita. Mama and Gene dated for about a year before they married in a civil ceremony at the County Courthouse in Wichita. There was one problem; Mama was still *legally* married to Chico. *What the heck was she doing?* She moved forward and changed her last name, *and* ours, to Vaughn, and we moved to Wichita to live with our new stepdad. All that Mama ever wanted was a better lifestyle, and security, for herself and her children, and she thought Gene could provide that for us. Seemingly unable to live without Mama, Chico followed her to Wichita where he lived across town with his girlfriend and their twin girls, who were infants at the time. Gene was never affectionate towards us; in fact, he rarely interacted with my brothers and me, but he was a *good provider* according to Mama. Even as a young child, I knew that something wasn't quite right with our life, but I couldn't put my finger on it. Everyone in the family was just happy that Gene took Mama, and her kids, off of their hands. Life for Mama was relatively easy while hitched to Gene. She didn't work, and yet and still, she drove a beautiful, shiny, new black Lincoln Continental, with "suicide doors," around town. She proudly drove Stefon and me to and from our private Catholic school on most days.

After getting settled in with Gene, Mama wasted no time going to California to retrieve her baby, Edris. Edris wasn't school age so while Stefon and I went to school during the day, he stayed at home with Mama, right where his spoiled behind wanted to be. She had missed her baby boy and I'm sure he missed her too. That same summer Uncle Sonny got out of the military and relocated to Detroit, Michigan, where he landed a great job at Ford Motor Company. Growing up, Stefon was a spitting image of Mama with his fair complexion, sandy brown hair and hazel eyes. He went through a brief pudgy spell, because he loved to eat and he thoroughly enjoyed Mama's good cooking; I on the other hand was a carbon copy of Chico with the same almond-shaped eyes. I was a slender little girl with long limbs just like Chico, but I was a lighter complexion like Mama. Edris was a cute little brown skinned boy with adorable features as if he took the best of both Mama and Chico. In the 1960's, people put a lot of emphasis on the color of black people's skin tone. The lighter you were, the better you were treated. So, Mama was *extremely* overprotective of her little chocolate boy. Life was relatively good for us in Wichita. Mama and Chico were still good friends, and I was able to visit with him, and his new family, on a regular basis. Mama would drive her big pretty Lincoln up to the side of Chico's house and I would get out of the car, like a little princess stepping out of a carriage, with my bags in hand. My hair was always freshly done and my clothes neatly pressed. I was happy to get away from Mama and Gene's house every now and then because they argued; and sometimes those arguments ended with Gene punching Mama, and that hurt me just as if he'd punched me. In my young mind though, I thought that perhaps that was the adult way of settling disputes, so I grew to believe that was the norm. Mama was a loving, sweet, and attentive woman, but she could be stern when situations called for it. For some reason though, Mama couldn't protect herself from Gene.

By the summer of 1965, Uncle Sonny was thriving in Detroit as a Foreman at Ford Motor Company. He and Mama were very close, so he wanted nothing more than to have Mama and her kids close. Uncle Sonny loved Chico too, but knew he was pretty useless. He did not like Gene at all because Mama complained to Uncle Sonny about the ongoing physical abuse. Often times I would hear Uncle Sonny trying to coax Mama to leave Gene.

"Listen Chachie," he'd say in his deep thunderous voice, "You do not have to put up with that Negro. I have plenty of room here for you and the kids. You can stay with me until you can find a place of your own. Gene has no business putting hands on you, especially in front of the kids." Uncle Sonny was upset and Mama could hear that, but she felt stuck in her situation.

"I know, Sonny," Mama replied. "But I was tired of struggling before I met Gene. He takes *good* care of the kids and me. So I'll just have to deal with it."

"But Chachie, I can take better care of you here in Detroit. You think about it and I will drive there and get you and the kids."

It didn't take too much coaxing to get Mama to move after a few more fights with Gene. The decision was easy actually, because Mama hated the thought of returning to Coffeyville, a place where the hypocrites went to church all day, every Sunday praising God only to turn around and sin all week long. So, Mama was ready to leave Kansas for good. Afraid to confront Gene, Mama waited until he went to work one day and checked us out of school. She parked her shiny Lincoln at the curb in front of the house and loaded us up into Uncle Sonny's fancy Buick Elektra 225, or as Uncle Sonny called it, his "Deuce and a Quarter," and headed to the Motor City.

Things started out great living with Uncle Sonny and his family, but before long crazy Gene followed Mama to Detroit. One day Gene pulled up to Uncle Sonny's house in the shiny black Lincoln in an attempt to lure Mama back to him. Gene pleaded and vowed never to hit Mama again if she took him back. Mama agreed on the condition that we live in close proximity to Uncle Sonny. Gene obliged and we moved into a beautiful duplex in a predominately black middle class neighborhood on the west side of Detroit. My brothers and I began to notice that there was always a huge difference in Mama's mood when she was with Uncle Sonny, which was happy and carefree, than when she was alone with Gene. It was a stifling environment when we moved back with Gene, and the boys and I definitely noticed. Mama re-enrolled Stefon and me in parochial school; Stefon was in the third grade and I was in the second. There was no kindergarten in catholic school so Edris had to attend a different school for a year before he could join Stefon and me at St. Bernard's. Mama resumed her role as housewife taking us to, and picking us up from school every day. I was a model student, and the teachers loved me. I wore my uniform with pride and could not wait until I reached the 6th grade so that I could remove the suspender type flaps from the top of my uniform, and just wear the plaid skirt with a crisp white blouse, that Mama ironed for me. Oftentimes, on the way to school, Mama stopped us by a local donut shop, where we got pastries to eat on the way to school. On days when she had errands to run, she would drop us off at a bus stop where Stefon and I took public transportation the rest of the way to school. Sadly, our Catholic school days came to an abrupt halt during our second year because Stefon started to rebel.

School Days Stefon, Tia 1965 and Edris (Bottom Center)-1969

He refused to complete his assignments in class, and when the Nuns chastised him about his deficiencies, he kicked and fought with them. The Principal called Mama and told her that Stefon could no longer attend the school, and they recommended that Stefon undergo a psychological evaluation. Mama was perturbed at the suggestion that her child see a "shrink." During that time period black people didn't go to therapy, unless they were "crazy," and no one ever thought they were crazy so Mama was offended by the suggestion.

"My son is not crazy," Mama defended. "So, I will not be taking him to a psychologist."

Stefon was 8 years old and had been kicked out of elementary school, and because of his expulsion, Mama said that I had to leave the school as well. I cried and pleaded with Mama to please let me stay. I *loved* that school, and I loved wearing my uniform. Leaving the school dashed all my hopes of ever wearing that cute little plaid Catholic school skirt. I was so angry with Stefon that I punched him in his chubby gut when we got home. *Where was Stefon's aggression coming from? Was the abuse we witnessed at home affecting all of us? Did Stefon believe it was ok to fight women; even at such a young age?*

Mama always told the boys that they were not to hit girls, but then they saw her get beat by Gene almost daily. So, how could she hold Stefon accountable for taking out his aggression on the Nuns? Mama thought about it and decided to take Stefon to see a school psychologist after all before she enrolled us in our new school.

"Stefon is bored," The psychologist told Mama. "He's in the third grade, but his tests for English and Math place him at a 6th grade level." Basically he was too smart for his own good so the school Psychologist suggested Stefon be advanced to a higher-grade level, but Mama disagreed.

"I don't want him to grow up too fast," Mama replied. "He's just a little boy, and he's not mature enough to advance."

Mama always coddled the boys. It was as if she knew that the world was going to be hard enough for them as young men of color, so she wanted to protect them as long as she could. It was the end of the first semester when we were kicked out of Catholic school and Christmas was fast approaching. Mama enrolled the boys and me in the same public school closer to the house, which actually made it easier on her. That year she bought a beautiful, silver artificial Christmas tree with a multi colored wheel that rotated underneath the tree. The red, blue, and green colors from the light, reflected onto the shiny tree. It was so pretty. Throughout the Christmas season Mama slowly added wrapped gifts under the tree, but they didn't look like toys. *Where were all the toys?* I asked myself whenever I looked at the tree. It was customary for Mama to put the unwrapped toys that were too big to wrap under the tree on Christmas Eve, after we went to bed, and that particular Christmas Eve was no different. We went to bed extra early, hoping that Christmas morning would arrive sooner. After we were in the bed for a few hours, I heard my brothers creeping in the hallway outside my door. Edris's little brown face peered around my open door jamb, and into my room, and suggested that we go into the living room to take a peek at what was under the tree. Excited for a sneaky adventure, I hopped out of bed and we tiptoed down the hall towards the living room. We were thrilled to see that unwrapped toys had magically appeared under the tree.

"Yay! Look at the bike," I said in a loud celebratory whisper. "Look at the basketball! Hey, where's my Chatty Cathy doll?"

We started pinching each other with elated anticipation of the next morning when we would be able to play with the collection of fun we saw under the tree, when we were stopped in our tracks. We heard noises coming from Mama's room, and were afraid of getting caught snooping, so we raced back to our respective rooms and jumped back in bed before we could be discovered. Once back in the bed, I drifted off to sleep thinking about what I would play with first on Christmas morning. A little while later I thought I was dreaming when I heard Mama's voice screaming in the distance. Then, I heard panting as if someone was being chased. Edris and I reemerged from our rooms simultaneously while Stefon remained sleeping in the boys' room. We tiptoed hurriedly down the hall trying to find out where the noise was coming from. As we approached the living room, we saw a large, dark figure, like an oversized, deranged wild animal tangled up with Mama struggling near the Christmas tree. I thought Mama was fighting with a stranger who might have broken into the house in order to steal our toys; but when I cleared the murky sleep from my eyes, I realized that there was no thief, who had crept in on that night. It was that monster Gene; and he was beating Mama with a high-heeled shoe near the beautiful illuminated Christmas tree. Six-year-old Edris decided to be Mama's protector and jumped on Gene's back to try to pull him off of Mama. I just stood there unable to do anything but scream. The tree fell over with the glass ornaments and lights shattering all over the shiny hardwood floor. Gifts and toys were scattered everywhere, with torn wrapping paper and ribbons strewn this way and that. Christmas was a bust. *Why did Gene have to ruin Christmas?* I hated him so much. Afraid to stay there another minute, we abandoned our home that night and headed for Uncle Sonny's home, in a taxicab. There she was in the dead of night, in the middle of winter, in a taxi with three kids, no job, and no work skills to speak of. Mama was barely 26, with only a high school education to boast, a failed marriage, and a toxic living situation. Her life was essentially a mess. Mama's arm was bloody and bruised from the vicious attack with the high heel, and Uncle Sonny was furious when he saw her.

"This is *exactly* why I wanted you to move to Detroit, away from him Chachie," he said in a worried but angry voice. "This man is evil and he's gonna kill you if you don't leave him."

The beatings were routine in Kansas and Mama dealt with it. Uncle Sonny wanted to protect her from Gene and he felt like he'd failed her at that moment.

"Gene is a good provider." Mama responded through her tears. Grandmother had always reminded Mama of Gene's ability to provide for her whenever Mama hinted at moving back to Grandmother's house with her kids, so Mama felt she had no choice but to stick it out with Gene at any cost.

After the Christmas from Hell, we stayed with Uncle Sonny again until Mama could find a job and re-establish herself.

"I'm never going back to that fool, Sonny." Mama pledged. "I can't continue to subject myself and my babies to the violence."

Our lives literally changed overnight. Uncle Sonny helped Mama move us into an apartment and she eventually got a job and went back to school to finish her college degree. Our new place wasn't in the *Projects,* but it was in a rough part of town, where most heads of households were single mothers, like Mama. Mama had been a battered woman, but her spirit was not broken. We were starting over but we were finally happy, and relieved to have a place of our own without crazy Gene. My brothers and I played outside on most days after school until it was almost time for Mama to come home from work. On most evenings I walked to the bus stop to meet Mama because we no longer had a car, and I didn't want her to walk home alone. Mama's hands were always full when she got off the bus. She would have her purse on one arm and grocery bags or her dry cleaning on the other arm. I would run to Mama and relieve her of the grocery bags or dry cleaning and carry them to the apartment. Mama was very prideful and made *us* take pride in the way we looked. When I turned nine years old, every other Saturday, like clockwork, Mama and I caught the bus to a local beauty shop to get our hair done. Mama would order up a *press and curl* for me and the beautician routinely pulled my freshly done hair up into a high bouncy ponytail after she had finished curling it. Mama also took the boys every two weeks to a local barber for a fresh *Quo Vadis,* a short-cropped hair cut, which people modernly refer to as the President Barack Obama haircut. I admired the way Mama took such good care of us. We ate well and always had nice clean clothes to wear. She was finally growing up. We weren't walking on eggshells at home, and we weren't scared to go to sleep at night, anymore. Most nights I cuddled up under Mama, in her bed like a kitten, while the boys slept in the room they shared. We were finally safe and I felt good about that.

CHAPTER 4

"Dysfunctional Family"

IT WAS THE SUMMER OF 1967, and life alone with Mama was still good. We had survived *the 12th Street Riot,* the violent public disorder, which turned into a civil disturbance in Detroit during the early morning hours of Sunday, July 23, 1967. The triggering event was a police raid of an unlicensed, after-hours bar then known as the *Blind Pig,* located on the corner of 12th Street-Rosa Parks Boulevard and Clairmount Street on the city's Near West Side. Police confrontations with patrons and observers on the street evolved into one of the deadliest and most destructive riots in United States history, lasting five whole days. I witnessed looters in the streets with shopping carts filled to the brim with food, and toppling over with appliances, TV's and furniture. People carried couches through the alleys and right into their homes as sirens from police vehicles and ambulances roared all day and night in the distance. I was clueless as to the gravity of the chaos happening around me. I continued to play outside while Mama was at work, and I watched nearby businesses being set ablaze while neighborhood anarchists ran through the streets with an excuse to wreak havoc across the city. On one of those afternoons, when Mama was at work, I walked up to the main Boulevard, where our neighborhood drycleaners was located. I saw the owner, a small Asian man, scurrying about attempting to close and secure his business as looters approached the door of the cleaners. Before the owner could secure the door, looters emerged and ransacked the place while the man stood by paralyzed by fear. I stood directly in front of the store scolding the looters.

"Hey, my Mama's clothes are in there," I shouted. "You better not take them!"

I was amazed as looters threw bubble gum from behind the counter through the broken front window, out onto the sidewalk in my direction. *Oh boy, free bubble gum.* Just as I bent down to pick up some of the *free* bubble-gum, I felt a familiar hand grab a hold of my skinny little arm, and yank me forward causing me to drop my handful of treats. I looked up into the piercing hazel eyes of my Mama. She pulled me so hard I thought I might have suffered a whiplash.

"Girl, I have been looking for you," Mama said angrily. "Get your ass home!"

She was furious, scared, worried and relieved, all at once, to have found me unscathed. I didn't realize how dangerous the streets had become, and I didn't know that those ignorant black folks were acting out in a manner contrary to what Dr. Martin Luther King, Jr. had often preached against. After the smoke cleared, some things returned to normal, but the neighborhood was in shambles. The once thriving businesses were now boarded up and the remnants of burnt and damaged goods lined the streets. No one cared that we had to live in that soot because, after all, *we* caused it. It was less than a year later, on April 4, 1968, that Reverend Dr. Martin Luther King Jr. was assassinated. I remember watching the news reports, announcing Dr. King's death. What a sad day in history. Little did I know that I would experience a similar riotous nightmare some 24 years later in Los Angeles, when civil unrest erupted following the notorious Rodney King beating. Both riotous events stemmed from police actions.

It had been a little over a year since we left Gene's house and he tried desperately to get back with Mama. She was very vulnerable; she was alone with 3 kids and her self-esteem was at an all time low. She was tired of struggling, but she just could not bring herself to go back with him. Uncle Sonny was definitely against Mama getting back with him, and he made that sentiment known.

"Gene, yes, you were a good provider," Mama told him. "But my kids are getting older and I have to think about their well being. We aren't safe with you." Mama told Gene during one of his begging sessions.

Like Gene Vaughn, Chico followed Mama to the Motor City. Chico lived with his new girlfriend Beverly a short distance from where Uncle Sonny lived, so we visited with Chico and Beverly often when we were in the neighborhood. During the winter of 1968, Mama, the boys, and I were at Uncle Sonny's house for a birthday party for one of his four boys. He lived in the upstairs unit of a duplex, or *two-family flat* as some called it. The front of the building had six stairs from the walkway to the porch. If you were facing the complex on the left side of the porch was the entry door to the downstairs unit, and on the right side of the porch was a steep flight of stairs leading up to the second story, where Uncle Sonny lived. It had been snowing outside and it was freezing cold. There was a pile of hard snow on the ground in front of the stairs, and the stairs themselves were covered with ice. As the evening hours approached, all of the boys and I, were bathed and in our pajamas. My white cotton knee length slip doubled as my nightgown on that evening. Uncle Sonny was a big teddy bear standing at six foot six and weighing about 350 pounds. I was the only girl in the mix so Mama and Uncle Sonny spoiled me rotten. Uncle Sonny would often lift me off of the ground and spin me around as if I were flying. I loved my Uncle Sonny.

The boys were playing loudly in one of the bedrooms with the door closed. I was in the living room with Mama and Uncle Sonny watching TV as Barbara, Uncle Sonny's wife, lay passed out on the couch. The shallow doorbell rang and, not expecting company, Uncle Sonny and Mama looked at each other strangely before Uncle Sonny went downstairs to answer the door. Mama heard Uncle Sonny's voice, and another familiar sounding voice so she got up to join them downstairs at the door.

"Stay here, Tia," Mama cautioned, pointing at me.

I was nosey and was ready to follow Mama to the door but I stayed put listening to Mama's footsteps on the wooden stairs, and almost immediately after she reached the bottom I heard her arguing with someone. I ran to the top of the stairs and bent down at the waist in order to get a good look at the front door and porch from where I was. Mama was standing in the doorway behind Uncle Sonny so I didn't have a good view of whom she was arguing with. I tiptoed down the steps quietly for a better vantage point. As I descended the steps, I saw Gene standing on the porch facing Uncle Sonny demanding to talk to Mama alone.

"She's my wife, Sonny," Gene reasoned. "I have the right to talk to my wife."

"Well, she's my sister, Uncle Sonny retorted. "And you aren't laying a finger on her ever again."

I crept downstairs and was hiding in the shadow of the doorway at the bottom of the staircase. I could hear the boys playing loudly upstairs but they had no clue as to what was going on downstairs. From my hiding spot, I could see a yellow taxicab with foggy windows parked and idling in the driveway. Mama stepped from behind Uncle Sonny in order to talk to Gene against Uncle Sonny's wishes.

"It's ok, Sonny," Mama soothed. "I'll just listen to what he has to say."

"Carmen, come back home, baby," Gene begged. "Things are different. I'm different."

Mama stood firm and refused to go with him. She was tired of talking to him and turned away from Gene to return to the house, when he pulled a long thin metal object from his coat pocket. Gene quickly grabbed Mama by her left wrist and stabbed her on her left forearm. Mama started screaming and tried to wiggle away from his grasp. She struggled trying to get back to the door and Uncle Sonny, when she slid on the icy stairs outside. Just as Uncle Sonny went to her aid Gene then turned his violent rage towards Uncle Sonny and began stabbing him with the same metal object he used against Mama. I was terrified watching this unfold. It was as though a monster from a past nightmare had come back to haunt us. I ran outside onto the porch where Uncle Sonny was lying in a growing pool of blood; I jumped off the porch and into the snow at the foot of the stairs as Mama wept hysterically by Uncle Sonny's side. She was so distracted that she didn't see me glide past her. She was bleeding profusely from her arm as she screamed.

"Oh my God!" She shouted hysterically. "Please call an ambulance!"

I was so frightened at the sight of all the blood, and the sound of Mama screaming and crying, that I took off running away from the house towards the main Boulevard with reckless abandon. I was barefoot and wearing only my slip and panties; and I was running for my life after the attack against

Mama and Uncle Sonny. Before I knew it I had run nine blocks to Beverly's house. I had been to Beverly's house so many times with Mama, I knew the way by heart. My sense of direction and recall was superb for a child my age. Mama said I always had a great memory, even as a toddler. Well, it served me well during Gene's late night attack. Upon reaching Beverly's home in the middle of the night, I was so cold I could hardly speak; I couldn't even feel my extremities. Finally, I was able to convey to Beverly what happened. She called Uncle Sonny's house and spoke with Barbara, who was awakened by the chaos. She told Barbara I was there. No one knew I had even left. Beverly put me in some warm clothes, and in a warm bed. I quivered for hours as my body slowly came back to life. The next day I was reunited with Mama and I was told that Gene stabbed her and Uncle Sonny with a screwdriver. Uncle Sonny was stabbed 17 times in the chest and back, and Gene escaped in the awaiting taxi. *What a lunatic.* Luckily, Uncle Sonny survived the horrendous attack. I never found out if criminal charges were ever sought or brought against Gene because that was the last time we ever heard from him. Mama kept Vaughn's last name, but she rightfully changed our last name back to Pugh.

In the spring of 1969, Uncle Sonny helped Mama buy a three-bedroom house on the west side of Detroit, and he got her a nice brand spanking new navy blue Chevy Impala. It was beautiful. Chico opened up a tailor shop on the west side of town, on Grand River Avenue, a short distance from our new house. Chico made suits for people in the music industry, and he was sharp every time we saw him, but he still wasn't paying child support. I was ten years old when we moved into our new house. The boys and I were excited about living in a house in a nice part of town *and* we had a car again, hallelujah. Mama didn't have to take the bus to work anymore, and she was able to go back to school on a regular basis, at night, to finish her college degree, at Wayne State University. Mama was working two jobs, so she took classes that fit in with her work schedule. She was always gone, and I missed her so much that on some nights I went to school with her. I sat in the back of her classroom and rested my head on an empty desk until class was adjourned. I could have stayed at home but I wanted to be with Mama as much as I could, especially after her attack. To help relieve some of her stress, I kept my room, and the rest of the house nice and tidy. I changed the sheets on our beds regularly and cleaned our one and only bathroom daily. My clothes were arranged neatly in my closet and my shoes neatly lined the baseboard inside my room. Mama didn't stand for us lying around in our rooms unless they were clean. We had to get up early everyday, get dressed and make our beds immediately, even on weekends.

"If you want to lie down after your chores are done," she'd say, "Make up your bed first and lie down *on top* of the covers after your chores are done."

Because of Mama's busy schedule, in addition to cleaning the house she relied on me to cook, to do her banking, and the laundry. Mama routinely sent me to the bank with her checkbook and her signed payroll checks, for me to deposit.

"Listen closely, Tia," she instructed. "Make sure you wait at the teller's window until the lady stamps my deposit in my checkbook."

"Ok, Mama," I responded, eager to please her and make her proud.

"It's real important that you get a receipt for Mama's deposit." she reminded.

That was my first lesson about independence and trust, and I was very obedient. All of the tellers at the bank knew me. I would stand on line and usher customers past me so I could get the same female teller every time. She was a pretty lady with blond hair. Some how, I thought we were friends. She always smiled and waved for me to come to the window where she reached down to take the checkbook from my little hands. I had a tight grip on that checkbook, as I stood there barely able to look over the counter. I always had a *no nonsense* look on my face, and attitude, as if to say, *I ain't going nowhere until you give me my receipt and stamp my Mama's book.* The laundry was my least favorite task because we had no working washer or dryer in the house, so my brothers and I walked to the nearest Laundromat to wash our clothes on a bi-weekly basis. The boys and I bagged up our dirty clothes, and piled the bags on top of each other in a red wagon. We pulled the wagon through the neighborhood, past all of our friends' homes and onto the busy street to the Laundromat. Once inside the Laundromat, I sorted the clothes and placed them in several washers at the same time, and then in the dryer once the wash cycles were done. The boys sat outside while I washed and folded the clothes.

Sometimes, if we had extra coins, they would go next door and buy *Hostess Cupcakes*, chips, and soda, to eat while we waited for the clothes to be done. There were many times that we got all the way home only to realize that we had left a dryer full of clothes behind. I felt like crying every time because we had to walk all the way back to get the clothes we had left. Laundry day was always a whole day ritual and I hated it. The only chore I was not allowed to do was take out the trash. That job was reserved for the boys, according to Mama. Mama was a stickler about maintaining an orderly home. She normally got home between 11PM and midnight from her second job, or earlier on days she went to school. When she walked in the house, if the kitchen was not cleaned to her standard, or the bathroom was dirty, she roared through the house like a lion. If we were already asleep, she woke us up and made us complete the chores that were not done. I had a good work ethic at an early age, so it was always the boys who got us in trouble for not doing *their* chores. School nights were extremely tough because we were usually awakened after midnight to clean, and then went back to bed only to get up again a few hours later for school. We were supposed to take turns washing the dishes and cleaning the one bathroom we all shared, but I was so livid about the boys' laziness, that I started doing all the chores myself just to make Mama happy. The boys loved that I resorted to doing all the work because it was less they had to do. Even on Sundays, if we weren't going to Church, we still had to get up at a reasonable hour; way before noon, and clean the house.

Speaking of church, when Mama was a child she lived in church all day on Sundays and sometimes during the week; but that wasn't as big a turnoff for Mama as the churchgoers themselves. Mama loathed one of the devoted, highly respected Deacons in the family church, who found time to molest her when she was only nine years old. Mama told Grandmother about the abuse but Grandmother didn't believe her. Those fine examples of Christians proved to be disappointing for Mama as she thought deacon was part of her *extended family*, and family didn't do that. When Mama left her hometown she vowed that she would never force us to go to church with such heathens. So with the exception of the short stint we spent in Catholic School, my brothers and I didn't attend church on a regular basis for many years while growing up. Mama was torn because she loved the Lord and she taught us right from wrong; she taught us to follow the Ten Commandments; and she instilled in us that we should forever be *God-fearing*, forthright people.

"You can worship God in any place, and at any time, babies," she'd say. "You don't *have* to go to church."

On the evenings I had to cook dinner, Mama would instruct me over the phone while she was at work. The first meal she taught me to cook was a pot roast with potatoes and carrots. She also showed me how to wrap and bake a potato in the oven; and how to make fresh broccoli with cheese. My food always turned out delicious using Mama's recipes. Mama and Grandmother were fantastic cooks, and I wanted to cook just like them. Mama's day job was as a clerical employee for the County, and at night, she was a Switchboard Operator at a hotel in downtown Detroit while she continued on in school. The hotel job was Mama's introduction to homosexuality and prostitution all at the same time. The location was a hot bed for heterosexual and homosexual prostitution, and drug activity. Mama was fascinated by the nightlife at the hotel. She was a very naïve little country girl, however, within a short period of time she became acclimated to the big city environment, and befriended several of the prostitutes, and one gay man in particular. Walter became one of Mama's best friends. Walter was what folks back then referred to as a big *sissy*. The colloquial term was used to describe particularly flamboyant male homosexuals; I had no idea, until I got to high school that it was a derogatory reference. Walter was a big man, who was tall and thick like Luther Vandross, in Luther's heavier days. In contrast, Walter's boyfriend was much smaller than he was, and Mama loved them both. Mama quickly transitioned from a small town girl into a grown woman living in a big metropolitan city with 3 mouths to feed. She shed her polite, girl next-door Coffeyville image, and developed a loud, fun-loving, larger than life persona that everyone wanted to be around. Mama's laugh could be heard for miles; she didn't smoke, but she drank sociably; and she was the ultimate social butterfly. She could not afford to overindulge in any way because she had the boys and me to care for, so a little Rum and Coke or Vodka and Orange Juice, were her drinks of choice every now and then. On special occasions, like Thanksgiving or Christmas,

Mama even allowed us a sip or two of her alcoholic beverages when we begged her long enough. She was usually in a celebratory mood, so she frequently gave in. She would hold her glass slightly tilted towards our eager lips so we could get a little taste. Those drinks danced on our young taste buds like fireworks on the Fourth of July, but it was that loose discipline that would one day come back to haunt Mama with my brothers. Mama's friendships with the cast of characters from the hotel exposed me to diversity, and she openly talked about sexual orientation, and lifestyles alternative to what was considered mainstream. Mama told us all sorts of stories about Walter and her street life friends from the hotel.

"I can't wait for you to meet your Uncle Walter," She'd say to us. "He's like a sister to me."

"A *sister*, Mama?" I asked, confused.

"Yes, baby, *a sister*. You'll see."

She was right. *Uncle* Walter was a sweetheart and he definitely loved Mama. He did in fact act and talk the way most women did, so the *sister* reference ultimately made sense. Whenever Uncle Walter came over, Mama would issue her standard warning:

"Walter, I will kill you if you even so much as look at my boys," she'd threaten playfully. "I'm not playing with you." Walter would giggle like a big old teenaged girl, and switch around with his big butt.

Another new friend of Mama's was a prostitute named Audrey, who was addicted to Cocaine. She was a very petite and pretty young woman, if you could see past the day old make up and tired raccoon eyes. Mama brought Audrey home one day after her pimp locked her out of her hotel room.

"Here's the deal, Audrey," Mama negotiated on the ride from the hotel. "When we get to my house, you have to call your mother, ok?" Audrey agreed without hesitation.

Mama was surprised when Audrey's mother arrived at the house to pick her up. Gloria was a beautiful, well-dressed woman. Mama and Gloria became friends and before long, Gloria introduced Mama to her brother, who lived with their elderly mother.

"Oh, Carmen," Gloria said. "My brother, Ronald would love you girl."

"Really?" Mama asked.

"Yes, but I have to tell you, he is recently divorced and has two young children."

"Ok." Mama responded, waiting for more information to leak out of Gloria's mouth.

"And...he likes to drink." Gloria said under her breath.

"I see. So, he's an alcoholic," Mama concluded. "Well what does he do for work?"

"He drives trucks and delivers merchandise," Gloria replied, relieved that Ronald's drinking may not be a complete deal-breaker for Mama.

Gloria introduced Mama to Mr. Ronald Ely, and after a few months they started dating. Thankfully, he was much nicer than old abusive Gene, alcoholic or not.

When Chico wasn't working at his shop he was always hanging around the house. Usually when Mama was working late he would come to the house to babysit us. It was at those times that I realized just how immature my father was. He was so playful he got on my nerves. I just wanted to be left alone in my room to play with my dolls, and allowed to make doll clothes. I would demand that my brothers give me the old clothes they no longer wore, and I used my own old clothes as well, to make my dolls' fashions. There was no way I was going to ask Mama to *buy* me doll clothes for my Barbie dolls when she could barely buy clothes for me. Chico and the boys took pleasure in annoying me. They tickled my underarms until they hurt, and they rough housed with me and taunted me until I was angry enough to punch one of them in the face. When Mama came home I pleaded with her to please save me.

"Please, Mama," I cried. "Please don't let Chico come over when you aren't here."

"Oh, Tia, calm down, baby," Mama replied. "Chico is barely here and you need to see your daddy."

As luck would have it, the situation resolved itself. Chico's visits became more and more infrequent, until they were almost non-existent, and that was cool with me.

The summer of 1968 came and went, and we had not seen much of Chico for months. Mama was not worried, so we went on with our day-to-day lives hoping that he would surface at some point. I had just started the 5ᵗʰ grade, Stefon was in the 6ᵗʰ, and Edris was in the 3ʳᵈ grade. Stefon and I attended Ford Middle School in Detroit, while Edris attended the nearby Parker Elementary. Ford was about three miles from our house but the elementary school was right down the street. Stefon and I took public transportation to and from school, and when the bus was too crowded we walked the 12 blocks to and from, together. School had been back in session a few weeks after summer break when I returned home from school one afternoon and saw a crowd of people lingering in front of our house. Fire trucks also lined the street, and smoke was billowing in the air. I was surprised to see the smoke coming from our house, which had caught on fire. Mama had been sleeping in between jobs when Edris returned home from school and decided to boil himself a hotdog. Instead of waiting for it, he decided to go outside and play while the hot dog boiled on the stove. A short time later Mama was awakened by smoke. When she got up to investigate she discovered the kitchen was on fire. Luckily, she escaped unharmed; but in terms of our house, what the fire didn't destroy the Fire Department did. I was so relieved to know Edris hadn't set the house on fire smoking cigarettes. He was only eight years old, but Stefon and I had caught him smoking cigarettes in his room before. He shared a huge room with Stefon in an unfinished upstairs attic. We discovered that Edris was smoking earlier in the spring after the winter snow had melted and we saw dozens of cigarette butts on the rooftop where Edris discarded them, from his bedroom window. No one knew exactly where he got the cigarettes. The fire turned out to be a blessing in disguise because the house was completely remodeled afterwards due to the smoke and water damage. We lost some personal items, that were all replaced, but at least we still had Mama unharmed. We stayed with Ronald and his mother for a few months while the house was being repaired. Ronald and his family were such wonderful loving people. Gloria loved Mama dearly, and felt indebted to her for helping Audrey escape from her pimp and accompanying reckless lifestyle.

By late January of 1969, we had moved back into the house and Mama enrolled me in a charm school at a nearby Department store called *Federals*. I woke up excited every Saturday morning, put on one of my cute mini dresses, and white pleather knee high go-go boots, fixed my hair, and walked to Plymouth Road to catch the bus to the store. Once there, I would go upstairs to the second floor into a big empty room where there was a plywood makeshift runway set up, and chairs that lined the walls leading to racks of clothes at the far end of the room. I learned how to walk the runway as part of the curriculum. I was challenged to walk straight with my shoulders back, and required to perform all the pivots and turns that were critical in modeling. The rigid instructor would check my posture by standing me flush up against a wall while she tried to drive her hand between the small of my back and the wall and twist her hand in the small gap. I also learned how to properly get in and out of a car with my legs together, like a true lady. At the end of the 10-week session, I participated in a fashion show right there in the store. The highlight of being in the charm school was that I got to keep the outfits I modeled. I loved clothes so I was thrilled. After charm school ended, several months passed and we still hadn't seen or heard from Chico. It was a cold day in late March of 1969, when Mama's neighborhood friend Art stopped by to visit on a Saturday afternoon. Mama, Art, Beverly, and Chico were all very close and they visited most often at Beverly's house. Since Mama worked so much, she hadn't hung out at Beverly's much so she wasn't aware that Chico was missing in action. I heard Mama and Art cackling in the living room, so I went to hear what they were talking about. I sat on the floor nearby making dresses for my dolls while Mama was getting caught up on the latest gossip from Art. Before long, Art brought up a rumor he had heard about Chico.

"You know Chachie, I heard through the grapevine that Chico's dead," Art said casually.

"Stop lying! That's not true." Mama quipped, nearly choking on the water she was drinking.

"Well, I know it's just a rumor, Chachie." Art continued. "But, I did hear he was shot and killed during a robbery." Mama never knew Art to lie or fabricate stories. He usually only reported the gossip that he had verified through reliable sources so he had her attention. "I know it might be scary," Art said. "But, maybe you should call the Coroner's Office to see if it's true."

I loved Art because he was very kind to Mama, the boys, and me. Whenever he came over I was stuck to him like glue. I'm pretty sure he was my first crush because he was very handsome. As I sat on the floor while Mama and Art had the conversation about Chico, I couldn't help but wonder why Mama didn't make me leave the room. I was so immersed in the adults' conversation that I had butterflies in my stomach as I anticipated Mama's call to the Coroner's office. Mama sat on the couch nervously rubbing the soles of her feet together. Mama positioned herself on the end of the couch closest to where the landline telephone was on the table. Mama sat the phone on her lap and steadied the bulky bottom part of the phone with her left hand as she picked up the receiver with her right hand. It was as if everything was moving in slow motion. Mama and Art continued to banter back and forth as to whether they believed the rumor about Chico. Art paced back and forth between the front door and the end of the couch where Mama was sitting. Every time Art took a drag from his Kools cigarette, he closed one eye to keep the smoke from stinging both eyes. He looked down at Mama with one eye open as she dialed the operator for information. After retrieving the number to Detroit's Wayne County Medical Examiner's office, Mama slowly dialed the rotator phone. She looked nervous.

"Hello...hello, I...I...I'm calling to see if you have someone...a dead someone...there by the name of Paul Higgins Pugh...?"

"Hold on honey, let me transfer you," the lady on the other end replied.

"Can I help you?" The man asked.

"Yes, I am calling to find out if you have someone there..." Mama asked ever so slowly with a tight grip on the receiver. I scooted my rear end closer to Mama while twirling Barbie by the hair.

"What's the name?"

"Paul...Pugh..."

"Nope, we don't have nobody by that name in our system.

Mama looked relieved but not really satisfied. She looked up at Art who was puffing feverishly on his cigarette, and mouthed, *I told you fool...* with her lips turned up in one corner. Mama was preparing to hang up when the man continued.

"We could have him as a *John Doe* if he was brought in without identification. Can you describe him for me?"

"Yes I can…He's a black man… 37 years old."

"Well, we do have a black man who has been here about a month. He was the victim of a gunshot wound… but he is about 65 years old."

"Oh no, the man I'm looking for is only 37 years old…so I know that is not him."

Mama had butterflies in her stomach. *John Doe* was a victim of a gunshot wound, and according to Art, Chico was shot, but Mama could not get past the huge age difference so she thought it couldn't possibly be him.

"Can you tell me when this *John Doe* was brought in?"

"Yes ma'am, he has been here since January 31st."

"Really?" Mama replied.

"This is all the information I can provide you over the phone so if you would like to come down and view the body to see if this is the fella you are looking for please do." Mama hung up the phone and turned to Art.

"Come on, you are going to the Morgue with me because they can't give me anymore information on the phone."

"You gonna buy me a half pint?" Art asked as he walked towards the front door. Art flicked his cigarette butt onto the front porch, and extinguished it with his foot.

"No, I'm not buying you anything. You came over here talking about Paul being dead so you are going with me but I'm not buying you anything to drink. Not even a soda pop."

Mama gathered her keys and purse and pulled her jacket closed to face the cold weather as she and Art left for the morgue; I wanted to go too, but Mama told me to stay home with my brothers. Ronald was either at work or somewhere getting drunk. Mama and Art arrived at the Wayne County Medical Examiner's Office just as they were preparing to close. The grim attendant stood behind the counter and peered over his glasses, which dangled on the bridge of his nose like a teeter-totter. Mama stood still and looked around the lobby of the morgue nervously. Just as her thoughts and fears started to over-whelm her, she was quickly snapped out of her trance.

"Go on, Carmen." Art urged in a whisper. "Tell the man why we are here, please."

Startled, Mama rolled her eyes at Art, and in her very proper white lady voice, she addressed the attendant.

"Is this where I can confirm whether a dead family member was possibly brought here?"

"Yes, what is the name of the decedent?" The man asked as he accessed his index card file.

"P-P-Paul Pugh."

"Ummm, let me see…there is no one by that name in our file, Ma'am."

"Oh ok," Mama replied, unsure of what to do or say next. "Can you please check the John Doe file for a possible match of a male black with a gunshot wound, who has been here for about 30 days? He's a 37-year-old male black and he's about 5'11."

The attendant flipped through the file cabinet behind the front desk and read the information out loud. "I have a male black John Doe, who was brought in here approximately 30 days ago, but he is listed at 65 years old."

"No, then that can't be Paul," Art inserted, "because he is only 37."

The attendant looked at Mama and saw the growing desperation on her face. Maybe he realized that she was looking for someone close to her; maybe he had a twinge of compassion that ignited in him; whatever it was, he started to seem more invested in assisting Mama in her search. "Does Paul have any identifying marks on his body?" The man asked as he looked at the file documents.

"Uh…well, he does have a half moon tattoo on the web of his left hand."

The attendant's eyes lit up. "Ma'am, the 65-year-old corpse that we have *does* have a tattoo on his left hand, see?"

The attendant handed Mama the index card he had retrieved from the file cabinet. As Mama read it, her stomach rose to her throat.

"Art, it says he has the same tattoo as Chico," Mama squealed.

"The Pachuco tattoo?" Art asked.

During his more active days with the Latin gang, Chico had gotten a crescent moon tattooed on his left hand to symbolize his allegiance to street life; Los Pachucos utilized crowns, five-pointed-stars, and moons and the left side of their body to display their affiliation or membership. If they wore a hat, it was tilted towards the left; if they put their hand in their pocket, it was the left hand inside the left pocket, and so on. Chico had a tattoo on his hand and so did the corpse.

"Yes," Mama responded, "that one." She was now trembling at the budding realization that her first love, the father of her three children, could be laying in a cold drawer in the very building that she stood in.

"Ma'am, can I show you some pictures and you tell me if this is the man you are looking for?"

Suddenly, Art backed away from the counter as if he had seen a ghost.

"What is your problem?" Mama whispered to Art.

"I don't think I want to see him like this... if this is him," Art replied.

"Get your scary behind back up here next to me!" Art rejoined Mama at the counter as the attendant pulled out two Polaroid pictures from the file and laid them on the counter. Mama reluctantly viewed the images of the dead body in the photograph. After a few seconds, her mouth fell open in disbelief.

"Oh my God!" Mama shrieked as she cupped her hands over her mouth. "That's him! That's Paul!"

There he laid, my father, the coroner's *John Doe,* dead from a gunshot wound to the right side of his head just below his ear. Mama could not control her emotions as she broke down and cried right there in the cold, dark lobby of the Wayne County Morgue. *How could they think he was so much older than he actually was? Was it the haircut they gave him at the hospital in preparation for surgery that may have revealed his prematurely grayed hair? Or could it have been the facial swelling that resulted from the gunshot wound to his face, which undoubtedly could have made him age instantly?* Whatever it was, it prohibited the medical examiners from properly identifying my dad. Anxious to hear the results of Mama's morgue trip, I tried to stay awake to wait for her to return, but after a couple of hours passed, I fell asleep on my bed with remnants of cut up clothing and my Barbie dolls all around me. I had to wait until the next day to hear all about Mama's trip to the morgue. After claiming Chico's body, Mama planned a modest funeral. Easter Sunday had recently passed, and Mama had bought me a pastel yellow pleated Easter dress with a Peter Pan collar, that I picked out of the Spiegel Catalogue. I decided I wanted to wear my Easter dress to Chico's funeral so Mama bought me a white lace veil to wear over my Shirley Temple curls, and my face, as the grieving daughter; and as the grieving widow, after all she was still legally married to Chico, Mama wore a matching black veil to compliment her black dress. During the service, I sat in the front row right next to Mama. When it was time for the viewing, I walked up to the casket and looked down at Chico lying there. I studied his face; and the bullet hole behind his right ear that was stuffed with flesh tone clay; and his eyelids and lips that were glued shut. I gently touched his face and it was cold and stiff. He looked different. The Chico I knew was tall and handsome with a kilowatt smile. His face was long, and not round; he had dimples and a goatee, but there were no traces of those attractive features lying there in the casket; they were forever gone. I was sad; Chico was my dad. As unconventional of a family as we were, I was still going to miss my Chico. The service ended and everything seemed so surreal. But God always has a plan. Chico's death resulted in child support payments, for the first time in many years, in the form of Social Security Survivor's benefit checks for my brothers and me. Mama received a lump sum death benefit check, as well as the monthly social security benefits for the boys and me. It turned out that Chico was more beneficial to us, and Mama, in death than when he was living. My brothers and I would receive our father's death benefits until we were 23 as long as we remained full-time students, otherwise, the checks would stop coming once we turned 18.

CHAPTER 5

"Moving to Cali"

THE MOTOR VEHICLE INDUSTRY WAS booming in early 1970 and Uncle Sonny was still working at Ford Motor Company in Detroit. Mama continued to work two jobs and she managed to finish college earning her Bachelor's Degree in Sociology from Wayne State University. Things were looking up in her life, both personally and professionally. In addition to the pimps and prostitutes, whom Mama befriended at the hotel, she also developed a friendship with a woman named Betty Clark, who worked with her on the Hotel switchboard. They remained close even after Mama left the hotel to become a full time Social Worker. A few months after Mama left the hotel job she received a call from Betty.

"Carmen, girl, you know me and Al are moving to California?"

"Oh, really?" Mama was a bit saddened by the news because her best friend was going to be moving out of state.

"Yes, honey. You know, I was thinking… maybe you and the kids should come with us to California."

"Oh, I don't know, Betty," Mama replied. "I don't know anything about California. I mean, I visited Sonny once when he was in the Army out there, but he brought me here to Detroit so I don't want to leave him."

"Girl, it's beautiful out there, and there are better job opportunities for Al so we gotta go. I can work at a switchboard anywhere *and* they need social workers everywhere so think about it." Mama paused as she contemplated the possible opportunities in California. "Ok, it's more than a notion girl. Let me think about it and talk it over with Ronald and Sonny, and I'll let you know."

Mama and Betty could pass for sisters as they were both fair skinned and on the plump side. Betty was so light that she almost looked albino. Mama thought about Betty's invite for a few days, and when she brought it up to Ronald he was on board with the idea of relocating because he knew he could find work as a truck driver in California with no problem. Uncle Sonny on the other hand didn't want Mama to leave, but he agreed there were better opportunities in California for Mama, and a better living environment for us kids. By that summer Mama was thoroughly convinced, and excitedly accepted Betty's invitation to move with her to California. For several years my brothers and I had spent every summer in Chicago with Aunt Juanda and Uncle Grant in order to give Mama a much-needed break from parenting. In the summer of 1970, Mama was making plans to move to California so instead of us returning to Detroit that fall, we stayed and started the fall semester in school in Chicago, while Mama got settled in California. Stefon was 12, I was 11 and Edris was 9. The plan was that we would join Mama in California in the middle of the fall semester. Ronald and Mama drove her Chevy Impala to California with just our clothes. The move to the west coast was a dream come true for me because I was ready to see movie stars, and live where the weather was *always* warm. The thought of no more snow was heavenly. My brothers and I worked that entire summer at Uncle Grant's restaurant, *Sully's Teapot,* a little burger joint located inside of the National Guard Armory on the south side of Chicago, that only opened on *Drill* weekends. That summer was our 4th year working there. The boys worked in the kitchen cutting potatoes and onions while Uncle Grant flipped burgers, fried Chicken, and made sandwiches. They hated working in the kitchen with Uncle Grant because he worked them to the bone.

"Man, Uncle Grant is a slave driver," Edris complained. "I can't wait to go back to school to get away from here."

Obviously there were no child labor laws back then because he definitely would have been in violation. I was the sole waitress at the restaurant and Aunt Juanda worked the cash register. When business was slow Aunt Juanda sat in the booths with some of the service men and talked, drank liquor and smoked cigarettes. I was tall for my age. I was about 5'4", very thin with long legs, and I wore a size *B* cup brassiere, which I was embarrassed about. I was very shy and hated to wait tables at the restaurant. I was completely disgusted by the old men, who were probably only in their twenties at that time, but they flirted with me and I was only 11 years old. Aunt Juanda protected me from the horny men like a prison guard. She had the mouth of a sailor, so she cursed them out from sun up to sun down if they looked at me too long.

"Listen here, this ain't Vietnam damn it, and my baby ain't no Mail Order Bride, so if you look at her too long I'm going to cut you!"

Uncle Grant's regular job was as the Head Chef on the night shift at a *Rodeway Inn Hotel* located off of a major highway in Chicago. Aunt Juanda did not cook at home so during the week Uncle Grant brought home leftovers from the hotel's restaurant for us to eat. He *could not* cook, but thought he could, and he would get mad when we didn't eat his hotel leftovers. Most other days, I cooked dinner for me, the boys, and Aunt Juanda before Uncle Grant got home. At other times we walked next door to the *Burger King* located at 87th and State, where I got my favorite meal: a fish sandwich, fries, and a coke; and the boys each got Whopper meals. Whether I cooked or we ate out, we made sure we were full by the time Uncle Grant got home. Aunt Juanda and Uncle Grant lived right across the street from the Dan Ryan Freeway, and the *L* train station so it was convenient for her to take public transportation to work at *Ecko Bake ware,* in the Franklin Park community of Chicago. Aunt Juanda left her pretty pink Cadillac parked inside the garage at home, and took the train to and from work instead of driving. She left every morning at about 5:00 AM and arrived back home at about 4:30 PM, Monday through Friday. Everyday at about 4:15 PM, I would stand at the window, and stare at the train station until I saw Aunt Juanda emerge from the subway. I watched her walk across the busy intersection towards the house smoking a cigarette and carrying her purse. I loved me some Aunt Juanda, especially when she was drunk, which happened to be everyday. She was a tall, light complexioned voluptuous woman. Uncle Grant, on the other hand, was not the most fun to be around. He was short and dark with crusty hands. He was ruggedly handsome in his younger days but he was very mean spirited and he frequently picked fights with Aunt Juanda. I was too young to really understand the dynamics of their marriage, but from my vantage point he was the bad guy. I was always excited when Aunt Juanda got home because it meant we would be hitting the streets making our rounds to her different friends' homes for long evening visits. There was one house that we visited at least once a week, and in that home lived an elderly woman and her middle aged son, Albert. We called Albert, Uncle Pee Wee but he was really Aunt Juanda's *boyfriend*. Yes, she had a man on the side, and I knew that at 11 years old. I probably would not have known anything had Aunt Juanda not sworn us to secrecy.

"Don't tell your Uncle Grant we came to see Uncle Pee Wee," she'd tell us on the way home from our visit.

"Why?" I asked innocently. "Uncle Grant doesn't like Uncle Pee Wee? He's so nice."

"Just do what I say Tia, damn." Aunt Juanda snapped. "Uncle Pee Wee is *my* friend and if Uncle Grant knew we came here he would be mad at *us*."

"Oh, Ok." I resigned "I won't say a word. I don't want Uncle Grant to be mad."

Uncle Pee Wee was a very handsome man, who Aunt Juanda dated before she married Uncle Grant. Uncle Pee Wee's mother had always wanted him to marry Aunt Juanda, but Aunt Juanda saw otherwise.

"I'm sorry but Albert is way too trifling for me," I heard Aunt Juanda tell her girlfriends. "I could never marry him. He can't hold down a real job, and doesn't handle his responsibilities like a man, so we would always be broke."

Although Uncle Pee Wee wasn't marriage material, he was definitely good enough for an ongoing fling and drinking partner. These little rendezvous' went on for the entire summer, *every summer*.

As the summer of 1970 ended, Uncle Grant closed down *Sully's Teapot* for the season. The boys and I took the money we earned all summer and went shopping for school clothes. We usually returned to Detroit with our new clothes, but that year we started out sporting our new fashions in Chi-Town instead. The change in our end of summer routine was not an easy adjustment. I missed Mama so much, and the only thing that kept me jazzed was that we were going to be joining her in *California*. Aunt Juanda and Uncle

Grant were always happy to see us come but more excited to see us go. Staying with them for the start of the school year meant they were totally responsible for us in ways they had never been before. Right away Aunt Juanda turned into a complete witch, as a full time mother figure, because in order for her to care for three school-aged kids effectively, she needed to be sober, and that was not what she signed up for. I quickly realized that the *drunk* Aunt Juanda was the woman I loved so much because the *sober* Aunt Juanda was no fun at all.

"I agreed to help Carmen," I overheard her complain to Uncle Grant one night. "But this is some bullshit. I have to make sure that *they* get to school, and back, *and* I have to make sure they do their homework and shit. I can't wait for her to send for their Asses."

School in Chicago was uneventful for the ten weeks that we were there, but it ended up being the longest ten weeks ever for my brothers and me. Mama sent for us at Thanksgiving time that year, and I was *not* going to miss Chicago at all. Mama didn't have a lot of money, so she had Aunt Juanda put us on the Amtrak train a few days before the holiday. I had never been on a train before, so I was excited for a little adventure across the country. Once we boarded the train, however, my excitement dissipated quickly. We were on that damn train for three whole days and four nights. By the time we arrived in California, I was sweaty, funky, and ready for a good old-fashioned bath. It was Thanksgiving Day, November 26, 1970, when our train pulled into Union Station in Downtown, Los Angeles. The beautiful landscaping, and majestic palm trees, swaying in the breeze mesmerized me. I was wearing corduroy slacks, a colorful print shirt, boots, and a big winter coat with a fake fur collar. I was warm and cozy when I left the Windy City; but when I stepped off the train in California, I was burning up. It was at least 85 degrees outside, and there I was walking out of the train station wearing what looked like a big jungle cat. I looked like a country bumpkin for sure. Mama and Ronald were waiting for us at the station and Mama was grinning from ear to ear. I was so happy to see her, and she was thrilled and relieved that her babies made it safely. We were all she had and she was all we had.

Mama had found a place for us to live in the Ladera Heights area of Los Angeles, a beautiful community surrounded by other beautiful areas; such as

Baldwin Hills and View Park, where affluent African-American doctors and lawyers, and some black celebrities like Ike and Tina Turner, and baseball great, Curt Flood lived. They had gorgeous homes with swimming pools and manicured lawns that anyone who passed by envied. Nearby Fox Hills, was an area mostly comprised of modern townhomes where the young and sexy jet-setters lived; and Inglewood another close community, was where middle class proud African-American families lived in modest homes and apartments. So, it seemed that Mama lucked up and landed us in the right community. Just a short distance away was an area the locals referred to as *The Jungle;* that name, at the time, was not indicative of the nature of the black people who lived there but rather named after the beautiful landscape and foliage that adorned many of the apartment complexes which lined the streets. Years later, the name became synonymous with the violent gang activity that took place in the streets and alleyways of the once beautiful neighborhood. When we moved to California in 1970, *The Jungle* was just starting to change for the worse. Betty and her husband had moved into one of the beautiful spacious apartments in *The Jungle,* so naturally that is where Mama looked first; but for some reason, Ladera Heights called to Mama, and that was where we settled. We lived in a very modest three-bedroom apartment on a busy thoroughfare. We spent the first weekend exploring the neighborhood, and preparing to check into our respective new schools. Things were different in L.A. compared to Detroit and Chicago. For instance, the concept of kids being transported by *school bus* to schools outside of the areas where they lived was foreign to me, unless you were a special needs child. Back east, if we were to take a bus to school, it was public transportation or we went to the school closest to our homes and we walked. In Los Angeles, the widespread city enabled families to apply for their kids to go to public schools farther away from their respective homes for a chance at a better education, should their home school be in a substandard environment.

On the Monday following Thanksgiving, Edris and I were enrolled in Orville Wright Junior High in Westchester, a predominantly white community about 10 miles west of Ladera Heights, and Stefon was enrolled in Crenshaw High School, located in the opposite direction from Westchester, in a black community east of where we lived. I didn't know anyone in California, so I was nervous about meeting new friends, especially considering the affluence that surrounded us. Although we were financially challenged, Mama busted her butt to keep good quality food on the table, money in our pockets, and fashionable clothes on our backs. Our clothes were inexpensive and mostly came from *Sears, Kmart, Zody's,* or other similar discount stores, but they were always cute and trendy. Mama pressed and curled my hair every week because we didn't know of a local beautician, and my brothers sported well-manicured Afros. When I got tired of the hot hair grease sizzling in my ear or searing my scalp, I too opted for an afro of mega proportions, or French braids adorned with white beads like Venus and Serena Williams wore as young girls in the 90s. I was in seventh heaven being in California and it didn't even dawn on me that I was living in such close proximity to so many well-to-do and famous people. The corner of Slauson Avenue and Overhill Drive was the first school bus stop in my neighborhood, so I walked up the long, steep hill from my apartment. I always grabbed a window seat on the school bus and hoped and prayed that no one sat next to me. I was so thankful that no one really noticed me because I would not have known what to say if they did talk to me. I sat on the bus every day staring out the window taking in all the scenery. The bus took a circuitous route through *the hills* of View Park and Baldwin Hills, and along the way it stopped in front of luxury homes, some of which stretched a block long. It was as if I was on one of those *Hollywood Home of the Stars* tours; it was all too amazing, but of course I couldn't show just how fascinated I was or the snooty kids on the bus would know I was straight off the train from Detroit. As each kid from those neighborhoods got onto the bus I thought to myself, *Wow, they are just as beautiful and well manicured as the houses they live in.*

During my first few days when the bus pulled up in front of the school, I saw several other school buses from other parts of the City lining the streets around the school. I noticed that some of the kids who got off those buses were not quite as beautiful, and not as well mannered, as the kids on my bus. I was somewhere in the middle of the two groups of people, I suppose. I wasn't beautiful but I was cute, and I was not dressed to kill, but I was matching, and if someone happened to make eye contact with me, I would at least give a shy smile with my straight white teeth. The kids from the other buses were the complete opposite. Some were loud and rowdy, others disheveled, and some just looked like they had woken up on the wrong side of the bed. *Oh, so this is what bussing is all about?* I realized. *Mixing up the races and classes of folks.* By the end of the first week, I had the routine down, but I still didn't have any friends. On the Friday of my first week there, I showed up to register for my Physical Education (PE) class, and to get a locker. The line was long and the girls working in the PE office were taking their sweet time and chatting it up a little too much. Finally, when I got to the front of the line the girl assigning lockers took my information card and inspected it as if she was a United States Customs Agent.

"Hey," she said, "you live on Slauson?"

"Uh…Y-Yes." I replied nervously.

"I think I live right next door to you!" She said excitedly.

"Oh really?" I asked. "That's cool."

"I'm Roslyn." She said with a warm smile.

"Tia."

"Do you take the school bus, Tia?" Roslyn asked.

"Well yeah." I responded. "Is there any other way to get here?"

"Well there is, but I was asking because maybe we can walk to the bus stop together. And hang out after school."

"Oh!" I laughed. "That would be nice. I'll see you later." I said as I waved coyly and walked away briskly.

That was the start of my very first friendship in California. Roslyn was a tall very busty girl with a huge gap between her front teeth, and she was a bit cockeyed. I didn't care about that, because I had finally made a new friend. We spent many days after school hanging out at Ladera Park playing softball, and catching the Metropolitan bus to the strip mall at Crenshaw and Martin Luther King Jr. Boulevards to shop at *Lerner's* trendy clothing store, and *Baker's* shoe store. Shortly after meeting Roslyn, she introduced me to her best friend, Pat. Pat lived in View Park, where I had seen all of the pretty people. She was a petite, brown skinned girl, who wanted to be Michael Jackson; she actually *thought* she could sing like the King of Pop but she was so wrong. She had older parents and several much older siblings, so she was spoiled rotten. She had a small music studio at her house where she had every instrument under the sun, but she primarily played the guitar and drums. Having a friend with a music studio was right up my alley because while in Middle School in Detroit, I was part of the school choir and right before I graduated my music teacher selected me to sing a solo during my 8th grade graduation ceremony. While rehearsing, the school principal came into the auditorium. She was so blown away by my voice, that she called Mama and told her she hoped Mama could make it to the graduation to hear me sing. Mama was so elated that she ran out and bought me the prettiest frilly white mini dress she could find for my grand singing debut. The dress and matching white shoes were beautiful but I didn't like how the dress showed off my knobby knees. So, here I was in California with my two new California friends who thought they were musicians. Things were also looking up in the friends' department for Stefon and Edris. They had met some neighborhood boys while playing ball at the park. When springtime arrived, Stefon signed me up to play softball, and signed up to coach my team. Stefon was a pretty good youth coach. He was organized and very responsible with getting me, and the team, to and from our games all over Los Angeles.

By January 1971, Mama and Betty were finding their way around the city and were meeting new friends as well so it seemed as if all was good with our new life in L.A. until one day, Mama received a call from Uncle Sonny.

"Chachie, I slipped on some ice and broke my damn leg," he explained. "I'm in the hospital going stir crazy. I need to get out of here because I need to go back to work."

"Sonny Eugene," Mama replied. "You need to stay your butt in the hospital until the doctor says you can go home. You need to stay off of your leg before you fall again."

"I know, but I got a family I need to take care of and I can't do that in this hospital."

"I understand Sonny, but you can't work if you can't walk, so stay your behind right there. I'll call to check on you in a day or so. Ok? I love you."

That was the last time Mama spoke to Uncle Sonny because a few days later, Grandmother called and told Mama that Uncle Sonny was dead.

"What? Mother, what are you saying?" Mama asked shocked and confused.

"Sonny left the hospital against the doctor's advice and as soon as he got home, he collapsed and they couldn't revive him. He's dead, baby... he's dead."

I could hear some of Mama's conversation and Grandmother was frantic. Mama crumbled to the floor weeping in our living room. Poor Mama was devastated. Her baby brother and protector were gone. Uncle Sonny was the youngest, and the first, of Grandmother's children to die. He was buried in Coffeyville; Mama flew home alone for the funeral. She couldn't afford for us all to go, so we stayed in L.A. with Ronald. We found out later that Uncle Sonny died from a blood clot that travelled to his heart. It was commonly known, by medical personnel that blood clots were a concern with leg and knee surgeries, which was why the doctor probably did not want to release Uncle Sonny prematurely. But it was too late, because he was gone and we never saw him or his boys ever again.

In the spring of 1971, Roslyn, Pat and I were having fun hanging out together. We even started a singing group in our spare time. Near the end of the school year we entered the school talent show singing *Betcha by Golly Wow,* a hit song recorded by the *Stylistics,* and we won first place. My stock went up after the talent show because I started meeting new friends and quickly became known as the "girl who can sing." I no longer had to stare out of the windows on the school bus rides because more and more people talked to me, and accepted me into their circle of friends. My short stint at Orville Wright was just the confidence booster I needed to prepare me for high school. In the fall of 1973, I matriculated to Westchester High School as a sophomore. During the first semester, I joined the girls' Junior Varsity Basketball Team but I was horrible at basketball, so I moved on to the Volleyball team. I was good at Volleyball but the season overlapped with my favorite sport, Softball, so playing Volleyball was also short lived.

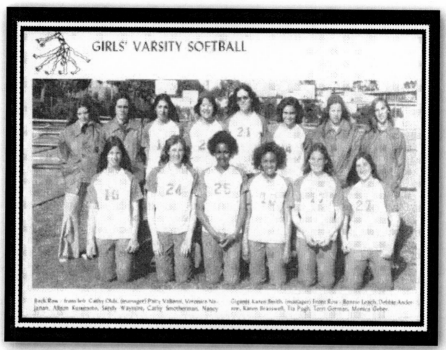

GIRLS' VARSITY SOFTBALL

Back Row - from left: Cathy Olds, (manager) Patty Valland, Veronica Na-janian, Allison Russman, Sandy Waynire, Cathy Smotherman, Nancy ... Gigantt, Karen Smith, (manager) Front Row - Bonnie Leach, Debbie Ander-son, Karen Braiswell, Tia Pugh, Terri German, Monica Geber.

My Varsity Softball Team- Tia #10 and my friend Karen #25

I was the proverbial beast in softball. I was a well-rounded in-field player; I caught well; I threw better than most of the boys on the varsity baseball team; and I ran fast. It was early in the school year when I befriended my teammates, Karen and Twyla. Karen and I were on the Varsity team, and Twyla was on Junior Varsity. Roslyn also attended Westchester, however, by 10th grade she had a steady boyfriend, that she hung out with most days, and I was busy playing sports and partying with my other friends, so my friendship with Roslyn waned during our high school years. Ultimately she and her family moved away from the neighborhood, so we didn't see each other at home anymore either. I was a tomboy through and through, and that notion did not sit well with Mama. She loved when people remarked that I should model as it validated her sentiments about how I should always look and carry myself. It was like pulling teeth to get Mama to come to my softball games when she was available. I knew she was tired most of the time, but I still wanted her to see what a good player I was. There was another girl on my team whose mother was at *every* game, and she would bring homemade cookies and praise us throughout the game. I *loved* it when she showed up and I would pretend that she was Mama sitting there in the bleachers cheering me on. I never told Mama how I felt because I knew she didn't have much spare time, and I never wanted to make her feel bad so I kept pretending that she was there. California was turning out to be the land of opportunities for me. One summer, my next-door neighbor, Irene, saw me leaving the house with my hair French braided.

"Hey honey." She called out to me. "Who does your hair?"

"I braid my own hair," I replied, smiling proudly.

"Oh really?" Irene asked. "Well my father and his new family just moved here from Chicago and they need someone to braid my 9-year-old half sister's hair for the summer. How much do you charge?"

"I will braid her hair for free." I chuckled at the thought of charging her. "I love to braid."

"Oh honey, please, I will pay you *something.*"

Irene was a pleasant woman, who waitressed at the *Hamburger Hamlet* in Beverly Hills. She made a pretty good living off of her salary and tips. I thought she would be a good friend for Mama to have, so I introduced them. When Irene got to know me she found out that I also liked to iron and make things look nice in homes, so in addition to paying me to braid her sister's hair, she also paid me to iron her sheets and pillowcases. I had found a way to make some extra spending change. Irene loved my work ethic for a young girl, and she later appointed herself as my *Godmother.* She wanted kids very badly but was unable to conceive, so she became a sort of surrogate mother to me and various other neighborhood kids who lived in her apartment building. Over the next several years Irene's and my friendship blossomed, and Mama and I often visited her at the Hamburger Hamlet where we ate lunch on occasion. Those trips were my introduction to Beverly Hills and Rodeo Drive. During Irene's daily dealings, she met all sorts of people, many of them wealthy. Irene thought I was a pretty girl and she insisted that I be a model so she took it upon herself to introduce Mama and me to an agent who was looking for girls and young women to model aboard a dinner cruise ship to Catalina Island, as well as other venues. I was 15 at the time. I was excited by the thought of finally utilizing all that I learned back in Detroit in charm school years earlier. On one occasion while modeling at an event in Inglewood, a woman in the audience prompted a young man from the audience to ask me to dance after the fashion show. His name was Darnell, and after we danced the woman who was with him approached me.

"Tia," the woman said tentatively making sure she had my name right. "I saw you dancing over there with Darnell. How would you like to audition to dance on *Soul Train*?"

"Yes, I would love that!" I screeched. I could hardly contain my excitement, but then I remembered one small detail. I needed to ask for Mama's permission. "Well, I have to ask my mother first, and she isn't here. Can I let you know sometime this week?"

Unlike in the movie, *Sparkle,* where the sisters sneaked out of the house at night in search of a music career, I knew I had better ask and get Mama's approval or I would never dance *anywhere* least of all, *Soul Train*. I could not wait to get home and tell Mama the news. She said *yes* without hesitation, so I called the woman and she sent me to the Gower & Sunset Studios in Hollywood for the audition. The audition room was a big empty space filled with about 200 *Soul Train* dancer hopefuls. I made the cut, and within a few weeks, I was dancing on *Soul Train* with Darnell Williams, the young man who had asked me to dance at the Inglewood event. Dancing on *Soul Train* was yet another dream come true for me. Before I left Detroit, I would often stay up until midnight on Saturdays in order to watch all the lip syncing artists pretend to be singing live, and watch Damita Jo Freeman robot her way down the infamous Soul Train line. A few short years later, there I was on that very show, dancing on national TV. I danced with Darnell for only a few episodes before he moved on to other partners, and later he became a series regular on the long running soap opera *All My Children*. He eventually stopped dancing on Soul Train and I never saw him again except on television. There were opportunities popping up everywhere for me so I was a happy camper.

Although Mama was working as a Social Worker for the County of Los Angeles, she still picked up a second job at an answering service on Vernon just east of Crenshaw Boulevard in South Los Angeles. Mama was familiar with the answering service job, and she drew from her experience at the hotel back in Detroit. The Answering Service in Los Angeles was different in that it was a service primarily to field doctors' off-hour emergency calls. Ronald continued working in the trucking business and landed a job at *Bayview Trucking,* so he was on the road often. Edris was fascinated with *big rig,* 18-wheeler trucks so sometimes during the summer months Mama let Edris go with Ronald on his short road trips. Ronald still drank alcohol heavily but was considered a functioning alcoholic. He was arrested several times for driving drunk during his spare time, so as time went on he became increasingly unreliable, which is why Mama kept two jobs to ensure she could make ends meet. My brothers and I were at home a lot by ourselves on most evenings, just as we were in Detroit the difference was that we were older and more responsible. We were good kids and Mama had us on a short leash.

By the spring of 1974, Stefon was in the 11th grade and had found his first job working at Ladera Liquors, a store a block away from home. Mama didn't really want any of us to work while we were in high school because she wanted us to just focus on school, but it was great Stefon was working because he didn't have to get money from Mama anymore, and he was a second revenue stream for me. After working for a few months, Stefon bought himself his first brand new car: a bright red Fiat with tan interior. It was a cute little five speed, and surprisingly roomy for such a tiny car. I had taken Driver's Education in the 10th grade, and learned to drive an automatic, but Stefon taught me to drive his new stick shift. I learned quickly, and it was a fun car to drive. Stefon readily became a taxi driver for my friends and I. In addition to driving us to our softball games, he took us to neighborhood house parties as well. It was great having Stefon at those parties too, because whenever wannabe thugs or other pesky characters annoyed me and my friends Stefon rescued us. It was especially helpful because usually the local gang members got pretty aggressive with us girls when we didn't go along with their program. If we weren't careful, and we stepped on their Stacy Adams shoes, or their shiny *Biscuits,* we had better standby because those minor indiscretions resulted in fights or worse yet, shootings. At that time, house parties were the "in" thing and all the local uninvited *Crips* and

Bloods, took pleasure in crashing those parties. It was after one of those house parties when we were in route to taking my friend Twyla home in South Los Angeles, when we were involved in a hit and run accident at Van Ness and Manchester while waiting for the red light to change. A drunk, old man in a big old raggedy car crushed the front end of Stefon's car but by the time we all came to our senses, the son of a gun had taken off; a classic Hit and Run. Thankfully none of us were injured. We drove Twyla home and continued on home with the front bumper dragging on the pavement. Several days later, the insurance company assessed the damage and totaled Stefon's car. He later went back to the same Fiat dealer, and got a bigger, better Fiat. This time he opted for a bright orange model. I lived vicariously through Stefon when it came to having a nice new car. All of the pretty, wealthy kids living in the hills were just starting to get their first cars too. One by one they stopped riding the school bus and drove to school instead in their new Datsun B210's and the like. When I would stand outside of the T.V. Studio in Hollywood waiting in line to go inside to tape *Soul Train*, I'd see my girl, Vicky, drive up in her brand new, bright green Volkswagen Sirocco. *Man, I loved that car*, I thought every time I saw her drive up. I wanted that car so bad. Vicki was one of the pretty people who lived up in the hills, but she was not stuck up she was cool. Whenever I couldn't use Stefon's or Mama's car, I caught the Rapid Transit District (RTD), bus in order to get wherever I needed to go. I wanted a job so badly, but Mama stood firm and didn't allow me to work.

"Tia, how many times do I have to tell you," she'd recite. "There will be plenty of time for you to work. Just focus on school. I don't want you to have to grow up too fast, baby."

"I know, Mama, but they're building a new shopping mall in Fox Hills, and I really want to work in one of the stores there. There's going to be a *Judy's* and a *5, 7, 9* store there." I begged Mama for weeks hoping she'd at least let me try it.

"Ok," she said, surprisingly. "But it had better not affect your grades."

"Ma, I *prrrromise* you it won't affect my grades," I replied, too excited to contain myself. "I promise."

With Mama's blessing, I marched my butt right down to the dusty mall the very next day after school. The construction was still going on while hundreds of people stood on line to apply for jobs at various stores throughout the mall. There were hiring signs all over the place, but I only applied to the aforementioned two stores. As it turned out, neither one of the stores hired me, so I stayed broke. Mama was relieved that I didn't get a job, but at least she gave me a chance.

During my junior year in high school, Irene caught me singing out loud while I was ironing some sheets at her house. Just as she had gotten me the modeling jobs, she mentioned my singing skills to another regular patron of hers, a foreign executive. I was sixteen, tall, thin, firm, and fit. I had transitioned from an awkward tomboy, to a really cute, teenaged girl. Before long, Mama and I met with the middle-aged executive from France, and his female partner. They heard me sing and loved my voice and my look. They immediately enrolled me in private voice lessons at a quaint music studio on La Brea Avenue in Hollywood. They also provided me with free clothes for a photo shoot, which took place at an unsuspecting home studio in Compton. Mama was very protective of me so she insisted that Stefon take me to the photo shoot and stay with me the entire time. The photo shoot went great. The male black photographer was very professional, and the house, which was converted to a studio, was very nice inside. Mama probably should have sent Stefon with me to the voice lessons too because the French executive who was preparing to launch a blue jeans pant line was in town one weekend and decided to stop by the music studio during one of my voice lesson sessions.

"Hey, Tia," he said in his slight French accent. "I thought I'd stop by to see if you wanted a sample of my blue jeans." He said slyly holding up a pair of windowpane jeans.

"You can take a quick break, T," my vocal coach said as he stepped out of the room.

"Thanks so much." I replied to the executive. "I'd love to try on a pair."

"Great, great." The executive said as he handed me the jeans.

"These are nice." I said loudly as I changed in the nearby bathroom.

"Let me see." He said as I exited the restroom to show him the jeans. "Oh, yes, they are perfect," he said as he slowly approached me to get a closer look.

I was shocked and disgusted however, when he leaned in and tried to kiss me. I backed away in disbelief.

"Ugh!" I screamed. "I don't think so!" I pushed him away from me as hard as I could and I ran out of the studio with the jeans still on. Needless to say, the voice lessons he was paying for ended abruptly. That stunt taught me a huge lesson that *nothing* in life was *free;* and I never accepted anything from a man ever again until I got married. I wasn't happy that my voice lessons ended, but I still had softball. I played at school and on weekends, *and* I still filmed *Soul Train* one weekend a month so I was good for extracurricular activities. During our high school years, my brothers and I remained very close. We had no other family in California, so it was important that we supported one another. Mama placed a lot of emphasis on what *she* wanted for Stefon's future, because he was so smart. He achieved straight A's without even studying, where I, on the other hand, was all over the place with my grades. I was a solid "B" student with little effort, but I had to put in some work in order to achieve A's unless it was English, Art or Biology. Those were all topics I was interested in, so I gave them my full attention, and did very well. Edris, had already flunked the 3rd grade, and he barely made it through junior and senior high school. Mama refused to accept that Edris was not college material. He was not lazy but he was emotionally *unstable,* in my opinion. Regardless of our level of potential, according to Mama, we were all going to college, and that was not up for debate. Mama declared early on that Stefon was going to be a doctor, but their plans were incongruent. Mama wanted me to go to college but she really never expressed *what* she wanted me to be in particular. I told Mama I wanted to be a Psychologist, but I needed to be proficient in math and science, and I wasn't, so my *Plan B* was to major in English or the Arts because I was good in both subjects. Stefon and I tried to get Mama to stop pressuring Edris about going to college because it was probably not going to happen. Her attempts to force him to go just made him despise me and Stefon, because he was very insecure and believed that Stefon and I thought we were better than him since we wanted to go to college. He didn't realize that we were *all* just looking out for his best interest. It was a good thing that he went on those ride-a-longs with Ronald in the big rigs, because at least he was exposed to an employment option that didn't require a college degree. Mama had high hopes for Stefon, her first-born, and her twin. During our high school years, Mama was very liberal, and faltered when it came to disciplining my brothers. When Mama found out Edris and Stefon were smoking weed she allowed them to drink alcohol *and* smoke marijuana at home and I couldn't believe it. Her philosophy was that she would rather they smoke at home so they would not get arrested doing so out in the streets. During the sixties and seventies "weed" was primarily the drug of choice amongst teenagers and young adults. I hated cigarette smoke. Actually, smoking in general was gross to me, so I didn't want to smoke any *hemp leaves, weed, marijuana* or whatever it was called. All of the girls I hung out with in high school either played ball with me or ran track, so most of us didn't smoke or drink anything. Mama had done a great job keeping us safe as young children, but in our teenaged years, it seemed that her parenting skills were on hiatus in some respects, when it came to her stance on allowing the boys to smoke weed. Unfortunately, Mama's free-spirited lifestyle laid the foundation for what was to come with both of the boys. Contrary to the boys' cultivating their weed and alcohol habits, my idea of fun was hanging out with my girlfriends on the weekends. We frequented the "Kappa House" on Crenshaw Boulevard for social events, birthday parties and dances; or we would spend time on college campuses, like Loyola Marymount University and West Los Angeles College, whenever there were parties at those venues; we sought out good clean fun activities, and didn't dare risk our livelihood playing sports, by drinking and/ or smoking weed.

I was the only one of my friends who lived in an apartment, and I was embarrassed about that, so I never volunteered my place for us to spend our free time. We were struggling financially, but I didn't fault Mama for our living situation because she was doing the very best she could. It seemed she was always in survivor mode. She had finally married Ronald, only, unlike when she *married* Gene, this time, her marriage was legal because Chico was deceased so she was free and clear to remarry. My brothers and I were teenagers and we were still getting our monthly checks from Social Security, so there was no way we were changing our names to *Ely*.

While Stefon and I didn't date in high school, Edris on the other hand started dating at 15. His first girlfriend, Tammi was an only child, who lived with her mother a short distance away from us. They lived in a very nice apartment complex in the Mid City area of Los Angeles. Mama always wanted to meet our new friends' parents as soon as she could in order to keep tabs on us. Mama quickly bonded with Tammi's mother because they were both single, and responsible mothers. Tammi and her mother were like bookends; they were both very petite, standing only about 4'9," and as cute as all get out. Edris had become a handsome young man and the girls loved him. He was about 5'6" tall, and all of 140 pounds, with a muscular physique and smooth brown skin. Edris and Tammi made a very cute couple, but it wasn't long before the ghosts of our childhood came back to haunt my baby brother. One weekend Stefon, Edris, Tammi, and I went to a house party when I saw the first signs of Edris's aggressive behavior. The four of us were having a good time dancing and chatting with our respective friends. We all stepped outside to get some fresh air, when Edris started arguing with Tammi for some unknown reason. Then, seemingly out of nowhere, he hauled off and slapped her as hard as he could right across her cute little face. I could not believe my eyes. I grabbed him and pushed him so hard he stumbled backwards and tripped over a tree root. Then I lit into him while Tammi stood behind me whimpering, trying hard not to cry.

"What is your problem, Edris?" I screamed. "What did Tammi do to you?"

I'm sure Tammi didn't believe what had just happened either and the poor girl had to be embarrassed. "How would you like it if someone slapped *your* ass in the face?" I asked rhetorically.

Edris's first act of aggression towards Tammi was the start of a vicious cycle he would repeat again and again and again for years to come. Needless to say Tammi broke off her relationship with Edris right away. As a young impressionable boy, Edris saw Gene beat Mama. Kudos to Mama for saying, *enough is enough* to the beat downs, and in spite of the struggles that lay ahead of her, she found the courage to leave Gene for good. Unfortunately Edris was impacted to the point of no return. Stefon graduated from high school in the spring of 1975, and his SAT scores were so high that several universities across the country reached out to *him*, especially the Historically Black Colleges and Universities.

Mama's income was so low that we qualified for all sorts of financial aid and grants and he and I took advantage of those resources. Stefon chose Tuskegee over Morehouse, because they offered him the best financial package so we packed his bags and sent him off to college in his bright new orange Fiat sedan. We were so proud of him, and Mama just knew her baby was well on his way to becoming a doctor. Meanwhile, Edris and I still lived at home with Mama and Ronald while we finished high school. It was Thanksgiving weekend and Stefon's freshman year at Tuskegee started out with a bang. Mama could not afford for him to come home for the holiday that year so he decided to take an 11-hour road trip to visit a new college friend in Pittsburgh, Pennsylvania. On his way back to Tuskegee, he was traveling through a one-horse town somewhere in Georgia when he hit an elderly woman's car. Mama received a call from the Sheriff's office.

"Ma'am, we have your son, Stefon here," the deputy said in his southern drawl. "He done run into the back of a lady, and will be arrested unless he pays the fine for causing this here traffic collision. *And* the boy says he don't have no money."

Mama looked confused as she tried to reason with the southern peace officer. "Well, he *doesn't* have any money. He's down there for school."

"Well gosh darn-it." The deputy's frustration spilled through the earpiece that Mama had positioned between us so that I could hear the conversation. "We're gonna need the money *rat* now or the boy is going to jail."

"Well, Sir, I've never heard of anyone going to jail for a traffic collision," Mama said. "Did he leave the scene of the accident?"

"Well no ma'am," the deputy responded. "Looks like he done fell asleep, that's all."

We were so afraid for Stefon, especially there in the South. It wasn't as bad as it was in the 50's and 60's in terms of outward racism, but still, Georgia was not liberal like California. Mama had done all she could to keep us safe, and her boys out of the legal system, and the first thing Stefon did when he was away from home, was get detained in arguably the worst place possible for a young black man, and for a traffic collision of all things. I thought to myself, *Stefon was probably high,* and I'm quite sure Mama thought the same thing. Nonetheless, she went to Western Union and wired money to Georgia to pay the *fine* and Stefon went back to school with a fresh new dent in his front bumper.

I was having a blast enjoying my senior year and looking forward to going to college. I ended my final softball season and I anxiously awaited the two crowning events of any high school senior: Prom and Graduation. Edris was in the 10th grade but he didn't like Westchester, so Mama enrolled him into Los Angeles High School. Ronald was still a drunk so his days with Mama were numbered. She had about enough of his coming home in a drunken stupor with his jacket on inside out, and upside down. Unfortunately, back then, no one thought of alcoholism as a *disease,* especially not black people. Black people just regarded alcoholics as plain old *drunks* like we thought of Ronald.

It was almost time for my Prom and I couldn't wait to go. I didn't have a boyfriend but I had several prom date options. My friend Roslyn suggested that her cousin take me and I was fine with that because I knew him for a couple years, and he was really handsome, so I knew my prom pictures would be cute. I had secured my prom date, but I needed a dress, and all the trimmings. I did not want to experience the same nightmare I had at Winter Formal in the 10th grade, when I bought a cheap dress from *Lerner's,* and five other girls showed up wearing the same dress. The only saving grace was that we all had different colors. We looked like a singing group from the 60's, but we weren't, so that was not cute. Mama and Irene had promised that I would get everything I needed for *every* event during my senior year, so Irene called me early one Saturday morning before she headed off to work. She wanted to take me shopping for my prom dress. I was jazzed about getting all dolled up for my prom so I hopped on a couple of buses and went to the *Hamburger Hamlet Beverly Hills* to meet Irene so we could hit the stores when she got off of work that afternoon. I sat in a booth at the restaurant, and waited while Irene finished her shift. Irene and I left Hamburger Hamlet and she drove north to the Sunset Strip. We parked Irene's brand new white Chevy Nova in a public parking lot and walked up and down the strip proudly. We went to various expensive boutiques, and I tried on dresses galore. I was amazed at the beautiful gowns, and the wonderful customer service. My eyes were as big as saucers throughout the entire afternoon. We went in and out of a number of posh spots until we came upon a small place where a woman welcomed us in with open arms.

"Honey, I have the perfect dress for you," the woman said in her heavy Persian accent.

Irene and I looked around the store while the woman disappeared into a back room. A few minutes later she came out holding a pale green dress with peek-a-boo square shaped cut outs from the high neckline all the way down the front bodice to just above the waist. I looked at the limp dress on the hanger, examining it, trying to figure out if I liked it or not. It was very plain and at first I turned my nose up at it.

"No, thank you. It's so plain."

"Honey," the boutique owner said attempting to butter me up. "You have a great body. You should try it on because clothes look different when you put them on."

Knowing that most customer service representatives used flattering tactics to get women to buy more items, I relented.

"Oh, ok."

Irene looked at me and shrugged her shoulders as if to say *give it a try*. I hesitantly took the dress from her grasp and disappeared into the dressing room. When I reemerged with the dress on I felt like a million bucks!

"She was right! It's gorgeous on you," Irene cheered, grinning from ear to ear and clapping like a proud Mama.

She loved me and wanted everyone to think I was her real daughter. The dress cost a whopping $250, and Irene pulled out a wad of cash and paid for it without hesitation. After seeing the dress, Mama took me to *Bakers*, where she bought my shoes and had them dyed to match my dress. To finish off my look Mama streaked my shoulder length hair with fresh blond highlights. My two maternal loves made me feel like royalty when I walked into Long Beach's Queen Mary ballroom with my date, who looked equally as regal.

Stefon returned home for the summer after a dreadful freshman year at Tuskegee, just in time to attend my graduation on Thursday, June 17,

1976. I was looking forward to Grad Night at Disneyland, but again, I didn't have a date, so Mama arranged for her friend's son, Patrick, to take me. He thought I was pretty, but I was not attracted to him at all. He was a nice yellow boy, but just *not* my type. I don't think I said two words to Patrick all night and that was horrible. It was a long, cold, night at the *happiest place on earth* and I regretted attending. Needless to say, I didn't hear from Patrick after that night. I was batting zero in the romance department throughout my high school years, but I had so much going on in my life I didn't have time to even think about a relationship, besides I was only 17, so I had plenty of time to find love. Once I graduated, my part time summer job at the Social Security Administration transitioned into a full time position that fall, which was great because I needed the money. I opted to attend school locally to stay close to Mama since Stefon was already away at school. There was no Internet when I applied to college so I conducted my college submission activity in person. I didn't have time to run around to the various local schools nor did I have the money to pay for multiple application fees, so I settled on Cal State Los Angeles, and only applied there. Once I was accepted, Mama and Ronald agreed to help me get a car. I was ecstatic about the thought of having my very own car and I could not wait. I wanted a brand new Plymouth Arrow right off the show room floor but it was $6000 dollars, and I could *not* afford that so I settled for a used Ford Comet, 4-door Sedan, Navy Blue with a White Vinyl top. It was so un-cool but it was within my budget. Mama and Ronald put $500 down, and my payments were $97.21 each month; that amount went up to $104 after my car insurance was added. As luck would have it, a couple of weeks after getting my first car, I got my first ticket. I made an illegal U-Turn in front of my apartment complex and there was an LAPD motor cop snooping around the neighborhood. He promptly and coldly stopped and cited me. I was only 17 years old and terribly afraid of the police, so I was traumatized. Mama was required to go with me to court in Hollywood to pay the fine, because I was a minor. That was the first, and last citation I ever received while *driving* a vehicle. I had plenty of parking tickets in my college days though.

I was enrolled at Cal State L.A. for the fall quarter, however, during the summer I signed up to take extra classes at El Camino College to get a head start on my General Education requirements. The fall quarter didn't start until October, so I had a little time to get my mind, and my wardrobe, right. I was scared of growing up but I was ready to start my *real* adult life. For starters I had my own money and my own car. Up until that point in my life I had lived off of Mama and my Social Security Survivor benefits. I was hoping to get that money until I was 23 years old so my plan was to remain a full time student. Starting college that summer at El Camino was instrumental in my transition from high school to college. I worked Mondays, Wednesdays and half days on Fridays at the Social Security office, and took classes all day on Tuesdays and Thursdays. That was a great schedule but the money I earned paled in comparison. I only made about $97, bi-weekly. That was just barely enough to cover my car payment and small bills. I was very responsible, and wanted to do everything the right way, so I budgeted as best I could. As the boys and I progressed through high school and college, things were starting to look up for Mama. We were more self-sufficient, so she started focusing on her own career. She also concentrated on shedding some weight, both literally and figuratively. Mama was done with Ronald. His frequent trips in and out of jail for Driving-Under-the-Influence, which oftentimes affected his job status, were trying her patience, and he knew it was just a matter of time before she kicked him out of the house. Other than drinking, he was pretty much harmless, which was why Mama put up with him for so long. When he worked, when he was sober, all was well. He assisted Mama financially, and he even gave the boys and me money when we needed it. One Saturday morning late in the summer of '76, Mama woke me up bright and early. I usually parked my car on the street in front of our apartment building but if no parking was available I parked in the raggedy parking lot behind the complex.

"Doll baby," she nudged me. "Where is your car?"

"Mama my car is parked out front." I responded in a groggy state.

Our apartment was located at the front of the building facing the street. I got up out of my bed and looked out the front window onto the street where I had parked my car the night before and it wasn't there.

"Hey, where's my car?" I exclaimed.

Ronald and the boys were still asleep so I dressed quickly, and hurriedly went outside and looked around for my car. After scouring the street, Mama yelled from the front door.

"Check the back lot, baby, sometimes you park it back there. Maybe you forgot."

I distinctly remembered parking on the street in front, but without any other ideas, I went to the rear parking lot and there it was: parked, and *wrecked*.

"Mama!" I screamed from the back parking lot and Mama came out to see what was the matter.

"What's wrong baby?" Mama asked as she reached the rear lot.

"Look at my car!"

"That damn Ronald, I know he did this. Hold on, baby." Mama ran back into the house and I followed. "Ronald!" Mama yelled as she shook Ronald. "Wake your ass up."

I was furious. That alcoholic, Ronald, had driven my car the night before and was obviously involved in a traffic collision. Mama and Ronald shared a Chrysler Le Baron that they bought shortly after the drive from Detroit. They traded the Impala for the Chrysler. Mama was at work the night before, so Ronald thought that he would take my car for a short spin. He ended up colliding with a pole so thankfully no one was injured, but Mama was livid; and so was I.

"I can't believe this fool wrecked my baby's car." Mama spewed under her breath as we waited for Ronald to emerge from the room. When he saw Mama and me standing there with my keys in hand he knew that was the last straw.

"I'm not dealing with this shit any longer," Mama scolded. "Every time I take one step forward I take two steps back with you. I have three kids to raise and you are getting in the way of that. You need to get your act together or get the hell out of my life."

"You're right Carmen," Ronald conceded. "I...I...know I got a problem. I'm sorry." Ronald turned towards me with tears in his eyes. "Will you please forgive me, Tia? Please, baby doll?"

Ronald was so apologetic I couldn't stay mad at him. He was a nice drunk, just careless. The insurance company paid for the car repairs so all was good however, the tension in the house between Mama and Ronald, continued to grow. While there was no arguing or fighting, it was evident that their relationship was very strained. One afternoon, right before summer ended, we were all at home when Ronald told Mama he was going out for a little bit. By the next morning he had not returned and that was long before cell phones, so all we could do was wait to hear from him. We figured he had been arrested for drunk driving again or worse, dead somewhere. Mama called tow yards to see if the car was impounded, and she checked local hospitals to see if Ronald had been brought into the emergency room. Fearing a repeat occurrence of what happened with Chico, Mama also called the Los Angeles County Morgue, but there was no sign of Ronald. Luckily for us, Stefon was still home for the summer so Mama had transportation to and from work. I needed *my* car to get to and from summer school and work, so sharing my car with Mama would have been difficult but we would have made it work. Ronald was gone for about a week when Mama received a call from the Sheriff's office in Lubbock, Texas. They called to tell her that her car was impounded in Texas. Apparently, Ronald had driven to Texas, and abandoned the car there. According to his mother he then flew to New York City, where he was staying with a family member, in Harlem. I felt so bad for Mama. *How could he do that to her after she put up with all of his drama, for all of those years?* I knew then what Mama meant when she would say, "A drunk ain't shit." Mama and Edris flew to Texas and drove her car back to Los Angeles. Thankfully, Ronald had not wrecked it.

The summer of 1976 was a wrap after all of Ronald's shenanigans. I had been out of high school for a few months and hadn't been physically active exercising or playing sports, so I had picked up a few pounds. I didn't mind the slight weight gain but I noticed too that my eyes appeared to bulge out of my eye sockets. My brothers, and their friends teased me about my bulging eyes, and I became increasingly more self-conscious about the change in my appearance; I wasn't feeling cute at all. I also noticed that my hair was thinning and I had no idea as to why, and I didn't know if any of these changes were connected. My hair was so affected that I walked into the salon inside the May Company Department store in Baldwin Hills, and told the first hair stylist, who approached me, a Japanese woman, to cut my hair into a very short pixie-like hairstyle. I *loved* the new look but I had not warned Mama about my makeover. Mama had taken great care of my hair over the years and had never allowed any hair stylist to cut more than a half-inch off due to split ends. When Mama saw my hair she had a fit.

"Tia, what did you do?" She asked rhetorically. "Short hair doesn't fit you, baby. Why would you cut your hair off?"

"Mom, it was thinning really bad and I don't know why," I explained.

"It's probably going through some shedding phase, that's all." Mama said, frustrated as she inspected my new hair doo. Funny thing was that she noticed my hair right away, but she *never* once mentioned how my eyes looked like someone had scared the bejesus out of me.

"Well you don't look good with short hair." Mama said as she rolled her eyes at me and walked away. I was an adult, but I still didn't dare talk back to Mama. So, as an unspoken compromise I wore scarves as a "fashion state-ment" for months until my hair regained some length.

I didn't think about seeing a doctor because I was young and otherwise healthy, so I thought like most young folks, the issue would resolve itself. I bought scarves to match *everything* I wore. I would wrap my scarf around my head, and twist it into a low bun in the back and I was good to go. I prayed for my hair to hurry and grow back so Mama would stop commenting on how much she didn't like my hair. A few weeks after my makeover, I was feeling a little better about myself, and I loved the low maintenance aspect of wearing the scarves. I was exceptionally chipper one day as I was walking out of my apartment building when I crossed paths on the steps with a young woman I had never seen before.

"Excuse me," she said as she motioned for me to stop. "I'm sorry but can I ask you something?"

"Sure, go right ahead."

"Well," she paused, looking for the right words to say. "This is going to sound so rude, but do you have any abnormalities?"

"Not that I know of," I chuckled. I was confused by her bizarre question.

"Well, I notice that your eyes are bulging a bit and your neck looks swollen," she remarked. "You might have a *goiter* because I had the same thing, and my eyes bulged just like yours."

My bulging eyes 1976

"Oh really? Ok, well thank you for telling me." I was polite but silently dismissed the woman's advice and went on about my day. I forgot about the encounter until a couple of weeks later, when I accompanied Mama to a doctor's appointment with her primary physician Dr. Sanders, whose office was a short distance from our apartment.

Mama had met Dr. Sanders, while she was working for the answering service. He subscribed to the service, and had stopped by to meet one of the switchboard operators, who had been flirting with him on the phone. The ladies all thought Dr. Sanders was *fine,* and the coolest doctor ever so when Mama was in need of a doctor he was at the top of her list of prospective caretakers. I accompanied Mama to Dr. Sander's office where I met his office manager and nurse, June. Over the years Mama and I became close with June and during my senior year in high school I often babysat for June's three children. I had not seen June since before I graduated.

"Hi June!" I exclaimed when I entered the doctor's office. "How are my babies? I miss them."

"Hey Tia honey, they miss you too especially that boy of mine. Lord Jesus he had a fit when I told him you had a real job, and couldn't babysit anymore." June replied as she looked up at me with a strange look on her face. "Sweetie, are you picking up weight?" June asked after the stare down.

"*Yeah,* I think I *have* picked up a few pounds," I responded a little embarrassed that the weight gain was so noticeable. "I'm not as active as I was in school." I felt my mood shift quickly as I took on a defensive posture. I was sensitive and didn't need anybody telling me I was gaining weight.

"It looks like your neck is swollen too, though," June said as she observed me closely. "You'd better go in there and let Doc take a look at you." It was like déjà vu. I shared with June my recent encounter with the young woman, who mentioned that I might have a *goiter.*

"I believe she could be right, Tia, you just may have a goiter."

"But I feel fine though," I reasoned.

"Well, goiters are usually painless, honey," June replied. "Go on in there and talk to Dr. Sanders."

By the time I left the office that day I was scheduled to see an endocrinologist at UCLA Medical Center a few weeks later. I didn't know what to expect with my visit to UCLA. I realized that it was the first time I had ever gone to see a doctor on my own without Mama. The UCLA staff performed a battery of tests, and ultimately diagnosed me with Graves Disease. The doctor told me that my thyroid gland was eight times enlarged, and they needed to treat me with a Radioactive Iodine capsule designed to kill my *goiter,* after which time he would start me on a daily dose of thyroid medication to bring my gland back to a normal level. Further assessment revealed that my Thyroid was Hyperactive with Hypoactive symptoms primarily resulting in fatigue and weight gain, when I actually should have been shaky and losing weight. Within a few weeks of my visit at UCLA my eyes retreated back into my big head, my weight started to drop off, and my hair became full and healthy again in due time.

CHAPTER 6

"Mama's Sick"

THE FALL OF 1976 FOUND Stefon back at Tuskegee University; I started my freshman year at Cal State LA; and Edris started his junior year at L.A. high school. Edris didn't have to take driver's education because he turned 18 during his junior year. He had gotten his driver's license so he thought it was the perfect time for Mama to get *him* a car. After much brow beating and guilt manipulation by Edris, Mama gave in and traded her car for a Cadillac Seville for the two of them to share. Edris had a way of making Mama feel bad about one thing or another due to his insecurities. He blamed Mama for his dark complexion; he wasn't as book smart as Stefon, or me, and he blamed her for that; he flunked the 3rd grade, and he blamed her for that. He always placed blame where it didn't belong, and it always started and ended with Mama. Mama knew Edris had major insecurities and she compensated by spoiling him rotten and taking all of the verbal and emotional abuse he dished out. Edris resented Stefon and me because, in his mind, we thought we were better than him. Mama never made a difference between any of us. She held a special place in her heart for each of us and had a different relationship with each of us. Stefon and I never considered that we were better than Edris because we regarded him was our cute little brother whom we loved so much. That insecurity issue turned out to be a life long struggle for Edris, even when popular culture deemed dark skinned men to be "in style" in the 90's, and then back in style, in the early 2000's with celebrities such as Tyrese, Tyson Beckford, Taye Diggs, and the like blazing across covers of magazines, billboards, television and movie screens.

Edris was 19 when he graduated from high school because of his back-to-back third grade attempts. As a young adult he was a hotheaded, ignorant, coward, who, by his late teens, was verbally abusive towards Mama, and physically abusive towards his girlfriends. Stefon was away at school during Edris's late teen years, so there was no other male figure in the house to help mold him and keep him in check. The bright side of things held that Edris's bark was much louder than his bite especially when he went up against other men. Edris never raised a hand to me or Mama because somehow he knew that would not be tolerated. He was strong but he would get a good fight out of me if he tried it. Mama's absence from home due to her work schedule did not help matters much. While she was no push over, Mama was very lenient. She essentially grew up *with* us as she had given birth to all three of us before her 21st birthday. I was a very cautious individual. I was afraid of getting in trouble, and afraid of the negative consequences that came with not following the rules. I wanted to *help* Mama and not add to her misery. Before the ink dried on Mama and Edris's new car contract, he completely took over the car. Mama was duped into thinking they would actually share it, but Edris barely picked her up from work on time, if at all, and completely disregarded their agreement. I ended up having to pick Mama up from work on most days, and taking her where she needed to go. Thankfully, I had gotten a more reliable car as I traded in my Ford Comet for a brand new 1977 Chevy Camaro, which was also more fashionable. After Edris graduated from high school, he took the car and moved in with a 26-year-old woman. Mary a single mom was 7 years older than Edris. She was an attractive dark skinned woman, who was very small in stature. She was a stereotypical ghetto girl, who lived in *The Jungle,* and she was as dumb as a box of rocks. She relied on public assistance via the Los Angeles County Welfare system, and she smoked cigarettes and weed frequently. She had a three-year-old daughter, Samantha, who we called "Sam," from a previous relationship and she had the most beautiful facial features I had ever seen on a dark skinned child. She was born with a hearing disability, and as a result, she had a speech impediment but she was otherwise healthy. Mary was meticulous about Sam's appearance and always kept her neat and clean. She was a well-mannered, sweet child, and Mama and I fell in love with her from the start. We didn't care much for Mary, or respect her, but we applauded how she cared for Sam.

Edris was with Mary for two years when she became pregnant. During the pregnancy, Mary continued to smoke weed and drink alcohol right along with Edris; and although they were excited about having a baby, they obviously didn't realize that drugs and alcohol were not recommended as part of optimal prenatal care. During the early part of her third trimester, Mary went into premature labor and gave birth to a 1 pound, 14oz. baby girl she named Erica. The premature baby was not expected to live, however, she defied the odds and survived; but she was wrought with multiple mental and physical disabilities. Erica was my first and only niece and Mama's only grandchild, and we were so angry with Edris and Mary for their reckless behavior. When Erica was well enough to go home Mama and I spent time with both her and Sam. As an infant, Erica was very tiny and she slept a lot, like most babies. Her disabilities weren't as recognizable until she grew older and started developing. She was unable to sit up on her own, crawl, or walk by the time she was a year old. Edris and Mary's relationship was short lived after Erica's birth. Edris was neither willing nor equipped to raise a child, let alone a child with considerable special needs. Within a few months Edris moved on to another woman who was 10 years older than him.

My entire college experience was nothing more than a second job for me. I lived at home so I barely communicated with or hung out with college chums, and dared not even think about joining a Sorority because I didn't have the time or energy. I declared my major as Criminal Justice with a minor in English because I was pretty sure I wanted to work in law enforcement in one capacity or another. While I was an all star softball player growing up, I never even considered playing sports in college. No one came out to recruit me; I wasn't offered a scholarship, and I wasn't aware of the concept of *walking on* to a team. As a result, my softball days ended with high school. I simply worked Monday- Friday during the day from 8-4:30 PM and went to school Monday-Thursdays at night from 6-10 PM. Due to my ongoing thyroid condition I was fatigued most of the time, so I probably would not have had the stamina required for collegiate sports anyway.

After living in the Ladera Heights area for the better part of a decade, Mama and I relocated to a beautiful, two-bedroom luxury apartment in Hancock Park, an exclusive area in Los Angeles where people with *old money* lived. Things were definitely looking up. Ronny Lott and Marcus Allen, who were college football stars at USC were roommates, and lived in the apartment next door to us. *Who knew they would go on to become famous pro-athletes?* Indeed, things were looking up for Mama and me. When I entered my final quarter in college in the spring of 1980, Mama and I were actually enjoying our time living together without the boys in our new space. Mama had a new boyfriend, an old childhood friend from Coffeyville, whom she reconnected with a couple of years after Ronald left. There was essentially no drama in the house with the boys and Ronald gone. Mama and I got along well and our bills were paid. As far as I could see, things were shaping up for the better. Mama never complained of any ailments in particular, but she remained diligent about her annual physicals. Over the years, she had picked up quite a bit of weight, and Dr. Sanders routinely talked to her about a healthier lifestyle. After unsuccessfully dieting, she decided to have gastric bypass surgery and was referred to Dr. Mathias "Mal" Fobi for her weight loss journey. Fobi hailed from Cameroon, West Africa, and was an expert at the bypass procedure. Many years later he earned the title of *Weight Loss Surgeon to the Stars*; when he helped celebrities, like Randy Jackson and comedienne Roseanne Barr, shed nearly 200 pounds combined. By September 1976, Mama had undergone the bypass surgery, and over the first few months following the surgery her weight loss was rapid. The more weight she lost, the better she felt about herself, but Dr. Sanders grew concerned about her rapid transformation.

"Carmen," he said after one of her regularly scheduled visits. "I'm a little worried about your rapid and extreme weight loss."

"Oh, don't worry. I feel great and I'm getting to a healthy weight like you wanted me to."

"Yes, you are losing weight," he said. "But, this is not the way I wanted you to go about it. I'm going to refer you to a colleague of mine for him to further assess your rapid weight loss."

Mama was referred to a Dr. Williams, who Sanders trusted immensely. He had the latest technology in his medical practice, and was considered young and cool by most of his patients. When Mama arrived at William's office, his office manager Rochelle Jackson greeted her. Rochelle was in her late 20's, and was statuesque, with long thick sandy brown hair. She was in Law School, and studied from her desk all day at the doctor's office when she wasn't busy dealing with patients. After examining Mama, Dr. Williams strongly recommended that she undergo a procedure to reverse the effects of the bypass surgery, to slow down the weight loss. He urged Mama to return to Dr. Fobi for him to address the weight loss issue and provide Mama with appropriate and safe treatment options. Mama contacted Fobi right away and he scheduled her for surgery to reverse the bypass. A few weeks later when Mama returned to Williams for a follow-up visit he told Mama that he felt a lump in her left breast, and he had Rochelle schedule her for a biopsy. I was in the kitchen cooking dinner when Mama came home from that visit.

"Hey Mama, how are you? How was your visit with Dr. Williams?" I asked joyfully. I was always happy to see her.

"Hey baby," Mama replied in a somber tone. "I *just* left his office, and he found a lump."

"A lump where, Ma?"

"In my left breast," Mama answered as she reached around with her right hand and felt her left breast indicating where the lump was imbedded in her breast tissue.

"O-ok," I stammered, trying not to sound fearful. The worried look on Mama's face scared me. "What happens now?" My heart was in the pit of my stomach.

"Well, I have to go in for a biopsy." Mama said as she walked away.

Mama headed for the bedroom to change her clothes. I could tell she was in her head. She was the biggest optimist I knew and even when things were bad, she always managed to find the silver lining in the situation. Mama didn't dwell on the negative no matter how bad things were. I loved that about her and I hoped this situation wouldn't be any different.

"I'm going with you ok?" I yelled to Mama from the kitchen.

Mama didn't have a husband she could rely on, so I was her only real support.

"Ok. I'll let you know when they call me."

A few days later Mama went for her biopsy and when the results of the biopsy came in, Mama and I went in to meet with Dr. Williams. This time I went with her. Rochelle greeted us as soon as we walked in. She and I hit it off right away when I met her. I was in awe of Rochelle and loved talking to her. She spoke with authority and kept it real. With her personality, I knew she would make a great attorney one day. Dr. Williams was very lighthearted in his approach when he discussed Mama's biopsy results with us.

"Okay Carmen, the results from the biopsy indicate a malignant tumor," he explained.

"What does that mean? I know what malignancy means, but what does it mean for *me*?" Mama asked.

"It means that you have breast cancer." Dr. Williams tried to remain lighthearted in his delivery until Mama started to cry. He then embraced her and assured her she would be ok. I stood by in disbelief.

Cancer? I thought to myself. I didn't know what to say or do, so I just stood there behind Mama, rubbing her shoulders as Dr. Williams consoled her.

Dr. Williams referred Mama to Dr. Harris, an Oncologist whose office was in Lynwood, California right across from Saint Francis Hospital. It seemed as if Mama was being passed around, from doctor to doctor like a hot potato. I was totally invested in Mama's healthcare and continued to make the rounds with her to most of her appointments when my schedule allowed. When we met with Dr. Harris he explained to Mama that because she had recently undergone the major surgery to reverse her bypass, the best option for her age and condition, was for him to perform a lumpectomy, followed by chemotherapy and radiation, rather than a mastectomy. Dr. Harris started Mama on Chemotherapy right away; he had a Port Catheter inserted into Mama's chest cavity for dispensation of the intravenous chemo drugs; and he placed radioactive rods in her left breast for the radiation treatments that followed. I didn't know much about Mama's prognosis at that time and

I didn't ask a lot of questions of Dr. Harris. I didn't know the "stage" of Mama's cancer and didn't know if her tumor had negative or positive receptors, which would have indicated the likelihood of her cancer recurring. All I knew about cancer treatment was that chemotherapy made your hair fall out. I lived with Mama during her entire treatment period, but I didn't ask her a lot of questions. I either took it for granted that Dr. Harris knew what he was doing, and I prayed for the treatment options to work, or subconsciously, I was afraid to know anything. I knew she was afraid enough for the both of us so I just wanted to be there for her. Mama drove herself to her bi-weekly chemotherapy treatments during the early morning hours when I was at work. She was strong, and never complained, so I never even asked if she needed, or wanted, me to take off work and accompany her to those grueling appointments. She continued to work full time, and even mustered up enough strength to exercise by going on long walks everyday when she felt up to it. She was determined to do whatever she could to beat the disease. Her recovery regimen also included attending church every Sunday where she got the spiritual feeding that she needed. Mama was raised in the church and after many years of not attending regularly, we finally found a church home at the First African Methodist Episcopal Church, better known as "FAME." For a few years, Mama volunteered her time in the church office at FAME. She was so enamored with the full-time staff that she decided to become part of their team.

In the spring of 1980 I had been so self-absorbed that I hadn't thought much about Mama's ongoing cancer treatment. I saw Mama everyday and she looked beautiful and appeared to be recovering well from what I surmised based on how she looked. That spring Mama became an ordained minister under the leadership of Reverend Pastor Cecil "Chip" Murray. I felt a sense of comfort in knowing that we were part of a wonderful spiritual family. I followed Mama to various church functions, such as the annual A.M.E. conferences, and I stood alongside her, feeding the homeless and handing out clothes in the church's parking lot. I enjoyed visiting Mama and Reverend Murray in the church office after services on Sundays. Mama loved FAME, and she was a faithful servant. Mama's weight was significantly low, but it had stabilized a bit. She was looking and feeling much better than she had been in a very long time.

Stefon had taken up residency in Washington, D.C., where he was well on his way to becoming a professional student at Howard University, while working for a major hotel chain. The boys loved Mama dearly but neither of them played an active role in her overall care. I was always there making sure she had everything she needed. After Mama was done with chemotherapy she endured 6 weeks of daily radiation treatments. By the end of the six-week period Mama's skin on her left breast, and on her chest was burnt and discolored from the radiation. My heart ached at the sight of her frail upper torso whenever I washed her back during her daily baths. Her disfigured breast was a constant vision in my mind. When I looked at Mama's perfectly shaped, smooth bald head, I tried to remember the beautiful thick locks of hair that once framed her face before the effects of chemo prevailed. I wanted to cry, but I couldn't. If she could smile and be positive then so could I. Mama *claimed* her healing, and told me repeatedly that the Lord was going to take care of her. Mama's illness forced me to think more clearly about where I was headed in life. I needed to stay focused. Mama was paying all of the household expenses, while I was only able to maintain my school and car expenses on my meager salary. I was 22 and my Social Security Survivor's Benefits, which I had always given Mama, were about to end so I needed to do something to better provide for myself, and to help Mama if need be.

By June of 1980, I was about to finish college and Mama had finished all of her treatments. She had just started working for American Airlines as a Reservations Agent and, for the first time in a long time, she was making enough money from one job, so, she quit her night job at the Answering Service after working there for about 10 years. She had her dream job and was able to travel as often as she wanted. Mama had great benefits at American Airlines, and we took advantage of the travel benefits often. Working for the airlines afforded Mama the opportunity to visit her sisters in Chicago, and Grandmother in Kansas several times a year. We travelled many times to New York City for long weekends *just* to shop for clothes and shoes. For most of my life we struggled financially, but Mama instilled in all of us the importance of eating healthy and buying good quality clothes and shoes. With that mindset, as an adult, I gravitated towards better quality clothing and shoes and I *loved* designer handbags. When we travelled, the flight fees were nominal, and we stayed at the best hotels using Mama's airline employee discounts. I finally felt as if we were climbing out of a hole of trials and tribulations laced with the sort of drama only found on reality shows. The boys were living their lives elsewhere and not impacting our livelihood too much; there was no man around mooching off of Mama or stressing her out; my health was back on track after my thyroid was under control; Mama was on the mend, and I was about to graduate from college. I was ready to embark upon a career in Criminal Justice and I really wanted to join the Federal Bureau of Investigations (FBI) as an Agent. I went to the Federal building in Downtown Los Angeles to get an application, and in small print at the bottom of the application, it indicated that in addition to having a Bachelor's Degree, I needed three years of law enforcement experience in order to qualify for acceptance into the FBI Academy. I felt deflated. I wasn't interested in being a street cop but I needed a Plan B. I had met several officers in my Criminal Justice classes at Cal State LA over the years, and had several instructors and guest speakers who also worked at local agencies. Hearing them talk about their jobs fascinated me. I was increasingly inspired and wanted badly to join the local ranks as my Plan B. Many of the local police agencies had tough hiring restrictions such as the Los Angeles Police Department. They had a 5'6" height requirement that I did not meet. After speaking with my law enforcement classmates, they mentioned that the Los Angeles County Sheriff's Department had a long history of hiring female deputies to staff their all female jail, Sybil Brand Institute. My goal was to get the required three years of law enforcement experience *somewhere* locally in order to pursue my dream career with the Feds. So, I started processing with the Sheriff's Department. My thyroid issues were under control with medication, and I had lost the pounds I had picked up after high school, so I was down to about 120 pounds, but I was completely out of shape. I had the nerve to saunter my narrow behind into the Sheriff's testing location in East Los Angeles as if it were a classroom at Cal State LA. The Sheriff's Deputy leading the testing cadre that day was a very cocky man, so I kind of tuned him out as he spoke about the testing process. I considered myself a pretty tough cookie, but I was very sensitive that day, probably because I knew I was *not* in shape. After everyone was signed in, and the Deputy finished his spiel he led us to the physical abilities testing area to show us what to expect should we make it that far through the candidate process.

"Alright, everyone listen up, you see that fence?" He pointed about 50 yards out onto a field where an 8-foot chain link fence was erected at the end of a long dirt path. "You all will need to get over that fence," the Deputy said in his booming voice. Command presence was a requisite for a job in law enforcement, and I immediately saw that the deputy fit the mold.

Oh, hell no! I thought. *He must be crazy; I can't get over that fence.* I got an instant attitude. But I was more upset with myself than with the baritone Deputy. I had let myself get out of shape, and that wasn't the Deputy's fault. *Girl, you need a job, a real one,* I thought to myself, *how could you be mad when you chose to do this? You better do what you need to do.* After the short conversation with myself in between the Deputy's instructions we returned to the classroom. I was looking for the nearest exit so I could make my escape. *No, you can't leave just because you are not in shape. You need to get it together.* My conscience berated me.

"If you don't want to work in the jails for the first five years of your career then you might as well leave right now." *Five years? No thank you.* That was my cue. Now *that was a good enough reason for me to leave.* I thought.

I only needed 3 years of law enforcement experience; and if I stayed there I would never get any field experience for five years so I got up and walked out. Just as I prepared to drive off, I heard on the radio that the City of Los Angeles had settled the Fanchon Blake Law Suit, which in part, dropped the LAPD's height requirement. I sat there and listened intently as they reported the details of the lawsuit. Ms. Blake's lawsuit was interesting. After almost 20 years on the Los Angeles Police Department, Fanchon Blake, a female Detective/Sergeant, had not promoted far enough up the chain of command as she had hoped. Like all Policewomen working under then Chief of Police, Ed Davis, Blake was forbidden from taking a Lieutenant's promotional exam.

"Sergeant" was the highest rank open to policewomen at that time, but Blake wanted to be a Lieutenant. She spent four long years taking her complaints before the City Council and the Los Angeles Police Commission with little results. Without seeing any progress, Blake took her case to the courts, and in 1973 filed a sex-discrimination lawsuit against the LAPD. Blake, then a 25-year veteran of the LAPD, won her lawsuit claiming that the City of Los Angeles, the LAPD, Los Angeles Board of Civil Service Commissioners, and Police Chief Ed Davis discriminated against her, and other plaintiffs, based on her gender. Blake cited the 1972 amendments to the 1964 Civil Rights Act, which compelled state and local government agencies to comply with anti-discrimination laws. As a result, the LAPD vowed to increase the number of women in their ranks until 20% of its sworn officers were female. Although Blake was white, at that time in LAPD history when discrimination was virtually commonplace, she was the driving force that gave more Latino, Black, and Asian officers opportunities to pursue and develop their careers in law enforcement due to her lawsuit. If not for Ms. Blake, minorities and women's roles would have remained minimal and not comparable with roles of their male counterparts. The Blake lawsuit, and resulting Consent Decree, set hiring goals, revised certain standards for the Los Angeles Police Department, and was a major catalyst for the progress of policewomen.

The LAPD hired its first policewoman, Alice Stebbins Wells, in 1910. Since then, women became a small but growing part of the law enforcement community. Through the 1950s, policewomen's duties generally consisted of working as Matrons in the jail system, or dealing with troubled youths while working in detective assignments. The early 1970's consisted of women being classified as "Police*women*" who did not work any type of field patrol assignment; and they were not allowed to promote above the rank of sergeant until Ms. Blake filed her lawsuit in the late 1970's. Following Blake's lawsuit the department eliminated the gender specific ranks of "Policeman" and "Policewoman." The policemen and women, who already held those positions, were grandfathered in and retained their respective classifications, but new hires, male and female were referred to as Police *Officers*. All new hires were field certified and qualified to patrol the mean streets of L.A. in a black and white patrol vehicle.

Race relations on the Department were also in a transitional period in the late 70's and early 80's. In 1886, the department hired its first two black officers, Robert William Stewart and Roy Green. Despite this, the department was slow at integration. During the 1965, Watts Riots, only 5 of the 205 police officers assigned to South Central Los Angeles were black, in the largest black community in Los Angeles. Los Angeles's first black mayor Tom Bradley was a former police officer and quit the department after being unable to advance past the rank of Lieutenant like other black police officers on the department during that time. When Bradley was elected mayor in 1972, Blacks made up only 5% of the LAPD and there was only one black Captain on the department, Homer Broome. Broome broke down racial barriers and became the first black officer to obtain the rank of Commander. He was also the first black officer to command a police station, Southwest Division, which contained historically black neighborhoods in South Los Angeles. When Blake's victory was announced, I figured it was time for me to join the ranks of the Los Angeles Police Department, so I went home and plotted my next move towards the LAPD. I started attending the daily physical workout sessions at the Police Academy to get in shape and things looked promising. I had been working for the Social Security Administration for four years and I was ready to move on. I was not about to get stuck behind a government desk processing claims and overpayments alongside college students or student workers from the Job Corp. I had my sights set on the LAPD.

The application process was surprisingly swift as LAPD was on the fast track to put systems in place to accommodate a growing number of women, and abide by the recent lawsuit-driven changes. In doing so, the need to accommodate the influx of women, many of whom were not as physically fit as their male counterparts, also became abundantly clear. The new co-ed academy structure was quite a challenge for the LAPD in that prior to 1980, *Policewomen* attended a separate academy from the men and in that environment no concessions needed to be made since all the women were pretty much on par with one another. But, in the new co-ed environment, adjustments had to be made to ensure that there was a level playing field for all parties. One of the initiatives the LAPD started following the Blake lawsuit was a physical training preparation course called the Crime Prevention Assistance (CPA) program, later renamed the Candidate Assistance Program, aimed at assisting women, *and* men, by training them for the physical abilities portion of the hiring process. That program greatly assisted the individuals, including myself, who took advantage of the free workout drill sessions. While there was no eight-foot chain link fence like at the Sheriff's training facility, there was a six-foot wall that had to be scaled by each candidate, and after much practice I was able to scale the wall and run long distances as required. Within a few weeks of starting my hiring process, I was notified that I was disqualified from the process due to my weight; I was only 123 pounds. When I inquired about my disqualification I was informed that I needed to lose six pounds in order to continue processing with the department. I had heard about "artificial barriers" but didn't understand the concept fully. I knew enough to know that employers like LAPD, were supposed to abide by the hiring and promoting rules and regulations set by the federal government however, instead they utilized unsubstantiated, or unofficial disqualifiers to hinder or remove candidates like me from the selection pool. Those artificial barriers prohibited women and other minorities from advancing their careers, or, as in my case, starting theirs. Being forced to bring more women on the job was not an easy pill to swallow for the mass majority of men already wearing the badge; and barriers, like my weight disqualification, ensured that, no matter how fit, or capable we were, we were never going to join the ranks of the *Good Ol' Boys Club* if the powers to be at LAPD had anything to do with it.

Police Chief Davis openly and sarcastically told police women that he would put them in patrol cars when the National Football League's Rams coach, Tommy Prothro put women on his team's front line. Blake stated in an LA Times article that the day the news of her lawsuit hit the media, she was terrified to death to even walk into the Police Headquarters Building (PAB). Once inside the building she saw that they had cleaned out her desk and removed her from her investigative assignment. She was ostracized and given a receptionist's job. The silent treatment was imposed and no one talked to her; no one even acknowledged that she was alive. When Blake started her new assignment at the reception desk, the phones rang off the hook with the media from all around the world wanting to interview her. Blake was under so much stress from believing the department had actually put a hit out on her life. The Department vehemently denied it, but Blake was convinced and ultimately suffered a stroke one day while she was working. At that time I was oblivious to all that was going on with Blake. After a few weeks of dieting and working out rigorously with the CPA program I returned to the City's medical facility for a weigh-in.

"I see you were disqualified for your weight," the middle-aged nurse mumbled as she looked back and forth between my medical file and me.

"Yes ma'am." I said as I stepped onto the scale with my fingers crossed. I didn't even want to breathe until the scale had settled.

"120 pounds," the nurse announced.

I was silent. *How could I have only lost three pounds?* I thought.

"You know what," the nurse said as she looked up at my boney face and narrow behind. "You will lose those last 3 pounds in the academy, honey. I'm going to clear you to move forward."

"Thank you! Thank you! Thank you!" I screeched. "Yes! Thank you Jesus!" I exhaled as I lunged forward and hugged the nurse tightly.

It was November 1980, and Ronald Reagan, former Republican Governor of California had just been elected President of the United States of America after defeating Jimmy Carter in a landslide victory. I was feeling patriotic, as my thoughts of becoming a civil servant were soon to become a reality. I had received my notice to start the Los Angeles Police Academy on Monday November 17, 1980, and I was nervous to say the least. On that fateful Monday morning at *zero dark thirty*, cop talk for really early, I reported for duty at the Los Angeles Police Academy in Elysian Park. I was familiar with the grounds because for months I had gone there to participate in the CPA workout program. I was one of a handful of women who showed up on that cold, dark morning as we all stood shoulder to shoulder on the infamous *black line* inside the Academy gymnasium. There I stood amongst 60 male and female recruit officers ready to face the notorious LAPD Drill Instructors, who were trained to whip us into shape and get us ready for field duty. Most of those instructors were brutal, vile, tyrants whose primary mission in life was to find a reason to have us fired, especially those of us whom they felt did not belong there, Blacks and women of all ethnicities in particular. Unfortunately, I had two strikes against me; I was black and female. I never experienced much blatant racism or gender bias in my previous clerical and student worlds, so I stood there blindly, not knowing what to expect. Darryl Gates was the Chief of Police and up until his administration, the LAPD was approximately 80% white, however hiring quotas began to change that percentage following the Blake lawsuit. That was a tough period for the LAPD as they unwillingly integrated more women into the workplace, in addition to promoting *Policewomen* to higher ranks. In December of 1980, after being in the academy for about one month, while wrestling with one of my male classmates, I sustained a leg injury after being tossed around like a rag doll by a big guy. On my way to the Training office to assess my injury I had thoroughly convinced myself that this job was not for me. I walked into the office and effectively resigned from the Los Angeles Police Department. After signing on the dotted line, the male administrator processed my resignation before I could change my mind. But by the time I reached the parking lot, I was summonsed back to the office.

"So listen up, Pugh," one of the training supervisors said. "It'd be a shame for you to have put in all of this work to get here and then let it go on account of a small injury like that."

"Well, I can't continue on, sir," I replied, looking straight ahead scared to make eye contact. I was unsure of what options I had.

"How about this," he continued, "at least sign up to work as a Crime Prevention Assistant until you have recovered from your injury and then come back."

"Ok, I'm good with that."

The CPA program had been revamped from a full workout program to a paid position wherein police candidates completed administrative duties at a Police station for four hours a day, and worked out at the Academy for the remaining 4 hours. I quickly accepted that offer because I had already quit my clerical government job and definitely needed the money to sustain me while I healed, and figured out how I wanted to proceed. The Department had already conducted a thorough background investigation on me, which I passed with flying colors so it would have been a huge waste of resources on their part if they had allowed me to quit and drive off into the sunset; and besides they had quotas to fill with hiring and sustaining women.

I had a blast working in the CPA program at Wilshire Division. I was assigned to the Detective Section and my leg healed fast. I was working out and getting stronger in my physical training and eventually regained my strength and confidence. I was *recycled* into the Class 1-81, which started on January 26, 1981. I felt like a new person the second time around because I knew the drill, *and* I was in shape. Once again, like a bad dream or haunting case of déjà vu, I showed up in the Gymnasium alongside my new recruit counterparts, but this time instead of 60 recruits there were 120 of us. Many of the men in my class joined LAPD after being laid off from the Detroit Police Department. *How ironic? I'm from Detroit.* The Department's recruitment efforts had expanded greatly and they reached out to a number of metropolitan cities around the country and definitely took advantage of the lay offs that were happening in Detroit, Michigan at that time. LAPD secured many of the Motor City's brightest, and some not so bright stars, and it sure helped increase the number of minorities because many of them were African American. My new class was so large, it was split into two classes: 1-81A and 1-81B. I landed in the B Class based on the alphabetical placing of my last name. My academy days were wrought with anxiety, "bubble guts," and dead legs too tired to drive home after a strenuous day of physical training (PT). The P.T. Instructors' voices rang loudly in my ears and penetrated the fog in my brain as I completed my daily tasks of running the hills in Elysian Park.

"Come on, Pugh," the faceless voices barked, "get up that hill! Stop sandbagging! You don't belong here, you damn panty waste!"

I tuned them out as best I could. I was in relatively good shape, so the long runs weren't exactly the problem. We were all more exhausted from the constant mind games they played with us all day long. There were many days I ran past my car that was parked along Academy Road, and I was tempted to get into my car, drive off, and never come back. But I maintained my stride and slowly fell back into formation. I was spared some humiliation during those long runs because there were so many *men* running *behind* me while I blended with the group in the middle of the pack. Before long, I was regarded as the fastest female sprinter in my class, and my running skills were often shown off when I was pulled out of formation in order to demonstrate the timed obstacle course for visitors and Command Staff personnel inspecting the academy classes progress. The obstacle course included scaling the dreaded 6-foot wall, diving into the dirt pit, crawling under, and hurdling over, barriers, and lastly, sprinting to the designated finish line. By the end of my Academy days my P.T. instructors encouraged me instead of berating me like they did at the start of the academy. They ran alongside me during the long runs.

"Come on, Pugh, you can do it!" They'd shout. "That's it! Get up there! That a girl!"

I was motivated, and I smiled to myself because I was proud of my gradual monumental improvement. On most days I found myself running back to the end of the pack and literally pushing the slowest runner, a 6 foot 3 inch dude across the finish line, so that we weren't *all* punished with extended P.T., because of his laziness. By April of 1981, the Department was overloaded with Academy classes as a result of the hiring frenzy; consequently, our six-month Academy was reduced to four months. So, instead of graduating in July of 1981, as originally planned we graduated in May of 1981. That meant we were introduced to the *real* world of policing that much sooner. When I learned we were heading out two months sooner I was excited. On May 11, 1981, I graduated from the Los Angeles Police Academy and started my tour of duty at LAPD's North Hollywood Division located in the San Fernando Valley. I had lived in the inner city for years and didn't know anything about the area that I was about to protect and serve. When I arrived at North Hollywood station, I was the only female police *officer* assigned to the field in Patrol. All the other sworn women were *Policewomen* working in the station as Detectives or as desk officers, and some of them even still wore *Policewomen* uniforms: navy pencil skirts, white blouses and black bow ties. They were cute, but looked like secretaries.

My LAPD Graduation May 1981 With Chief Daryl Gates

CHAPTER 7

"Married With Children"

By January of 1982, I had been working in North Hollywood Division for about six months and my probationary period was going very well. Each month, a new batch of officers, who had graduated from the Academy, transferred into divisions all over the city.

My Rookie Days at North Hollywood Division 1982

One morning, I was in roll call waiting on the Watch Commander to start our shift. It was an unspoken, or an unwritten rule that all rookies sit in the front of the roll call room. Hazing was an acceptable practice back then, so my rookie peers and I had to brace ourselves for the shenanigans, and intimidation directed at us from tenured officers, seated behind us. Sometimes the antics were funny, but sometimes they were flat out rude and obnoxious. I was one of the more senior Rookie's at the division at that time so I was accustomed to the routine. On this cold winter morning officers were filing into the tiny old Roll Call room, one by one. My head was down as I made notes in my Field Officers Notebook and after a few minutes I looked up to see what was taking the Watch Commander so long to get the party started. Just as I looked up I noticed a new male officer walking towards the front of the room. He was very handsome and obviously in shape since he just graduated from the academy. We weren't officially introduced but I observed his nametag: Morris. Officer Morris stood about 5'11, and he looked like he weighed about 185 pounds. He had big brown eyes and shiny curly black hair. I was thrilled to see another black officer at the division, and it didn't hurt that he was easy on the eyes. It was a requirement for an officer to wear a tie whenever wearing a uniform jacket. Well officer Morris was wearing a short sleeve shirt with a jacket and *no* tie, which was against uniform guidelines, so I took the liberty to tell him that he was out of compliance. I called myself "pulling his coat" because I honestly did not want him to get in trouble so soon after transferring into the division.

"Hey," I said trying not to talk too loudly. "You know you need a tie on if you are going to wear your jacket with that short sleeve shirt."

Morris kept walking towards his seat holding a Butterfinger candy bar in one hand and a cup of coffee in the other. He paused momentarily and looked at me as if I had a third eye growing in the middle of my forehead and without saying a word, he turned away and kept on strutting towards his seat. A bit offended, I turned around and went back to minding my own business. *Ok then,* I thought. *Get in trouble. I don't care.* After that disastrous meet I tried to steer clear of Officer Morris, and within a couple of weeks we were moved to different shifts. During our shift changes on some days we passed each other in the station parking lot, and after a few weeks Officer Morris spoke to me.

"Hey, I'm PJ," he said, slowly letting his guard down.

I introduced myself and from that day on, we spoke often, mostly casually in passing. Our small talk eventually morphed into laughing and joking with each other, and soon afterwards we started talking on the phone for hours at home. I wasn't dating anyone exclusively but I was open. It was during one of our conversations that PJ told me he was engaged to a woman who was not on the police department.

"That's cool," I replied. *We're just friends anyway.* I thought

By March of 1982, PJ and I were actually seeing each other every day on and off duty. One day after work PJ said he had something to tell me.

"I ended my engagement," he said sheepishly.

"What? Why?" I asked.

"Well, *she* doesn't want me to be a Police Officer and I can't have some-one trying to control my life. Whoever I marry has to be on board with my career, and if not, then we can't move forward." he explained and I understood.

We had become very close in a short period of time, and I appreciated him sharing with me the reasons for his personal decision to end his engagement. I still had a few months to go before I was due to transfer out of the division that June and I was having an amazing time working patrol. I was treated well by my training officers, peers and supervisors, and I felt like I was meant to do the job of a police officer. My partners, who were primarily older white men thought I was smart; I was an excellent writer; and most importantly they respected how assertive I was in the field. PJ, on the other hand, was starting to feel disrespected after a few months in the field.

"I can't do this, Tia," he said after a few daunting weeks with a not-so-nice training officer. I think I'm going to quit."

"Are you crazy?" I replied. "You went through that long hiring process and you want to quit because of *one* jerk? No, no, no. Don't do it. Trust me, it will get better." I tried to motivate him, as I had been where he was with a really bad training officer.

PJ was frustrated but after he calmed down and looked at the situation for what it was, he realized it was all a game that he had to play in order to pass probation. After moving on to another training officer, PJ adjusted to the atmosphere and began to thrive. A few weeks after dumping his fiancé, PJ and I started dating exclusively and after about six months, he asked me to marry him. I didn't have to think about it twice because it felt right. However, we had to keep quiet about our relationship until I transferred out of the division. The department was very leery of officers who dated each other while working at the same division. They didn't want any off-duty issues to become on-duty problems.

Our Engagement Party Photo 1982

PJ grew up in Stockbridge, Georgia, a small rural town located on the outskirts of Atlanta. Unlike me, he grew up in a two-parent household with one sibling. PJ followed his sister to California a few years before joining the department. After working a few jobs, and owning a small cleaning business, he decided to join the ranks of the LAPD. A couple of years after PJ moved to California his parents also relocated to Los Angeles from Georgia.

When PJ's dad, PJ Sr., moved to California in 1979 he was working for United Airlines. Due to contract negotiations he was forced to transfer from their hometown in Atlanta, Georgia, to either Hawaii or California in order to keep his job. He chose California since PJ and his sister Cheryl-Ann were already living there. When I met PJ he was living with his parents, PJ Sr., and Virginia, his mother, in the San Fernando Valley. They had a big beautiful two-story home located on a busy street in a rural part of the east San Fernando Valley. One morning, I had to testify in criminal court for one of the cases I was involved in at work and since the courthouse was in the Valley PJ invited me to stop by his house afterwards to meet his family. I was not familiar with the area of the San Fernando Valley where PJ lived, but I pulled out my department-issued Thomas Guide and successfully navigated my way to the Morris's Manor. PJ's sister and a family friend were also living there when I stopped by, so I was able to meet the *entire* family during that first visit.

PJ, PJ Sr. and Virginia

"Hello, darlin'," PJ, Sr. said as he opened the front door. He was a southern gentleman. "You must be Tia. Come on in. Spote, well…I call him Spote, he's in the room with his mother." PJ Sr. called PJ, *Sport* as a boy growing up but when he attached his southern drawl, it became *Spote*.

"Thank you," I responded as I entered the double doors into the foyer.

When I walked into the house I took it all in: the smell of breakfast being cooked by PJ Sr. while other family members roamed about the house. As I walked further into the hallway I caught a glimpse of PJ lying on the bed next to his mother in the downstairs bedroom. Virginia lay there laughing and talking with her son waiting for breakfast to be served. PJ motioned for me to come into the room where he introduced me to Virginia.

"Look at you. Just as pretty as you wanna be." Virginia said smiling.

Virginia's speech pattern was affected by a stroke she had when PJ was only 13. The stroke also affected her ability to walk amongst other things. As I sat there witnessing their interaction I remembered Mama telling me to watch how a man treats his mother and I would have a pretty good idea as to how he would treat me. PJ was so attentive and loving towards his mother, so naturally, I thought, *he is a keeper*. Virginia and PJ, Sr. turned out to be two of the sweetest, most loving people I had ever met. On the other hand however, I had the most interesting introduction to PJ's sister that day. Cheryl-Ann was six years older than PJ and his only sibling. She had just moved back home most likely for financial reasons because her car, a cute little sporty Mazda RX7 had just been repossessed. PJ Sr. had already worked a deal with the bank to get the car out of hock so PJ asked if I would follow him to the tow yard to pick it up for his sister. Since Cheryl-Ann had already defaulted on her payment several times PJ, Sr. had to pay the balance of the car loan in order for the bank to release the vehicle; those were the only terms acceptable to the bank. I didn't know Cheryl-Ann, but it was obvious to me that she had either fallen on hard times or was just irresponsible. I could spot hard times a mile away because I grew up in hard times, so I was in no position to judge her at that point. Nevertheless, and in spite of the awkward first meeting, she, and the rest of Morris family, welcomed me with open arms. I left there feeling optimistic about my new relationship with PJ and couldn't wait to tell Mama all about him.

"Mama, you will like him," I said emphatically. "I went to his house the other day and met his whole family, and you will love his mom and dad. They are a bit older than you, and his mom has been sick, but PJ is so sweet with her. I remember what you told me about men who treat their mom's right."

"Well I can't wait to meet them, and don't get me wrong, I mean there are some exceptions to that mother/son thing, but for the most part he will treat you right if he treats his mom right."

A few days later PJ came over to visit, and met Mama. He was riding a motorcycle that he called an *ass rocket* because of its tapered look and speed. I never liked motorcycles, but he was young, single, and daring so I understood his fascination with bikes. When I opened the door for PJ, Mama was standing in the kitchen. PJ flashed a big wide grin and greeted Mama with a big bear hug.

"It's a pleasure to meet you." He said.

Mama saw firsthand what I meant about his loving nature. She thought PJ was very handsome and she knew he had a good stable job, so that was good enough for starters. Within a few weeks, PJ and I took Mama to meet Dad and Virginia and although there was a 20-year age difference between them and Mama, they got along like old friends. By that summer PJ and I were officially engaged. We hadn't known each other very long, but Mama was ecstatic to hear that we were getting married. Any concerns she had were set aside because she trusted my judgment, and could see PJ was pretty level headed. Besides, PJ was already vetted by the LAPD before they hired him so their background investigation was surely way better than any investigation that I could have conducted. If the LAPD thought he was ok to hire, I was pretty sure he was good to go. When PJ met Stefon and Edris he accepted them as his brothers and they all got along famously. PJ and I were open with each other about everything. I'd shared with him about my dysfunctional upbringing, and how it was difficult for Mama to defeat the obstacles that most single parents faced; and how Mama wasn't as lucky in love as his parents were. PJ was down to earth and he wasn't hung up on the superficial so he never judged my family. Instead, he embraced my family as his own. In the months following our engagement, I was all over the place trying to plan a wedding. I knew it was customary for the parents of the bride to pay for the wedding but Mama was in no position to pay for a *courthouse* wedding, let alone an extravagant wedding, and I had bills, so I was on a super tight budget as well. I had just bought myself a brand new 1982 Camaro, and financed it for only three years, so my car payment was a little higher than normal. I gave Mama my older model 1977 Camaro since Edris had swindled her out of the car they were *supposed* to share.

In June of 1982, I transferred from North Hollywood Division, to Jail Division, where I was assigned to the Female Jail Section. A couple of months later, PJ transferred to Communications Division at Police Headquarters. I was relieved that we were no longer working together because I didn't want anything to interfere with our personal relationship. Besides, I was bound to get on his nerves with my wedding planning, so it was best that we had our space. PJ was fine with the idea of having just a *civil ceremony* at the Justice of the Peace, but I explained to him that it was always my dream to have a big wedding, and I was Mama's only girl, so she wanted me to have a wedding too. PJ understood and agreed to help me pull *something* together for a winter wedding in February of 1983. After hearing of our wedding plans, and the short time frame; and understanding the underlying financial concerns, Dad willingly chipped in a few dollars. My self-appointed Godmother, Irene also became an active contributor to my wedding planning operation. Earlier in the year, I had attended a wedding at a venue called the *Ivy House*. It was a home in a residential area of Inglewood, California that was converted into a small cottage with a Victorian twist. It boasted a beautiful backyard garden with a gorgeous, flower-laden gazebo that was fit for a heavenly wedding, and when I saw the wedding pictures I was completely sold. I told my friend who invited me to the wedding that I wanted to have my wedding there and I later expressed my interest in the location to Mama and PJ. I told Mama and PJ they had inexpensive packages for the complete wedding and reception, and they even had their own photographer. I was excited, but having the wedding *and* reception there in the limited time frame they allowed just wasn't grand enough for the type of celebration I longed for. I needed a bit more. So, PJ and I reached out to Cheryl-Ann's boyfriend, Eric, and asked if we could have an after party on his yacht. Eric and Cheryl-Ann had been dating for a while when I met the family, and they were planning to marry a few months before us. Eric was a car salesman at Lou Ehlers Cadillac and he owned, and lived on, a beautiful 60-foot yacht, which he docked in the Long Beach Harbor. PJ and I had gone out on the Yacht with Cheryl-Ann and Eric several times, and we always enjoyed our leisurely cruises on the Pacific Ocean, so we thought the Yacht would be a great place for an after party for our family and closest friends. Eric was very accommodating and agreed to the after party. Although Cheryl-Ann and I had just met we agreed to be in each other's weddings. I mean, she wasn't going to be my maid of honor but I was happy to have PJ's sister take part in the ceremony as a bridesmaid.

"So, you can be in my wedding and I will be in yours," Cheryl-Ann said matter-of-factly. "Eric and I want to get married in August. When do you and PJ want to get married?"

"Well, we were thinking about next February because that would give me enough time to plan and save a little more money," I explained. "But PJ doesn't really want to wait that long. So, we may push it up to November around Thanksgiving."

"I'm so excited for the both of us!" Cheryl-Ann shrieked. "Let's go soon and look at wedding dresses."

"Ok cool." I agreed. "But I have to see when my mother is available because I definitely want her input." Our excitement was electric. We were both on cloud nine.

PJ and I did in fact move the wedding to November because we didn't want to wait until February. The planning of our weddings created somewhat of a bond between Cheryl-Ann and me early on. Whenever we saw each other, we found ourselves discussing our wedding ideas, browsing through bridal magazines, and comparing wedding dresses that fit our individual tastes. A few weeks into our planning phase, there was a rift in our short-lived harmony. It was one afternoon in the middle of July 1982, when Cheryl-Ann went to visit Eric on his Yacht. She was going to surprise him but instead the surprise was on her because she found him in bed with another woman. Cheryl-Ann was devastated, and upon hearing the news that her wedding was off, her sadness turned into unexplained anger towards me. Cheryl-Ann moved out of the family home and back to an apartment in the city after realizing she wasn't getting married anytime soon. She remained very cold and distant towards me and she *never* mentioned anything about my wedding ever again. As the summer ended it dawned on me to ask Cheryl-Ann if she was still going to *be in* my wedding so I called her.

"Hi, Cheryl-Ann," I began trying to gauge her attitude. "I was wondering when you were going to be able to go to the bridal shop for your dress fitting."

"You know, Tia," she replied coldly, "I think your bridesmaids should be *your* very close friends."

"Well, ok. So sorry I bothered you." I said as I went to hang up. I felt bad. "Hey, I'm sorry things didn't work out for you and Eric." I said earnestly and then I hung up.

My feelings were hurt and I was taken aback because what happened with her relationship had *nothing* to do with her being involved in her own brother's wedding. I continued planning the final details of my wedding with Mama and Irene. I was not going to let Cheryl-Ann's rotten attitude steal my joy.

November 27th was the date we agreed upon for the wedding. It fell on the Saturday after Thanksgiving, so it turned out to be a very festive holiday weekend, and a mini family reunion of sorts. I was very happy that Grandmother and Grandfather were well enough to travel and Mama's airline benefits made it possible for them and my aunts to fly in as well. PJ and I were both hopeful that Virginia would be able to attend our wedding. Sadly, however, in late October, a few weeks before the wedding, she suffered another stroke, which further affected her speech, and resulted in her being completely bedridden. Dad rented a hospital bed and hoist for Virginia that he set up in the downstairs den of the family home. Dad was still working when Virginia fell ill so he brought his elderly aunt to live in the family home to help care for Virginia. There was no way the family was putting Virginia into any assisted living facility or nursing home when she had so many people who loved her. PJ was so sad, and worried about his mother that I felt guilty having to celebrate such an important event without her there. It rained the entire week leading up to the wedding, including on Thanksgiving Day, so I was getting anxious about how the inclement weather would impact my outdoor wedding ceremony.

"Oh my goodness, Mama," I vented. "Why did I plan a doggone garden wedding this late in the fall? What was I thinking?"

"Calm down, Doll Baby," Mama said. "I'm sure it'll stop raining soon. Stop worrying about things you can't control. Aren't you excited that your Grandmother is here?" Mama was attempting to divert my attention from the weather with small talk.

Our wedding party was comprised of my closest friends from high school, college and work. Twyla was my best friend and Maid of Honor. We met at Westchester in the 10th grade during P.E. and remained extremely close throughout high school and college. My grandparents, Uncle Grant, Aunt Juanda, Aunt Laberta and her son, my favorite cousin, Will, Jr., Stefon, my cousin Darryle, PJ's cousin Dirona, and my good friend Denise all flew in for the wedding from Kansas, Chicago, DC, Atlanta, and Florida respectively. Stefon, Edris, my cousin Darryle, and a few of PJ's closest friends were all groomsmen. PJ's LAPD academy classmate, Lamotta "Daddy Jack" Jackson, was PJ's Best Man. I was excited to see everyone, and loved the idea of having all of the family together for Thanksgiving Day.

Grandmother and Mama got up early on Thanksgiving morning and cooked up a grand feast with all the trimmings, and the drinks were flowing nonstop from sun up to sun down. I marveled at how Grandmother never used a measuring cup or spoon for anything. *A pinch of this and/or a pinch of that* was her perfect measuring ritual.

"Grandmother that Lemon Meringue pie is tart just like I like it," I squealed like a schoolgirl. "Woman, how do you get that crust so flaky? Mmm. Mmm. Mmm It's so good." I loved talking to my Grandmother. She said I was her "pride and joy," and I made her laugh.

"Chile, you better leave that pie alone, or you ain't gonna fit into that pretty little wedding dress," she laughed. I was so happy Grandmother was there.

After stuffing my face all day, I only had one day left to tie up loose ends while I managed our out of town guests. The first order of business was making sure my bridesmaids had their dresses, accessories, and satin ballerina slippers I had bought for them as gifts. The ballet shoe selection was perfect for the Yacht party since all guests were requested to wear soft sole shoes. I had all of the shoes, so it was my responsibility to take them to the wedding location. All was going well until that Friday afternoon, the day before the wedding, when I received a call from Twyla.

"Hey T," she said in a low monotone voice. "I'm sick and I don't think I can be in your wedding."

"*What*? What are you talking about? Twlya, I get married *tomorrow*!"

"I know, T," she explained apologetically, "but I've been throwing up all day and I don't think I can make it. Maybe you can have your friend from Florida wear my dress."

"Twyla, really? Denise is *way* too small to fit your dress," I said, "and we have no time to have it altered." I said as I started crying. I was furious and definitely did not expect this drama.

"I'm sorry T," Twyla offered. "I will let you know if I feel better, ok?"

I wasn't mentally prepared to move forward without my Maid of Honor and I really couldn't be mad because she couldn't help that she was sick. It was a hectic week and, in spite of Twyla bailing out in the 11th hour, and Virginia's unfortunate absence, I was still ecstatic about my impending nuptials. I took inventory of all that I needed for the ceremony, reception, and after party. Mama and Irene stayed up late into the night preparing food for the party while I gathered all of my things for the wedding. I placed all the bridesmaids' shoes in my car along with some other items so that I would be ready to go the next morning. I stayed up half the night with Mama, Grandmother, and my aunts laughing and talking, and nibbling on Thanksgiving leftovers while listening to the constant heavy rainfall until I drifted off to sleep. I prayed for the rain to stop. Early the next morning I was awakened by the blinding sun piercing through the slivers of the mini blinds in my room. All I could do was scream with excitement because the rain had stopped. It was bright and quite beautiful outside. It was a little crisp but the sun shined so bright it stung my eyes as I walked to the car with my wedding dress draped over my arm. The Limousine arrived right on time to drive me to the Ivy House. The Limo would later take PJ and me from the Ivy House to the yacht, where we would set sail for a few hours. PJ drove my car to the Ivy House and then had one of his buddies drive it to Long Beach so that PJ and I could drive to our honeymoon in Vegas after the party. My bridesmaids showed up looking beautiful and ready for my special day and to my surprise, Twyla was there in the bridal suite with Mama when I arrived.

"Aw, I'm so happy you could make it. Are you sure you are feeling up to this?" I asked playfully.

"Girl, I'm three months pregnant," Twlya grumbled under her breath. "That's why I was sick as a dog."

"What!" I exclaimed, "Congratulations! I'm so happy for you. Oh wait, are *you* happy about it?"

We bantered back and forth until we were interrupted by a knock at the door of my bridal suite. It was Irene.

"Hey Tia, the girls want to know where their shoes are."

"Oh," I said, "I have them right here in my bag." I turned and unzipped my duffle bag, but the shoes weren't there. "Wait a minute, I know I put them in here last night."

I frantically searched for the shoes and could not find them amongst my things. I was sure I had brought them with me. Then I remembered putting them in my car the night before. That's when it dawned on me; they were on the back seat of my car that was parked at the pier in Long Beach.

"Irene, please ask PJ to have someone go to the pier and get the girls' shoes out of my car." I was starting to panic hoping that my recall was right. *There is no way we can start the wedding if my bridesmaids didn't have their shoes*, I thought.

Luckily the shoes were right where I said they were and they were delivered with time to spare. The wedding and reception went off perfectly. During the reception I looked amongst the faces in the crowd when I realized something was wrong.

"PJ, where is Cheryl-Ann?" I asked quietly, as we greeted our guests on the receiving line.

Cheryl-Ann was *not* at our wedding. We later found out that she went to her friend's wedding instead, which was on the same day at the same time as ours. I was beyond offended. She went from being *in* our wedding to not even attending.

It was clear that Cheryl-Ann took out her frustration over her failed relationship on PJ and me. You would have thought *we* put the other woman in bed with Eric.

Our Wedding Day, November 27, 1982

To add insult to injury, when PJ and I arrived at the yacht that evening for the after party, Cheryl-Ann and several of her girlfriends, all whom had just come from the other wedding, were already on the yacht with Eric. I was angry at the sight of Cheryl-Ann.

"What is *she* doing here?" I asked PJ.

"I don't know, but she has to leave."

Me and Dad, Me PJ and Eric at the Yacht Party 1982

PJ wasted no time in throwing Cheryl-Ann and her friends off the yacht.

"Cheryl-Ann, this is a *private* party," PJ explained coldly to his sister. "You and your friends are not welcome here."

Cheryl-Ann stared me down as I stood beside PJ then she motioned for her lackeys to follow her to exit the yacht. The shade of it all had me shaking my damn head. It was unbelievable. She always wanted to be an actress and she could have won an Emmy for her performance that night. At that moment, Cheryl-Ann was pure evil in my eyes and that was just the beginning of many challenging years we faced while trying to build a healthy relationship with her.

PJ and I moved into the family home right after the wedding so we could assist with caring for Virginia, and PJ could spend as much time with her as possible. One evening a few days after the wedding PJ and I were at Virginia's bedside talking to her.

"Baby, you know I love you. I heard your wedding was beautiful and Cheryl-Ann said that Tia looked gorgeous." She spoke slowly as her last stroke made it harder for us to understand her but PJ and I heard that lie loud and clear. How dare Cheryl-Ann be that wicked? "I want you to know that you are going to be alright. I'm leaving you in good hands," Virginia continued.

"I know Mama," PJ said with a heavy heart. "I'm not afraid anymore because I won't be alone. Tia and I have each other."

In a previous conversation with Virginia, PJ had silently pleaded with her to just hold on and stay with him until he found a wife that she would approve of. It was as if our wedding and Virginia's fondness of me was all the reassurance that she needed. In April of 1983, 6 months after we married my sweet Mother In Law, Virginia Helen Rice passed away. Virginia was buried in Atlanta in one of the family's burial plots. The piece of sacred ground was also where generations of Dad's kinfolk were buried. Losing Virginia was especially hard for Dad because he and Virginia had been married for 35 years. After Virginia passed away we slowly reconnected with Cheryl-Ann because she was, after all, PJ's only sibling, and even though she treated me horribly on several occasions *I* was not going to stand in the way of their relationship. Following the wedding debacle, Cheryl-Ann *never* found it in her wretched heart to even acknowledge boycotting our wedding. PJ and I agreed to forgive her but we vowed to never forget. She on the other hand carried on like nothing ever happened.

PJ and I wanted our own home, however, we stayed living with Dad after Virginia died. Living with Dad worked best at that time because we had minimal expenses *and* we were able to spend time with Dad, who was alone. Dad had friends he worked with who lived nearby so they turned out to be a great support system for him as well. It was while visiting one of his neighborhood friends in January of 1985, when Dad became aware of a home in the neighborhood that was facing foreclosure. The custom-built 4-bedroom, tri-level home was only about ½ mile from the family home where we lived. The house was built in 1970, so it wasn't too old at the time; however, it was dated with shag carpeting and wrought iron banisters, and the property inside and out was severely neglected. The out of work Chiropractor, and father of five, who owned it, could no longer afford the property's upkeep or mortgage payments. He had an assumable loan so he welcomed the bail out offer from Dad. Dad thought it would be a great home for Cheryl-Ann, so that she could live in a house versus an apartment. Dad told Cheryl-Ann he was purchasing the property for her and to our surprise she accepted.

Cheryl-Ann had a new live in boyfriend, who would also be living with Cheryl-Ann, and Dad was okay with that. Rodney, Cheryl-Ann's boyfriend was a sweet-spirited, legal professional and part-time clairvoyant. The two of them worked in different law offices in downtown Los Angeles. The caveat for Cheryl-Ann accepting the house was that Dad would live there as well. Dad moving in with Cheryl-Ann meant that PJ and I took over the family home in its entirety. We were happy to have our own home *and* still have Dad close by. Cheryl-Ann could *not* afford the home Dad purchased for her without his assistance because she hadn't handled her finances well in the past and not much had changed. While Cheryl-Ann loved her Dad, *sharing* was not something she was accustomed to doing with anyone. She reluctantly agreed to the arrangement primarily because she knew that Dad was about to retire, and he would be returning to his hometown in Georgia, which meant she would have the house all to herself in due time. Dad promised that he would finance the remodeling, and upgrade the home to Cheryl-Ann's specifications and satisfaction, which really sealed the deal. Dad divided up their household responsibilities, and bills. He agreed to pay the mortgage, and all Cheryl-Ann had to do was pay for the utilities and cable etc. Cheryl-Ann had the liberty to make any and all changes that she wanted in upgrading the house.

Cheryl-Ann chose beautiful designer wallpaper, custom colored pastel paints, French doors to replace an old window, wood flooring in select areas, new carpeting in the living room, and marble floors in the entryway of her blossoming home. It was simply gorgeous. There was no denying Cheryl-Ann's first class taste. She did wonders with updating the house and making it her own. The family home that PJ and I stayed in had been maintained very well, so all we did was add *our* furniture, change the window treatments, and change out the carpet for wood floors. We were all happy with our living situations thanks to Dad. PJ and I wanted children right away, but for almost three years, I had no luck in conceiving. My doctor thought my ongoing Thyroid issues were adversely affecting my fertility, so at one point the doctor alluded to us accepting the fact we would not be able to have children. In the vain of a childless couple we both traded in our sedans and bought matching two-seater sports cars. The ink on the sales contract hadn't even begun to dry when I found out I was pregnant so within short order I switched out my sports car for a more family-friendly sedan. I was rounding the corner at 4 years on the job and working in an administrative assignment at LAPD's Traffic Coordination Section, where I reviewed and responded to Assembly and Senate Bill propositions that, if passed, affected Law Enforcement in some capacity. Due to my pregnancy status, I was considered "light duty," which meant that I was temporarily exempt from qualifying/shooting on the firing range with my duty weapon. I hated shooting on the range anyway because while in the Academy, the stress on the shooting range made me anxious. Firearms instructors would prowl the lanes screaming and barking orders to get the recruits riled up before firing rounds down range. The department's stance on the stressful training was that in a real life situation, things would not be calm; they would be chaotic, fast moving and stressful, so it was futile for us to *not* practice that way. Due to the influx of women coming on the job, the advent of a new maternity uniform came about while *I* was pregnant, and *I* bought the first one. It was a regular old uniform with pleats added to the sides of a formerly fitted shirt, and an elasticized fabric replaced the zipper on the pants. It was cute.

My LAPD Maternity Uniform 1985

During the remodeling phase of Dad and Cheryl-Ann's home PJ and I visited with them often on the weekends and all seemed to be going well. As the remodeling was winding down Dad retired after 29 years with United Airlines, and he was preparing to go back to live in Georgia. It was early in April of 1985, when Dad came to our house one day and he was exasperated. He told us that the utilities and cable at his house had not been paid in several months and when he discussed the issue with Cheryl-Ann, she told him that she had not paid them because she no longer wanted to live there. She said that she was not married and didn't have a family, so the *suburbs*, where we lived, were not where she wanted to live. Soon after that conversation Cheryl-Ann and Rodney left the house and moved back to an apartment in the mid city area of Los Angeles. I thought that Cheryl-Ann was very inconsiderate to abandon Dad like that when he had spent a lot of time and money trying to make her happy.

Dad was perfectly happy in the family home before he secured the property for Cheryl-Ann so she should not have accepted the house under any conditions if she was not going to hold up her end of the bargain. Since Dad was going to be leaving California he suggested that we switch houses with him.

"The new house is on a quieter street; and newly remodeled so with the baby on the way, I think it's best, if you all switch houses with me. I will do a "quick claim" deed putting the house in you and Tia's names and y'all can assume the loan from me." Dad reasoned.

I loved the original family home, but moving to the newly remodeled house on the quiet secluded street really appealed to me, especially since Cheryl-Ann didn't want it anymore. We agreed to the switch and scheduled a day to swap houses. Dad and PJ rented a large U-Haul truck and we took load after load of our personal belongings from our house to the other, and vice versa with us taking Dad's personal belongings back to the family home. The move between houses was a bit hectic and I couldn't do much physically because I was pregnant. PJ and I settled into our new home pretty quickly. We helped Dad get back situated in the family home and we checked in on him regularly to make sure he was ok. He lived alone, but his aunt, who cared for Virginia before she died, still came out for long visits from time to time. After a few months, one of Dad's former coworkers, Mr. Copeland, who had relocated to California at the same time as Dad in 1979, went to live with Dad in the family home. Mr. Copeland, who went by "Cope" was within a few months of retiring, and was planning a move back to South Carolina, where he was from. Cope's wife had already gone back home in preparation for his impending retirement, so Cope moved in with Dad to save some money. It was a great arrangement because Dad, in turn had a companion. All of Dad's friends knew that he was pretty much financially secure, and that he owned several properties in Georgia. They often reminded him of how much money *he* had. They were a mess. Soon after Cope moved in with Dad, he, and some of their other friends thought Dad needed a female companion, and according to them, they had just the right woman in mind. Dad was open to meeting her because he had been a widower for almost 5 years and was open to having a relationship. Enter Ms. Neomi, a 50-year-old *gold digger* straight out of Compton. She *allegedly* owned a liquor store in the Compton-Lynwood area with her soon-to-be ex-husband, who was the father of her eight-year-old son and youngest child. Ms. Neomi had a few adult children too, but her pride and joy was her eight-year-old angel, Jason, whom I referred to as "Little Lord Fauntleroy." I called him that because he was extremely proper for a ghetto boy. Whenever he wanted eating utensils at the dinner table, he asked for *cutlery*. I didn't know of any child, who asked for *cutlery* so he was a bit much. Jason was a handsome, well-mannered little boy who was ill for most of his childhood due to issues with his kidneys. Neomi was an attractive dark complexioned woman, 15 years Dad's junior, and she thought she was royalty, which accounted for Jason's precociousness. Neomi wore *the best* ghetto designer fashions she picked up at the Slauson Swap Meet, and she drove *the best* older model, big body Mercedes-Benz, but it was all a façade because she was flat broke. It would be a while before Dad realized she was an imposter. A few months after swapping houses, Dad called PJ in a panic.

"Hey Dad, what's up?"

"Are you sittin' down, Spote?"

"No man, I ain't sitting down," PJ responded. "I'm outside talking to Henry from next door.

"Spote, I just been served with papers from some attorney's office," Dad explained. "This notice is advisin' me that we are being sued."

Who is being sued Dad?"

"Where's Tia?" Dad asked avoiding PJ's question.

"She's in the house, Dad. What is going on?"

"Spote, go in the house and call me back when you are with Tia. She needs to hear this too." When we called Dad back, he told us that Cheryl-Ann had filed a lawsuit against the three of us.

"Wait, what?" I exclaimed. "What is she suing *us* for?" PJ and I were blown away; we hadn't done anything to warrant being sued but it was Cheryl-Ann so we weren't surprised.

"Cheryl-Ann wants to be compensated for her *interior design* of the house, son." Dad continued.

"So, she's mad because we moved into the house that she voluntarily abandoned?"

What a selfish, spiteful woman, I thought to myself. It became clear to me that she had some deep-rooted issues, and that she needed some deep-rooted therapy, or Jesus, or both. We weren't rich, and black people just didn't sue their parents. It was horrible. First, we had to deal with Cheryl-Ann dissing her only brother on his wedding day, and then she decided to sue for her "interior design." I was certain she had lost her damn mind. That stunt made bad matters worse between her and PJ. I felt bad for him and Dad. After reviewing the confusing legalese, and meeting with Dad to discuss Cheryl-Ann's nonsense, he decided to settle the lawsuit out of court for $25,000 in order to spare our family from a possible long drawn out court proceeding. I was becoming used to Cheryl-Ann's antics, but it bothered me that Rodney was okay with Cheryl-Ann's foul nature especially in this instance. His acquiescing to her behavior spoke volumes for his character. Had I been Dad in that situation, I would have let that mess play out in court. That was some nerve she had.

My first trimester was particularly uneventful. The summer was fast approaching and I was shopping for furniture for the nursery. The guys at work were good for finding wholesale merchants who offered police discounts. They took me to an inconspicuous furniture warehouse in Downtown Los Angeles that sold to high-end children's specialty stores. I wanted a gold trimmed white, wrought iron day bed and the matching baby bed, both of which were very expensive on the retail market. The warehouse had *everything* I needed and more; and at a third of the price with my police discount, so I was in heaven. That 4ᵗʰ of July, Aunt Juanda came to California for a short visit with Mama. I had not seen her since my wedding, and I missed her crazy behind. She had recently retired from Ecko Bakeware in Chicago after 25 years, and she and Uncle Grant, who had become disabled from a chronic heart condition, had moved to Coffeyville to care for Grandmother in her old age. Grandfather had died, some years prior, and Grandmother was living alone so Aunt Juanda and Uncle Grant bought the house directly across the street from her to make things easier for all of them. During her visit, I took Aunt Juanda to Long Beach to visit her aunts on her dad's side of the family, just as I did every time she came to L.A. She was ecstatic that I was pregnant, and she said she couldn't wait to spoil my baby. There was a calmness in her demeanor, that I had not witnessed before, but I thought maybe she was just happy in retirement, and happy to be home in Coffeyville with grandmother and other relatives. I was sad to see Aunt Juanda leave after her weeklong visit, but I figured she would be back after my baby was born.

I remained very active throughout my pregnancy, and by the end of my second trimester I had only gained 26 pounds. My doctor wasn't overly concerned, and opined that my baby was going to be small. Then my feet started to swell, which made her pay closer attention. By the end of July, my OBGYN was concerned that my swollen ankles and high blood pressure were consistent with Toxemia. I only had three months left to go as the baby was due October 12ᵗʰ. By mid August, however, my doctor took me off work and put me on complete bed rest. A few days after I was placed off work I got a call from Mama telling me that Aunt Juanda had dropped dead from a heart attack right there on her front porch only a few months after relocating to Coffeyville. She was only 55 years old. Mama and Aunt Laberta believed she had liver disease due to the many years of heavy drinking. Still, it was a surprise, and devastating at the same time. PJ and I travelled with Mama to Coffeyville for Aunt Juanda's funeral after clearing it with my doctor considering my medical issues. I was pretty bloated, and uncomfortable during the trip but I was glad I was able to attend the funeral. After returning home I was back on bed rest for about two weeks and I was bored, so I begged PJ to let me ride with him to the drug store one evening. He had to go to Sav On Drugs for one thing or another, so I walked into the drugstore and was milling around the store with my tight belly and semi-swollen ankles when I came across a blood pressure machine in the pharmacy section. *I should check my pressure since it was elevated during my last doctor's visit,* I thought. I sat in the chair and placed my arm in the sleeve and waited for the machine to read my results. When the machine was done sucking the life out of my arm, I looked down and shrieked.

"Oh, my God! Oh my God!" I was freaking out because it was way higher than it was at the doctor's office during my last visit. PJ heard me yell and ran over to see what was wrong.

"Girl what is your problem?" He said as he looked at the machine.

"My blood pressure is 205/105!"

"Ok. I'm taking you home."

I didn't argue with him because I was scared. As soon as we got home, I called my doctor and she scolded me and told me to get back on bed rest. Later that night, I went to use the bathroom and it felt like I urinated for a long time. When I stood up, I saw a bloody mucous discharge in the toilet and I completely panicked.

"PJ!" I yelled from the bathroom. "I'm bleeding!"

Well, I wasn't *bleeding,* but there were traces of a bloody discharge present, so I called the doctor again and she told me to go to the Emergency Room at Holy Cross Hospital where she would meet me. My baby wasn't due until October 12th and here it was only August 24th and I was in premature labor. PJ was a nervous wreck by the time I was admitted. He thought both the baby and I were going to die. It had taken me so long to get pregnant, and he thought he was going to lose us both at the same time. PJ called Mama and told her I had gone into labor and she rushed right over. By the time she arrived at the hospital PJ had completely lost his composure; he cried; then Mama cried; everyone who came to the hospital cried. I was having contractions closer and closer together, which meant I was definitely in premature labor.

"Ok, Mr. Morris, we have to perform an emergency C-Section because the baby is too small to deliver naturally. PJ and Mama stood by while I was whisked away to the OR. About 45 minutes later my doctor reported to PJ.

"Mr. Morris, your wife and your daughter pulled through."

"Oh, thank God," PJ said relieved. "Wait, my *daughter?*"

"Oh, yes," Dr. Perez smiled. "Looks like we got it wrong on the ultrasound. You and your wife have a beautiful baby girl. Congratulations."

During one of my prenatal doctor's visits Dr. Perez indicated that per the ultrasound she was 99% sure I was having a boy. We had picked out boys names and bought everything in blue and yellow for the nursery, so it was a surprise when she announced that we had a girl. I was elated because I prayed for a girl. On the morning of August 25th 1985, Brittany was born at 6:15AM weighing three pounds, three ounces. She was tiny, but she was a healthy "preemie." I was in the hospital for five days recovering from surgery while Brittany baked in an incubator in the neonatal unit.

"Oh, Mrs. Morris, don't worry," said one of the nurses in the neonatal unit. "Girls who are born prematurely, usually fight to survive and end up thriving. This little angel doesn't even have jaundice, or any other issues normally associated with preemies. She just needs to remain in the hospital until she is an acceptable weight.

My baby shower was planned for September 7th, and since the invitations had already gone out before I went in the hospital, I went forward with the shower. When my guests arrived, they were surprised to see that I had the baby already, and my stomach was as flat as a pancake. My girdle worked wonders. For two weeks, PJ and I visited Brittany everyday for hours as she lay in a warm incubator until we got there to cuddle and feed her. Within those two weeks, she had grown to a little over five pounds and was finally released from the hospital. When she was released from the hospital, she looked like the little E.T., with her long curled fingers and long head. PJ poked fun at her flyaway hair, and bulging eyes, in her hospital release photo. She was a sight for sore eyes but she was my little angel. It was fun watching her grow. Her chubby cheeks grew to match her chubby thighs and I loved watching the transformation. That C-Section, however, was the start of my many surgeries. I had survived the childbirth crisis only to face another episode two months later. I was experiencing excruciating stomach pains, and I thought maybe the doctors had left a surgical instrument in my gut or something but after several trips to the emergency room, and no resolve I followed up with Dr. Perez, who delivered Brittany. She conducted a quick analysis of my pain and sent me for an ultrasound.

"Mrs. Morris, looks like you have Gall Stones," She explained. "Although, you don't exactly fit the criteria to have a faulty gall bladder."

"What are the criteria?" I asked.

"Well, unofficially, we refer to it as the Three F's: Female, Fat, and over 40," she replied. "But they are starting to link Gall Stones to pregnancy when they occur in younger women, who are of child-bearing age. We think it's due to the increase in your dairy consumption."

"So, how do you treat Gall Stones?"

"Actually, I recommend we surgically remove your Gall Bladder," Dr. Perez responded.

"Oh my, another surgery?"

I followed the doctor's recommendation and had the surgery. I could easily hide the bikini cut scar from the Cesarean, however, the new mid abdominal scar I received when they removed my Gall Bladder brought my mid drift top wearing days to a screeching halt, at the ripe old age of 27. I recovered well, but I proclaimed then that I did not want any more children. After the scare with Brittany, and the back-to-back surgeries, I was "gun shy." Ten months after Brittany was born, however, I was pregnant again.

"Well, it looks like you are a pro at this pregnancy thing." Dr. Perez said smirking. She knew the problems PJ and I encountered trying to conceive Brittany, so she was happy for us.

"Yes ma'am I think I got it mastered now Doc," I said with a chuckle.

"You did well last time with your weight only gaining 26 pounds but you also delivered early, so I'm going to keep a closer eye on you this time. You had an emergency C-Section before, so we should schedule you for another, since there is an increased possibility that you could rupture your uterus if you try to deliver naturally."

"That's fine. I trust you," I replied. "While you are in there you can tie my tubes because I'm done having children after this one. Two is enough. PJ always says 'the kids should not outnumber the parents,' so we will be maxed out with two."

My second pregnancy was a piece of cake. I gained very little weight again, and stayed active the entire time. I danced, I bowled, and I ran after

Brittany, who was all over the place as a toddler. I literally worked until the day before I went into the hospital for my scheduled C-Section. On March 16, 1987, Natalia was born. That delivery resulted in my 3rd abdominal surgery in as many years. I was so grateful that I was a fast healer, and kudos to whoever invented those girdles because I wore one for months after each surgery, and it provided great support for my fragile midsection; I had no jiggle and no pain.

Tia, with Brittany and Natalia at home in 1988

By the time Natalia was born, Dad and Neomi were in a full blown dating relationship. We tried to get to know Neomi, but she was a fake, so it was hard being around her too long. It was obvious that she had an agenda. Dad was preparing to move back to Atlanta and Neomi was on board to move with him. Before they finalized their moving plans, Neomi *told* Dad they were getting married, so she gathered up all of *her* kids, and their families and they went to Las Vegas. PJ, Cheryl-Ann, and I were neither told about the wedding nor were we invited to join them. We found out about the wedding a few days after they returned from Vegas. It was shameful. Neomi immediately started taking control of Dad's finances, which she had her eye on for a while. She was quick to tell us that the Trust Fund Dad had in place before they got married was no longer valid because it referred to Dad as a *widower,* and he was no longer a *widower. The senior citizen gold digger was crazy,* I thought. Neomi thought Dad had millions stashed away and she was determined to find the money. By the time they left for Georgia, Neomi had *lost* or *sold* the Liquor Store that she allegedly owned, *and* she had pulled out all of the equity from Dad's family home that we had lived in. That was just the start of the financial drain that she imposed on Dad.

After arriving in Georgia, Dad and Neomi settled into the home that Dad and Virginia had built in the 70's that PJ grew up in. The house was paid off until Neomi got a hold of the deed. Before long there was a whole new mortgage on that property as well as all of Dad's other Georgia properties. PJ and I were not surprised when we found out that Neomi and Cheryl-Ann had become friends. We understood the importance of them being on friendly terms for Dad's sake, but they were a little too close for comfort. PJ only communicated with Neomi when he needed to check on Dad, or when we were in town and wanted to visit him. It was difficult to watch Neomi conquer Dad like that, but he was grown, in his right mind, and could make his own decisions; so we minded our business.

CHAPTER 8

"The Boys Got Issues"

IT WAS THE SUMMER OF 1987, and Dad, Neomi, the senior citizen gold digger, and her cute little 8-year old, Jason, were getting settled in Atlanta. Two of Neomi's grown daughters also moved with her to Atlanta, with plans, to open a hair salon. When Dad and Neomi left California, PJ and I were living in the house vacated by Cheryl-Ann, and we took over the original family home that Neomi had pulled the equity from. We rented the house a couple of times to families we knew, and when we tired of hunting them down for the monthly rent, Mama rented it, which allowed her to be closer to us. I was happy Mama was living there, but I did not want Edris to move in and take advantage of her. He was so disrespectful, and I would not be there all the time to protect her from his verbal brow beatings. Obviously, it didn't matter what I wanted though because as soon as Edris broke up with the woman he was dating, he moved right in with Mama against my wishes. Edris was 27 years old and a full-blown alcoholic. His criminal record at that time only included a number of traffic warrant arrests and DUI's. My brothers knew that PJ and I were police officers and that I was not going to allow their antics to adversely impact our careers. I warned them often not to call me if they were ever arrested because I'd never bail them out. I needed to put my family first, which meant I did not want to do *anything* to jeopardize my job.

It had been seven years since Mama's last cancer treatment and she was doing well, except that she had started to complain about stomach pains. I thought maybe she was stressing out because of Edris's ongoing drama so I stayed close by to keep an eye on her and Edris. Stefon was still in D.C., and as far as we

145

knew, he was going to school and working. After one of her visits with Stefon, Mama came over to tell me about her trip. We laughed about Stefon's messy apartment, which he shared with two other young men. Mama confirmed that Stefon actually worked at the Waldorf Astoria Hotel because he'd always put Mama up in the Five Star Hotel when she visited. Mama loved seeing Stefon, and Stefon loved it when his *Baby*, as he affectionately called Mama, came to visit him. Thanks to American Airlines, Mama got to see Stefon regularly but it wasn't long after that last visit that the warmth and fuzziness Mama had experienced with Stefon came to an abrupt halt.

It was mid July 1987, and I was about to return to work after being off on Bonding Leave for four months with Natalia. PJ was working 77th Division Vice, and always had plenty of gritty stories to tell me about with his encounters with the street prostitutes, who just loved his green-eyed partner, William. Within a short period of time we fell in love with William, his wife Wanda, and their two girls Miya and Stacie. Coincidentally, Wanda worked for American Airlines with Mama, and I had met her before PJ and I met William on the job. PJ and I were coming up on our 5th wedding anniversary and up until then Stefon had been living back east, so our in-person communication with him was limited. It was late on one afternoon in July 1987, when Mama called me.

"Hey baby," Mama sounded exasperated. "I need to go to Washington D.C. to check on Stefon."

"Mama, you just came back from there," I replied. "What happened? What's going on?"

Stefon was about to turn 30 and was *still* in college. Mama was starting to have health issues again so it wasn't the best thing to have her going back and forth across country to *check* on Stefon. It was just ridiculous to me.

"I think he might be on drugs Tia," Mama confessed. "I have to go and see for myself what's going on with him."

I knew Stefon smoked marijuana but I was stunned to hear about any other drug use. I thought Stefon was just indecisive about what he wanted to do with his life, but I hadn't thought about him dabbling in hard drugs. I loved my big brother and I didn't want anything to be wrong with him, but, if in fact, Stefon were on drugs, then it would explain why he had become a perpetual student.

"Why do you think that Ma?" I asked with a growing concern.

"Bobby, one of Stefon's roommates, called me and said he thinks Stefon is *strung out* on drugs and that I need to come and get him some help." Mama said mocking Bobby's indignant tone.

"Strung out? Are you serious? On what?"

"Bobby thinks he's on crack, and that he's not even a student at Howard anymore." Mama shook her head in disgust as she recalled her conversation with Bobby.

"Cocaine?" I asked incredulously.

Mama had just visited Stefon, and his roommates Bobby and Jerrod, and other than their place being a mess, which was typical, she didn't think that anything else was askew. At least when she briefed me on her last visit, she didn't let on that anything was out of sorts, and that had only been a few weeks before.

"Bobby practically begged me to come get Stefon," Mama relayed. "So, I have to go get him."

Mama booked a flight to D.C. right away and I suddenly had a gut wrenching feeling in the pit of my stomach and couldn't stop thinking about what was going on with Stefon. *Stefon cannot be a drug addict.* I thought. It was such a sad situation, especially for Mama: one son, an alcoholic and woman abuser, and now, the other a possible drug addict. What broke my heart was that Mama had such high hopes for Stefon. She knew he was highly intelligent, and *she* had always proclaimed that *he* was going to be *a doctor*. Stefon would agree with Mama to appease her if nothing else but I never really believed that was *his* goal because he was lazy, and Mama knew it. I always believed Stefon would finish college because he was so smart, but I also knew he wasn't motivated about anything except smoking weed and reading anything he could get his hands on; that's *all* he wanted to do. He was extremely well versed about a lot of topics that no one really cared about. He stayed up on current events, and knew a tremendous amount about sports trivia and the like but now, according to his friend, he was on crack. Mama flew into D.C. and took a taxicab to Stefon's apartment where Bobby was anxiously awaiting her arrival.

"Hey Ms. Carmen." Bobby said acting surprised, so he didn't tip Stefon off that *he* called Mama.

Bobby slowly opened the door to the cluttered apartment, which was when Stefon saw Mama standing there looking beautiful in her double breasted, winter white wool maxi coat, and black patent leather high heel pumps. Whenever Mama flew using her American Airlines employee benefits, otherwise known as "Non-Rev/Standby," she always took a *carry on* bag, in case she was bumped from a flight; and the mandate for Non Revenue passengers was that they abide by a very strict dress code, which included the men wearing ties, so Mama was always dressed to kill whenever she flew American. Stefon was sitting casually on a frumpy old couch when Mama stepped into the apartment carrying her purse with one hand, and a small carry on bag with the other.

"Hey Baby, what are you doing here?" Stefon asked as he looked up from the newspaper he was reading; he was surprised to see her.

"I'm here to get you," she replied. "I'm taking you back with me. You aren't working; you are not going to school; and Bobby is tired of you lying around on him." Stefon gathered his newspapers and rolled them tightly into one hand like a baton, and slowly got up from the messy couch. He walked towards his bedroom and as he passed Bobby near the kitchen he pointed the newspaper baton in his direction.

"You're an asshole, man." Stefon said angrily.

"Man, I'm trying to get you some help," Bobby said as he positioned his body to defend himself in case Stefon lunged at him. "I'm your friend, Stefon."

"Stefon, get your things and let's go." Mama urged. "Don't forget to put on a suit jacket and tie. I have us booked on a flight back to Los Angeles this evening so shut up and let's go." She then turned to Bobby. "Thank you so much for calling me, Bobby. I'm going to take him home and get him some help."

"Ok Ms. Carmen," he said. "I'm so sorry. I mean we all smoke weed, but he's on that crack and I can't get with that."

"I know, I know." Mama replied.

"I don't know what happened at the hotel," Bobby continued. "But he ain't been to work in a while and Jerrod and I can't afford this place by ourselves, so we have to get another roommate to replace Stefon. I called you to come get him because I didn't wanna just put him out on the street."

"Well, I appreciate you for calling, honey," Mama said as she hugged Bobby.

"Yeah, I appreciate you too, bro," Stefon said sarcastically as he walked out of his bedroom and towards Mama, with his overstuffed suitcase. Mama and Stefon got into an awaiting taxi and rode to the airport.

Stefon was silent in the taxi, but his mood lightened up by the time they arrived at the airport. They opted for the curbside baggage check-in for Stefon's bag, and Mama held her breath when they weighed that sucker. *God knows what is in that bag.* Mama thought. It barely made it, weighing in at 49.8 pounds. Most of the flights she took to and from D.C. were wide open so she wasn't worried about Stefon making it onto the flight, and she almost always got upgraded to First Class if space was available. Once they boarded the plane, they got settled into their First Class seats for the long flight back to California.

"Mama," Stefon said after the plane took off. "I'm not on drugs. I swear. You know I smoke weed. I will always smoke weed because the *government* can't even tell me I can't."

"Ok, now you sound like a straight fool Stefon," Mama said in a harsh whisper as she snapped her neck in his direction. "You're talking about the *government* can't tell you what to do. You *sound* like you're on drugs. That's just ignorant, Stefon. I wish I had never allowed you and Edris to smoke weed at home. I see I've created a monster. You need to get your ass back in school somewhere, and finish your damn degree," She said. "And, get a job to take care of yourself."

Mama continued preaching to Stefon as he nodded off to sleep. Mama looked worn down and frail when she showed up at my house with Stefon the day after they returned. I was concerned because of her resurgence of health issues. She didn't need the stress that Stefon's antics caused her. I looked at Stefon with a side eye as he passed through the door into my foyer. *He looks pretty healthy for a dope-head,* I thought. Considering that the narcotics abusers I encountered on the job were usually scrawny, ashy, and just plain dirty, and Stefon wasn't any of those things. I had never associated with drug addicts in my personal life, so I didn't realize that all drug addicts didn't *look* strung out. I understood how the affects of alcohol abuse affected a person, but I did not fully understand the affects of crack cocaine. I needed to know what was going on with my brother, so I did a little research and gleaned information from my

Narcotics training I had at work. I read that Cocaine Hydrochloride, which is crack's clinical name, is both a local anesthetic and a stimulant to the central nervous system, and that it directly stimulates the brain and gives the user strong feelings of alertness and energy. Crack cocaine takes about 8-10 seconds to get to the brain when smoking it. Actually smoking any drug delivers higher doses of it into the brain more quickly than any other route of administration. The high received from cocaine "freebasing" lasts only 2-5 minutes followed by a rapid depression, and a craving for more of the drug, similar to the effects of snorting cocaine powder. With cocaine freebase however, the symptoms are more severe and in many instances, individuals become rapidly addicted to cocaine freebase, and exhibit severe psychiatric reactions such as paranoia, deep depression, and emotional instability. *Oh, my God. Mama said Stefon's moods were switching up on the ride to the airport in D.C.*

During the 1970's in Los Angeles, "crack" was prepared by using what was termed, "The Baking Soda Method." Cocaine powder was mixed with baking soda and water to form a paste. The mixture was then heated until dried. When dried, the product became a rock-like substance that was broken into chunks and then smoked. The method was used for at least 10 years before it reached the east coast, where Stefon lived at the time. It was given the street name crack because when heated, the rocks made a crackling sound. In the early 1980's, when the baking soda method of preparing cocaine freebase was used, the product was packaged in small clear vials, and sold on the streets, which is where Stefon scored his fixes in D.C. By 1986, crack cocaine use was considered to be in epidemic proportions in New York City, which is very close in proximity to D.C. In a short period of time, crack cocaine became a household word that was often equated with crime, violence, and medical problems, and sometimes led to death. Thanks to Bobby, we became aware of Stefon's unhealthy habit, and it wasn't long after arriving back home before his drug problem reared its ugly head.

Stefon went to live with Mama and Edris. The boys were 27 and 29, and neither of them was working, so Mama was supporting the three of them. Edris finally found a job, but Stefon was just *chillin'* as he tried to decide what to do to feed his drug habit, that he claimed he didn't have. Of course Stefon was in denial, and because he didn't look like a stereotypical druggie, I even fell for his "I ain't on no drugs" proclamation. Stefon spent a couple of months looking into getting a Series-7 license, which enabled him to sell all types of securities products. The exam to obtain the license covered topics such as, investment risks, taxation, equity and debt instruments, packaged securities, options, retirement plans, etc. Stefon was definitely smart enough to pass it, but I wondered how his brain cells were affected by his alleged drug use. He studied and passed the darn test on his first try. If I had not seen the test results myself, I would not have believed him. *Maybe he's* not *on drugs,* I continued to think. Mama was hopeful as well. After securing his Series-7 license, Stefon got a job at a Security Exchange company in Beverly Hills. I took him shopping at the Broadway Department Store in Panorama City so that he would have suitable business attire for his new career. I bought him dress shirts, ties, slacks, and a beautiful London Fog trench coat. He was good to go. Things were off to a good start, but the proverbial white elephant remained in the room whenever we were all together. *Is this fool on drugs or not?* I asked myself. He was getting up and going to work every day. I worked in Downtown L.A. at the time, so I drove half a mile to Mama's house everyday and picked up Stefon, and drove him to a bus stop on Wilshire Blvd for him to take public transportation the rest of the way to his office. That carpool arrangement went on for a few weeks until, as luck would have it, a friend of Mama's let Stefon borrow her older model Datsun B210 coupe, for transportation. Although I didn't mind the carpooling with Stefon, I was glad that he had his own ride.

It was September 1987, and Stefon had been home for about 3 months. One Saturday evening Stefon was driving his loaner Datsun in the East San Fernando Valley, close to Mama's house when he failed to stop for a posted stop sign at Foothill Blvd and Osborne Street, near the famed Rodney King beating site. Some of my brothers in blue were close by, observed the traffic violation, and conducted a routine traffic stop. I was in bed when the phone rang; it was Mama.

"Stefon's been arrested."

"For what Mama?" I asked in a groggy state.

"I don't know. The police won't tell me anything." Mama was worried.

"Don't stress yourself Mama," I said, "I will see what I can find out," I reassured Mama.

PJ and I made some calls and found out that Stefon had been arrested by LAPD's Foothill Division for an out of state warrant, which was discovered during the traffic stop. Apparently, before Stefon left D.C., he was arrested for buying crack cocaine from an undercover officer, and when Mama picked him up from Bobby's apartment, he failed to tell her that he had a pending court case, and needed to return to D.C. a month later in August 1987. When Stefon missed his court date there was a Bench Warrant issued for his arrest. It was confirmed for me then that Stefon was on drugs even though he denied it when Mama picked him up. Bobby was right. A few days went by as Stefon sat in the Los Angeles County Jail while the Federal and the D.C. authorities decided what they were going to do with the incidental fugitive. The Feds were involved because Stefon fled to another state after he agreed to testify against his drug dealer. Ultimately, the authorities in D.C. decided not to extradite and Stefon was released with only his local traffic violation to deal with, but I still confronted Stefon.

"Stefon, are you stupid or what?" I asked, angry and confused. "Or, do you think I am stupid? You are starting to piss me off with this crap about not being on drugs. Just 'fess up damn it."

"T, I'm not on drugs," Stefon continued to proclaim his innocence. "And I'm tired of you guys accusing me! I've been working and everything, so I just need you and Mama to stop accusing me." Stefon was rather indignant. It wouldn't be long before I got more firsthand proof of Stefon's addiction.

After Stefon's arrest, he continued to work as a stockbroker, and still lived with Mama. I was watching him closely because I no longer trusted him. As the months went by, things seemed to be back to normal for the most part; however, it was just the calm before the storm.

In early 1988, PJ and I were working and raising our girls, and keeping an eye on Mama *and* my brothers. It was about 2am on one Saturday morning when our doorbell rang.

"Who could that be at this time of the morning?" I asked PJ, startled by the early morning knock at the door. We both raced to the door, and after seeing Mama through the peephole, I frantically opened the door to see her standing there, stoically in the darkness. We quickly ushered her into the house, and I made sure she wasn't physically injured in anyway. Mama walked slowly towards me and broke down sobbing. My heart sank down into my stomach. Mama was wearing a long red fleece robe, which zipped up the front, red terry cloth slippers, and a multi-colored silk scarf, which she often wore to wrap her hair at bedtime. It looked like Mama got right up out of bed and drove the short distance to my house in a trance.

"Mama, what's wrong?" I was afraid to hear her response.

"Stefon is strung out on drugs," Mama exclaimed through her tears.

The look on Mama's face was heartbreaking. I guided Mama down the steps into the living room and had her sit on the sofa across from where PJ and I were sitting. I listened intently as Mama told us how Stefon had stolen money from her wallet, and left the house *after* she refused to *give* him the money. I instantly became furious and wanted to take my gun and go look for Stefon right then. I grew up watching Mama get hurt by the men in her life, and now her very own sons were carrying on with that same affliction. Mama never hurt anyone, and she did everything for us. She worked her fingers to the bone so that we didn't want for anything, and we didn't. *How dare these assholes bring her such heartache?* I sat there shaking my head, fighting back the tears.

"Don't worry, Mama," I said as I moved to sit next to her. "I'll figure something out."

I hugged her and wanted her to stay at the house with me but she said she needed to go home. I loved her so much and wanted to protect her always. In spite of the drama at home, Mama was thriving at American Airlines. She loved her job and was blessed to promote into a supervisory position. Stefon returned home after his thievery, as if nothing happened. He had an impending court date due to charges stemming from his LAPD arrest. He had been driving without a valid license, and was found to be under the influence of a controlled substance, a felony violation. Mama was afraid he was not going to meet his court obligation so to ease her stress PJ and I decided to have Stefon stay with us so that we could ensure he went to court. While staying with us,

Stefon tried his best to convince us that he was clean and sober. He was going to work everyday, but the loaner car he was using was returned to Mama's friend following his arrest. As a result, I started back giving Stefon rides into downtown where he would catch his bus to Beverly Hills. When the day came for Stefon to go to court PJ and I were in attendance because we wanted to hear for ourselves what was going on with him. The prosecutor wanted Stefon remanded, but to our surprise, and dismay Stefon's attorney told the Judge that he was staying with his sister and brother-in-law, who were LAPD officers. We were trying to be incognito, but he ratted us out and I was furious with him for that revelation. PJ was always supportive of Mama and the boys even though the boys were a consistent pain in the butt. The Judge in open court acknowledged our status as law enforcement officers and praised us for being there for our family member.

"Stefon, if your sister and brother-in-law will sign for you," the Judge said, "then I will release you to their care and control until your next court appearance."

PJ and I looked at each other and he gave me the affirming nod before he spoke up.

"Your Honor," PJ replied, "my brother-in-law has a stable job as a stockbroker and in an effort to help him maintain that job, I will sign for him." *That*, I thought, *is the reason I married that man.* Not because he got my brother out of jail, but because he had a big heart and he had so much compassion for people; especially the underdog.

We returned home with Stefon and made sure that he was *never* left alone with our girls, actually we tried our best never to leave him alone *period*. Most days when we were at home, he was in the den reading the newspaper. About a week after Stefon's court appearance, I went with Stefon to meet with a Probation Officer, who was assigned to complete Stefon's pre-trial report. Since PJ signed for Stefon's release, we had every right to know what was going on with his case, and the Probation Officer agreed. The Probation Officer was a very sharp woman, and she and I developed a great rapport from the start. She was very informative and told me exactly what I needed to know about Stefon's case. I was tired of him lying to me so I was glad I made that connection. A few weeks went by, but it was still long before Stefon's next court date. On one Saturday morning, PJ went outside to start his usual weekend chores of cutting the grass and washing cars.

"Tia! PJ yelled back into the house from the garage door. "Where's my truck?"

PJ had bought an old pickup truck at a police auction. We shared the truck with our friends and neighbors when they needed to haul miscellaneous items. Our next-door neighbor, Henry, had the spare key so that he could use it at his leisure. It was an old bright orange Cal Trans vehicle that PJ fixed. He had it painted a nice chocolate brown and he replaced the weathered vinyl bench seat with a nice new one. It was a great find, and other than the gas gauge not working, it ran just fine. Although Stefon was staying with us, he still went to Mama's on occasion to escape our oversight so it wasn't odd that he wasn't at the house when PJ discovered the truck missing.

"I don't know, honey," I yelled back. "Maybe Henry has it."

A few moments later Henry emerged from his residence ready to partake in his Saturday outdoor ritual of cutting grass and washing cars, with PJ.

"Hey PJ, what's up, man?" Henry asked when he saw PJ.

"Hey, bro I'm good. Man, where's the truck?"

"Man, I thought *you* had it until I saw you outside." Henry chuckled as he walked towards PJ.

"I'll be right back," PJ ran into the house leaving Henry standing in the driveway.

"Hey my keys are gone." PJ yelled to me as he walked back outside. "I think your brother took the damn truck."

"Huh? What are you talking about?" I asked as I ran outside to meet PJ and Henry standing in the driveway. "Oh damn." I went back inside and called Mama. "Mama, Stefon isn't here. Is he over there?"

"No, I thought he was with you." There went my stomach again.

It was clear to me that Stefon had stolen the truck. We didn't see Stefon take the truck, but we *knew* he had it. PJ and I talked about what we needed to do about the missing truck, that was now in the hands of a dope head.

"I'll wait for a day or so to see if he comes back," PJ decided.

PJ actually waited for two days and by the second day, when the truck was not returned, PJ and I reported it stolen. We were so conflicted because it felt like we were making a false report, which if proven to be true, could have jeopardized both of our jobs, but it really was stolen because it was taken without our permission, and in our opinion the thief's intent was to permanently deprive us of our property, so it met the reporting criteria and we made the right decision. At that time we didn't have proof that Stefon took it but regardless of who took it we needed to protect ourselves from any potential liability stemming from the thief's actions. Stefon and the truck were missing for three days, and during that time, I discovered that he had also stolen money from me. I had placed $300 cash in a book in my panty drawer as emergency cash. When I discovered the money missing, I thought back to one day when Stefon was laying on the floor in the den. Our house was tri-level, and the den was on the second level with the kitchen and dining room, and my Master Bedroom, was on the third level. From Stefon's vantage point, he had a clear unobstructed view, right into my bedroom. I vaguely recalled standing at my dresser inserting the money into the book, and as I closed the drawer I just *happened* to look up and out the door, when I caught Stefon watching me. I didn't think anything of it at the time because he had been reading the paper, so I thought he just *happened* to glance up at me at the same time that I looked at him. Stefon was clocking my every move, and whenever he had a moment alone, he was rummaging through our bedroom drawers. We were on pins and needles while Stefon was gone. On the third day we observed the truck parked back in the driveway with the keys left inside, but Stefon went back to Mama's and acted like nothing happened. I called Mama and told her that Stefon had stolen $300 from me *and* had stolen our truck.

Since the truck had *reappeared*, we needed to cancel the stolen report. To avoid any suspicion cast against us, since it was returned to our house, we called a friend who was an officer at the nearby station LAPD's Foothill Division, and he came right over and completed a vehicle recovery report. I hated to involve our friend in Stefon's drama, but it was our only option to avoid unnecessary scrutiny by the Department, and our friend understood our dilemma. Stefon's court date could not come fast enough. We were still bound by the Bond PJ signed for Stefon, so we *had* to keep tabs on him until his court date. He was no longer allowed at our house, which made for a horrible babysitting situation. By this time Stefon was barely going to work, so I abandoned our carpool arrangement. I made sure to check in on Stefon and Mama everyday mainly to keep tabs on him. About a week after Stefon returned with the truck PJ came home in a huff. He rushed in and went directly to our room, where he searched feverishly through the drawers of his bedside table. I followed him into the room.

"Dang it! This mofo has been all up in here going through our things!" PJ was outwardly frustrated. I knew he was talking about Stefon because he was the only *mofo* around. "He took those fake American Express Traveler's checks, that were assigned to me for that undercover operation I recently worked on. They were in my bedside table."

"Awww man, I am so sorry...I," PJ interrupted me.

"It's not your fault," PJ said as he shook his head. "My supervisor came to me today to ask me about the checks because he was notified that they were used at the Pink's Motel on San Fernando Road, and at a liquor store down the street from the motel. I told him there was no way because the checks were in my bedside table."

PJ kept searching the drawer as he continued to explain when he found the empty blue vinyl American Express check cover in between miscellaneous mail in the drawer. PJ lifted the vinyl cover over his head signifying that he found what he was looking for.

"The checks were in here, and now they're gone." PJ said in an exasperated tone.

We didn't know what Stefon was up to when he took the truck, but it became abundantly clear as time went on that he was on a binge. He used my $300 for drugs, and PJ's fake Traveler's Checks for food, and room and board. I was convinced he was a major drug addict. On top of that, PJ and I knew that only dopers and prostitutes hung out at the Pink's Motel so that was further confirmation. It was at that point that I felt uncomfortable being responsible for ensuring that Stefon went to court. PJ had only agreed to sign the Bond because Stefon was *my* brother. I desperately needed to rectify this mess so I contacted the Probation Officer in the pre-trial services section and I explained what was going on with Stefon.

"What do I need to do to for my husband to be released from his obligation to guarantee Stefon's court appearance?"

"You would have to *physically* surrender Stefon to the court."

I was so angry with myself for allowing PJ to accept the Judge's offer to have Stefon released to us. I didn't know how I was going to surrender him, but I had to do something. PJ and I devised a plan and waited for a few days before I called Stefon.

"Hey, T," he said. My blood immediately started to boil. *Breathe, Tia*, I coached myself, *you have to be calm for this to work.*

"Hey Stefon, I just got a call from Probation and they need you to come in for an interview before the trial."

"Uh, ok. But why?" Stefon seemed to be a little suspicious, but I was adamant that he was going to follow my plan.

"Because damn it, that's their mandate and PJ signed for your release, so I have to take you personally." I said annoyed by his nerve to question me.

After much coaxing, Stefon reluctantly agreed to go. I told him I would pick him up the next morning and take him downtown to the Federal Building. Although I did not trust Stefon, I was not afraid of him. I was mad as hell, and I would have killed him had he gotten out of line at that point in our relationship. He was no longer the loving brother I knew growing up; he was like any other random hustler on the street and I could not wait to wash my hands of him.

"You better be ready tomorrow morning Stefon, because I have to take you on my way to work."

"Damn T, I will be ready," he said as if I were bothering him.

I couldn't sleep that night. But I was ready for battle that next morning. I got dressed, and strapped on my gun around my waist nice and tight. PJ had already left for work and the girls were at home asleep with the Nanny. I drove down to Mama's, and I was relieved to see that Stefon was there, dressed and waiting for me. Stefon walked out wearing a clean, starched white dress shirt and nicely creased slacks, with a newspaper rolled up in his hand. I unlocked the doors and he entered on the passenger side of my Acura Legend. I needed gas so we stopped on the way.

"I'll pump the gas T," Stefon offered as he went to get out of the car.

"No, no." I said hastily. "You just stay right there, I got it." I replied curtly. I didn't want him trying to leave, and I didn't want his crack headed behind handling anything flammable, so I got out and pumped my own gas.

The drive to the Federal Court Building was quiet. I acted lighthearted, and talked about forgiveness for his latest thievery, but I was pretending big time. I was still mad about him violating my home. Stefon smiled with relief and read the paper as I drove, believing he had me fooled. PJ and I had car phones in each of our vehicles so I called the probation officer, and let her know that Stefon and I were on our way. Stefon was listening but he had no idea she was in on the plan. When we arrived at the Federal Building, the Probation Officer was waiting for us in one of the courtrooms rather than in her office. Stefon looked puzzled as the Court Marshals immediately ushered him into a holding tank just outside the courtroom. I breathed a sigh of relief when I heard the door lock as it closed behind Stefon. He turned, looked at me and shrugged his shoulders, and mouthed: *What's going on?* I shrugged my shoulders with my palms up and mouthed back: *I don't know.* But I knew exactly what was going on. He didn't share with me that he was going to steal my things, so we were even. I sat on a bench across from the holding tank, and watched as Stefon paced back and forth across the width of the small space that he shared with one or two other idiots. I was anxious to see what happened when he went before the Judge. Finally, after waiting for about an hour it was time for Stefon to meet the Judge. I waited around so that I could make sure that PJ was released from that responsibility. The Judge openly acknowledged that I was *surrendering* Stefon based on the fact that he was still using drugs; and that he burglarized my bedroom, and stole my truck. Stefon became visibly angry because he then realized I had tricked him into surrendering. He denied all of my allegations, but, of course, the Judge didn't believe his lies. The judge was as cool as a cucumber and very diplomatic. I liked him.

"So, you are telling me your sister is lying Mr. Pugh?

"Well, I don't know what she is doing." Stefon looked down and around at nothing and totally avoided the Judge's rhetorical question.

"Well answer this Mr. Pugh, are you under the influence of drugs right now?"

"No, your Honor, I am not." Stefon vehemently denied any drug use.

"I'll tell you what then, I'm going to release your brother-in-law from this Bond and I'm going to give you a drug test." Stefon fell silent with eyes as big as saucers. "If you test negative for narcotics in your system, then I will release you on your *own* recognizance."

I breathed a sigh of release as the Judge released PJ from this obligation. I stood by as the Marshals ushered Stefon past me, but I kept looking straight ahead, and I showed no remorse for having tricked him. The Marshal took Stefon to another room where a drug test was administered, and when they returned to the courtroom a short time later the Judge looked up at Stefon and read the results.

"Sir, you say you are not using drugs right?"

"No...No...Sir," Stefon responded while looking down at his feet.

"Well, sir you tested positive for cocaine, so I am having you remanded until your next court date."

The Marshal's immediately took Stefon into custody, and he was livid when he realized that I was the reason for his being there.

"That's fucked up, T," Stefon said as he walked past me staring at me with his angry hazel eyes.

"Fuck you," I said back to him as I walked away without a single regret.

After Stefon's case was adjudicated a few weeks later Stefon was set free and was placed on probation for that case, which was plea-bargained from a Felony to a Misdemeanor.

In the summer of 1988 we planned our first of many summer vacations with William and Wanda. We took our four girls, all under the age of seven, and went to Maui, Hawaii. We all had flying benefits since Mama and Wanda both worked for American. The times that we travelled together the flights were never full so we usually took over a couple of the center rows on the large DC10 planes, for our girls to play with their dolls, and color. They ate junk food for hours while us grown folks sat nearby enjoying a few libations while we laughed and talked during the 5½-hour flight. Once we landed in Hawaii we got our rental Van and drove to the Sands of Kahana resort where we shared a three-bedroom condo for the week. After getting settled in we headed off to the Safeway Supermarket in nearby Lahaina where we loaded up our baskets with booze and food. The next order of business was for me to braid all the girls' hair so we didn't have to deal with that daily ritual of combing hair. We spent many hours at the pool, where all of the girls splashed around until they actually learned how to swim right there in Hawaii. We enjoyed traveling, and thanks to Mama, we travelled often. We took the girls to Disney World in Florida, and on several Disney Cruises to the Bahamas. Those vacations were priceless and very inexpensive.

We were trying to enjoy our lives, but my brothers were still up to their usual mess. Stefon had totally lost his job so all he did was lie around. One day both boys were sitting idle at home when Stefon asked Edris to drive him to the nearby 7-Eleven store so he could get a pack of cigarettes. Mama was asleep, so they took her car because Stefon didn't have one, and Edris had wrecked his. They figured they would be back before Mama realized they were gone, so they didn't bother to ask. The store was so close they really could have, and should have walked. Edris drove into the parking lot at the 7-Eleven and sat with the car idling while Stefon ran inside. A few minutes later, Stefon ran out of the store like a bat out of hell, and entered the passenger side of the car frantically telling Edris to drive away. As Edris drove from the store, he saw the store clerk, through his rearview mirror, run out from the store with a cordless phone held to his ear. Stefon had committed what is known as an *Estes Robbery*. Stefon pretended to buy cigarettes, and when the clerk opened the register he reached over the counter, grabbed money from the cash drawer, and attempted to run from the store as the clerk grabbed Stefon's hand. They struggled a bit over the cash before Stefon pulled away and made his escape. In California, an Estes Robbery is when a shoplifter tries to take merchandise from a store, and is approached by store security or a loss prevention officer, and then either pushes past, or uses force against the security guard in an effort to get away. It's a robbery whereby the suspect's original taking of the goods or merchandise is non-forcible, but then he subsequently uses force to retain possession of the goods. When that happens, a minor petty theft offense turns into a very serious robbery offense and Stefon was guilty of that crime. Edris drove about 2 miles up the road away from the house and parked the car in a secluded location in a residential community called Sun Valley. It wasn't long before the LAPD Air Unit hovered above in the vicinity, while the ground units quickly set up a perimeter. Officers went in search of *two male blacks, who had just committed a Robbery, and fled, eastbound from the location in a late model gray vehicle,* which is how the 9-1-1 dispatcher described the incident. The search effort went on for a while, and just as the Air Unit pulled away from the area and things quieted down, Edris grew impatient and decided to come out from hiding. When Edris emerged from his secluded location on foot, he was immediately spotted by one of the ground units that stayed in the area looking for the two *robbery suspects.* As soon as the officers spotted Edris, he was taken into custody by the very police agency that PJ and I worked for.

Edris maintained that he had not done anything, so he cooperated with police and directed them to Stefon's location. Before long, they were both in custody. Edris said he did not know Stefon was going to *rob* the 7-Eleven. Up until that point, Edris had only been arrested for traffic related warrants and DUI; and Stefon had only been arrested for the drug charges in D.C., and he was on probation for the local LAPD charges stemming from his arrest the year before. I could not believe they were arrested for Robbery. I was embarrassed, and Mama was devastated. She didn't raise us to steal, and she worked extremely hard to provide for us so we didn't want for anything. I was done with both of them. While I felt guilty turning my back on them, I had to protect myself, and *my* family. Months went by and my brothers' respective court dates approached. They were both assigned public defenders. The public defender's strategy for Edris was to tell the court he had a drug problem so that he could enter into a nine-month Diversion program as his sentence for his part in the botched *robbery.* Stefon was sentenced to state prison, and garnered the first strike on his criminal record pursuant to California's Three Strikes Law. Stefon was sent to the California Correctional Institute – Tehachapi where he served a few years. I didn't like the idea of my brothers being incarcerated, but at least they weren't causing any trouble for the time being. It was sad, that both of them were in the prison system at the same time. I couldn't imagine how Mama felt. Her babies were locked up, and neither she nor anyone else could do anything to make the situation better.

CHAPTER 9
"Mama's Sick Again"

By late 1989, Cheryl-Ann and Rodney had finally gotten married, and unlike her boycott of our wedding, we took our girls to Las Vegas to witness their nuptials. Cheryl-Ann used the proceeds from the $25,000 lawsuit and purchased a small home in south Los Angeles, and a nice gold Mercedes to park in the tiny driveway. It was sad that Cheryl-Ann didn't have the money, house or car for long.

Detective Tia and LAPD Chief Bernard Parks 1989

I promoted to Detective in August of 1989, along with several of my friends, so we planned a huge party to celebrate. Mama wasn't feeling well so it really dampened my spirit. Mama was very proud of me, and was hoping that she was feeling well enough to help me host the party. I bought Mama a cute olive green jumpsuit with goldenrod low heel pumps to match the bodice area of the jumpsuit. On the night of the party she looked pretty snazzy, and really tried to enjoy herself, but she complained that her stomach hurt so much that all she could do was sit still. I thought she was stressing over the boys being locked up, but her abdomen was actually bloated, which concerned me greatly. After weeks of complaining, Mama and I went to see Doctor Fobi because we thought that maybe her stomach issues were related to her gastric bypass reversal procedure.

"Looks like there's a lot of fluid building up in your abdomen, Ms. Carmen," Dr. Fobi said. "I'll run some tests."

After running a battery of tests, Fobi still could not figure out the cause of the fluid build up so he admitted Mama into the hospital and performed exploratory surgery. I had established a great rapport with all of Mama's doctors, and she made it clear to all of them that they were to give me any and all information I asked for about her condition. Back then there was no such thing as the Health Insurance Portability and Accountability Act, better known as HIPAA, which later set the standard for protecting sensitive patient data, so the doctors were very accommodating when *any* concerned party, family or not, wanted information about a patient's condition. After the surgery, Mama remained in the hospital for over two weeks as the fluid continued to accumulate in her body. Fobi analyzed the fluid and finally got to the root of the problem.

"Ms. Carmen, wake up, beautiful." Dr. Fobi nudged Mama as she slept in her hospital bed. "The fluid in your belly tested Category Level 5 on the cancer suspicion scale, but we can not locate exactly where the cancer is."

"*What*? But I have been cancer free for 8 years." Mama said as she struggled to sit up in bed and comprehend what Fobi was telling her.

"I know you have been having routine breast exams, and there is no evidence of a recurrence in either breast, but there could be some metastasis so we will conduct further tests and get to the bottom of this ok?"

"Ok, Doctor. Please tell Tia everything." Mama was groggy as she drifted back off to sleep. Doctor Fobi motioned for me to follow him into the dimly lit hallway.

"What does Category 5 mean doctor?" I asked, expecting the worst news.

"Category Level 5 means the fluid assessment is *highly* suspicious of cancer malignancy." Fobi calmly replied.

Dr. Fobi had known Mama for over ten years and he cared about her well-being. Dr. Fobi was concerned but didn't want to alarm me unnecessarily, so he chose his words carefully. His assessment also revealed that Mama's blood was not reproducing properly so he conducted further tests to include a bone marrow tap to figure out *why* Mama's blood was not reproducing. It was discovered that Mama had a condition called Aplastic Anemia.

"Ms. Tia," Dr. Fobi said sitting across from me in the hallway outside of Mama's room. "Bone marrow is a sponge-like tissue inside of the bones that makes stem cells that develop into red blood cells, white blood cells, and platelets. Aplastic Anemia is basically bone marrow failure. If Mommy's bone marrow can't make enough new blood cells, then it can cause a whole host of problems." Whenever Dr. Fobi spoke to me about Mama, he affectionately referred to her as *Mommy* in his African dialect. "This disorder can cause arrhythmias, an enlarged heart, heart failure, infections, and bleeding. But in Mommy's case, her body isn't producing enough blood cells or platelets because her marrow is damaged most likely due to her past radiation and chemotherapy treatments."

"Oh goodness."

"This is a rare, but serious disorder, and is normally treated by blood transfusions or bone marrow transplants. Unfortunately, Mommy also has what we call Metastatic Breast Cancer and it has spread to her bones, which is causing this anemic condition."

"So, her cancer has spread?" I felt like, a Mac truck had just plowed into me.

"Yes, Ms. Tia, and, because of her terminal status, we can only treat her with a blood transfusion because a bone marrow transplant is not a treatment option."

"Wait, what?" I interrupted the doctor. "Mama is terminal?"

"Yes, Ms. Tia, I'm so sorry."

"Oh, my God!" I exclaimed. Hearing the word, *terminal* took my breath away.

"So, the blood transfusion will treat the anemia, but it won't *cure* her because the cancer is everywhere right?" My stomach felt queasy. I needed to lie down.

"Yes," Dr. Fobi solemnly replied. "It is most probably *everywhere*. It is evident that it has spread to her bones, *and* she has a quarter size mass on her liver as well."

Eight years had passed since Mama was first diagnosed with breast cancer. We had celebrated her 5-year mark, when we believed she was cured from her first bout with cancer. What I surmised from Dr. Fobi's information was that there was nothing doctors could do. I couldn't bear leaving Mama in the hospital alone after hearing that news, so I sat in the hallway outside of Mama's room trying to gather my thoughts, and control my emotions before I approached Fobi again.

"So how long until...?" He cut me off because he knew where my line of questioning was going.

"Only God knows, baby doll." Fobi said with a caring glance. I appreciated the fact that he didn't put a time stamp on Mama's life because, if nothing else, it gave *me* a little hope.

In the summer of 1990, PJ promoted to Detective, and I was working as a Detective II Supervisor at Internal Affairs Division, where I investigated fellow officers accused of wrongdoing. I quickly earned the title, *The Black Widow*, because, for some odd reason, I was assigned a string of Domestic Violence cases that resulted in several male officers being terminated. I only had nine years on the job, but I was a skilled and dedicated investigator. I was ok dealing with criminals at work, but the sad part was that I had to deal with them at home too, and that frustrated me. Edris had finished his *diversion program* and was back out in the world to continue his mischief. He started dating a woman named Shelly who Mama introduced him to, but Mama's introduction was *not* intended for them to make a love connection. Mama had met Shelly at church, and during one of their conversations Shelly mentioned she was moving back home, to the San Fernando Valley where she grew up, to help her mother, who was battling breast cancer. As a result, Shelly was looking for someone to sublet her studio apartment to. It was located in South LA and Mama thought it was a perfect place for Edris, so she sublet it from Shelly. Edris was with Mama when they met Shelly to look at the place. Shelly was very nice, but very arrogant for an unattractive girl. She graduated from high school and went right to work for Wells Fargo Bank as a teller. She was instantly attracted to Edris when they met, and when I met her I thought they were perfect for each other. Shelly had a cute little petite figure just like Edris liked, so he forged a relationship with her even though he often said aloud that he didn't find her attractive. In fact, he called her *ugly*, which I thought was mean and hypocritical because she wasn't too ugly for him to sleep with. It had been about 2 years since Edris and Stefon hit the 7-11, and Stefon was still in prison. For some unknown reason Stefon was transferred from Tehachapi State Prison to Corcoran State Prison, both located in California. I didn't feel bad about Stefon being locked up anymore because he was a thieving drug addict, so prison was the best place for him.

Before Fobi released Mama from the hospital, he consulted with Mama's Oncologist Dr. Harris, who started her on a second chemotherapy regimen to immediately address her Metastatic Breast Cancer. Mama's treatments were bi-weekly, and in between some of those treatments, she had to return to the medical facility to have fluid drained from her lungs. Drs. Harris and Fobi didn't understand why the fluid was still building up in Mama's abdomen nor why it was happening so frequently, and they didn't know why the fluid build up was always following her chemotherapy treatments. I opined that Mama's body was simply breaking down. It's no secret that chemotherapy is a radical form of treatment designed to kill cancerous cells, but it also kills good cells. I was older and wiser, and much more dialed in when Mama underwent chemo the second time around. I asked all of Mama's doctors a million questions including what I could do to help her at home. By the time my inquiry was done I was well informed, but I still didn't fully understand the gravity of all of the chemo related side effects. I knew about the anemia and hair loss issues but nothing about the discolored brittle nails, blackened skin around the nail beds, mouth sores, hot flashes and aching bones; and I didn't understand how much any of the side effects interfered with Mama's daily routine, however, I knew all too well when I was similarly stricken with some of the same side effects years later.

By early 1991, Mama had completed her second round of chemo treatments, but she was still unable to return to work. Instead, she continued her volunteer duties at church, which was right where she wanted to be anyway. Mama and her hometown friend, who she was dating for a few years, were no longer in a relationship but they remained very good friends. FAME's ministry *Beyond The Walls* provided a service where the ministers checked in on their sick parishioners at home. It was during one of those beyond the walls visits that Mama met Frank. Frank's parents were members at FAME and lived in the Mid-Wilshire area of Los Angeles in a duplex they'd owned since Frank was a child. Frank's mother was bedridden and his retired father was her caretaker. Frank lived in a very small meticulous house on a hillside in the exclusive area of Silver Lake. After knowing each other for about a year, Mama and Frank started dating. Frank and I shared the same birth date, October 25th, but of course, he was old enough to be my father. Frank was a decent enough guy, and boyishly handsome but he had a very cold personality, which is why I was surprised that Mama was attracted to him. Mama on the other hand was a hoot. She loved to talk and laugh out loud. She loved people, and people loved her, so her connection with Frank seemed very odd. Before Frank dated Mama he had only dated white women exclusively so the switch in his dating pattern was also cause for pause for me. By January of 1992, after dating for about a year Mama and Frank were engaged. I wondered what he really wanted with Mama, and why all of a sudden he was interested in marrying a black woman for the first time in his 50 years of life? There was nothing wrong with dating outside of your race, but my gut told me something was fishy with him changing up at this point in his life. Mama later confided in me that Frank had some financial challenges, and that he was using credit cards to pay some of his bills.

"Girl, this man is robbing Peter to pay Paul," Mama told me.

"Yeah, that *is* really robbing Peter to pay Paul if he's paying bills with his credit cards."

That told me he was really in dire straits, and that revelation kind of confirmed my suspicion that he wanted something more than companionship from Mama. The man needed help. Also, he asked Mama to marry him *knowing* she was terminally ill, battling cancer. I figured he knew Mama had great medical and life insurance. I couldn't bite my tongue for long.

"Mama," I probed when the two of us were alone one day. "Does Frank know your prognosis?"

"Yes baby. We already talked about it and he doesn't want anything from me. We agreed that he is leaving what he has to his kids, and I'm leaving what I have to mine."

Mama was rather convincing when she assured me that Frank had no ulterior motive for marrying her at that time in her life. I felt bad having that conversation with her, but I couldn't stand the thought of Frank using her. Regardless of my feelings for Frank, PJ and I spent time with Mama and Frank on occasion, usually on Sundays after church. We all got along just fine, but he was nerdy and weird. The boys were no longer living with Mama and she didn't have a roommate. She complained that the house she was renting from us was too big for her to stay in by herself, so she moved out freeing it up for us to rent to another family. Mama stayed between our house and Frank's house while she feverishly planned her dream wedding. It was the spring of '92, and thirty-five years had passed since Mama's shotgun wedding to Chico at the age of 17. I'm quite sure Mama had no say in planning *that* wedding, so she went all out for her upcoming wedding. She procured a beautiful Ivory wedding dress and veil, and assembled a huge bridal party made up of her dearest friends and family members, including me and PJ, Shelly and Edris and our girls. Mama's health had declined significantly, and noticeably, in the months leading up to her wedding. I worried most about her inability to keep food on her stomach. I cringed every time I looked at my poor Mama, but I masked my pain by being overtly excited about the wedding.

On Saturday, April 11, 1992, Mama and Frank wed in a beautiful church ceremony at First AME (FAME) Church, officiated by Mama's mentor, Reverend Cecil "Chip" Murray with about 200 people in attendance. Pastor Murray was jubilant during the joyous event, and the church was lively. Grandmother, Aunt Laberta, and my cousin, Will Jr. all flew in for the wedding and I was excited to see all of them. Mama loved her sisters so much, and Will Jr. was her favorite nephew so I know they offered a sense of comfort for her.

"I now pronounce you husband and wife," Reverend Murray recited as he held his hand up and out towards the audience. "I present to you, Mr. and Mrs. Speights!"

Mama reached for Frank's hand but before their hands connected she collapsed right there at the altar. *Holy Mary Mother of God!* I exclaimed to myself. *What's happening, please don't take her now, Lord, please!* Everyone gasped in unison as Mama's legs buckled beneath her and she slowly sank downwards into the folds of her pillowy gown. Thankfully, Frank caught a hold of Mama before she hit the floor as we all watched silently. Grandmother shrieked so loud that all heads in the room turned away from Mama and in her direction. PJ consoled Grandmother as I ran towards Mama. Mama was frail, and her breathing was shallow when I held her in my arms. I cradled Mama's head trying not to cry as Frank and Reverend Murray stood over us and fanned her face. It seemed like a nightmare. I thought Mama suffered a heart attack, however, when paramedics arrived they ruled that out.

Mama on her wedding day April 1992

They said that Mama's vitals were good, so she wasn't even transported to the hospital. Mama had been fighting her illness consistently for

2 years, this second time around, so she was simply exhausted and weak. Mama was a trooper, though, because she did not let that episode stop her from moving forward with the Reception.

Aunt Laberta, Grandmother and Cousin Will April 1992

Edris, PJ and Tia at Mama's wedding April 1992

Once Mama regained her normal breathing pattern and regained her footing, we all went downstairs to the church banquet room for the Reception. I watched Mama like a hawk throughout the evening and all was well. She pranced around like a love struck teenager but she looked worn. The next day Mama called the house bright and early to make sure we were ready for church as she was preaching at the 10AM service. Mama's sermon was entitled, *"So, You Wanna Be A Hero, Huh", and h*er message was powerful. Grandmother, Aunt Laberta, Cousin Will, PJ, the girls, Edris and Shelly and I all enjoyed her sermon immensely. I was proud to see Mama in her glory, and was happy that Grandmother got to hear her baby preach. PJ and I took the opportunity to have the girls baptized during that same church service. We wanted it to be significant for the girls to be baptized on a day their *Mimi* preached.

It didn't take Mama long to get settled into her new home with Frank because she was already semi-living there while they were dating. Mama stayed occupied at the church on most days and only visited us on the weekends when she wasn't too busy or tired. Over the years we'd relied so heavily upon each other that I was never too far away from her because we were all each other had for a very long time, and I couldn't imagine living without her. We talked throughout the day, everyday; and on my way home from work during the week. I didn't allow too many days to go by without seeing her. I made sure she had what she needed, whether she was at my house or at home with Frank. Oftentimes I stopped by Frank's place to check up on her, and spent time with her before heading home. On those days she was usually resting in bed, so I would curl up on a floor pillow next to her bed, and hold her hand as it dangled over the side. Frank worked for the Gas Company during the day, and moonlighted as a self-employed handy man on most evenings so he was always still at work when I visited.

"I don't know what I would do without you, baby," Mama said every time we were together.

"I hope you never have to be without me, Mama," I responded. "I love you Chachie May." I teased, calling her by her maiden name.

A few weeks after her wedding, I was visiting Mama when she received a call from Stefon.

"You have a collect call from a California State Prison Inmate," said the loud automated recording on the phone. "Will you accept the charges?"

Mama pushed the appropriate button on the handset to accept the call.

"Hey Ma, how are you?" Stefon asked.

"I'm good baby." she replied. "It's so good to hear your voice. I'm sorry I haven't been up there to see you, but it's just too far."

"Don't worry about it I'm going to be released in a few days, Baby," Stefon continued. "But I will be on Parole, so I will let you know where I will be staying. It will be somewhere in LA. I can't wait to see you."

"Ok. I'm so happy to hear that. I look forward to hearing from you," Mama said.

"Mama, I-," Stefon was interrupted by the recorded message, which indicated that the call time was almost up. "Ok Ma, Tell T, PJ, and Edris I said hi, and I will see ya'll soon. I gotta hang up now." Stefon continued after the recording ended.

A few days later, Mama received another call from Stefon telling her that instead of being released he was actually just being transferred to Chino State Prison to start serving another two-year prison sentence based on a charge, which ran consecutive to his other sentence. Mama was very disappointed that Stefon was not being released because she longed to see him. Mama was dying, and I was witnessing her disappear right before my eyes. It seemed that Stefon's news took a little more of her life away at that very moment. When Mama stayed with me, I saw that she was still not able to keep any food down no matter how small the meal was. She had finished her second regimen of chemotherapy so I thought that maybe the vomiting was a result of her stomach, or esophagus being affected by the spread of the cancer. By that summer Mama and Frank's marriage wasn't going well and they had only been married a few months. Mama complained that Frank was mean spirited, and she didn't feel comfortable in the house she shared with him because he was so territorial. That broke my heart, especially because I thought he had ulterior motives anyway. Mama started to come and stay at my house on most weekends and eventually those weekend stays became week long stays and that was perfectly fine with me because I wanted her with me, PJ and the girls, so I could take her where she needed to go without her driving all over the place. She was very weak, and just needed to rest, so I pampered her when she was with me. Mama stayed hopeful about the marriage, *and* continued to claim her healing *in the name of Jesus,* but I believed the marriage was a bust. Mama's illness had slowed her down quite a bit, but she continued to go get her nails done every two weeks like clockwork. Her hair had started to grow back. It was short and very fine in texture, but it was beautiful. It was salt and pepper, shiny and silky, and it lay on her head like a newborn baby's crown. Mama maintained her stance against short hair so she experimented with different styles of wigs rather than wear her natural hair, pretty or not.

"You know what?" Mama asked one evening.

"What, girl?" I responded playfully.

"Now that Stefon is closer, I would like to go see him. "Will you please take me?"

Mama's request caught me off guard.

"I want to see him too, Mama, but I'm torn because, I mean, I am a police officer and I can't jeopardize my job, *and* I'll be straddling the fence if I step one foot inside of a prison to visit an inmate, even if he *is* my brother. I miss him too but I don't know Mama. Let me think about it." I said as I gritted my teeth and grimaced. I was instantly riddled with guilt as I looked at Mama's face. Then I thought really quickly, *she's dying, and all she's asking is to see her son.*

"I understand." she said, quietly looking down and away from me. "I don't ever want you to jeopardize your job."

After a few days, I decided that I didn't want to regret not having done my best to fulfill Mama's last request so I prayed to God for guidance and almost immediately I felt compelled to take Mama to see Stefon. I had only been to a few prisons before while in my official capacity as an officer of the law, so I didn't know what to expect from a visitor's perspective. Regardless of my job, I agreed to make the 40-mile trek from the San Fernando Valley to Chino State Prison with Mama posted up in the passenger seat. We'd get up early on the Saturdays we visited and Mama happily gathered her things. Mama would sit the entire way humming along with whatever music I was playing. I remember our first trip. I was playing Vanessa Williams' Comfort

Zone Album the whole way. Mama loved the song "Comfort Zone" and I did too. I guess I was a little too quiet, so Mama started feeling me out with random conversation.

"She has such a pretty voice," Mama remarked about the sea foam green-eyed beautiful R&B singer. "I saw her once at the NAACP awards, when I went with Reverend Murray. She is skinny as a rail, but she is very pretty."

"Yes," I replied. "I *love* her music. I'm so glad she bounced back after the Hustler Magazine nude photo scandal. She's such a classy lady."

Mama was lighthearted all the way to our first visit to see Stefon. I was apprehensive about walking into a prison while off-duty, but the way I saw it; I had no choice. As we approached the prison, I saw the barbed wire fencing, the long driveway, and remote controlled gate that led into the joint. There was a one-story building just outside the gate close to the parking lot, which was the reception area for visitors. After parking, Mama and I walked arm in arm to the reception area, and completed the necessary forms for admittance. I was embarrassed and didn't want the guards to know that I was a law enforcement officer. If Mama were healthy, I would have let her go inside alone but I needed to accompany her inside to make sure she was ok. Mama had already checked to verify the visitation requirements and prohibitions. She even asked me to make food to take for the next visit with Stefon. *Oh, hell no,* I thought, as I rolled my eyes when she turned away after asking. I was seething, but I couldn't show it. *This is for Mama. This is for Mama,* I kept reminding myself. Between May and July of 1992, I took Mama to visit Stefon every other Saturday. On one Saturday in mid July it was extremely hot outside, and I wore white jeans and a t-shirt to visit. I was abruptly stopped at the gate.

"Ma'am you can't wear those jeans in here," The Deputy politely said to me when Mama and I reached the front of the line.

"Are you serious?" I asked in amazement. I was aware of the *No Blue Jeans* policy for visitors because sometimes inmates wore blue denim also, and the staff needed to ensure that prisoners and visitors were distinguishable from each other, so I understood. The regulations were also aimed at minimizing the prisoners' excitability and apparently, the white jeans were too provocative in that you could possibly see through them.

"Oh, Ok." I replied nonchalantly. "Well, I don't have a change of clothes so, Mama I will wait in the car because I don't want you to miss your visit with Stefon. Take your time and enjoy your visit." *Hallelujah!* I thought. I didn't want go inside in the first place. Those trips were for Mama.

I stood off to the side and waited until Mama made it through the checkpoint, and then I happily skipped back to my car. I waited for several hours while Mama visited her baby. She really didn't understand how those visits wreaked havoc with my personal values, and she didn't know how much it repulsed me to stand on line at a prison waiting to visit an inmate. Mama was getting weaker by the day. She was tired all the time, but remained as active as she could in church. It eventually got to the point where she slept in on Sundays when she was supposed to be at church, and *that's* when I knew she was slipping away, because she *never* missed church. As Mama's condition worsened, she *still* wanted to visit with Stefon; and I obliged against my better judgment. It was the last weekend in July and it was ridiculously hot outside. I gathered our things *and* packed food to take with us. Mama dozed off and on during the ride. She was tired. The heat outside at the correctional facility magnified the funky smell of cow manure emanating from the nearby cattle farms in Chino that morning. I made sure I dressed appropriately that time because I needed to go in with Mama since she was so weak. Once inside I sat in the prison picnic area across the table from Mama making small talk while we waited for Stefon. Thank God the area was covered to shield us from the sun. I had set the table so to speak with the home cooked food I prepared, while we waited and watched intently as the prisoners appeared, one by one, from behind the barbed wire gate. After a while I was tired of watching inmates walk towards their loved ones in the picnic area while we waited patiently for Stefon to appear.

"There he is Mama." I said when Stefon finally walked from behind the gates to hell.

Mama smiled and tried her best to perk up, but she couldn't muster the strength. She was happy to see him, but it was a muted joy. Stefon looked very thin wearing navy pants cinched at the waist with a faded black belt and a neatly pressed light blue button down shirt. *Hey, I wore the same outfit in the police academy*, I thought, laughing to myself at the irony. The only difference was that my academy shirt had cut outs for a badge. Stefon's neatly trimmed beard was completely gray, and his hair was cut close. He had beautiful hazel eyes just like Mama, and they were crystal clear that day as he was clean and sober by default. I knew prisoners could get drugs inside, but they weren't as plentiful as on the outside, so I believed Stefon was really sober in spite of that possibility. When Stefon got closer to the patio he scanned the area until he saw Mama and me. When he got to the table I stood up and hugged him tightly while Mama remained seated. Stefon appeared puzzled as he looked past me at Mama still seated. I stepped aside and he bent down to hug Mama.

"Hey Baby, how are you feeling?" I loved when I heard him call her Baby. After seeing Mama being abused when we were younger, Stefon vowed that when he was old enough, he would protect Mama. He adopted the nickname "Baby" for her because she was the queen of his heart, and his baby. When I heard him call her that, it reminded me that my brother was still inside that drug-addicted cavity somewhere. Stefon loved Mama so much. Yes, he stole from her in his binge state but he never verbally disrespected or berated her like Edris had on so many occasions. I felt bad Mama had to see her pride and joy in that environment.

"I'm not feeling well Stefon," she replied, "I'm very tired."

"You'll get better, Baby. I'm sure T is taking good care of you," Stefon said with a worried look on his face and a side glance at me.

"She is, but this will probably be my last visit for a while ok? I love you but I can't come for a while." Mama's eyes were glassy and little beads of sweat started forming on her forehead. She was not handling the heat well at all. I removed the Hawaiian dinner rolls from the cardboard container, folded the cardboard in half and used it to fan Mama.

"Here, boy," I said playfully. "You better eat up because we can't sit in this heat much longer."

We tried to enjoy our visit under the circumstances but the heat was draining. Stefon enjoyed the food, but said he couldn't eat much because he had been having issues with his stomach. That explained the weight loss. I was a bit concerned about Stefon's stomach issues considering Mama's bout with the fluid build up, however it was secondary to my concern for Mama sitting in that heat. She looked at Stefon the entire time as if it was going to be her last time ever laying eyes on him. I hated those visits. I also hated leaving Stefon there but he deserved to be there based on his criminal behavior. My heart softened whenever I saw his handsome face though. I prayed for the Lord to forgive me for not wanting to visit him. By the time we left that day, Mama was moving much slower than she was when we arrived. I clutched her arm with one of mine as I carried the bags of leftover food and my purse on my other arm as we walked towards the parking lot. The air conditioning in the car felt amazing as we made our way back to the Valley. Mama napped while I drove and reflected on life. I took off work that following Monday so I could drive Mama to a follow up visit with her Oncologist. Doctor Harris examined Mama.

"Well, I think I found the culprit of the fluid build up. You have an abscess between your lower bowel and your colon Ms. Carmen."

"Really?" I asked. He said Ms. Carmen, but I responded.

"Yes, and that's also why she hasn't been able to keep any food down."

Whew. I felt relieved because at least there was no new mass in her tummy. Mama's body was breaking down, but we were determined to fight for as long as we could. She had great medical insurance, and supplemental disability insurance, which allowed her to get excellent in home care.

"Ok, so what has to happen now?" Mama asked. "I can not go through another surgery, I just can't." She said as she started to get choked up.

After the last round of chemo, she had the fluid build up on her lungs, which she had drained every two weeks until it subsided. Then the abscess surfaced. My poor Mama couldn't catch a break.

"Well in order for the abscess to heal, I need you to completely rest your bowel," Dr. Harris said. "So here's what we are going to do: I'm going to put you on a liquid diet via intravenous fluids; you will get all the nutrients that you need that you have been devoid of due to all of the recent purging; I am going to insert a tube into your abdomen to allow for drainage of the fluid and hopefully get this thing dried up so you can feel better. You will have to be on the IV fluids for 12 hours a day, and off for 12 hours a day," he continued. "Don't worry, I'm going to have a nurse come to your house for those daily visits. She'll come once in the morning to change your bandage and hook you to the IV, and then she will return 12 hours later to take you off and change your dressing. The nurse will show you how to manage the machine and clear any malfunctions," Dr. Harris explained.

"Oh, I don't know if I'll be able to do all that." Mama said sounding apprehensive about the extensive instructions.

"Don't worry Mama," I said. "You will stay with me and I will operate the machine. You just focus on getting better."

I saw the fear in Mama's eyes grow as she lay on the table looking down at her belly as Dr. Harris inserted the tube. He bandaged her up and afterwards helped her sit up on the side of the bed.

"There you go," he said kindly. "We will get this thing taken care of and you will be back to eating in no time at all."

"Thanks Dr. Harris, we will see you in a couple of weeks," I said as Mama and I walked out of his office.

I got Mama home and into bed fairly quickly. She was tired, and so was I. I still had a five and seven-year-old I had to attend to, and they were a handful. The girls were happy that their Mimi was staying with us for a while. They knew about her illness, but didn't understand the extent of her medical issues. I was still working at Internal Affairs as an investigator and studying for the Sergeants exam so my plate was full. My hours were flexible so I went in late so I could be there to meet the nurse during the morning visits. The doorbell rang right at 7AM sharp on that first morning. The nurse was bright and cheerful and wore a starched white uniform with bright pink clogs.

"Hi, my name is Rita," the jovial nurse said. "Are you Ms. Carmen?"

"No, I'm her daughter," I replied just as jovial. "But she is upstairs. Please come in."

I liked Nurse Rita immediately. She was very kind and attentive and she and I, and Mama talked like we were old friends.

"There you go Ms. Carmen," Rita said. "Hopefully the bandage adhesive won't start to irritate your stomach. I will come daily at 7AM and again at

7PM to make sure everything is ok. I'm going to get your IV set up, and I will be back this evening to change your dressing and take you off the IV. Now, I need to show you how to clear the various malfunctions that can occur with the machine." I stood near as Rita spoke softly to Mama. Mama looked at me pleading for me to intervene as she was too drained to pay attention to any instructions.

"Um, Rita?" I interrupted. "If at all possible, could you put Mama on the IV at night when I am home, so that I can clear any malfunction; and take her off the IV during the day so that she can get around when I am at work?"

"Absolutely. I will get her IV started this evening when I return. Until then, only liquids like Ensure or Chicken broth, ok?

"Ok, I'll make sure of it."

After Rita left I went through some old boxes and found my old baby monitor that I used when the girls were infants. I positioned it close to the bed in Mama's room with the corresponding receiver in my bedroom so I could hear Mama if she needed help during the night. I didn't want her tripping over the cord and possibly pulling the IV needle out. PJ took the girls to school when he left at his normal time that morning. I got Mama situated and then went on in to work. Nurse Rita returned promptly at 7PM that evening; changed Mama's bandage and connected her to the IV.

Although I was up throughout the night checking on Mama, she tried her best not to bother me but I couldn't sleep anyway. Mama's illness and my demanding job assignment and studying for Sergeant, on top of raising a family and maintaining my marriage, made for a very stressful period in my life. I suppose that is why I started seeing more and more gray hair, and I was only 34 years old. Chico grayed early so I believed it was hereditary, but stressing over Mama didn't help. Before I had the gray hair, I thought I wanted salt and pepper hair because it looked beautiful and classy. While my gray came in evenly for the most part, I was still too young to sport gray hair, and besides, Natalia hated my gray hair.

"Mommy, are you old?" She'd ask whenever she looked at me. "Are you going to die?"

"No, little girl I'm not old, and yes child, we all gonna die. I just hope not soon, baby." Watching her Mimi deteriorate caused Natalia to become obsessed with *me* being old. It scared her.

Thank goodness Rita trained me because we had a couple malfunctions with the machine and I was able to clear them all. After a couple of weeks, Mama was going stir crazy in the cute little room I set up for her, because she wanted desperately to eat solid food. Mama had always enjoyed cooking and eating, so the liquid diet via the IV was sheer torture for her. There was absolutely *no* cheating allowed in this process because it was counterproductive to the healing process. One evening Nurse Rita arrived to change Mama's bandage.

"How's my star patient today?" Rita asked as she slowly and carefully removed Mama's dressing. There was visible waste on the bandage in addition to the drainage. "Oh it looks like somebody has been snacking," Rita remarked as she held the soiled bandage face up in the palm of one hand.

"I was hungry, so I just ate a few Ritz crackers." Mama said with tears in her eyes.

"Of all things, richly flavored Ritz Crackers?" Rita asked. "Ms. Carmen, that's not good, hun. I want you to heal." Mama's sad, sunken face was pitiful and my heart ached for her as she looked up at Nurse Rita.

One morning I was getting ready for work after Nurse Rita left and Mama was in the bathroom purging. I rushed to the bathroom to see if she was ok. Nothing but phlegm came up because she had no solid food in her system. I heard the deep throttle in her chest as she gagged. Brittany and Natalia were up and running around and heard her in the bathroom. After Mama returned to her room, I broke down and cried right there, on the bathroom floor. Brittany stood in the doorway looking down at me with a puzzled expression because she had never seen me cry. I didn't want to scare my girls but I was distressed. Over the next couple of weeks our routine was like clockwork. Mama was still frail, but she looked much better because she was getting nutrients in her daily IV fluids. Her eyes were sparkling and her face was a little fuller. August rolled around and we were getting ready for Brittany's 7th birthday party. It seemed as if Mama was adjusting well to her liquid diet, and she was up and about during the birthday celebration watching the kids run around on their sugar high. The next day was a bright beautiful Sunday. I got up early as usual to check on Mama and the girls, who were worn out from the party. After Nurse Rita arrived I entered Mama's room and she advised me that Mama was not as talkative as usual.

"Hey Mama, how you feeling honey? Do you want me to help you with your bath when Ms. Rita leaves?" I asked.

"No baby," Mama replied, "I showered already." Mama usually bathed, or showered, daily and sometimes twice a day, but on that morning I knew she had neither bathed nor showered.

"I suppose you partied too hard yesterday with the munchkins, so you don't feel up to a bath this morning, huh?" I jokingly said winking at Rita as she changed Mama's bandage. I passively challenged Mama about her shower, but she was distracted watching Nurse Rita, so she didn't answer me.

"You are healing well Ms. Carmen," Rita said looking down. "How are you feeling?"

Mama did not respond to Rita either.

"Ms. Carmen?" Rita looked up and saw that Mama had dozed off just that quick. I thought it was odd, but I let it go. I figured she was tired from the festivities the day before.

I let Mama sleep after Rita left, and a couple of hours later, Mama walked into the kitchen where I was preparing dinner.

"I'm going to go get my nails done." Mama said matter-of-factly.

"Umm Ok." I responded, as I looked her up and down.

Mama was wearing her long red velour zip front robe, which she wore around the house on most days, and was holding her wig in her hand like a rag doll. She didn't have far to go because my neighbor across the street had a nail salon set up in one of her spare rooms and she had quite a big clientele, including Mama and me. After seeing that Mama was stable enough to walk across the street I helped her down the short flight of stairs and into the foyer. She stopped briefly in the powder room, shook out her wig, slipped it on, and headed out the front door. I walked with her to the curb. We looked both ways, and then she crossed the quiet street gingerly as if she was walking on hot coals. About an hour or so later, Mama returned with her nails freshly painted bright red. She wore her nails long, and the color looked beautiful against her pale skin. Mama sat up and waited for Rita to come for her evening hook up to the IV. After Rita left, the girls and I stayed in Mama's room visiting with her as she lay there in a daze. The girls were bathed and ready for bed wearing white tank top t-shirts and white ruffle panties, which doubled as their summer jammies. It was too late for Mama to have her daily bath because she was back on the IV for the evening. Out of the blue Mama started to cry.

"I'm *so* hungry. I just want something to eat," she pleaded as I gently pulled her close to me and hugged her.

"You'll be able to eat again soon Mama." I didn't know what else to say. *God, please help her because I can't.* I prayed.

The girls and I stayed in the room a little while longer talking to Mama when she peered up at Natalia.

"Aw, look at her little panties. They're so white," Mama said then she drifted off to sleep. *That was a random comment,* I thought then I dismissed it and went to bed after she was asleep for a few minutes.

Monday morning came, and it was a typical, beautiful, sunny, summer day. I was off work that day. Rita arrived at 7AM. Mama was very sullen, and quiet that morning, and she stayed in the bed after Rita left.

"Baby, give me some ice chips please." Mama requested.

I thought she just wanted *something* to chew on, so I obliged and gave her a large cup of ice. I watched her closely as she lay there chewing on the ice. I was doing my best not to look concerned. I sat on the side of the bed making small talk, when I noticed Mama lay back with her eyes glazed over, and the cup tilted in her hand. As she talked to me, she started mumbling and jumbling her words. My adrenaline started to pump as I panicked trying to make sense of what she was saying. PJ was at work, so I called him on the phone.

"Honey, Mama's talking gibberish and her eyes are glassy. I'm scared!" I was practically screaming into the phone.

"Ok, first calm down, ok?" PJ coached. "Call her doctor and call me back and keep me updated."

I called Dr. Harris and he told me to call the paramedics and he would meet us at the hospital." I called my long time friend, Myrna, who came to the house right away to get the girls so I could focus on Mama. When the paramedics arrived to transport Mama, I crawled into the ambulance and listened to them ask Mama a series of simple questions that she could not answer. It was clear that she was confused about details such as what day it was, her name, and her birth date. I remained hopeful that she would get to the hospital and be all better; but clearly I was in denial. I was ushered out of the ambulance so that they could leave. I called PJ, updated him, and then jumped into my car and followed the ambulance to Saint Francis Medical Center in Lynwood. PJ arrived at the hospital shortly after I did. Once I got Mama admitted, and settled into her room, I made notifications to family members, local and out of state, as well as to Reverend Murray, Pastor Green, an associate pastor at FAME, and other ministers at FAME. Pastor Murray and Reverend Green had consistently prayed with, and for Mama during her illness, so I knew she wanted them close. It was especially hard for me to call grandmother. She had already witnessed Mama faint at her wedding five months prior. Family and friends knew Mama was undergoing cancer treatment, but no one knew her prognosis.

I couldn't wait for Dr. Harris to arrive to tell me what was going on but he didn't arrive until about 5PM. I was annoyed by his delay. I was grateful however, that Mama was at least getting medical care in the hospital so that alone calmed my nerves a bit. I stayed in the room when Dr. Harris assessed Mama.

"Ms. Carmen, how are you lady?" Dr. Harris asked. "I'm going to do what I can for you, but most importantly I want to make sure you are comfy and getting the best care possible. Your daughter has taken great care of you at home, but we need to manage your vitals and get you stable ok?"

Mama nodded slowly in affirmation. She was slightly coherent and drowsy.

"Thank you Doctor," Mama said slowly. "Please tell my daughter whatever she needs to know ok?" Mama looked up at me as I stood by her bedside. Her breathing had become more and more laborious as she lay connected to a respirator.

"Well, in order for us to allow your daughter to make decisions on your behalf, I will need for you to sign this form authorizing her to have Power of Attorney."

Harris held up a clipboard for Mama as she signed the form in her beautiful cursive handwriting. *She's still in there*, I thought, *look at that handwriting.*

Dr. Harris motioned for me to follow him out of the room while the nursing staff attended to Mama.

"Mrs. Morris," he began cautiously. "What's happening is, basically, your mother's organs are failing." I remained silent staring at the doctor. I had no words.

"I'm so sorry, but there is not much more we can do for her. So, in addition to the I.V., I am going to authorize a Morphine drip to manage her pain. Now, should your mother *Code* while she is here, how do you want to handle that?"

"I don't know." I replied, still trying to grasp the gravity of the situation.

"As her physician, and based on her condition, I recommend that you consider signing a Do Not Resuscitate, or DNR, Order." Harris handed me a clipboard with the DNR directive for me to read and sign.

"Ok. So, what do I need to consider in terms of her short term or long term care?" I was too numb to cry, and had a lot of decisions to make in a short period of time. I thank God I had PJ because my brothers were no help.

"I give her about three to six months to live, so you may want to consider putting her into Hospice." I was frozen in place as the doctor's words pierced my heart like a knife.

"What is Hospice?"

"Hospice is a specialized type of care for those facing a life-limiting illness. The service provider will address your mother's physical, emotional, social, and spiritual needs." Dr. Harris explained.

"Oh ok…thank you so much."

I was not prepared to watch Mama die over the next three to six months. I didn't know what the hospice thing was or how it worked but I knew if I took Mama home and she died in the house, I would not be able to live there. I worried about how my girls would be affected watching their Mimi die at home. It was too much to think about. By that evening Mama was placed on life support, and she was still struggling to breath. I could barely watch her, but at the same time I couldn't take my eyes off of her. One thing remained constant after Mama checked into the hospital was her desire to see Stefon.

"I want to see my baby. I want to see Stefon," Mama repeated during her bouts of clarity.

PJ and I stayed with her until she fell off to sleep late that night. Edris worked as a truck driver and was finally doing well for himself. He had come to the house whenever he was in the Valley area, and had seen Mama at my house before she was hospitalized, so I called to update him on Mama's condition.

"Hey T, I'm on the road right now, so I will get to the hospital as soon as I can."

"Ok, I will let you know if anything changes." I told Mama, Edris would be there to see her as soon as he could. She smiled and blinked with gratitude.

Over the next couple of days Mama grew increasingly weaker, but kept insisting on seeing Stefon. I didn't know how I was going to make that happen but I had to try to see what I could do. It was early on Wednesday morning, September 2nd, when I called the prison to see if it was possible for Stefon to attend Mama's funeral should she die while he was still incarcerated. The prison representative told me they had provisions for prisoners to either go to visit a dying parent in the hospital *or* attend the funeral. The caveat was that I had to pay for two Deputies for a minimum of five hours to transport Stefon to the location of his choice, the hospital or the funeral.

The prison official allowed me to speak to Stefon to ask which he preferred. I told Stefon the tragic update about Mama's most recent prognosis. Through his tears, I could hear him reasoning with himself trying to make a solid decision.

"Aww man T, is she *that* sick?" He asked, hoping for a different answer.

"Yes Stefon, she is *that* sick," I replied. "They are giving her 3-6 months to live."

"I would rather see her alive at the hospital, than go to her funeral," Stefon said. "I can't have my last image of her be in a casket." Stefon said as he started crying uncontrollably. I could hear the sound of prison doors closing in the distance and buzzers in the background as I spoke to Stefon.

"Ok, honey, I'm going to start the process to have you transported to the hospital before Mama is discharged," I said. "Keep your head up ok? I love you Stefon."

I had a pounding headache. PJ stayed in the waiting room right next to Mama's room as friends, family, and fellow church members started to cycle in and out of the room. Myrna brought the girls to the hospital, but I didn't want them to see Mama with all the tubes draping her face.

"You need to let the girls see their grandmother. What if this is the last time?" PJ urged.

"You're right. What if they never get a chance to see her alive again? I can't do that to them." PJ led Brittany and Natalia into the hospital room, where Mama was lying and struggling to breathe.

"Hi, Mimi," Brittany said in a soft, shaky little voice.

Mama tilted her head in the direction of her grandbabies, whom she loved so much. She didn't say a word, but her breathing quickened as she looked at her little doll babies.

"She's talking to you, girls," PJ softly informed them.

"I love you, Mimi, I hope you feel better soon," Brittany said. Natalia was too young to understand what was happening, and just quietly stood there next to Brittany trying to hide in her shadow.

"She loves you guys so much, too." PJ answered for Mama and then guided the girls back into the waiting room.

The next morning, which was a Thursday, I left PJ and the girls at the hospital while I made the drive to Chino Prison and paid $750 cash for Stefon's transport to the hospital. Deputies were scheduled to leave the Prison on the following Sunday morning, September 6th at 5AM. I didn't know how long Mama would be in the hospital, but I was in no hurry to get hospice set up. By the time I returned to the hospital that afternoon, Mama was speaking completely in gibberish. Reverend Earl Green was sitting beside her bed just as he had been everyday that week after he finished his church duties.

"Honey, she is talking to God," Reverend Green said looking up at me over his oval rimless glasses. I couldn't understand a word she was saying, but

I figured *she* knew what she was trying to say and that's all that mattered. Before Mama fell off to sleep I reassured her.

"Stefon's coming Mama. He's coming real soon to see you."

After she fell off to sleep we left to go home to get some rest. We had been at the hospital the entire day but we had close friends who stayed with Mama around the clock. The labor-day weekend was fast approaching and the girls were due to start back to school that same week. It was Friday and Mama had been in the hospital since Monday. The girls were at the hospital with me while PJ went on to work. That evening, he came to the hospital after work as he had done every evening that week. PJ was my anchor and I appreciated him so much. The girls were at the hospital with me, but thankfully they were more focused on Wanda and William's daughter, Stacie's birthday sleepover party the next day so they were excited about that event rather than focused on Mama. Dr. Harris made his rounds late that evening and I updated him on Mama's gibberish rants and what changes I had noticed in her demeanor.

"Tia, you need to prepare yourself," Dr. Harris said firmly.

"Prepare myself how, doctor?" I asked growing anxious and confused.

"I give her 24-48 hours to live," he responded.

"Hold on, you said 3-6 months in *hospice*, and now you are telling me 24-48 hours? Really?"

"I'm so sorry, Tia," Dr. Harris replied as he moved to console me.

"Oh No! No, no, no!" I screeched. I collapsed into the doctor as PJ ran to see what happened then I turned to face PJ.

"They are giving her a day to live," I said.

I buried my head into PJ's chest and cried until my soul ached.

A million thoughts danced in my head; I was beat. That was the longest, most dreadful week of my life. I needed to call Edris; I needed to call Grandmother; I needed to call the prison for them to let Stefon know that Mama may not make it until Sunday. At the top of my list were Edris and grandmother. My Aunt Linda, Mama's best friend and quasi baby sister, was already at the hospital at Mama's side.

"Don't you worry, Carmen, honey," Aunt Linda said to Mama, who had already slipped into a coma. "I'm gonna look after your Doll Babies. I'm gonna look after them for you."

On the morning of Friday, September 4th, Mama was in a coma but hanging in there. After hearing the devastating news that Mama's time was near I felt the need to update the prison since I had the wheels in motion for Stefon to visit. I was frantically trying to reach the Warden's office in case she passed away before Sunday. The Warden's office was closed due to Labor Day weekend, so the staff was not due to return until the following Tuesday. I had heard that comatose patients were aware of what went on around them so I kept talking to Mama. By the fluttering of her eyes it appeared as though she was trying to respond. I wanted her to rest so I stopped talking and just stayed by her side and held her hand so that she knew I was there. I didn't want her to feel alone in what could have possibly been her last hours. By Saturday afternoon, Mama was resting comfortably with a consistent dose of Morphine being pumped through her veins. I had fallen asleep next to her bed and when I woke up I saw Edris walk into the room.

"Hey T, I got your messages, what happened? I thought you said they gave Mama 3-6 months to live?"

His eyes searched mine for confirmation that Mama was going to pull through. He reminded me of that clueless little boy I remember back in Detroit, who flunked the third grade, and ran after Mama's car whenever she'd leave to go to work. I felt sorry for him because she had always been there to pick up the pieces for him. The little brother I saw standing there appeared to be vulnerable. The thought of him losing Mama was bad enough, but actually *watching* her die was even more devastating for him.

"Edris, her organs are shutting down," I explained. "She's been suffering for a long time and I don't want to see her suffer like this."

"Oh my God," he said as he sank into a chair in the corner of the room.

"The Sheriffs are bringing Stefon here in the morning to see Mama," I continued.

Edris covered his face with his hands and started sobbing.

"Don't cry, Edris. We'll be alright." I said as I hugged him. He was shaking like a leaf. I didn't know if it was from the grief or the alcohol. *Poor thing,* I thought. *My poor baby brother, what's he going to do without Mama?* My heart went out to him.

Edris and I stayed in the room for a while talking to Reverend Green while Mama lay there. We held a vigil at Mama's bedside until late Saturday evening. I prayed that Mama would make it till daybreak to see Stefon even if she could not communicate with him. Stefon would be in shackles with two uniformed strangers joining him at Mama's bedside, so I hoped that would not confuse her. PJ and I were at the hospital all day with the girls and they were antsy, so we thought it was a good time to drop them off at Wanda's for Stacie's sleepover, and then we could go home really quick to shower and change clothes while Aunt Linda stayed at the hospital with Mama. It was about 11PM when we pulled into the driveway at home after dropping the girls off. I showered first and then got dressed. Afterwards, I sat on the side of the bed while PJ showered. Just before midnight, we were preparing to head back to the hospital when the phone rang. It was Aunt Linda.

"She's gone baby," she said through her audible tears.

"Noooo!" I screamed, as PJ stood watching me with a startled look on his face. "Mama's gone." I uttered as I lay the phone down.

PJ and I returned to the hospital right away. Mama was gone but I needed to see her because I couldn't believe she was gone. My head was spinning. I had just left and she died before I could get back. I was always there for Mama and that one time I wasn't there for her. I started thinking that I shouldn't have left the hospital. I felt horrible. The drive back to the hospital was long. When I finally got to Mama's room she was laying there with the sheet pulled over her face. I tentatively walked into the room, and gently pulled the covers away from Mama's face when I saw a beautiful Angel peering back at me. The breathing apparatus and all the wires that once adorned Mama's petite face were removed; her eyes were partially opened, but she wasn't struggling to breathe anymore; and her skin was gorgeous. I examined Mama as if she were a foreign species I had never seen before. I pulled the sheets completely off of her so I could get one last look at my precious Mama lying there. I wanted to see her legs and her feet one last time. As I pulled the sheets back I tugged at her gown to ensure she was not exposed. I raised Mama's hand that was closest to me and placed it on my cheek. Mama was at peace after 53 years on this earth. My earth Angel had gotten her wings. After examining Mama I pulled the sheet back up and tucked the corners neatly under Mama's shoulders, and walked out of the room. I was so sad, but I felt a sense of relief because she was not suffering anymore.

"Oh man!" I shrieked. "Stefon!" I said aloud in a panic as PJ and I walked towards the elevator.

It was about 2AM, and the Deputies were scheduled to leave Chino at 5AM to bring Stefon to the hospital. I called the prison and let the phone ring, ring, ring until someone answered.

"Hello sir, I have arranged for my brother, inmate Stefon Pugh, to be transported to Saint Francis Hospital in a couple of hours and I need to stop the transport because my mother has died." I couldn't believe the words that were coming out of the mouth. *My mother has died.* I repeated over and over and over again in my head.

"Ma'am, I am sorry to hear of your mother's passing, and I will most certainly stop the transport. Would you like to speak to Mr. Pugh and tell him about your mother's passing?"

"Yes," I said surprised that they would allow that at that hour. "I would appreciate that very much, sir. Thank you."

I heard the deputy sit the phone down, and I heard voices echoing in the background as the sounds of metal doors opened and closed. I heard the prison guard politely advise Stefon that he would step out of the room to allow Stefon some privacy.

"Hey T, what's going on?" Stefon sounded sleepy.

"Stefon, Mama died. She's gone."

"What are you talking about, T?" I'm sure Stefon heard me.

"She died a couple of hours ago, so they are not bringing you to the hospital. Ok?"

"I.. I.. I.. didn't get to see her while she was alive T." Stefon said as he burst into tears. I felt helpless. There he was, locked away. I felt horrible, but

I couldn't imagine what he was going through. I prayed for God to help him, and help *us*.

"I can see if they will allow you to come to the funeral since I paid already, ok?"

"No, no, no," Stefon said. "I can't see her in a coffin. I can't, I can't, T. I don't know what I'm going to do. I failed her. She raised me to be better than this. I'm sorry… I'm sorry. Man, I can't live without my Baby."

"I know honey," I said, fighting back tears of my own. "But you have to stay strong. I hate that you couldn't be here with her, but you have to be strong ok?" Stefon continued to cry uncontrollably.

"Mr. Pugh, hand me the phone please," the Deputy, said in a soft tone.

"Ok, I'm ready to go back now." Stefon replied in a somber tone. Stefon had to come to terms with never seeing Mama again. We all did.

"Ma'am I have stopped the transport," the Deputy said when he returned to the phone. "And Mr. Pugh does not wish to attend the funeral. Per our policy we can not issue refunds for the transport however, the funds you paid will remain on the inmate's books."

"Oh, ok," I replied. "I don't have a problem with that, and I'm sure Stefon will be ok with that as well. Thank you, sir."

"You're welcome, Ma'am. Again, I am very sorry for your loss." The line went dead.

CHAPTER 10

"Mama's Gone"

THE THOUGHT OF PLANNING MAMA'S funeral was surreal. It was as if I was in the twilight zone. Mama had not pre-planned her funeral, and we never talked about it. Dad had made all the funeral arrangements when Virginia died, so PJ had no firsthand experience in planning a funeral either. As a result, we started from scratch, and with no help from my brothers. There was no need for an autopsy because Mama was terminally ill and her doctor willingly signed off on the death certificate, so we were able to move swiftly with scheduling Mama's service. Aunt Linda, Reverend Murray, and Reverend Green were with PJ and I every step of the way as we made arrangements. I called Angelus Funeral Home, in South LA, bright and early that Sunday morning, and requested they pick up Mama's body from the hospital. Angelus was an aesthetically beautiful building on the inside and out. The white Spanish Colonial building was one of Los Angeles' Historic-Cultural monuments. It had large gold double entry doors; a large ethereal chandelier in the main entrance, and furnishings trimmed with gold, plush couches, decadent chairs and tables, set on richly textured carpeting; and classical French paintings hanging on the walls. It was a regal establishment, so it was the best place for my Queen to lay her head. Later that Sunday evening, we picked up the girls from the sleepover. I rode in the back seat with the girls because I just wanted to hug them. Boys II Men's song, "End of the Road," was playing on the radio during our ride home. *How fitting*, I thought. Once we got home, PJ encouraged me to lie down while he gave the girls their baths, which is when PJ broke the news about their Mimi's death. The girls then got into bed with us.

"Mommy, are you sad?" Brittany asked as she lay next to me. She was so cute.

"Yes, honey, mommy is sad, but Mimi is in heaven now. I'm going to miss her but she is in a better place."

"Yeah, Brittany," five-year-old Natalia chimed in. "Mimi is in heaven now. Mommy, don't be sad, she is watching over us," Natalia said bravely. She reminded me of Mama so much, and she was very spiritual even as a child. She liked to preach in the shower, and it was hilarious, but she was serious, and passionate about praying.

"I'm glad Mimi won't be throwing up anymore," Brittany admitted. "But, I'm gonna miss my Mimi."

My little thumb-sucking divas cried themselves to sleep, as they lay between PJ and me.

Order my steps Lord, I repeated over and over again as I moved forward with planning Mama's funeral. Mama was legally married to Frank when she died, so I asked for his input from time to time during the brief planning stage. Angelus notified me after they retrieved Mama's body, and PJ and I immediately went there and selected a beautiful ivory casket with praying hands embroidered on the interior lining above Mama's head.

"I like that one. It will go perfectly with Mama's robe." I chose to bury Mama in her ministerial robe, which was Ivory colored with a gold trimmed sash with praying hands stenciled on one side.

"Ok," said the funeral home director. "That one is $4800, does that fit your budget?"

"Yes sir, that's fine." I was less than enthused about the process, so he could have said the cost was $10,000 and I would have agreed. I was not in the mood to bargain.

"Ok ma'am let's go to my office where we can go over all of the associated costs and burial details," he replied.

Frank had a family burial plot at Lincoln Memorial Park Cemetery, which was paid for. He told me he wanted to have Mama buried there. I was a bit apprehensive when he told me the cemetery was located in Compton, because it was so far from where I lived, but I went ahead and agreed to the arrangement without seeing the burial site. I dreaded going to the cemetery because I had visions of throwing dirt on Mama's casket and saying goodbye forever, and that was eerie to me. I was vaguely familiar with gravesites as I had been to Inglewood Park and Forest Lawn Cemeteries, where the grounds were extremely well manicured, so I figured the gravesite Frank offered was comparable and I was grateful that he was willing to offer any assistance.

The funeral director and I discussed the details of the impending funeral as we walked the long hallway from the casket room to his office.

"The service will be on Friday at 11AM at First A.M.E. Church," I advised.

"Ok," he replied, "That's good you are having the service on a weekday because usually, Interment costs more on the weekends."

"My Mom's husband has made arrangements at Lincoln Park Cemetery for the Interment."

"Ok, very good, I will need for you to bring me your mother's clothes including shoes and brand new undergarments. The undergarments must be *new*, ok? We will have her ready for viewing by tomorrow evening, but we will not allow anyone to view her until you have done so first. Once you approve, we will schedule viewing hours on Wednesday and Thursday for family and friends."

"Ok," shoes and *new* under garments. I got it. I'll bring her wig also."

Tears welled up in my eyes, and my voice quivered as we ended our conversation. I couldn't believe I was leaving Mama there in that cold dark room. I needed to see her eyes open, and I needed to hear her hearty laughter. I was starting to go stir crazy but PJ's presence kept me sane. PJ and I left the mortuary and went a short distance away to meet with the printer for the Obituary. Frank's cousin, Wilma owned a small print shop, and she was fond of Mama so she was very accommodating, and very kind throughout the process.

"Hey Doll," Wilma said, "Let me show you some sample obituaries. I really like this staggered folded one," she said holding up the sample Obituary. "What do you think?"

"Oh, I *love* this style and the layout. It's beautiful." I couldn't believe I thought an *Obituary* was beautiful.

Mama's Obituary-September 1992

I was exhausted, but my work was far from done. PJ and I returned to Angelus on the next evening, and we were directed to *Slumber Room No. 4.* There she laid, my Mama, fully made up with her hands crossed over her chest. Her nails had a fresh coat of red polish on them. She had gotten them done just days before her trip to the hospital as if she knew that she was getting ready for her funeral, and knew that her manicure would be on display.

"She looks beautiful, but can you please remove some of the make up? It's a little too much," I whispered to the funeral director, who was standing close by cheesing as if he had just painted a masterpiece. As strange as it was, I didn't want to talk too loudly so I wouldn't disturb Mama.

"Of course," the director replied, "I'll take care of that right away. Is everything else ok?" The funeral director asked as he reached for tissue at the foot of the casket, which he used to gently wipe some of the make up from Mama's face.

"Now, *that's* perfect." I said as I looked up at PJ, who was standing beside me.

"Yeah, Mom looks beautiful," PJ echoed as he lightly stroked Mama's cheek with the back of his hand.

When we left the funeral home that evening I felt encouraged. I felt I had the strength to make it through that rough patch. PJ held my hand as we drove away. A sense of calm and acceptance gradually crept over me and I needed that because, once the funeral was over I had to return to work and resume my study program for the upcoming Sergeant's exam. The funeral service was a lively celebration of life. Reverend Murray eulogized Mama and it was amazing, and the choir was incredible. Lincoln Park, on the other hand, was appalling. When we approached the cemetery, the grounds were horrific. The unpaved dirt roads leading to the scattered graves resembled a scene right out of a Tim Burton movie. I couldn't even focus on the Interment because I was so angry. I couldn't believe that Frank thought that place would be acceptable for Mama.

"I don't care if the *Pope* is buried here, Mama is not staying here," I told PJ under my breath. I came close to interrupting the Interment because I was that furious. I couldn't wait for the graveside ceremony to be over. On my way back to the limo, I walked up to Frank and lightly tapped him on the shoulder.

"Frank, my mom is not staying here. This place looks like a pet cemetery. I will be having her moved." I said in a low angry tone.

"I'm sorry, Tia," he replied clueless. "I was just trying to help."

"Don't get me wrong," I said apologetically. "I really appreciate your gesture but this place is unsatisfactory, and you *have* to see that."

I quickly snapped back to civility because I realized I was being rude, and that was not my intent. I was ornery, because I was hurting and like they say, *hurt* people, *hurt* people. On the Monday following Mama's service, I was on the doorstep of Forest Lawn Hollywood Hills right when they opened for business, and I made arrangements to have Mama moved from Lincoln Park to *their* beautiful location. I then called and notified Lincoln Park of the transfer. They advised me I would have to pay a $550 fee to have Mama's casket exhumed and transported to Forest Lawn. I didn't care. The appointment was set, and on the afternoon of the move I stood by as they exhumed Mama's vault from the gravesite at Lincoln, and I followed the mortuary van to Forest Lawn, where I watched Mama's second interment on a beautiful hillside on the street called *Gentleness.* I was pleased about Mama's new resting place. I sent out notecards to family and friends notifying them of Mama's change of address.

It was November of 1992, and I was adjusting to life without Mama, and the City of L.A. was recovering from the 1992 Riots. I had returned to work and had resumed studying for the Sergeants Exam. I eventually wanted to promote to the rank of Lieutenant and wanted to do so from the rank of Sergeant versus Detective so I needed to make Sergeant. Traditionally, the Senior Command Staff frowned upon individuals promoting to Lieutenant from the Detective rank, because most detective assignments employed functional, administrative supervision versus line, or patrol rank and file type, supervision. They felt that substandard functional supervision made it more difficult for someone with a detective only background, to manage police officers in the field. Also, *women* always had a harder time promoting into leadership positions anyway, so I made it a point to follow the path most taken by the men, in order to afford me more credibility in leadership roles. When I returned to work I sat at my desk at Internal Affairs and thought about how awkward it was that life had continued on, as if Mama were never here. Everyone was moving about completely un-aware as to the horrific week I had just endured. *Such is life, I suppose,* I thought. It showed me that you never know what people are going through. By late November, Edris married Shelly in a civil ceremony in downtown Los Angeles. We were all still on decent terms with Frank, so Shelly and Edris rented the upstairs unit of the duplex from Frank's parents. Things started out great with the two of them. Shelly started an in-home childcare business, and she helped Edris start his very own trucking company; Pugh Trucking. They purchased a pre-owned big rig truck, and Edris set out on road trips just as he did when he accompanied Ronald back in the day. I was so proud of the both of them, and thought that just maybe Edris was growing up and mellowing out. Frank was still living in Silver Lake at the time, and Stefon was due to be released from prison within the next few months. That first Thanksgiving and Christmas without Mama was extremely hard for me. Thanksgiving was Mama's favorite holiday because she loved to cook and eat, and Thanksgiving was the perfect opportunity to do both.

In February of 1993, Shelly told me that she was pregnant, and in the same conversation she told me that Frank, whom I had not seen since Mama died, had suffered a massive stroke, which left him physically disabled. Frank could no longer maneuver around his hillside property without help, nor could he maintain his handyman business that he needed to augment his Gas Company salary, so he sold his home and moved in with his parents in the downstairs unit beneath Edris and Shelly. Although he wasn't the friendliest individual I still felt really bad for him. I didn't think his intentions for Mama were genuine, but I still didn't wish him any harm. I know it was not my place to judge him, but I did, so shame on me. By the summer of 1993, I passed the Sergeants Exam and was placed so high on the list that within 5 weeks from the list being published, I promoted to Sergeant and was assigned to Newton Division in South Los Angeles.

Chief Willie Williams (RIP 2016) and Sergeant Tia Morris 1993

The moniker for Newton Division was "Shootin' Newton," because of the number of shootings that took place in that area of the City. I bore witness to some of those shootings early on as a brand new field Sergeant. I remember one of the first shooting calls I responded to; while en route to the call, I actually saw muzzle flashes from a shotgun near where the call came out. I was a supervisor, which meant I wasn't expected to get to the scene first. Besides, I was riding alone, so I let the officers do their job, and I fell back and provided back up and supervision. By the time I rolled up on the scene, I was calm, cool and collected. I never let the officers see me sweat. I was enjoying being a Sergeant, but there were some men in the division who were not ready to accept me. I was in roll call one night when one of them challenged my qualifications to be a Sergeant in front of the Watch Commander and everybody else. I didn't need to respond.

"Don't worry about her qualifications," the Watch Commander said in my defense. "All you need to know is that she is *your* supervisor, and you need to focus on how to do *your* job."

I did not want to respond to the officer's ignorance in that forum, so I was relieved that the Lieutenant set the stage for the others who were present. *I bet they'll think twice before trying to embarrass me again in front of that watch commander.* I thought. Right after roll call, a big cuddly, male white police officer named Gil Egan approached me.

"Hey, Sarge," he said. "I just want to let you know, that guy was completely out of line in there. Welcome to Newton."

"Well, thank you," I smiled. "But I'm fine. It comes with the territory, you know?"

"Yes, ma'am. I know," he replied. "But it *shouldn't* come with the territory. We're all on the same team." *What a pleasant young man*, I thought. "Anyway, I just wanted to welcome you the way you should have been. I'm Gil Egan."

"Thank you for your professionalism, Gil," I replied. "And nice to meet you. Be safe out there."

I hadn't been at Newton for very long before I received a call from Chief Bernard Parks' office advising me that they wanted me to work on a special task force. I didn't understand why *I* was chosen or whether I should accept because I had just gotten to Newton.

"Can you tell me anything about the assignment?" I asked the office administrator who called me.

"Not yet, ma'am," he replied. "It's a very sensitive investigation, so all will be discussed when the entire team is assembled."

"Ok, well can you at least tell me why *I* was selected?" I asked perplexed.

"To be quite honest, ma'am, we needed a female supervisor with an excellent investigative background, and you were recommended by your former lieutenant at Internal Affairs."

"Oh ok," I chuckled. "Well, I guess I would be a fool to turn the Chief down, huh?"

"Uh…yeah," he responded. "I will be in touch to advise when and where we will meet. Your *loan* has already been approved by your Commanding Officer at Newton."

"Ok, thanks. I'm looking forward to the meeting."

When my male peers at Newton division found out about my new temporary assignment, they were not happy. I had not completed my six-month probationary period as a Sergeant yet and they couldn't understand *why* I was selected to go work in the Chief's office so soon after making Sergeant. *There's no doubt in my mind that they would have taken the job had they been offered the opportunity but, they weren't asked, and that was not my fault.* I thought. When I reported for duty in my new loan assignment I was told that the task force was assembled to address ongoing *racial* issues at West Los Angeles Division (WLA). *How ironic.* I thought. I told Chief Parks that I was assigned to WLA in 1983, when those same issues persisted, when Detective Martin Foster spearheaded the hate groups, "Men Against Women (MAW)" and "WASP (White Anglo Saxon Police)." Those groups targeted minorities and females and unfortunately I fit into both categories. I sat there during the meeting and reflected back on that horrible time early in my career when I met the infamous Martin Foster. Foster and I were both Police Officer 2's (PO2's) assigned to the mid pm shift from 6PM to 3AM. That shift was primarily staffed with PO2's, because we were no longer on probation, and we were capable of working independently, on foot beats in and around Westwood Village, at critical sites throughout the division, and in cars with peers who didn't require much guidance or supervision. The camaraderie on the mid watch shift was normally outstanding because we were usually a cohesive team that provided coverage during the change of watch for the primary shifts. When I arrived at WLA I was told about Officer Foster, who was on our shift, and was known for hating minorities and women, which is why he spearheaded the groups MAW and WASP, which I thought was despicable. The department was still reeling from the aftermath of the Fanchon Blake lawsuit, which had recently opened the floodgates for more women and minorities to join the rank and file of the Los Angeles Police Department, and people like Foster were not having it. I was so green at the time and so accepting of everyone, except for mean spirited people, that I had no clue about the potential fallout from that lawsuit as it related to minorities and women in the workplace. I had been treated surprisingly well on probation at North Hollywood Division, and I didn't have any issues when I transferred into Jail Division. However, when I arrived at WLA in March of 1983, I swore I met the devil. I started to witness Foster's racist and sexist activity so I tried to avoid him as best I could. I was at WLA for a few months and had developed a great rapport with officers I met there, and I reconnected with several of my male classmates, whom I had not seen since we graduated from the academy. I was having a great time work-ing there but that happy feeling was short lived when I came face to face with Officer Foster. I arrived for work one evening, and while in roll call the watch commander was calling roll and assigned me to work with Foster, as partners in patrol. I sat there scribbling my assignment in my field officer's notebook when I heard Officer Foster yell from the back of the room.

"I'm not working with Morris, Sarg." Foster said in an angry tone.

"You *are* working with Morris," replied the Watch Commander, Sergeant Bichlmeier, an old tenured male white Sergeant II, who seemed as menacing as Foster.

I sat there mortified. I didn't even bother to look up, and didn't know what to say. The way I saw it, the fight was between the watch commander and Foster and not me and Foster. I was embarrassed and humiliated, and the watch com-mander obviously didn't get it, because clearly the problem was way deeper than he cared to recognize at that moment, which should have been addressed with Foster. Instead, Bichlmeier continued on with calling roll while Foster notice-ably ranted and raged in the back of the room for everyone to see.

"This is bullshit and you know it Sarg! C'mon, *she* doesn't belong here and you know that."

"Foster! Please sit down and shut up. You are working with Morris, so get over it."

I started to grow a little concerned because I didn't know what was in store for me in the field that night. Foster was clearly angry, and I was scared of what Foster might do to try to sabotage or ambush me in the field. After roll call I met Foster at the KIT Room where we got our radios and shotgun. Foster grabbed the shotgun and walked away with his chest poked out daring anyone to cross his angry path.

"Meet me at the gas pumps, Morris." Martin barked.

I looked at him with a scowl on my face, and without saying a word I grabbed my things and walked across the street where Foster was standing outside of our assigned black and white vehicle pumping gas. I noticed that the shotgun was on the roof of the car slightly under the light bar. I placed my police equipment in the trunk, and got into the passenger seat and started to write on my Daily Field Activities Report. A few minutes later Foster entered the driver's side, slammed the door behind him and took off like a maniac. After driving off I noticed the shotgun was not in the rack.

"Hey, where's the shotgun?" I asked.

"Goddamn it!" Foster yelled as he abruptly applied the brakes.

Just then I heard an object hit the pavement on my side of the car just as the car came to a screeching halt. I opened the door, and saw the shotgun sliding down the pavement in the middle of the road.

"What did you do with it Morris?"

"*You* got it from the KIT room, so you should have loaded it and placed it in the rack."

I said as I got out and retrieved the shotgun. I loaded it and placed it in the rack as Foster accelerated away.

"That's exactly why you don't belong here. You need to go be a secretary somewhere, or at home barefoot and pregnant. What are you going to do if we get into a fight? I can't trust you with my life. I will challenge you and all of your female buddies to a fight at the academy, and I bet I will choke you all out in minutes. You are no match for the weakest man. How can you measure up in a fight with a man much bigger and stronger than you? Huh Morris? What you gonna do?" Foster went on about a ten-minute rant as he sped aimlessly up and down Santa Monica Boulevard, and to and from various radio calls.

"Well, I guess I'll just have to shoot their *big ass* huh Foster?" I responded.

I was not scared of Foster, but I was scared of what he would try to do *to* me or get me involved in that night. Foster was known to go into gang territory, remove his badge and name tag and beat down local gang members and especially minorities, so I figured he would try to have me initiated or beat down to prove a point. The straw that broke the camels back was about two hours into our shift, a Code 2 "Prowler There Now," residential burglary call came out on the radio and it was in the Mandeville Canyon area of WLA, where there are large homes secluded behind gates. I acknowledged the call, and we were rolling. When Foster pulled up to the residence he parked right in front of the residence, which happened to not be gated, he turned off the engine and just sat there in the darkness. I bolted out of the car, and drew my weapon to a *low ready* position with my finger along the frame. I scanned the area as I walked towards the residence with both hands at the low ready, and turned quickly to see where *my partner* was. To my surprise he was *still* seated in the car shining his flashlight here and there. I motioned for him to get out of the car and he shooed me away. I could not believe what I was experiencing. As I got closer to the door I saw the owner quickly walk out of the front door of the residence. She advised me that the *prowler* had run off, so I got her information and completed a crime report. When I returned to the car I was fuming and Foster laughed like a wicked monster. I demanded that he take me back to the station immediately. Once at the station I went right into the watch commander's office where I reported Foster's negligible behavior.

"Lieutenant, I refuse to go back out in the field with Foster because I don't feel safe. I will go home sick right now if you make me work with him."

"Ok Morris, you can go back out as a report car and I'll talk to Foster." The Watch Commander said casually.

Foster and I never worked together again, and after that night whenever I worked with one of Foster's friends he would send me messages via the Mobile

Digital Terminals in our police vehicle reiterating that I didn't belong on the force, and that I should go dance on *Soooooooouuuuul Train*. He would stretch out the word *soul* just as I indicated. This activity went on for months until one night I was working and the morning watch commander Lieutenant T. King came on duty. He sent messages to me and all the other female officers working that night, and directed us to meet him at the 7-11 parking lot on the corner of Santa Monica and Bundy. Once assembled, Lieutenant King directed our male partners to continue patrol until we were done speaking with him. His sole reason for meeting was to address the *rumors* about the ongoing racist and sexist activity he was hearing about that was occurring primarily on mid watch and morning watch, spearheaded by Foster. After a very candid conversation, he vowed to open an investigation and assured us that he was going to put a stop to the foul activity. In spite of the Lieutenant's efforts Foster continued to openly express his hate for women and blacks in the workplace. His outward disdain for women is what prompted the department to launch a large-scale investigation due to the organized efforts initiated by Foster with MAW and WASP. Foster ostracized male white officers who talked to black officers, and female officers of all races. On the heels of the Department's investigation, Foster's actions piqued the interest of a Los Angeles Times Staff Writer who authored an article in 1986 entitled *LAPD: Despite Gains, Race, Sex Bias Persist: More Blacks, Latinos and Women Are Hired but Tension, De Facto Segregation Continue.* The journalist, David Freed, reported that the police department's population consisted of stifled, once-ambitious veteran minority officers, who no longer sought advancement in the department because they considered the effort futile. Freed interviewed more than 100 patrol officers, detectives, supervisors, and administrators, who painted a vivid portrait of a police force not completely comfortable with affirmative action, non-whites, women, and particularly, blacks. Minority officers contended that the lack of acceptance from their white counterparts sometimes escalated into hostile situations, such as the one I experienced with Foster. Freed specifically addressed the issues at West L.A. division. He stated that at West Los Angeles police station, black and female officers complained to their supervisors that white officers, who belonged to Foster's clique, "Men

Against Women," were harassing them. There was one black female rookie officer at the station, who alleged that she was maliciously soaked with gasoline by a white officer at the station's fuel pump. Additionally, she stated that she was assigned to more than 32 training officers during her probationary period, some of whom never spoke to her during their long shifts at WLA. After the article was published, an investigation revealed that the rookie's accounts were found to be true.

The Police Department's chief spokesman at the time of that activity, Commander William Booth, conceded that a *couple* of white officers were involved in various small *pranks* at the station. Booth claimed that the individuals involved were strongly counseled, and that the hate group was disbanded soon after allegations of misconduct were raised. Booth's comments were disingenuous. The incidents of ostracism went way beyond *pranks*, and none of the actions were intended as a joke as Booth stated; they were mean spirited and lasted longer than a couple of months. Freed reported that a number of white officers in WLA, and elsewhere on the department, argued that the ill treatment complained of by minority and female officers had little to do with racism or sexism. Those officers believed, and some said publicly, that a sizable number of women, and non-whites, who were hired during that time to fill the department's quotas were simply unqualified to wear the Los Angeles Police badge. Freed quoted former Captain Roy M. Randolph, a 28-year veteran at the time, as saying, "the simple, real fact of life… is that (the department) is taking in minorities who are not as qualified as some Caucasians. Some of them have been actual functional illiterates; they're trying to teach minorities to write. These are people with lower intellectual abilities, with an inability to assimilate the information an officer needs to do his job." To me, it seemed as if Captain Randolph was stuck in the 1950's and totally ignorant. Here I was sitting in the room with Chief Parks, and his task force comprised of all supervisors, ten years after those racist and sexist organizations first reared their ugly heads at WLA. Chief Parks contended that many of those same issues *still* persisted in the workplace, and he felt it was necessary to address the activity once again.

I had just made Sergeant, however I was studying again, and this time for Lieutenant. Thankfully, many of my peers from Newton, reached out to me often for us to share study materials. During the few months that I was assigned to the task force, I regularly received phone calls and messages from one such Sergeant, D. Nunez, a very short, overly friendly, religious fanatic, and divorced father of two young boys. Nunez knew I had a wide variety of administrative experience, so he often asked me for exemplars of various types of Department audits, and other administrative documents. I obliged, and always delivered the information to the station for him as time permitted. We weren't friends, but it was a professional courtesy on my part, especially since he took the time to call and ask. One day, when I went to the station on one of these routine delivery missions I went into the women's locker room to get something from my locker. When I tried to open my locker I realized that someone had changed the lock. Just as I turned to leave the locker room a young female police officer, Cherita Niles approached me.

"Hi Sgt. Morris," she said. "I saw a note taped to your locker, and it was not nice." I was completely caught off guard. "Yes, Ma'am, it had some really hateful comments on it. I was scared to take it off but *someone* removed it."

Officer Niles could not recall the exact verbiage on the discarded note but based on the tone of the note, which was available for all to see, it was clear that it was authored by one of my male peers, who took the liberty to breach the privacy of the women's locker room just to harass me. *How dare they violate my space?* I was angry, but I was afraid as well because I didn't know who was watching me, and didn't know how far they would go to harm me because of their disdain for me. I went directly to the Watch Commander's office to check my assigned Sergeant's box, which housed my work-related mail and other miscellaneous items. I noted that all of my belongings were discarded, and my name was removed from the box. Those issues seemed minor or petty on the surface, but there was a huge underlying problem that I needed to explore. Accordingly, I took my concerns to the Captain's office to address.

"Well, Tia," Captain Trotter began in response to my complaints. "You need to come back and prove yourself to your peers."

I couldn't do anything but stare at him because this was the same red headed Captain, who requested that I be assigned to his division in the first place because he knew that I would hit the ground running with my experience; *and* he was the same forked tongue devil who approved me going to the damn Task Force in the first place.

"Sir," I replied. "With all due respect, what are you talking about?" I asked looking at him intently.

"You know Tia, the *guys* feel slighted because you just got here and haven't finished your probationary period." He explained.

I was fuming because he obviously didn't seem to see how hypocritical he was. *Is this some sick joke?* I thought. It was clear that my male peers had gotten to the Captain, and in his cowardice he turned on me instead of telling them the truth about how *he* was the one who approved of me going to the task force before I was ever approached by the Chief's office.

"Sir, this has to be some kind of initiation prank or something right?" I laughed out loud because it was unbelievable. "Well sir, did you express your concern to the Chief's office when they called you and got *your* approval?" I asked calling him on his nonsense. "Because I sure did. I told them I had just gotten here, and I didn't want to leave so soon and that's when they told *me* that *you* had already approved my loan, so why would I object at that point?" Trotter didn't have an answer. He just sat there turning red.

Trotter was married to a female Lieutenant at the time, and she had not worked the field in many, many, many, many years. In fact she was working in a nice cushy job at police headquarters at the very moment that he chided me. *Would he have had this same conversation with her?* I wondered. *No, he wouldn't have.* I locked eyes with him, and without saying another word, I got up and walked out of his office. Bottom line was I was still a black woman in a profession dominated by male whites at the helm. I was the lowest on the totem pole in terms of respectability. Obviously not much had changed since Fanchon Blake's discrimination suit in 1977. The only good thing was that her lawsuit at least made it possible for me to even compete for Lieutenant, and I was grateful for that.

It had been over a year since Mama died and life was rolling full steam ahead. On January 17, 1994, the Northridge Earthquake rocked Southern California. We were living in the San Fernando Valley and were very close to the epicenter. Our home sustained major structural damage resulting in a red flag designation. Two weeks after the devastating earthquake that ravaged the city, Edris and Shelly welcomed a baby boy, Edris II, whom we called "Junior," into the family. He was the most adorable little boy. Shortly after the birth of his son, Edris's drinking started to affect his trucking business, *and* his relationship with Shelly. He had been arrested several times in the past for Driving Under the Influence, and, the looming monster, Domestic Violence, once again, reared its ugly head. Edris began directing his frustrations at Shelly, and I'm sure the grief didn't help. At one point Edris slapped Shelly while she was holding Junior, and Shelly was so frightened that she called the police. Edris sat in jail for a few days after that incident, which gave Shelly just enough time to move in with family members. It was so sad to see that Edris was still tip toeing around in that cycle of violence, which had unfortunately been ingrained in him as a little boy, when he witnessed that same violence against Mama. It appeared that Edris was the most affected by the curse of domestic violence that we all witnessed whereas Stefon was a gentle soul who only hurt himself.

Dad had been back in Atlanta for a few years with Neomi and her ghetto family and we talked to him frequently. Neomi clocked Dad's every move, so we knew whenever we called she was always close by listening in on Dad's conversation. Neomi wanted to know what he was talking about with *his* children. As a result, Dad waited until Neomi wasn't around before he called to talk to us. It was crazy. When Neomi's son, Jason, was about 16, he lost his battle with kidney disease and passed away. I disliked Neomi wholeheartedly, but I felt bad for her losing her baby boy, especially at such a young age. He was truly a gifted and intelligent child. Not long after losing Jason, Dad slipped and fell while he was at home. The fall resulted in a neck injury making it painful for him to walk, so he started using a wheelchair to get around, and due to the injury, he required assistance in completing some of the most basic daily tasks. After a couple of years of dealing with Dad's restricted lifestyle, Neomi called Cheryl-Ann.

"I can *not* take care of your dad anymore," she exclaimed. "It's just too much for me. I think you guys need to come and get him."

"Ok Neomi," Cheryl-Ann replied. "Let me call PJ."

Over the years Cheryl-Ann had developed a friendship with Neomi, so it was easy for Neomi to call and complain to her. Cheryl-Ann didn't have a plan when she called PJ but they discussed what was going on and came up with one before PJ talked to me.

"Cheryl-Ann just called, and she said *we* need to go and get Dad."

"What do you mean *we* need to *go and get* Dad?" I asked. "What's wrong with Neomi?"

"I don't know. She's saying he's too much for her to handle."

"What happened to *for better or for worse*? So *now* he's too much for her to handle? Really? That's horrible."

"I know, but Cheryl-Ann said Neomi sounded overwhelmed."

"Let me get this straight," I said. "She and her family take Dad to Vegas without our knowledge; they get married; then she mortgages all of his properties to the hilt and takes all the proceeds; and now she is overwhelmed? No, she just has no more use for him."

"That sounds about right," PJ replied.

"Un-be-lievable!" I was livid.

My frustration wasn't directed at Dad because I loved him and truth be told, he needed to be with us anyway because according to Dad, Neomi was not providing appropriate care for him, and her actions bordered on neglect. After I calmed down and put things into perspective, I became excited about the prospect of having Dad back with us.

"Well, you know what, it'll be nice for the girls to have their only living grandparent close by," I told PJ and he agreed.

Cheryl-Ann and PJ decided that he would fly to Atlanta and bring Dad back to L.A. and that Cheryl-Ann and Rodney would provide primary care for Dad because PJ had a family to take care of and Cheryl-Ann and Rodney had no children.

It had been several years since Cheryl-Ann purchased her house, and luxury car with the proceeds from her lawsuit, and she had since lost them both. *I guess that's what happens when you buy things with ill-gotten gains,* I surmised. When Dad arrived back home, Cheryl-Ann and Rodney were back living in an apartment. They moved a few more times *with* Dad before settling into Neomi's old house in San Dimas. Neomi had owned the home with her ex-husband and tried to soften the blow of abandoning Dad by making it possible for Dad, Cheryl-Ann and Rodney to live in the home. The home was facing foreclosure, so Dad really bailed *her* out by assuming responsibility of the house. That was by far the only decent gesture Neomi ever made, but it was still for selfish reasons. Cheryl-Ann and Rodney took great care of Dad but his retirement funds helped greatly with the household expenses so it was no real sacrifice for them.

In early 1994, I was scheduled to take the Lieutenant's exam, which was administered at Fairfax High School. It was a beautiful, sunny winter morning, and my study partners and I met for breakfast at a deli near the school right before the test. We needed our bellies full so that we could concentrate. I had studied and exchanged a massive amount of materials and information with coworkers and my study partners for months, so I was ready. The task force I was working on ended, and instead of me going back to Newton working for the red headed hypocrite, Chief Parks made it possible for me to be reassigned to Foothill Division, which was closer to my home. It had been a few months since the Northridge earthquake and my home and other damaged properties throughout the city were in various stages of repair or demolition, and ours was under construction. By April of 1994, the results of the Lieutenant's Exam were in. However, instead of getting my pass/fail notice in the mail, I received a letter advising me that I was *disqualified* and unable to continue on in the testing process. I was in disbelief. I later found out that a disgruntled individual had initiated a complaint against me, saying that I failed the meet the qualifications to compete for lieutenant because I had not finished my year in the field as a Sergeant. I contacted Personnel Department to inquire further about the disqualification, and expressed my desire to appeal the Department's decision. It was true, that I had not completed my year as a Sergeant; however, I met the qualifications with my Detective Supervisory experience, while working at Internal Affairs Division for more than two years, which qualified me to compete, so my time in grade as a Sergeant was irrelevant. When I submitted my formal Appeal, I was informed that two other female candidates, both minorities, were also disqualified. The complaint specifically named, and targeted me, but they were collateral damage and they too were completely blindsided. I wanted the coward to reveal him or herself but they didn't. Within a few weeks, the rumors started. The most outrageous were those that accused me and the two other female detectives of *cheating*, which was the furthest thing from the truth. The Department launched an investigation and then Lieutenant Charlie Beck, who was working in the Police Commission, led the inquiry. Beck determined that the basis of our disqualification directly conflicted with a practice that had been allowed for the previous 15 years, which was that Internal Affairs Detective Supervisory experience could be used, in lieu of Sergeant experience, to qualify candidates for the Lieutenant's exam. Beck advised the powers to be that the complaint challenged the validity of the alternative supervisory qualifier but the Department maintained that we were still disqualified. They acknowledged that the disqualification was unfair to the three of us, and, as a result they tried to come up with a just remedy for the situation. One suggestion was to re-administer the entire test and the masses went ballistic. Our peers were adamant that we *cheated*, and they vehemently protested against the City giving a new test. Many of them angrily appeared before the Police Commission and the Police Commission told the mob that the disqualifications were due to a systemic issue and not an integrity issue, but they *still* upheld the faulty decision and disallowed us from continuing on in the process, and the new test remedy was abandoned because it was easier to upset three minority women and satisfy the remaining candidates. We were encouraged by a high-ranking Department official to file a lawsuit against the Department; however, we didn't want to commit career suicide by doing so because the LAPD was known for its retaliatory practices.

I was still reeling from the injustice done to me when, literally one month later, a great promotional opportunity became available. A Detective III position as Officer-In-Charge of a Traffic Collision Investigations Unit was being vacated by one of my former bosses, who was retiring. Len, a longtime Detective, reached out to me and encouraged me to apply for the position. I was working as a field Sergeant at Foothill Division and I wasn't ready to leave there, but I couldn't pass up the opportunity for a promotion, *and* the 11% pay raise that came with it. After a grueling interview with the Captain at the traffic division, and an exhaustive background investigation conducted by the Captain himself, I was selected for the job. They say that the best revenge is success, and within one month of the Lieutenant's exam disqualification, the three of us *cheaters* all promoted to the rank Detective III at different divisions.

Detective III Tia Morris 1994

I was excited about my new position but I was apprehensive about taking over the unit of tenured investigators, some of whom were my competitors, all male detectives, who had much more time and experience *in the field of traffic* than I did, but I had way more well rounded and supervisory experience than all of them. When I was chosen they were so angry that they banded together and filed an Employee Grievance stating that I was not qualified for the position. The grievance was not based on merit, so they did not succeed in ousting me.

Our house was still under construction and in order to make the structural repairs we needed to move out for about 4 months. Fortunately, Edris was living alone after Shelly left, and he had two bedrooms to spare. What I didn't know was that Edris had lost his trucking license due to a recent DUI, so he was not working and he needed financial assistance.

"T, yeah, you guys can come stay here until your house is finished," Edris offered. "I could use the help and summer's coming so I can watch the girls while you and PJ go to work, while I look for a job."

The girls were seven and nine years old, so they were pretty self-sufficient. They loved their Uncle Edris and his famous buttery, fattening grilled cheese sandwiches, and they loved playing outside with the kids who lived in his neighborhood, so we took him up on his offer. The same week that we moved in with Edris in June of 1994, former NFL great, OJ Simpson, was arrested for allegedly killing his ex-wife and her male friend. I watched the news as Al Cowlings drove his distraught friend all over town to avoid his pre-planned surrender. Later on during the trial, it was all over the news that Detective Martin Foster, who had garnered a reputation for being an *alleged* racist, had tampered with evidence at the Simpson crime scene. As part of the defense's strategy, Simpson's *Dream Team* of Defense Attorney's became aware of Foster's involvement in racist banter at WLA in 1983, when he was a young officer. That's when the media turned their attention towards me. They found out about my previous issues with Foster so they tried relentlessly to get me to confirm that Martin Foster was in fact a racist. Various Media outlets camped outside of my office in Downtown L.A. for weeks hoping to get an interview with me, and they stalked me at home as well. Johnny Cochran was attempting to discredit Foster's testimony when he said he never used the "N" word. They tried to show that Foster's disdain for black people was a motive for framing OJ. Cochran's investigators, many of them retired LAPD detectives, attempted to persuade me to tell them about my personal account of Fosters purported racist activity with MAW and WASP. As far as I was concerned, Cochran's crew had what they needed when they uncovered Laura Hart McKinny's taped interviews of Foster wherein they proved he used the "N" word so they didn't need me, and I was staying out of it to protect my career. Many years had passed since that humiliating time in my career, and there Foster and I were, pitted against each other during the O.J. Simpson trial. I wanted no parts of that circus so I took the high road and I refused to speak with the media or Cochran about Foster. In spite of my prior experience with him, I was not going to be used by the defense, and I was not going to ruin my career, or compromise my integrity, by being spiteful. I had moved on from Foster's ignorance and bullying, and did not allow myself to be lured into his cycle of hate, which perpetuated the racism, sexism, and bigotry on the department.

In September 1994, we returned home after the construction was completed. Shelly and Edris reconciled a few weeks later and she, and Junior, moved back in with Edris after we moved out. Stefon got out of prison late that September and went to stay with Edris and Shelly. I divided Mama's insurance money with the boys after the burial expenses were paid, and they were happy to receive the monetary assistance at that time. I also paid off Mama's car and I gave it to Edris. The summer was over and it was wonderful being back at home, with all of the beautiful cosmetic improvements, and it was just in time to get the girls ready for school. The girls attended a small Christian school near our home, that was a moderately diverse environment, with a good mixture of middle class Caucasian, African-American, Latino, and Asian families represented. The girls loved their school and were excited when PJ and I were able take off of work in order to join them for the school's chapel programs on Friday mornings. PJ and I liked the idea of the Christian school atmosphere, which reinforced the spiritual values and beliefs that we had established at home. We had always emphasized the importance of honesty, and told the girls that whatever mischief they engaged in was not worth lying about because that would only make bad situations worse. We explained that our jobs consisted of arresting the liars of the world and we didn't want them to be like those bad people. Brittany understood our advice and abided by it; but Natalia was another story altogether. One Sunday evening we were all at home. PJ, Brit and I were in the den. I was braiding Brittany's hair while she and PJ watched television. The den was on the second level of our tri level home and Natalia was in her bedroom on the third level of the house. All of a sudden, PJ became alarmed.

"Hey, do you smell smoke?" PJ asked. I paused for a moment and began sniffing the air in order to see if I smelled smoke.

"Oh my God, I *do* smell smoke." We immediately went into investigation mode.

"Natalia!" I yelled up the stairs as I walked in the direction of the girls' rooms. As I got closer I could see small wisps of smoke billowing from her room, and out into the hallway. I quickly entered her bedroom, where the smoke was coming from. "Natalia, are you playing with matches?" Natalia was startled as she turned and looked up at me.

"No, Mommy," she replied with her hands behind her back.

I walked further into the room towards the white dressers that lined one wall, and I observed two fresh burn marks on the top of one dresser as well as several burnt matches in the trash can, next to the dressers. PJ and Brittany followed me into Natalia's room; then the *real* interrogation began.

"Are you playing with matches?" PJ intervened.

"No, Daddy," Natalia said mimicking the tone she used when answering my initial inquiry. She was not budging.

"Natalia, tell the truth," PJ warned. "We can smell the smoke, and we can see the burn marks on your dresser. There are fresh matches in your trash can, and you are the only one up here. So just tell us the truth."

Natalia continued to deny that she was lighting matches, and denied that she had burnt her dressers. I could not believe she was not coming clean and continued to lie to the point that it infuriated PJ and me. I had never spanked either of the girls because I couldn't bring myself to hurt them even when they were naughty. PJ, however, was the disciplinarian, and he had no problem spanking them. In our version of "Good cop, Bad cop," all I had to do in order to get them to act right was to threaten them with telling their daddy. I know, I know. It wasn't right, but I took the easy way out. The interrogation went on for more than two hours, and even with the threat of a spanking looming over Natalia's head, she kept lying.

"Natalia, I promise, you will not get a spanking if you come clean," PJ offered.

Then, as if she couldn't take the stalemate any longer, Brittany attempted to rescue Natalia.

"Ok, Daddy," nine-year-old Brittany said. "Let me talk to her and see what's going on."

Often times, when Natalia found herself in a sticky situation, Brittany attempted to save the day. She wasn't always successful, but she kept trying. Brittany talked us into giving her a specified amount of time to convince seven-year-old Natalia to tell the truth. After a short time, the girls emerged from Brittany's room and came to our room.

"Daddy, Natalia has something to tell you. Go ahead and tell Daddy what you told me Natalia." Brittany was standing proudly as if she had won a Nobel Peace Prize, then Natalia spoke up.

"Daddy, I was *not* playing with matches." Brittany's jaw dropped, as she was clearly shocked that after 30 minutes in the room with Natalia she *still* refused to admit to playing with matches.

"Natalia!" Brittany screamed. "That's not what you just told me!"

I lost it. I smacked Natalia across the side of her little face with my open hand. It wasn't hard enough to hurt her, but firm enough to get her attention. Just as I was drawing back my hand from her face, she turned to run away and ran right into my bedpost. She fell to the floor and ended up with a knot the size of a quarter in the middle of her forehead. I couldn't believe I smacked her. But she deserved it because we were not raising liars. PJ then spanked her and took her to her room where he explained his actions. He was dumbfounded so he wanted to see what was going on inside of her head to make her lie. They bonded for about two hours.

"Maybe you just struck one match, baby girl," he said, trying to understand Natalia's curiosity. "Now tell me what happened ok?"

"Daddy," Natalia began with a tear-stained face, and a growing knot on her forehead. "The devil got into me."

"What?" PJ asked, confused and a bit concerned.

"The devil got into you too daddy when you spanked me." At that point PJ could barely contain his laughter. He ended their conversation and left Natalia's room shaking his head and laughing out loud.

"That girl is crazy," PJ said. "We need to get her some counseling or something." He was laughing but we were both really concerned. We had seen and heard too many stories of children who claimed to be possessed by the devil when they murdered their parents in their sleep, and stuff like that, and we were not going out that way.

"Now *that's* clever," I replied. "I think she is a con artist, and I'm really scared about that."

The next morning, I dropped the girls off at school and went on to work. When I returned to the school that afternoon to pick them up, the Principal called me into the office.

"Mrs. Morris, can I talk to you?"

"Sure, what's going on?" I asked.

She seemed a bit apprehensive but she seemed pleasant enough, so I wondered what she needed to speak to me about.

"I hate to tell you this, but Natalia came to school this morning with a bruise on her forehead." *Oh shit,* I thought, *I know where this is going.*

"As a mandated reporter, I had to notify the Department of Children Services for suspected child abuse." The Principal was very apologetic as she continued, "Natalia's teacher asked her what happened to her head and she told her that you slapped her."

I was not surprised but it was obvious Natalia did not tell the teacher that *she* caused the knot on her forehead from hitting the bedpost.

A few days later I received a call from a Detective, who happened to be a friend of mine. We had worked together a few years prior in the Abused Child Unit, of all places. She told me that based on her interview with both girls, and no evidence of previous abuse, it was an open and shut case. I knew I hadn't abused Natalia, but I was glad the investigation by my Department was cut short. A few days later I was at home with the girls when the doorbell rang at about 7:30 PM. PJ was still at work. I answered the door and in the pouring rain there stood a Social Worker on my porch.

"Mrs. Tia Morris?"

"Yes."

"I'm a social worker from the Department of Child and Family Services and I need to come in and inspect your home and your children."

"No problem. Come on in." I responded intending to cooperate fully.

After interviewing and visually inspecting the girls, she wrapped up her visit.

"Ok ma'am, I'm closing this case because it's obvious your children are not in an abusive home. They appear to be healthy and happy."

"Thank you," I replied sarcastically as I rolled my eyes.

"But, you have to promise me you are not going to hit her again."

"I'm not going to promise you that," I said stubbornly. "I didn't *spank* her. I *slapped* her and I did not leave the mark on her forehead. I will promise you *this*, if she tries to burn my house down again, I will *beat* her. My kids are not abused, but they will continue to be disciplined so, you can leave now."

The woman looked at me like I was crazy as I stared her down.

"But Mrs. Morris, you *have* to promise me or…" I ushered her out of the door before she could finish her sentence. I locked the door and turned off the porch light.

I knew she was just doing her job, but I was mad that she was trying to tell me how to raise my children, so I was not promising her anything. *Goodnight lady*, I said to myself as I walked away from the door just like Loretta Devine walked away from Gregory Hines in the movie Waiting to Exhale.

It was mid 1995, and it had been several months since Shelly and Edris reunited. Shelly resumed her childcare business, and she and Edris tried to make their marriage work. Unfortunately, however, Edris was still an alcoholic, and he was in and out of jail over the next year and a half for domestic violence episodes he had with Shelly, and for DUI related offenses. In late 1996, Edris and Shelly got into one of their heated arguments and Edris threatened to throw her off of the balcony of their upstairs apartment. During the altercation, he flung two-year-old Junior across the room by his arm, because Junior was crying. Shelly admittedly slapped Edris first, anticipating his rage, but when the police arrived, they hauled *him* off to jail because of his previously reported domestic incidents. Afterwards, Shelly wasted no time securing a Restraining Order against Edris, to ensure that he kept his distance. Although they were not together anymore, I maintained a friendly relationship with Shelly, so that I could still spend time with Junior. Shelly and Junior remained in the duplex over Frank and his parents. When Edris was released from jail he went to stay with friends. Shelly was very protective of Junior, so she begged me not to allow Edris to come around when Junior was in my care. As a mother, I understood her concern and honored her request. I thought Shelly was very responsible and admired that she had built her childcare venture into a thriving at home business. When the time came for Junior to start school Shelly home schooled him because she had limited support and could not afford to take him to and from school. When Shelly shut her business down for the day, she made herself available during the evening hours to assist with caring for Frank's mother, who was bedridden. Shelly would sponge bathe her, and braid her hair. Shelly knew that Frank, who was also her landlord, did not approve of the Child Care business in the upstairs unit, so as a fair compromise, she felt the need to help with his mother. He in turn stopped griping about the noisy kids.

By Thanksgiving of 1996, Shelly and Edris had been split up for a couple years. Shelly had plans for the holiday weekend, so I agreed to keep Junior for her. She came to the house early on Thanksgiving morning and when she pulled into the driveway, I happily met her at the car. I noticed that she was driving Frank's car with him in the passenger seat, which was odd. She was wearing a robe and had her hair tied up in a scarf as if she had just rolled out of bed, and that too was odd. As I looked at her, I thought, *I know she did not drive all the way from LA to the Valley in her pajamas with Frank in the car.* Junior exited the rear passenger door after wiggling out of his booster seat, and Frank, whom I had not seen since Mama died, slowly exited through the passenger door of his car. I felt sorry for him as he was disabled from the massive stroke he suffered. We greeted each other and then he got back in the car. I was quite thrown off by the entire scene. I wondered why Shelly was wearing a robe, and why she was driving Frank's car? I tried not to judge the situation before I knew the facts. Before I could put my feelers out there, Shelly offered, during our brief conversation, that Junior was *jealous* of the time she spent with Frank, and that he *acted out* whenever Frank *spent the night*. At that point it was abundantly clear that Shelly was sleeping with Frank, my mother's widower. I felt she was stupid for revealing that to me, and I thought of how desperate and disrespectful she was for engaging in that relationship. She was a single parent trying to raise her son, and he was a widower, recently disabled, and of course desirous of companionship, but I was still dumbfounded by their decision to date each other. I didn't expect much from Frank, but how could *Shelly* stoop that low, and then tell me about it? I couldn't place all the blame on Shelly because it takes two to tango, so Frank was just as responsible for the ongoing booty call as Shelly was. They were both wrong in my opinion, so I *was* judging. Before Mama died, she and Shelly had a great relationship, or so I thought. Shelly's decision bothered me greatly, but I did not say anything to her about my opinion. Shelly must have felt guilty because after she picked Junior up from that weekend visit, I received a letter in the mail, which said in part:

Hi Tia, I wanted you to know that since I have been helping Frank with his mom we have become very close. I know it doesn't look right but he needs my help. I wanted you to be the first to know that he wants to marry me and I am considering it since I need to secure a home and future for Junior and me. I just figured that if I marry Frank I would inherit the duplex one-day and not have to worry about my future. I love you like a sister and hope that you can understand where I am coming from. I want you in my life and Junior needs you too.

I guess she was dumb enough to think that by cozying up to Frank, and combing his mom's hair, she was going to inherit the family property and live happily ever after. Of course I cared about Junior's future too, but securing it in that way was wrong on so many levels. Not once did she mention anything about love between the two of them. I showed the letter to PJ.

"Wow. Is she on dope or dog food?" He asked jokingly. "Is she *that* desperate to use him like that? You said they were messing around and I guess you were right."

"Yeah, she *has* to be desperate and that's sad that she feels she has to use him to secure her future when she needs to do that for herself. When she was here the other day she told me how they went to Disneyland and poor Frank was trying to eat an ice cream cone with his good hand, and she said she had to keep wiping his hand because ice cream was dripping all over the damn place faster than he could lick it."

"Oh shit, they went to Disneyland? Oh, they are serious huh?"

"Yes, boy you are crazy. I'm really torn about abandoning my relationship with Shelly. I mean out of respect for Mama I feel I should. I just don't want to sever ties with Junior, but now that I received this little courtesy explanation I'm good with severing ties."

I believed situations always worked out for the best. I never responded to Shelly's letter and we maintained a very distant relationship from that point on. I just prayed about it.

Remember, Tia, I reminded myself, *Romans 12:19 in the King James Bible says, "Dearly beloved, avenge not yourselves, but rather give place unto wrath: for it is written, Vengeance is mine, I will repay, saith the Lord; Leviticus 19:18 says, "Do not seek revenge or bear a grudge against anyone among your people, but love your neighbor as yourself. I am the LORD, and Deuteronomy 32:35 says, "It is mine to avenge; I will repay. In due time their foot will slip; their day of disaster is near and their doom rushes upon them."*

I felt better after I prayed about it. A few months went by and Edris contacted me from jail. It was obvious he had not learned his lesson because his crazy butt was in custody again for a domestic violence incident involving *another* woman; a fellow alcoholic druggie chick, who he started dating after he and Shelly split up. Edris called me because he wanted me to facilitate a call from him to Junior. Edris and Shelly were not yet divorced, and I forgot she still had the restraining order in effect prohibiting Edris from contacting her, or coming to within 500 feet of her. When I refused to make a three-way call for Edris, he asked me to arrange a visit with him and Junior at my house when he was released from jail.

"No Edris," I said. "I am so tired of dealing with you and Shelly's crap, so I'm going to give you Shelly's business phone number and you call her yourself and work out your custody issues. I don't want anything to do with either one of you or your drama."

I didn't have the heart to tell him that his soon-to-be ex-wife was sleeping with his former stepfather. Apparently, Edris called Shelly immediately after hanging up the phone with me, because shortly after my conversation with him Shelly had the nerve to call me.

"Tia, why did you give Edris my phone number?" She asked without so much as a salutation. "I have a restraining order against him so he is not to contact me or come to within 500 feet of me, or Junior. I really don't appreciate you giving him my phone number."

"Girl, he can't do anything to you because he's in jail," I advised. "You all need to work out your child custody issues and leave me out of it. I want nothing to do with either one of you." I hung up on Shelly before she could say another word. I was sick and tired of her and Edris.

I was still working as a Detective Officer-in-Charge at Central Traffic Division, but I was getting bored in that assignment so I decided it was time to study *again* for Lieutenant. After I was disqualified from the previous test, I had time to think about what I really wanted to do with my career as I had about 15 years left to go before retirement. The girls kept us busy at home taking them to dance recitals, Tae Kwon Do, and basketball tournaments, but it was time for me to decide where I wanted to end up on the department before it was too late. I hadn't seen or heard from Stefon after Edris and Shelly broke up. Stefon moved out of their apartment when Edris went to jail, and Shelly got the restraining order. Stefon had already violated our home so he was not welcome to ever step foot in our home again. I didn't know where he was.

CHAPTER 11

"The New Millennium"

By the start of the summer of 1999, I reflected back on things that had gone on in my career as I prepared to enter the new millennium. I had already gone through the sexist and racist crap at West L.A. in the early 80's; and the hate mail drama from my peers at Newton in the early 1990's; and at the current time in '99 I had been dealing with workplace issues at Central Traffic Detectives for a few years. The male detectives, who worked for me, did everything they could to make my work environment a living nightmare because they did not want to work for a woman. I had been there for six years but I still had not mastered how to handle all the nonsense they were throwing my way. Luckily for me the Captain who hired me was very supportive and stood beside me all the way trying to protect me at every turn. What I really liked about his leadership was that he did not intervene and take up for me, but rather he listened to how *I* wanted to handle each situation and then he offered his opinion and/or direction, which he thought was optimal to handle the situation at hand. The best advice he gave me was to *document everything* because whatever was not documented did not happen, so I did just that. He also reviewed all of my negative documentation before I served it on an employee to ensure that I did not come across as emotional or angry. It was about the three-year mark that the Captain, who hired me, transferred out of the division; but before he left, he briefed the new Captain on the ongoing problems in my unit, as well as the barrage of complaints from the malcontents about my leadership. I met with the new Captain right away after he transferred in.

"Nice to meet you Detective Morris. You know, Captain Slater briefed me on the plethora of issues that are going on but I need to see for myself what the problem is in detectives. I think I am going to request that the Department conduct a workplace assessment to identify the issues rather than take action myself based on someone else's observations. How does that sound?" Slater was a stuttering nerd, but he seemed harmless, so I gave him a chance before I judged him.

"Ok, Captain. Sounds good to me," I replied. "I welcome the oversight. During my first 3 years here I have been subjected to consistent tomfoolery and pure sabotage. I have worked painstakingly hard to try and alleviate the problems here and the problems still persist. So *please* do the workplace assessment."

The assessment actually turned out to be a good thing for me. One of the Department psychologists was assigned to conduct the assessment and, as with most bands of crooks, the institutional terrorists who were causing the problems in my unit fell apart when the Psychologist got each of them by themselves. They did not disappoint. They turned on one another and accused *each other* of being *the problem* in detectives and not me. By the time the 2-month inquiry was complete, I was completely vindicated and found to be quite competent. Most importantly, I was praised for doing things the *right way*. I had great systems in place, which held employees accountable; and those systems also ensured that quality service was provided to the citizens we served. After *my* interview as part of the assessment, the psychologist discussed the results of the entire inquiry with me.

"Detective Morris," the Psychologist said. "How did you survive in that unit for the past three years? I don't understand why you didn't just leave. I have never seen anything like this before. My investigation revealed that the problem back in detectives is that there is ongoing racial and gender bias directed at you."

"So, let me get this straight Dr. Cross," I replied. "*They* are misbehaving so *I* should have left? Why would I let them run me away from *my* job? I will *never* give them the satisfaction."

"I guess you are right Detective." He said as he laughed embarrassingly.

I later thanked Captain Slater for having the inquiry done. He was relieved that there was no systemic problem in the unit, just as my previous

Captain had reported; but the bigger issue was that there *was* racial and gender bias identified and yet there was *nothing* done about *that*. I didn't push the issue. I was just happy I was vindicated and it was documented.

My family and I had spent a lot of time on the weekends with Dad, Cheryl-Ann, and Rodney, most often at their home in San Dimas, or out and about, when Dad felt like getting out of the house. We hadn't had a negative episode with Cheryl-Ann in a while so we, in our forgiving spirits, allowed her back into the family fold. We always felt comfortable at Dad's house, and Dad loved being surrounded by PJ and Cheryl-Ann, and his grand children. We especially loved going to Rodney's New Moon celebrations that he hosted when his witch and warlock friends came to the house as part of their clairvoyant rituals. We all participated in what we considered to be a fun, hocus pocus type event, but the clairvoyants considered it to be some serious psychic networking. Cheryl-Ann and Rodney still considered themselves to be God-fearing people and not devil-worshippers as depicted in some movies when psychics were involved. Even some of PJ's coworkers joined us at the New Moon celebrations on occasion because Rodney had met them and had become their personal psychic. Apparently Rodney was pretty good, and that is why people came from far and wide to see *Dr. Rodney* as he called himself. PJ and I would sit on the floor with our backs against the wall and eat and drink and watch the witches and warlocks prance around the room. They were weird, but fascinating. It was truly a sight to see. During each celebration, we participated in the banishing bowl ritual where we placed our handwritten proclamations into a large decorative bowl and banished all that was negative in our lives at that time. When Rodney set fire to the contents in the bowl we watched intently as the smoke emanated from the bowl, and floated up into the rafters of the 20-foot high ceiling beams in Dad's living room.

It had been a few years since Dad was back with us and in spite of his jovial nature and excellent care his physical condition worsened over time. He had bone spurs in his neck, but his mind was as sharp as a tack. By early July 1999, he was hospitalized and within a day or two he fell into a coma. Because his prognosis was not good, Cheryl-Ann called Neomi and told her what was going on so Neomi hopped on the first thing smokin' and landed her ratchetness back in California a few days later. PJ and I, and Cheryl-Ann and Rodney held a vigil at Dad's bedside every day for about a week. When Neomi arrived he was still in a coma and, for PJ and I, it was like déjà vu because we had dealt with a similar situation with Mama. One day when PJ and I arrived at the hospital I was walking slightly ahead of PJ and as I was about to walk into Dad's room I poked my head into the doorway first to make sure the coast was clear for visitors. Just as I did, I saw Neomi standing over Dad's bed squeezing his hand. I paused because I didn't want to intrude. So, as I went to knock on the doorjamb suddenly Neomi started talking to Dad.

"Where's the money Percy? Where's the money? Come on, tell me, where's the money? Percy, where's the money?" Neomi repeatedly asked in an exasperated tone. Of course Dad didn't answer because he was in a coma.

Neomi quickly and slyly looked around the room and towards the door. PJ and I backed away into the hall so she wouldn't see us. I could not believe my ears. That crazy old gold digger always thought Dad had millions stashed away somewhere, and she was determined to find them before he left this earth. I wanted to say, *you spent all of his money, remember?* But, instead, we just stood listening to Neomi badgering Dad. We waited for a moment and then loudly walked into the room to avoid causing an awkward moment for Neomi in the middle of her diatribe. She didn't see us standing in the doorway, and we didn't let on that we had heard her.

"Oh, hey, Neomi," PJ said with no expression as we walked into the room.

"Oh, hey, I just got here." Neomi said. "He is looking good." She said looking like the cat that swallowed the canary. She had no clue we heard her. It was a shame

We visited with Dad for a few hours before heading home. The morning after the shameful inquiry, Dad miraculously awoke from his coma. Doctors couldn't explain it, but his vitals were in the normal range for his age, so he was discharged. Disappointed and still broke, Neomi returned to Atlanta on that same day. Dad was pretty much bedridden after that because it was too painful for him to sit up for long periods of time. Cheryl-Ann hired Wilbur, a middle aged male caretaker, to look after Dad when she and Rodney were at work.

"Daddy," she said. "I got you a caretaker, so you are not at home alone when me and Rodney are away."

Neither Cheryl-Ann nor Rodney could independently come home during the day to check on Dad because they were glued at the hip most of the time. Rodney didn't drive, so he rode to and from work with Cheryl-Ann everyday and as a result, they were always together.

"Girl, don't you bring no woman up in here to wipe my butt," Dad whined playfully. "I need a man who can lift me up, so I can wipe my own ass." Dad said grinning from ear to ear. He was quite a character.

"Oh Daddy, knock it off. You are a mess. I got a *man* so he can help you to the bathroom where you can wipe your own behind." Cheryl-Ann replied as she laughed heartily at Dad's candor.

Dad and Wilbur quickly developed a great rapport and Cheryl-Ann and Rodney trusted Wilbur as they could see he was doing a great job responding to Dad's every need. One day in mid July 1999, Cheryl-Ann and Rodney had gone off to work and Dad was at home *shuckin' and jivin'* with Wilbur, as usual. Dad's room was on the first floor of the two-story home and it was just a stone's throw away from the kitchen.

"Hey son, can you go get me some water?" Dad requested of Wilbur.

"Ok, I'll be right there Mr. Percy," Wilbur replied. "Let me finish getting these clothes out of the dryer ok?"

Wilbur continued folding clothes in the downstairs den before getting Dad a glass of water. Dad lay silently on his side with his back to the door when Wilbur returned to the room.

"Here you go, man," Wilbur said as he sat the water down on the bedside table. "Percy, here take your water, man," Wilbur repeated as he reached up to turn on the lamp. When Dad did not respond, Wilbur gently grabbed Dad's shoulder, and pulled him onto his back so he could see Dad's face.

Wilbur then realized Dad's breathing was shallow so he shook Dad but Dad remained solemn. Wilbur ran back into the den and called 911, and then called Cheryl-Ann. A short time later, Cheryl-Ann called PJ and told him Dad was dead.

We packed an overnight bag and loaded up the girls and rushed over to Dad's house. When we arrived at the house, Dad's body was still there lying on the floor on his back in the den, and he was covered with a sheet. The paramedics and the sheriffs had already left the scene. They had moved Dad to the floor in order to facilitate life saving efforts on a flat, hard surface. The girls were preteens, so they clearly understood what was going on. Dad was their last living grandparent, so his death definitely created a void in their lives.

"Well guys," Cheryl-Ann said. "Doctor Moore is still going to sign off on the death certificate even though he just gave dad a clean bill of health. Do you think we need to have an autopsy done?"

"Why? Do you think Wilbur killed him or something?" PJ responded facetiously.

"Hell naw!" Wilbur retorted. "Ya'll hired me 'cause the man was sick. Don't try to put no case on me." Wilbur exclaimed as he sat on the couch.

"No Percy. I don't think Wilbur killed Daddy," Cheryl-Ann replied embarrassed that PJ would joke like that in front of Wilbur. Whenever Cheryl-Ann scolded PJ, she typically used his full first name. "Why would you say something like that Percy?"

"I'm just kidding girl," PJ said. "But, no, we don't need an autopsy unless we suspect foul play." PJ started laughing uncontrollably as Wilbur walked towards him. Wilbur stepped over Dad's body and playfully pushed PJ out of his way.

"You damn Homicide Detective," Wilbur mumbled as he walked towards the door to go out for a smoke. He was amused by the levity in the room.

"So, Cheryl-Ann who's coming to get Dad's body?" PJ asked as he straddled Dad's body.

PJ pulled the sheet away from Dad's upper torso to get a better look at him while me and the girls circled Dad's body as if we were conducting a science experiment. We walked around the house for hours as if Dad was just sleeping on the floor, but when the mortuary arrived late that afternoon, and loaded dad onto the gurney, we all broke down and cried as the realization sank in that he was gone. They transported Dad's body to Angelus Funeral Home where Mama was also prepared for her burial. The only difference was they prepared Dad to be flown to Atlanta where he was buried in the family plot next to Virginia. Neomi stayed in Atlanta and awaited the arrival of Dad's body versus heading to California when Dad died; and we all flew to Atlanta for Dad's funeral. Unlike Neomi and Cheryl-Ann, PJ and I were self-sufficient and we never asked Dad for anything. He didn't owe us anything, so when he died we did not look to inherit a thing from his estate. Neomi made sure the Trust Fund, Dad had before he married her was null and void so that was gone. Neomi was living in the family home in Georgia and it was in her name after she refinanced it, so that was gone. PJ didn't know of any other real assets to be divided between him and Cheryl-Ann, except for some unoccupied land the family owned in Georgia, which was in PJ and Cheryl-Ann's names, which PJ signed over to Cheryl Ann, so that was gone. Cheryl-Ann and Rodney and Neomi all benefitted monetarily from Dad's death. When PJ asked Cheryl-Ann how much was her inheritance, Cheryl-Ann replied, "Oh, Percy I don't want to say." Clearly whatever Dad left behind should have been split between the two of them, but since Dad lived with Cheryl-Ann and Rodney, she felt entitled to 100% of all of his personal property. So Cheryl-Ann and Rodney took their riches and ran to Atlanta.

On New Years Eve 1999, the country was a buzz about the New Millennium and everyone was anxious to see what, if any, fallout there would be at the turn of the century. PJ and I were antsy waiting for the countdown, which was still hours away, so we decided some Tito's Tacos would rest well in our bellies, and calm our nerves. I didn't like going out on New Years Eve because of the idiots firing bullets into the air, and all the drunk drivers on the road, but the craving for Tito's Tacos was overwhelming. PJ didn't feel like the 25-mile ride to the restaurant from our house, so I agreed to go and bring food back. The girls were in San Bernardino spending New Years Eve with my Aunt Linda and her girls, so off to Tito's I went, alone. The restaurant was located in Culver City just east of the 405 Freeway. It was about 8PM when I left, so there was plenty enough time for me to get back home before the craziness started at midnight. It was chilly and dewy in Culver City on that Friday night, and Tito's was just as busy as ever. Rather than parking in the tiny cramped parking lot, which was always full, I parked at the curb west of the location, where my SUV was only partially covered by the 405 Freeway overpass. I went inside the restaurant and after waiting in line for about 10 minutes I heard what sounded like a huge explosion. There was a loud bang and tree branches, and other unrecognizable debris went flying everywhere outside. Everyone in the restaurant gasped, and then paused, as we all tried to figure out what was happening. *Was the New Millennium starting off with a bang, literally?* I wondered.

Just as the dust settled several of us ran outside to see what was going on and there it was, the front of my SUV flattened like a pancake. There was a black mustang involved in a collision on the 405 Freeway just over the area where my car was parked that broke through the guardrail and landed on top of my car. I couldn't believe my eyes. I was so thankful that my girls were not with me because they probably would have stayed in the car while I went inside. *I hope that this is not a sign of things to come in the New Year?* I thought prayerfully. I called PJ and told him what happened and he *had* to get up and come to Tito's after all. I was relieved that he did not want to come with me in the first place, because, he would have been sitting in the car waiting for me to get the food. After Culver City PD finished the traffic collision reports and towed my vehicle away we finally made it back home just in time to watch the clock strike midnight. Wait for it, wait for it. Hey, nothing happened so the transition into the New Millennium ended up being uneventful.

We started 2000 without Dad. PJ and I loved our siblings, but we couldn't count on any of them for anything. Cheryl-Ann and Rodney became empty nesters when Dad passed, and Neomi, the witch, was able to *move on* for real. Dad loved Cheryl-Ann more than anything in this world, and she could do no wrong in his eyes, so it was good that she was there to provide *him* with lots of love and attention during his final years.

On March 19, 2000, my Aunt Laberta, Mama's older sister died of breast cancer. I had spoken with Aunt Laberta from time to time while she was going through cancer treatment, and all she said she was that she had a cancerous lump on her back, so I never knew that she had *breast* cancer. My cousin Will Jr. later told me that she had noticed a lump in her *left* breast, in the early 90's, but she was afraid to get it checked out like so many African American women, who die from the disease all too young. Aunt Laberta finally got up the nerve to seek medical attention, but, unfortunately she waited much too long. She had her left breast and her underarm glands removed and after the operation, she bounced back very quickly. She was in remission for five years and living her normal active life, however, her symptoms returned and her health declined rapidly after that recurrence. Ironically, unbeknownst to us Aunt Laberta and Mama were battling breast cancer at the same time in the 90's. Aunt Laberta was literally in cancer treatment when she came for Mama's wedding. That made me very sad in hindsight.

By late 2000, I had been studying to take the Lieutenant's exam again. In addition to my boredom in my detective assignment, rumors persisted about the department's intent to disband Traffic Detective Units throughout the City, so I was looking forward to promoting out of the unit instead of being displaced. Things were going well at home with PJ and the girls. Brittany was a sophomore in high school and doing extremely well academically; and she was playing Varsity Basketball at Campbell Hall, a prestigious private school in North Hollywood. Natalia was in the 8th grade at a public middle school in Northridge, an upscale Valley community, and she was also doing well in school. Natalia excelled in the performing arts and English, but she was not into Physical Education or sports. PJ and I encouraged the girls' individual aspirations, so we were fine with her not gravitating towards sports.

By the spring of 2001, Natalia was about to graduate from middle school. Earlier in the school year she had befriended a beautiful biracial girl named Shantal. Her mother was a very attractive black woman, and her estranged father was a Hispanic bootleg limo driver. Shantal lived with her mother Taylor, her older sister Lonnie, and younger half brother Jeremy. They lived near the middle school that Natalia and Shantal attended; in an older one story home in a very nice neighborhood. Taylor 's much older, very successful real estate broker boyfriend, Mikael, owned the house where she lived with her three children. Taylor was a few years younger than I was, and she was very lenient with 13-year-old Shantal and14-year-old Lonnie. Taylor was the type of mother, who wanted to be best friends with her teenaged girls, so she acted as such by personally taking them to their boyfriends' homes for evening visits on the weekends, and she would pick them up at about midnight following those visits. I personally would not have done that with my girls at that age, but that was her parenting style. Shantal spent many weekends at our home with Natalia, and she accompanied us to Brittany's basketball tournaments around the city just to hang out with Natalia. Natalia had no choice but to go with us because we were not leaving her at home alone. We saw what the streets had to offer young people, so we held our prize possessions, our girls, close to the vest as much as we could. Shantal was very sweet, and in a short period of time, her mother Taylor and I had fostered a good relationship. It was obvious that Taylor loved her children, but she was misguided herself because of her upbringing. Taylor was off work on disability from an injury she sustained while working in the real estate office where she met her boyfriend Mikael. Taylor maintained a very clean home and her children were always very neat and well put together.

Earlier in the school year, Natalia and I had discussed where she wanted to attend High School because she was not interested in attending Campbell Hall with Brittany. Natalia wanted nothing to do with the uniforms and the stuffiness of prep school and the lifestyles of the rich and famous kids. She wanted to be able to spread her wings at a public school where she could wear what she wanted and meet all kinds of kids bussed in from all over the city, so Hollywood High School was right at the top of her list. Brittany and Natalia were like oil and water; total opposites in every way. They couldn't have been more different except for their love of dance. They both embraced the various styles of dance and both were excellent dancers; that was the only thing they had in common besides their parents. Brittany was shy and socially awkward in that she thought she didn't fit in with any clique of girls outside of the basketball arena. Natalia was not shy, and was fascinated with the kids from *the hood*, and I didn't quite understand that. Hollywood High was a Performance Arts Magnet, and when I submitted the admissions application, Natalia was entered into a lottery type system. We prayed that she got in because several of her friends also applied to Hollywood High and many of them had danced together for years as part of a dance troupe; and they all took dance classes at the Millennium Dance Complex in the artsy section of trendy North

Hollywood. We were notified by the Los Angeles Unified School District (LAUSD) that Natalia was number 8 on the waiting list for Hollywood High School. I contacted the school and was told that there was a great possibility that she would get in because she was so high on the list, and that they always made it through about 20 on the waiting list. All of Natalia's friends, who applied, got in during the initial lottery so I knew Natalia would be devastated if she did not get a chance to attend, so we crossed our fingers, toes, and eyes and waited patiently. Natalia remained confident and was excited about attending Hollywood High School, and excited about all the high school activities that came along with high school. She started asking me about the various high school activities and specifically asked me if I would allow her to attend a High School Prom while she was still in middle school.

"No, you are only 14," I told her. "You will attend prom in due time. Like when you are in high school."

"But, I'm almost in high school now Mommy. What's the difference?"

"There's a time for everything Natalia, and it's not time for a prom just yet. End of story."

I thought it was odd for her to be pressing the issue about attending a prom but I just thought she was excited about high school. Natalia and Shantal were going to be attending different high schools but they expected that their friendship would remain in tact. As the school year ended Taylor had broken up with her boyfriend/sugar daddy and she and her children had moved out of his home and into an apartment in the same area. Mikael was nice enough to assist her with securing an apartment in the same neighborhood so the kids could finish out the school year at their respective schools and he even agreed to pay the rent at her new apartment for six months to give her time to get on her feet. I felt bad for her and her children being uprooted and having to live in an apartment after being in a more stable environment, but they seemed to make the best of the situation.

PJ had become a Delegate for our Police Protective League, and he and I made plans to attend the League Delegates Conference in Palm Springs in late May of that year. Brittany had a basketball tournament that very same weekend, so we made arrangements for her to stay with her high school basketball coach

Freda, who was also a longtime friend and our neighbor. Freda had recruited Brittany to play for her at Campbell Hall, which was largely the reason she went there. We had planned on taking Natalia with us to Palm Springs, but she had different plans. Taylor asked me if Natalia could stay with Shantal on that weekend since Shantal had stayed with us on so many occasions. PJ and I were hesitant because our parenting styles were so different from Taylor's, but we relented and allowed Natalia to stay with Shantal that weekend. Natalia was 14 years old, and we trusted that she would be ok. After getting the girls squared away on that Friday afternoon that we left for Palm Springs, PJ and I set out for a relaxing weekend in the beautiful desert community. Taylor and I agreed that she would pick Natalia up from school that Friday afternoon when she went to get Shantal, and she would take Natalia to school on the following Monday and I would pick her up after school as usual. Sounded like a good plan to me. I had left my contact information with Taylor and Freda, and even called them when we arrived in Palm Springs to ensure all was good with the girls. They each assured me that all was well. I called again on Saturday evening just to make sure the girls were still okay, and once again they each verified all was well. Natalia was exceptionally perky on the phone that evening, which piqued my interest a little bit but not enough to comment on it. The weekend getaway was great, and by the time Monday rolled around it was business as usual. I arrived a little bit early at Natalia's school that Monday afternoon as I always did, and I waited in my car at the curb right in front of the entrance to the school. After sitting there for a little bit, I spotted Taylor across the way in her car, and within minutes she was knocking at my car window so I talked to her for a bit and asked her about how the weekend went.

"Oh girl, we had a great time this past weekend. Everything was good." Taylor said.

Taylor looked worn out and seemed a little preoccupied. She found it hard to make eye contact with me, but I just figured she was embarrassed because of her recent split from her sugar daddy. Over the next few days during our curbside meetings Taylor shared with me intimate details of her split.

"Are you and the kids ok?" I asked. "I'm just shocked that you and Mikael split up."

"Yeah. But I guess he had every reason to kick me out." She said as she leaned into the passenger side window. "A few years ago, I was at a family party girl and I got drunk so my cousin took me home. I was so damn drunk that I had sex with my cousin and I got pregnant, and I finally told Mikael about it when he repeatedly asked about my son's father."

"Wow, really? That's a trip." I actually felt sorry for her, but that's all I could say.

The week flew by after our Palm Springs getaway. On that Friday evening Natalia and I were at home while PJ and Brittany were at basketball practice. Natalia was upstairs in her room with the door closed while I sat in the downstairs den watching TV when the phone rang.

"Hi, may I speak to Mrs. Morris?" Natalia and I picked up at the same time.

"Mommy, it's for you." Natalia yelled.

"Ok got it." Natalia hung up the phone when she heard me on the line. "Hello?"

"Hi Tia? This is Donna."

Donna was the mother of a young boy, who was one of Natalia's closest friends in middle school. Randy was a sweetheart and he and Natalia considered themselves to be like brother and sister. Randy, at that time, was Shantal's boyfriend, so the three of them spent a lot of time together at school and at home. I had known Donna and her husband for as long as Natalia and Randy were friends, as we often ran into each other at the kids' school events. Donna knew that PJ and I were cops, and she also knew that we kept a tight reign on Natalia. Donna and I did not talk on the phone so I was surprised that she called.

"Oh, hey Donna," I replied. "What's up girl?"

"Are you alone? I don't want Natalia to know that I'm calling."

"Yes, I'm alone," I said. "PJ and Brittany are not here and Natalia is upstairs in her room."

"Ok, good. Well, did you know that Natalia went to a Prom last weekend when you were gone?"

"Come again." I said as I gripped the phone tighter.

"I have been pondering over this all week, and because I know the kind of parents you and PJ are, I decided that I needed to say something." Donna continued.

"What are you talking about Donna?" My heart was pounding.

"Well, I talked to my husband and he said for me to stay out of it, but I decided to tell you because I figured you didn't know, and I would want someone to do the same for me if it were my daughter," Donna explained.

I was getting mad as Donna continued to talk because I didn't know what she was talking about, but I was starting to understand that it was about something inappropriate that Natalia had orchestrated.

"You know on Saturday night when you called to check in on Natalia? Well, I was there and there was a huge undertaking at that time by Taylor to get her ready to attend a Prom at Hollywood High School," Donna explained. "I took Randy to Taylor's apartment to pick up Shantal because she was coming back to the house to visit with Randy for a couple of hours while Natalia went to the Prom. When we got to the apartment, I walked to the rear bedroom, where Taylor was getting Natalia all dolled up. She gave Natalia a long black dress to wear and some shoes that were actually too big for Natalia's small feet, and she fixed Natalia's hair in an up do style. I stood by for a little bit in awe of what was going on when Taylor turned to me and said, 'Whew if her momma finds out I let her go to this prom I'm going to have to get out of town. Hee hee hee!'"

"Donna, are you kidding me?" I asked, infuriated at the thought. "Oh I can't wait to call Ms. Taylor and find out why she allowed my child to go to a prom. That is wrong on so many levels!" I was fuming.

"Yes it is and to top it off Taylor was supposed to pick Shantal up from my house by 9PM, but she didn't get to my house until well after midnight." Donna sounded disgusted.

"Well, Donna, thank you so much for calling me. I know you went against your husband's wishes and I'm sorry Natalia put you in this position."

"No problem. I put myself in your shoes and I would want you to tell me. Take care."

I couldn't wait to get off the phone to see what Natalia had to say. I gathered my thoughts before I called her downstairs. I thought back to a few weeks earlier about the brief conversation I had with her when she asked if she could go to a prom, and I told her "No", not at 14. I didn't know she had plans already, and had been scheming for a while. *She had better not lie to me.* I thought. It had been seven years since the school called child services on me and that was not going down again. I was glad that PJ was not home when I got the call because it gave me time to hear from Natalia and try to save her from PJ's wrath. I calmly called her downstairs and I watched her closely as she walked into the den.

"Sit down." I said with an authoritative tone, as I watched her sit gingerly on the edge of the sofa across from where I was sitting on the matching love seat. I had a dilemma because I didn't want to out Donna for telling on her, but there was no way around it.

"Listen, and don't you lie to me."

"What Mommy? You're scaring me."

"Did you go to a prom last weekend when I was away?" I stared at her without blinking an eye.

Before she could lie I started repeating Donna's story and Natalia readily admitted to going to the prom with a *friend*. She then immediately started begging.

"Mommy, please don't tell daddy, please!"

"Girl, are you crazy? I'm not keeping this from your father. Now, tell me how this prom came about after I told you, you could not go to a prom at 14."

"Mommy, I met this friend on *MySpace* and we have mutual friends at Hollywood High. He knows I want to go there for high school, so he asked me to go to prom with him, so I asked Taylor if I could go. I knew she would let me go because she lets her girls do whatever they want and Taylor said it was ok. She made my date come up to the apartment so she could see his driver's license; and then she went down to the car and got his license plate number. Oh yeah, and she gave me her cell phone so that I could call her in case of an emergency, and she told me to be back by midnight."

As Natalia told the story, my stare became more intense and I got mad all over again just listening to her tell that bullshit story.

"What were *you* thinking?" I yelled. "And, why did she let you go without my permission. You asked me if you could go to a prom and I had said NO! What part of 'NO' did you not understand?"

Natalia sat there nervously as I called PJ. Brittany answered his cell phone.

"Where are you guys?" I asked trying to stay calm.

"What's wrong mommy?" Obviously Brittany heard something in my voice even though I tried to keep my composure.

"Oh nothing, just wondering how long before you guys get here, that's all."

Brit knew I was lying, but she went with it. Within minutes they were home. I asked Brittany to go to her room and then I began telling PJ about Natalia's prom. My mind was all over the place. Unlike me, PJ was calm and extremely strategic whenever he dealt with adverse situations. He approached this situation from a fear standpoint. He sat Natalia down and explored every possible scenario that could have arisen when she ventured out without our approval. PJ explained to her that she could have been gang raped; she could have been in a stolen vehicle or involved in some other unfortunate situation that perhaps she could not have escaped. Natalia appeared to get it, but what she didn't get was that this revelation was just the beginning of the fall out from her little indiscretion. After discussing the situation at length with Natalia and PJ it was time to call this crazy, no parenting skills having, sleeping with her cousin, tramp, and find out why she put my child out in those streets like a common whore. I went right in. I didn't even bother to say hello.

"Taylor, why did you let my child go to a prom without my permission?"

"She said *you* gave her permission to go."

"Stop lying, it's insulting. I already talked to Donna, so I know *everything*. She saw you dressing my child up like a freaking jezebel, and you made comments that let her know I was not aware. I'm not done with you." I said as I slammed the phone down.

Taylor deserved a beat down. But I would never stoop to that level because I was not a fighter. I was angry and I needed to do *something*. PJ and I talked about the situation for a couple of days and then we filed a police report against Taylor for "Contributing to the Delinquency of a Minor." She should have known better than to allow my hormonal child to go to a prom without our permission and our oversight.

The school year was about to end and Natalia had to go back to school and face Shantal with our families at odds. By the time they graduated Taylor and her girls became aware of the crime report we filed against Taylor. Taylor was scared, and her girls turned on Natalia with a vengeance. Shantal's friendship was a huge loss for Natalia as they were very close at school and at home *and* they travelled in the same circles. The only saving grace was that they were attending different high schools in the fall so they didn't have to see each other too much if at all. The prosecuting agency set the matter for a City Attorney Hearing rather than a Criminal Court Hearing, and that was good because it meant that we would at least meet with a mediator, and Taylor had to formally face the music for her actions. I insisted that Natalia attend the hearing with us, and I told her to apologize to Taylor for putting her in that situation. I explained to Natalia that she should never have asked to go to the prom knowing that PJ and I did not approve. Taylor continued to try to lie during the hearing until the Hearing Officer, an ex LAPD Detective shut her down. He placed her on probation and required her to attend parenting classes.

During the summer months, Natalia tried to adjust to having no close friends to hang out with so she occupied her summer with unlimited dance classes at the Millennium Dance Complex where she reconnected with her former BFF, Kayla, who was one of the friends going to Hollywood High in the fall. Natalia was notified early that summer that she was accepted at Hollywood High School so she was ecstatic, which helped to boost her spirits. Meanwhile, several Division I colleges were considering Brittany for sports scholarships, but they all expressed that she needed to play against better competition such as that experienced in the public school sector, so we took Brittany out of Campbell Hall and enrolled her in a public High School near our home in the San Fernando Valley. I wasn't happy about her leaving Campbell Hall, but the public high school actually turned out to be a great decision for Brittany. She took as many Honors classes as her schedule allowed; she excelled in basketball and academics; and was speaking, reading and writing fluently in Spanish. She actually taught herself to speak Spanish at the age of 7. I would tell the girls about their grandfather they had never met and how he had immigrated to the states from a Spanish-speaking country.

"Where is Cuba, Mommy?" Brittany asked as a precocious second grader.

"It's in the Caribbean, honey," I replied.

"Oh, so they speak Cuban?" She asked.

I chuckled. "No, they speak Spanish."

"Well then I have to learn Spanish if I'm Cuban, Mommy."

She watched Spanish language cartoons and used audiotapes PJ had laying around the house that he got from a training course at work. When Brittany got to her new public high school is when she added formal Spanish classes to her regimen. Within a short period of time she had mastered the Spanish language well enough to be appointed as the president of the Spanish Club at her high school, which was predominantly Hispanic. I was very proud of how she adjusted to her new school environment. That fall, at the start of Brittany's junior year PJ and I bought her a car. We had busy schedules so it helped for Brittany to drive herself to and from school, and she picked up Natalia from the bus stop when we could not make it to her in time. It was an expensive relief for us but necessary.

I thought Hollywood High would be a great fit for Natalia because she could pursue her dreams in the Arts, at a school where stars like Judy Garland and recording artist Brandy had attended. The icing on the cake was that she had friends, she had grown up with, and danced with, who were also going to Hollywood High so she was happy to be amongst friends again after the disastrous end to her 8th grade school year with Shantal. The school year started off in the right direction and was sure to be fun with all of the dance performances, and meeting new friends in the process. Early on in the school year Natalia complained that Kayla was acting strange towards her. The two were literally BFF's since the age of 4 when they met in preschool during Chapel at their Christian elementary school. Kayla's mom, Brenda was a professional woman, and business owner and her dad an airline pilot. Natalia and Kayla were pretty much inseparable from ages 4 through 11. They separated briefly to attend different middle schools, but they were still very good friends.

While the girls were growing up, Brenda and I worked hand in hand to make sure they were occupied with all kinds of wholesome activities. By the time they were in middle school Brenda was no longer working full time, but she was not idle at home because she was involved in every civic activity in the San Fernando Valley. Brenda knew everybody, and as a result, she came upon the best opportunities for our girls whether it was an educational opportunity, or an opportunity for them to attend an exclusive social event. Oftentimes Brenda was given tickets to the annual Soul Train Music Award shows, which turned out to be a treat for us mommies and daughters to attend. Brenda and I had fun on our mommy-daughter dates throughout the girls' pre-teen years. Even though Kayla and Natalia attended different middle schools they still remained very close, and then came back together in school at Hollywood High. Natalia was perplexed by Kayla's sudden cold shoulder so she asked Kayla what was going on. Kayla explained to Natalia that *Brenda* didn't want them to be friends anymore, and it was completely out of the blue.

"What do you mean Brenda doesn't want you all to be friends anymore?" I asked Natalia when she came home and told me what transpired.

Natalia was very hurt, and on the heels of losing her other good friend, it was a crushing blow. I was confused because I considered myself to be very close to Brenda *and* her children. Obviously, Brenda had given a lot of thought to her decision, and Kayla was right to listen to her mother. Kayla was a very cute girl, and a sweet child, and to my knowledge she and Natalia had never fallen out about anything serious enough to destroy their friendship. I was hurt and disappointed that Brenda didn't have the decency to talk to me about the change in her feelings towards Natalia. So, I called Brenda, and our conversation was just as cold and ambiguous as the reason for Brenda ending the girls' friendship. One thing that came across loud and clear was that Brenda didn't like that Kayla was following Natalia's lead whenever they were together. Funny thing was that I knew neither of the girls were angels, so Natalia was not a bad influence on Kayla. After our brief conversation, I knew there was no salvaging the relationship between the girls, or Brenda and myself; and the timing could not have been worse for Natalia. Within months, she had lost all of her close friends, and she was terribly lonely, so it made perfectly good sense when she told me she wanted to leave Hollywood High. I always told my girls to be careful what they wished for, and that first year at Hollywood High brought that point home all too well for Natalia. She decided to attend Cleveland High School where many of her friends from our neighborhood attended, and it ended up being a great choice actually.

By the fall of 2002, Natalia started her sophomore year at Cleveland. The change of schools was a real blessing in disguise because Natalia had hopes of being a film director, and the school was starting a brand new Film Academy that year. It was very cool that Natalia was able to join the film academy at its inception, with motivated instructors and state of the art equipment. Natalia was excited and I was excited for her. I had always told Brittany and Natalia that the 10th grade year was the most critical year in high school, relative to laying the foundation for college. Brittany listened, but Natalia chose to ignore my advice. Natalia was strong-willed from day one, and although I loved her independent spirit, high school was not the time to be hard headed. Instead of being a model student in the 10th grade, Natalia decided that she would just have fun. For starters she was adamant about taking public transportation, which I didn't agree with, but that's what she wanted to experience, and I felt I needed to let her grow up. There wasn't a bus stop close to where we lived, so PJ or I took Natalia to a nearby bus stop in front of a community library, and cute little neighborhood Coffee Shop, located in a new strip mall. I chose that location so that Natalia could go to the Library after school, and do her homework while she waited for one of us to pick her up. It was a safe location and it was close to Brittany's high school, so some days Brittany picked Natalia up for me. By the time Natalia got to Cleveland she was hungry for new friends. I didn't know what to make of some of her new friend choices because I didn't know them like I did Kayla and Shantal. I wanted Natalia to be happy, so I kept an open mind. One new friendship Natalia had was with a young girl named Clarice. Clarice lived in a huge apartment complex on a busy thoroughfare in the mid valley area called Van Nuys. Clarice was a pretty biracial girl, whose mother was black and father white. Her father was deceased leaving Clarice in the care of her mother Sherry who was disabled. Over time I found out that Sherry was basically a shut in and an alcoholic. I was no stranger to alcoholism growing up with an alcoholic step dad, so I knew I needed to get to *know* Sherry to make sure I was comfortable with allowing Natalia to spend time with Clarice in their home. I felt some comfort in that Natalia was older and she was not easily influenced or swayed unless it was something Natalia, herself, wanted to do, so I gave Sherry the benefit of the doubt as far as providing appropriate oversight for the teenaged girls when they were in her home. Sherry was a very sweet person and a hoarder of sorts, who cooked everyday. Natalia loved Sherry's home cooked meals, especially her fried fish. Sherry had so much food and other clutter in that hot little kitchen that I couldn't catch my breath the one and only time I went inside for a quick visit. One thing for sure was that Sherry loved her only child. Thankfully, she and Clarice had a great support system with a grandmother and aunt, who lived close by, and they helped make sure that Clarice didn't want for anything. Natalia and Clarice were typical dumb teenage girls who thought they knew *everything*. Clarice was way more streetwise than Natalia because Clarice had no choice but to take public transportation for most of her life and/or walk everywhere she went, and she had to deal with the transiency of apartment living versus Natalia's middle class home environment, and private transportation options. Clarice's free lifestyle fascinated Natalia because it allowed her more freedom when she visited with Clarice than she was afforded at home. I recall one Saturday night/Sunday Morning, Natalia was spending the night with Clarice. It was about 2AM and PJ and I were asleep when the phone rang. It startled me because of the time of night. It was Sherry.

"Hi, Tia?" She said.

"Hey Sherry," I replied. "Is everything ok?"

"Well, it would be fine, but these girls are missing." Sherry's shaky voice was slurring from the alcohol.

"Sherry, what do you mean they are *missing*?" I asked as PJ sat up in the bed with an inquisitive but annoyed look on his face.

"Well, they left here yesterday evening and said they were going to visit some friends and I have not heard from them since."

After asking Sherry a litany of questions I told her that PJ and I were on our way to her house so we could try to locate the girls together. PJ immediately started blowing up Natalia's cell phone, but repeatedly got her voicemail after only one ring, indicating that the phone was most likely turned off. We didn't know what the girls were up to. On occasion Natalia would ask if she could catch the bus home with Clarice after school and I would pick her up from Clarice's house on my way home from work, and on some Fridays Natalia spent the night and I picked her up the next day. That night was one of those times when Natalia went home with Clarice on a Friday. When we arrived at Sherry's none of us had heard from the girls and it was about 3AM. I didn't know whether to be scared or mad. We had already gone through the prom drama with this girl and now this *missing* crap? Sherry got in the car with us and after driving around the area for a while we took Sherry back home and PJ and I sat in the parking lot adjacent to Sherry's apartment complex and waited for a while to see if the girls would return home. Sure enough at about 3:45 AM Clarice and Natalia appeared from the darkness walking towards the apartment. They were strolling like it was 12 Noon. It wasn't until they saw me and PJ lurking in the parking lot, that they became visibly shaken. Needless to say Natalia went home with us after drilling the girls for a little while about their whereabouts. They independently told the same story that they caught a bus to a friend's house at 11PM and they remained there until returning home in the wee hours of the morning. Natalia swore that her phone battery died, which is why her phone kept going straight to voicemail but PJ swore they were probably hanging with some boys so he went into detective mode and confiscated Natalia's phone. Once he was able to charge the phone he checked the call log and discovered that Natalia was telling the truth about whom she had called, and he saw that there was no activity for hours just as she said. We were relieved but we explained to Natalia that two young girls catching public transportation at those hours of the night was not only in violation of their curfew but also very dangerous, and as parents, we were accountable. I couldn't blame Sherry because they told her they were going nearby to visit a friend and that was normal for Clarice. I couldn't blame Clarice for being a bad influence on Natalia because Natalia was old enough to know better, and I'm sure she could have just as easily been a bad influence on Clarice, with her independent nature. Natalia was off to a poor start in her sophomore year. My concerns were valid, because during the second semester of Natalia's sophomore year I was contacted by the school's attendance office. They told me that she had skipped school and/or missed homeroom at least 23 times, and after talking to Sherry the same rang true for Clarice. Although

Natalia denied that track record, I was still livid because even one unexcused absence was too much for me. *I'm not sure how long this girl is going to live,* I thought. She was pushing all of my buttons; and all the wrong buttons at that. I was so ready for that school year to be over because I had more important things to deal with and I was sick of Natalia's antics.

It was March of 2003, and after 20 plus years of living with uterine fibroid tumors, it was time for them to come out. I was tired of the bouts of heavy bleeding every month and the abdominal pain that came with the territory. I had been having mammograms since I was 25 years old, due to my strong family history of breast cancer. My doctor made it clear that with my family history, it was best that I undergo a *full* hysterectomy and remove everything including my Cervix to avoid the chance of ovarian and/or cervical cancer. It was harder to diagnose ovarian and cervical cancer in a timely manner, so I was good with having the full hysterectomy. Removing the one grapefruit size benign fibroid was like giving birth as the doctor accessed the blob via the same scar used for my two C-sections. The fibroid had attached itself to my ovaries so the doctor really had no choice but to remove *everything*. I was already 44 years old, and I had no plans of having any more children, so there was no emotional attachment, nor any need to come up with a strategy to spare those body parts. The only problem was that I was forced into instant menopause because my estrogen producing mechanism was removed. I was off work for three months following that surgery and that was the first time I had used sick time since my pregnancy in 1987 when I had Natalia. By July 2003, I was happily returned to work.

Brittany had just graduated from high school, and only had a few weeks before she was due to start her freshman year in college. The exposure Brittany received at the public school helped her garner a full athletic scholarship to San Jose State University, so the Division I college coaches were right about the exposure she received by attending public school. It was Wednesday July 23, 2003, when we drove Brittany up to San Jose for her day long Freshman Orientation. The school was nestled in the middle of a small quaint downtown area, which had all the markings of a college community, with fast food restaurants and coffee houses. It was a bit old and not too big, which PJ and

I thought was good for Brittany since she was going to be away from home for the first time on a semi permanent basis. San Jose became notable during the 1968 Olympics when Olympians Tommie Smith and John Carlos attended San Jose, and during the closing award ceremony at the Summer Games in '68, they protested over the treatment and conditions of *Black Americans.* During our tour we were advised that black power statutes made in Smith's and Carlos's likeness would soon adorn the lawn in front of the newly built sports center to commemorate their legacy. We walked the campus and looked at the old dorms, one of which Brittany was to share with another female athlete. There was excitement on campus because newer dorms were under construction, and the models looked amazing. After making our rounds on campus, and in the nearby community, we joined other families in the Student Union for the Orientation.

When I took the Lieutenant's exam 2 years prior, I placed high enough on the eligibility list to make Lieutenant early on during the life of the list, however there was an employment freeze due to the City's failing budget so I was frozen on the list from 2001-2003. My eligibility was about to expire that summer so I was prepared to take the exam again within the next few months. I was a firm believer that everything happened for a reason, and if it were meant for me to make Lieutenant, then it would happen; and if not, then God had something else planned for me. It was about 1PM as we sat in the Student Union waiting for the university staff to get the show on the road. I was excited for Brittany, but sad that she would be away from home and me. There was idle chatter all around as we waited for the Orientation to start. I heard my phone ring and dug around in my purse to find it before it became a distraction to everyone else. It was my office calling and I suddenly became annoyed by the call. *Why are they calling me?* I wondered. I hurriedly stepped outside to take the call. To my amazement, it was a co-worker calling to tell me that I had been promoted to Lieutenant. My annoyance quickly transformed into excitement. I was grinning from ear to ear when I hurried back inside. As I sat down, I whispered the good news to PJ and Brittany. It was a great day. It had been 9 years since I was disqualified from making Lieutenant, in 1994, and I felt good about finally overcoming that hurdle in my career. I couldn't wait to get back to work and get started in my new assignment. On that following Monday I walked into my office with my chest poked out because in less than 10 days I was going to be crowned one of the newest Police Lieutenants, and I would be one of only 4 black female lieutenants on the 10,000 member Department, so it was a proud moment for me.

I was assigned to Central *Patrol* Division, which was great because I knew the 4 square mile area of Downtown Los Angeles very well, and I knew many of the people who worked at the division, so my transition was a lot easier than if I was assigned to another division. When the time came, I assumed my new role but there were some people who were not ready for me. I was met with open arms by the majority of officers who already knew me from seeing me around the station in my previous Detective assignment, which was in the same building. I was a 22-year veteran however, it didn't matter how much time I had on, I was still a woman, and I was black, so I had to prove myself again and again at every juncture throughout my career. Needless to say I was immediately met with resistance especially from one grouchy old male Sergeant, affectionately referred to as Sarg by the troops. Sarg was one of my subordinate supervisors, or shall I say insubordinate supervisors? When I passed him in the hall before assuming my new role I felt comfortable reaching out to him because I had not felt any ill vibe personally from Sarg, directed at me in all the years we had passed each other in the halls. As Sarg approached that day I extended my hand.

"Hey Sarg, it looks like we will be working together." I said smiling from ear to ear.

I was over the moon with excitement, and I was sincere in my approach. My new role as watch commander was critical and in order for me to be successful I needed everyone's cooperation. When I extended my hand, Sarg looked down at my hand as if it was a foreign object. He then looked up at my face with his hands down by his side, and his lips pursed, he turned and walked away without uttering one word. *Wow... really? How unprofessional.* I withdrew my hand, and continued to walk down the hall hoping no one saw that exchange. All I could think of was that I was in for a real challenge.

I had already experienced racism and sexism in my previous assignment, and I made it through that, so I thought I was just destined to that way of life for as long as I worked in a male dominated profession, and for the seemingly racist LAPD. It wasn't right but I was part of the minority so *I* had to adjust.

My Promotion to Lieutenant 2003

Early on in my tour as watch commander I was told that Sarg openly opposed management in general, and that he kept a tally of the number of Lieutenants he had *run out* of the Division. I was led into the Sergeants' work area on my first day and shown the chalkboard on which Sarg maintained his written tally of the Lieutenants he had ousted. I could not believe that Sarg was allowed to maintain such an open display of hostility towards management in the workplace. There were a few Lieutenants who preceded me, who had allowed Sarg to run the ship rather than fight with him. All I wanted to do was go to work, do my work, and go home safely. I didn't have time for his crap. I was high on principle and integrity, sometimes to a fault, because everything was not that serious, and I had to learn to discern between the BS I needed to address, and that which I didn't. It took me a while before I realized that some battles were just not worth fighting, and that I should really choose them wisely, or I would stand the chance of minimizing everything, because I fought for everything. By the time I made Lieutenant I had 13 years of supervisory experience, so I was pretty good at determining whether an issue needed to be addressed but sometimes I faltered. Sarg was one of those battles I needed to fight. He was a former military man who still thought he was some sort of Drill Sergeant. He was disrespectful to his superiors, including me, and I received an abundance of complaints from his subordinates who accused Sarg of mistreating them in one way or another. Sarg and I needed to be on the same page for the good of the Division, and for my sanity. I discussed my new work situation with PJ because he was always good at providing me with sound advice, and even played the devil's advocate in order for me to come to a good decision myself. PJ agreed with my plan to move forward with handling the situation with Sarg. PJ never led me astray, and he agreed that something needed to be done about Sarg.

"You need to make Sarg your first project." PJ said firmly.

"I like that." I said shaking my head in agreement.

From the moment I put those bars on my collar and I sat in that watch commander's seat I was confident; calm and calculated in my response to Sarg's blatant disrespectful actions against me, and others, but I really didn't need that stress in my life. Removing Sarg's tally from the board was my first order of business, so I personally erased the rhetoric. From day one I had mini battles with Sarg but I never allowed him to take me out of my character in front of anyone. I assessed all the venom he spewed my way and addressed only the real issues. I ignored all else. My actions at every turn were firm, swift and well documented, and reported up the chain of command. After several months of Sarg's open display of aggression the Captain was compelled to move him out of my chain of command and into an environment that was

more conducive to his style of leadership. Sarg was furious about his reloca-
tion and his new subordinates were equally unhappy that they had to work for
him. The field troops working for me were elated and bowed down to their
new queen, for Sarg was dethroned.

Life as a watch commander turned out to be a great experience. I wore
a uniform daily so maintaining my wardrobe was low maintenance, and I
welcomed the break from my high fashion detective days. Everyday, I arrived at work about an hour early wearing jeans, a white t-shirt and running
shoes. I sat at the end of the bench in front of my locker and put a high shine
on my black leather police boots each and every day, and I touched up my
leather belt with Kiwi Black shoe paste if I needed to. I loved the feel of my
fitted wool uniforms and always made sure that my bars and buttons were
sparkling. I felt so officious. My days consisted of conducting roll call and
assigning officers and supervisors to their field assignments; providing training, conducting audits, and questioning arrestees each and every time one
was brought in:

Do you know why you are here?
Are you sick, ill or injured?
Do you have any questions for me?

These were mandatory questions to protect the arrestee and the arresting
officers as well. What I hated most was that there were so many transients
that were brought into Central station, and I had to greet every one of them
as the watch commander. I was constantly sanitizing my hands and holding
my breath while speaking with them; but I always treated them with respect
just as I hoped my brothers were being treated while they were in the prison
system. I had not heard from Edris since he called from jail and wanted me
to connect him with Junior, and Stefon was still missing in action since he
moved from Edris's place. I worried about both of them and prayed that they
were ok in their own worlds. I was sitting in the watch commander's seat one
morning at about 11AM when I received a phone call.

"Hey T, it's me Edris. I'm outside your station."

"What are you doing here?" I asked attempting to keep my volume down.

"I just got out of jail and I don't have any money and no place to go."

I was not expecting Edris to call me and I was not sure of what I was willing to do to help him.

"Ok so why are you *here* at my job, and how did you even know I was working today?"

Edris was always very neat and clean so I was never ashamed of how he looked but he had just walked out of jail, so I didn't know what he was going to look like. I was hoping for the best.

"I remembered you worked here so I called and they told me you were across the hall. So you got a promotion huh? That's good girl," he said, sounding proud.

"Yes, Edris. Well, I'm happy that you are out, but I need to call PJ and see what we can do to help you. Where are you?" I asked.

"I'm across the street at a pay phone."

"Are you hungry?"

"Yeah, I could eat. I ate one of them nasty prison burritos before they released me because I didn't know when I was going to eat again."

"Ok, I will meet you outside and give you some money, so you can go get something to eat and then meet me back here at 4 when I get off ok?"

Surprisingly, Edris looked great *and* he was sober. I gave him a hug and money and hurried back inside and called PJ.

"Honey, we can't just leave him out in the street," PJ said. "Bring him to the house and let me talk to him and we will go from there."

"Ok, but I don't know if I want him staying with us."

I was glad that PJ was so accommodating. Edris had never done anything to hurt us, but our lifestyles were different so I didn't want to be bothered with his domestic violence drama and his drinking issues. He was an alcoholic and very irrational in his thought process all the time, and I did not approve of any of his girlfriends, who were usually alcoholics as well. I finished my shift that day and met Edris in front of the station. We drove to the house and PJ was home when we got there. Natalia was a senior in high school and Brittany was away in college. We had a guest bedroom, which I used only for my extensive wardrobe, so we clearly had room for him to stay. By the time PJ and Edris were done talking that evening we all agreed he could stay with us for six months to help him get on his feet. We were comfortable leaving Edris in the house alone while we were at work because he wasn't a thief; and I knew he would clean up behind himself. Edris was prohibited from bringing anyone to our house and was warned that if he brought *any* drama our way that he would have to leave. Edris accepted those terms and vowed he would abide by the house rules. We had bought Natalia a car so whenever she was at home her uncle Edris would sometimes bother her to take him to get cigarettes. PJ helped Edris get his driver's license renewed so he could get a job and a car. Edris was a truck driver and in order to renew his Class A license he needed a physical exam, so he headed off to the nearest County Hospital, Olive View Medical Center. During that visit to Olive View, Edris met his next casualty, Tyra. Before long he was in a relationship with Ms. Tyra. Within a short period of time Edris got his medical certification updated, found a job and bought a used car. He was getting back into the swing of life on the outside. I was happy Edris was getting back on his feet and Natalia was happy that he was not bothering her anymore for rides to the store. A few months went by and everything was going well until one evening when I was at home and I received a call.

"You need to come get your brother!" The woman yelled into the phone.

"Excuse me, but who are you?" I asked as I tried to figure out what was going on. Then I heard Edris in the background engaged in a screaming match with this unidentified woman. Edris then got on the phone.

"Tia, she is crazy. I'm just trying to get out of here and she won't give me my car keys."

Edris was drunk and Tyra was screaming in the background, 'he put his hands on me and he ain't leaving until my brother get here.'

"Edris, this is exactly what we warned you about. You are never going to learn. If that woman calls the police you are going back to jail, and that is so ridiculous. Why are you fighting? As soon as you get out of that situation over there you need to come here and get your things because you can't stay here any longer." I called PJ, who was not at home, and I told him what was going on. PJ and I agreed that it was time for Edris to go. When Edris arrived at the house later that night I had already packed his things.

"Awww T, can't I stay for the night?" He pleaded.

"No! You got a car and a job now so you go get you a room at a hotel and figure out your life. We told you not to bring any drama here and you didn't listen so we can't help you. Bye." I said as I ushered Edris out the door.

"He just can't help it can he?" PJ said shaking his head.

"No, he can't." I affirmed.

CHAPTER 12

"Large and In Charge"

IT WAS EARLY JANUARY 2005, and LAPD was scheduled to open a new Division in the San Fernando Valley later in the year. It was the first new station built in 28 years so everyone around the Department was excited about the possibility of working in the new state of the art building. LAPD was known for its run down, dirty, raggedy stations, so it was going to be great having all new surroundings and brand new equipment. The Department always operated with old broke down furniture and overly used supplies unless a community member or organization donated new equipment and/or furniture. I hadn't thought much about the new station except that I shared in the overall excitement of my coworkers, about possibly working in a brand new division with brand new amenities. Chief Bill Bratton assigned a Captain to head up the *Transition Team,* which cadre was assembled to open the new station. That Captain was then charged with selecting his management/leadership team. As time went on more and more positions were staffed in order to prepare to get the station fully up and running, and that's where I came in. I was about 18 months into my tour as a watch commander in downtown LA, and I was enjoying my time back in the field. It was a slow Friday morning when I received a call from the Detective Division Commanding Officer, a Lieutenant II, who was already a member of the *Transition Team* for the new station. Lieutenant Ellems was a male black who looked white. I knew who he was but I had never worked with him. We had seen each other in passing when we worked in the same building earlier in our careers. Anyway, he called me and said they were looking to bring a Lieutenant I Assistant Detective Commanding Officer on board with the Transition Team and my name came up. I was flattered that I was recommended, but at the same time I was apprehensive about the move because I didn't know the Captain and I didn't know Ellems, so I wasn't sure if it would be a good move. Within a few days, after talking it over with PJ, and weighing the pros and cons I made the decision to join the Transition Team.

Natalia was in the second semester of her senior year in high school and in spite of her 10th grade shenanigans she became more focused in her junior and senior years thanks largely to the film academy. In addition to her interest in film, Natalia demonstrated a passion for writing. As a young teen she wrote songs and poems, and by her high school years she was writing scripts for the school's weekly telecasts. Natalia was excited about her upcoming senior film project, which she decided would be a feature film but she didn't know what story she wanted to depict. One afternoon while at a hair salon, Natalia was under the dryer flipping through a Teen Glamour magazine and there she found a story for her movie so she called me.

"Mom. I know what I want my movie to be about."

"Ok tell me about it."

"Well, I need you to pick up a magazine for me. There is a *really* sad story about a 16-year-old football star, who stabbed his 15-year-old girlfriend to death at school after she tried to break up with him. It is a disturbing story about teen-dating violence. Mom, it's so sad and heart wrenching."

"Oh wow, ok I'll pick it up. I can't wait to read this story."

The domestic violence hit close to home for me because I witnessed it as a child involving my mother and stepfather, and again it was ever present with Edris bullying his girlfriends over the years. I picked up the magazine on my way home and later that evening I read the story. Although my family situations did not end in death I was very much moved by the story. Then the reality set in. I didn't see how in the world we were going to make this movie so we definitely needed the help and guidance of the school's film academy staff. After discussing the project with PJ and the school administrators we were all on board to help Natalia make the movie. Natalia finished the first draft of the script and the teaching staff read the script to make sure the project was suitable based on the school district's standards. Since the script was based on a true story, the school suggested we get the script vetted by an Attorney. The school knew we had no budget for producing the film so one of the teachers referred us to an Entertainment Attorney who, for a small fee, agreed to review Natalia's script for us. The Attorney asked a series of pointed questions about the story and we in turn asked a lot of questions about meeting our responsibility as writer and producers. After a short discussion and clarification on both ends we were good to go. We felt good knowing that we were on the right course to proceed with the project.

On January 21, 2005, I received word that Grandmother died of natural causes. I had not seen her since Mama's funeral in 1992, due to distance, but we talked on the phone often, and she wrote me letters regularly. It was storming in the Midwest when Grandmother died, so I was not able to attend the funeral due to commercial flight delays. I was heart broken but she *was* 97 years old, and had outlived all of her children except for Aunt Della.

The film academy at Cleveland had state of the art Apple computers and other filming equipment, which the students all knew how to operate. We had vetted the screenplay, which Natalia entitled "Beast," signifying the rage that was depicted in the story. I didn't know anything about filmmaking but I was willing to spend my free time to help get the project off the ground. The second order of business after meeting with the Attorney was that PJ and I meet and discuss the details of the project and logistics with the film school teaching staff. One teacher in particular was totally committed to seeing the film come to fruition. Mr. Gleaton was a dedicated teacher who was in charge of the Film Academy. He admired Natalia's talent and expressed his full support. Mr. Gleaton allowed us to use the school's equipment and provided us with a full film crew made up of students from the Academy. I was responsible for ensuring that the filming equipment was returned and secured at the school at the end of each shooting day. Filming went on for about 10 weeks at various locations throughout the San Fernando Valley. I knew the *concept* of the school's film academy was great but I wasn't aware of its real potential for the students, until I witnessed it for myself during the filming of the movie. Working with the young talented students was refreshing and a much needed break from police work. The end of the school year was upon us but the film editing was not yet complete. Natalia spent most weekdays editing the film but there was no way that she would be done before graduation. It was great working in the Valley because it was exciting being a part of the transition team for the new station, and it put me closer to Natalia as she ended her school year.

It was amazing to watch the new station being built. My new partner, Lieutenant Ellems was a typical male chauvinist, who was really moody for a guy. He loved to gossip, and took offense to everything someone said or did that he was not in total agreement with. Ellems didn't have much experience managing detectives, so over time he felt threatened by my extensive detective experience, and management skillset. The detectives and civilians under our command oftentimes came to me for advice and direction instead of going to Ellems, and that didn't sit well with him. I thought the assignment, as the Assistant Commanding Officer would be a great opportunity for me, which it was, except for my relationship with Ellems. On May 1, 2005, the new Police Station opened as scheduled and I saw how it immediately took hold in the Community. The opening of the new station came and went with a lot of fanfare, on the Department and in the Community. Shortly after the station opened, Ellems became embroiled in an ongoing dispute with his Administrative Assistant, Marva. Immediately after a closed-door meeting that he had with her, alone, Ellems came to me and told me about the meeting, and said he wished I had been in the meeting with him. The meeting went sideways, and it was only the two of them in the room, so he feared it would come back to bite him in the butt. Apparently he lit into Marva about some office management issues, which he felt had gone awry. A few days after the faulty meeting Ellems went on vacation, and as soon as he left, Marva, who was still visibly distraught about the meeting, came to me and accused Ellems of sexual harassment. Marva alleged that he made comments of a sexual nature, and said that she was offended. *Oh boy.* I thought. *This is not going to end well.* This was a serious allegation and I knew Ellems was going to be pissed about it but as a supervisor I was compelled to make a formal complaint about the *alleged* inappropriate sexual comments. Did I believe that Ellems was guilty of sexual harassment? No, but Ellems was stupid for meeting with

Marva alone because he knew how emotional she was. In Ellems's absence I discussed the issue with our Captain and initiated a complaint on Marva's behalf. I was really torn because Ellems was already intimidated by me so I felt like a bigger wedge was forced in between us by me having to file the complaint. I felt like a traitor for not being able to give him a *heads up* about the complaint but I didn't want to interfere with the investigation nor instill distrust in the system at Marva's expense. Besides, it was the Captain's responsibility to advise Ellems of the complaint against him, not mine, so I let the system work the way it was supposed to and I went on about my business. Well, sure enough when Ellems learned about the complaint he was livid with me, and he felt he had a good reason to openly express his dislike for me because I didn't give him the *heads up*. I really didn't give a care about him not liking me because I did the right thing. I continued to work as the Assistant Commanding Officer with Ellems in Detectives and I was still happy being there in spite of his coldness towards me. The detectives were awesome, and they trusted my leadership so I was good with working there.

By the summer of 2005, Natalia had graduated from High School. When school ended the filming of the movie was done but the editing process was not. We didn't own an Apple computer and had not planned on purchasing one at that time. The teachers in the Media Academy were excited about the film project being completed so the first option was to allow Natalia to go to the school during the summer months to work on the film however, the teachers did not want to commit to opening the media room; and/or commit to remaining on campus with Natalia in order for her to work on the film. Ultimately the staff agreed to allow us to take one of the Apple computers home for the summer. I vowed that I would be completely responsible for the computer and liable if anything happened to it. Natalia spent the summer months editing her film and we were *all* looking forward to seeing the finished product. We then had to decide what we were going to do with the film, as it was a very relevant topic and it definitely needed to be seen in order to acknowledge the hard work done by the incredible students. I was very touched during the filming process, and even the adult actors who were cast were amazed at the quality of the story written by a teenager. Not only had Natalia done an amazing job of writing the story she had also done an amazing job of directing, and editing the film. It was really quality work for a novice filmmaker.

Brittany was away in college during the filming of the movie but she came home for the summer while Natalia finalized the film. During Brittany's sophomore year at San Jose she had started dating a young man who was also a student at San Jose State. Mark was from San Diego and grew up in a dysfunctional family, kind of like I did. Mama got pregnant at 17 with Stefon, and Mark's Mama got pregnant with him at 16. One main difference between our dysfunction was that my brothers and I all had the same father, and Mark and his three siblings had four different fathers, so that was like dysfunction on steroids. That summer we met Mark for the first time when he came to the house to visit Brittany. I was impressed in that he took the opportunity during that visit to personally ask PJ if he could date Brittany. We thought that was a noble gesture for a little black boy from the ghetto. It was during that same summer that Brittany met Mark's family when she travelled to San Diego for a visit. Brittany fell in love with Mark's family just as they did with her. I thought Mark was harmless in that he appeared to be a really nice guy. He was not an honor student like Brittany nor did he play any organized sports in college, but he obviously wanted a better life than he was accustomed to in San Diego, and I admired that. Mark had very sweet supportive paternal grandparents, and they were so proud of him having been the first in the family to attend college. It was great having the girls home for the summer, and meeting Mark. I was happy that Brittany was happy in love.

I was sitting at my desk in the Detective squad room at the new station in August of 2005, when one of my old friends, Jen walked into the room. She was a Captain assigned to Internal Affairs Division (IAD), but I had known her since 1983 when she was a brand new rookie officer, and I a more tenured officer assigned to West Los Angeles (WLA) Division working patrol. Jen was one of the "Men Against Women" targets at West L.A. during the Martin Foster heyday. She was a woman, she was really short, *and* she was not cute so Foster and his followers targeted her to ostracize. They openly chided Jen for being ugly, and for being too short to be a police officer. She was on probation and had no recourse. I was furious at the angry men's display of aggression directed at all the female officers which is when I came to realize that it was not just a black and white issue with Foster and his followers, but rather a *hate* and sexist issue in general. Jen and I had developed and maintained a good friendship over the previous 25-year period, but over the years she had become more and more sarcastic about everything. She had become jaded due to bad relationships and issues with her promotional opportunities that she didn't feel came fast enough. Although I liked Jen, she was a big mouth hateful little woman who used humor to mask her hatefulness. She made it known that she hated her elderly parents, and she hated kids even more, so she and I didn't really have much in common except for our bond as young female officers forced to band together to defend ourselves against our male counterparts at WLA. Jen was passing through the Detective squad room admiring the new division when she saw me sitting at my desk. She immediately came over and struck up a conversation.

"Hi Tia." Jen said in her Chicago-born Jewish dialect.

"Hi Jen. What brings you our way?"

"What a nice station. How has it been on the Transition Team? How do you like working with Ellems?" She whispered. But she moved on with the conversation when she saw the grimace on my face. "Hey, I have a Lieutenant II position that I think would be perfect for you. You would be in charge of a team of investigators at our criminal section in Burbank. Please come work for me."

"Jen, I am only 5 minutes from home working here, and I don't want to commute to downtown again." I was spoiled because I had literally no commute, and was working in a brand new station in Detectives, which I loved, but the job Jen was recruiting me for was an upgrade with a 2 ½ percent raise.

"In addition to the upgrade, you will have a take home car, so does that make the commute sound better?" Jen asked as she playfully punched me in the shoulder.

"That sounds pretty tempting lady but I just got here and they hand picked me so I don't feel right about leaving so soon." I said as I rubbed my arm to smooth out the wrinkle Jen left in the sleeve of my cute jacket.

I debated whether I should leave my current assignment so soon after being hand picked for the job, but this was the second time Jen had offered me this same job within a 3 month period.

"It's an *upgrade* for you so no one will fault you for leaving this assignment. Ok, well if you turn me down this time I'm not going to ask you again." Jen said under her breath as she slowly walked away.

I thought to myself… *hmmm, an upgrade and take home car?* That was a no brainer.

"Ok, I'm in." I exclaimed from across the room as Jen continued to walk away.

A couple of months went by before I was scheduled for an interview at Internal Affairs. Jen sent me to speak with several Lieutenants already assigned at Internal Affairs Division in preparation for my interview, so that I was well versed on the ins and outs, and nuances of the job. On the day of my interview I showed up at my appointed time at Internal Affairs Headquarters, otherwise known as, The Bradbury Building. I felt comfortable knowing that Jen would be sitting on my interview panel along with the head Chief at Internal Affairs. As I sat nervously in the waiting area the doors to the interview room opened up and a black motor Sergeant, and a black professionally attired female walked out of the room and into the waiting area where I was sitting. I knew the Sergeant who was embroiled in several lawsuits and I figured the woman with him must have been his Attorney. I spoke to the Sergeant and as the woman passed I looked at her thinking, *she looks awfully familiar.* I couldn't stop staring at her wondering how I knew her so before she walked completely out of the office I stopped her.

"Ma'am, what is your name?"

"I'm Attorney Rochelle Jackson." She responded in a deep husky voice as she looked at me with a slight smile on her pretty face.

"Get out of here! Rochelle, it's me, Tia." I said. "Oh, wow, you did it. You finished law school and now you are a big time Attorney. What a small world!" I exclaimed."

Rochelle was in law school and working as the Office Manager at Dr. Williams's office when Mama was first diagnosed with breast cancer in the early 1980's. Rochelle and I chatted for a little bit while I waited to be called in for my interview. I told her of Mama's demise and updated her on PJ and the girls and she spoke of her daughter and two granddaughters. We exchanged business cards and vowed to keep in touch. It brought back such fond memories when I saw her. I thought Rochelle was the coolest person ever when I went into the doctor's office with Mama. After our chance meeting, Rochelle and I talked on the phone frequently and over the course of a couple years Rochelle told me she was battling late stage breast cancer. I was heartbroken for her. Within a few months of me finding out about her breast cancer, Rochelle died before we ever reconnected again in person.

By summer's end both Mark and Brittany had enjoyed their respective families and returned to school as a happy young couple. Natalia was enrolled at Cal State University Northridge and living on campus. After successfully interviewing for the position at Internal Affairs I broke the news to my current bosses that I was selected for the position, and off I went to Internal Affairs Division. That was the first time that a black female Lieutenant held a Lieutenant position at Internal Affairs. Although it wasn't a decision made based on race it was a milestone for women of color on the job. I assumed command of the investigative section at Internal Affairs Division, where I was in charge of 17 sworn and one civilian employee, and it was crazy busy from the start. I got along well with Jen, as well as the female investigators in my unit, however, I guess I rubbed some of the male investigators the wrong way as I tried to encourage them to get with *my* style of leadership. I was a very experienced Detective, and had been a supervisor for a lot of years so I knew what I was doing, and that's why Jen recruited me. The unit I was in charge of like most small units was very cliquish and the guys just wanted to continue to do things *their* way. My predecessor was a male white Lieutenant, Jim Barker, who I suspect got along with all of the guys. I mean, they complained that he was never there but they were ok with that because they could do whatever they wanted in his absence. Barker obviously didn't care about what the investigators did because rumor had it, *and* Jen believed, he was too busy screwing Jen's self proclaimed best friend, Dana, another female Captain in the division. Jen was quite jealous of Lieutenant Barker and Dana's relationship, and oftentimes she made mention of how appalled she was at their closeness since both of them were married to other people, and actually Dana's husband was also on the job in a management position. Jen obsessed over the alleged sexual relationship between Dana and Lieutenant Barker. According to her it had been so long since she had sexual relations, she joked about cobwebs taking up space in her vagina. I laughed at Jen's humor because she really was very witty.

It was a sad reality that whenever a non-white and/or female supervisor of any ethnicity assumed a leadership position on the LAPD, they weren't as readily accepted as their male white counterparts were, and they always had to prove themselves and/or win over the good ol' boys by allowing them special favors, accommodations or by cowering down to them. Whether good or bad I pretty much followed the letter of the law, and Department protocol to a tee. I took pride in being a fair supervisor even if I didn't like a subordinate. Basically I stood true to the set standards. Was I maybe a little inflexible? Yes, maybe sometimes. I could not afford to be flexible because I was scrutinized far too much, so I had to tow the line or risk faltering. It was easier to just follow the rules and not deal in the gray area, which would have most likely promoted a healthier work environment on the surface. My reputation for being *by the book* was fine with me because I challenged anyone who cried foul when I did as I was expected to do. Within a few months of the investigators adjusting to my style of leadership I slowly won most of them over, and gained their respect as they saw me as a hard working exemplary leader. Slowly but surely those who didn't like my style or me, left the unit and that was better than good.

The summer had ended and it was time to study and prepare for the upcoming Captain's exam. I had about 5 years to go before retirement, so PJ and I had decided to look into buying our retirement home. Early on in our marriage PJ had talked about us relocating to his hometown of Atlanta, Georgia when we retired. But after Neomi made a mess of the family's property and assets, PJ lost interest in returning to Georgia. On the weekends we looked all over southern California at new home communities from the most eastern parts of southern California like Rancho Cucamonga to the West Valley, and also out in the Antelope Valley. We loved looking at the new home models, but we didn't love some of the inflated home prices. We had a lot of expenses at that time like Natalia's college expenses, and all of our car and insurance expenses were huge. We paid about $8,000 a year in car insurance alone for all of our vehicles. I didn't want either of the girls to work during college like I had to so we paid all of their expenses while they were in school. Completing their college degrees in 4 years was a top priority so PJ and I dealt with the temporary hefty expenses. PJ and I were most familiar with the San Fernando Valley since that's where we had lived since 1982, so we pretty much focused on the San Fernando Valley, and an exclusive area of the Antelope Valley, called Quartz Hill. The Antelope Valley was known for huge homes that were more affordable than like properties in the City of LA or other communities around southern California. We found a new community in Quartz Hill, that we fell in love with, and after several phase releases we finally got the model that we really wanted, but it meant that we *had* to sell our existing home. The new home wasn't built yet so we had a little time to accommodate our contingency sale. The housing market was booming in late 2005, just as it was in the early 90's so I looked forward to the move and the excitement of the blossoming new home market. Our existing home was a new home when we purchased it 5 years prior, in a gated community in the eastern part of the San Fernando Valley so we were excited about getting another *new* home. With all that was going on at work, selling our home; getting Natalia settled into college and helping Brittany overcome her Sophomore year homesick meltdown, I had obviously failed to schedule my 2005 mammography appointment.

I was looking forward to the upcoming Captain's exam, which was scheduled to take place in February of 2007. It was a little over a year away but with my work schedule, I needed all that time to study right. After the girls returned to school we planned to have a formal screening of Natalia's movie "Beast." We invited school officials; and were hopeful that teachers would bring high school students from around the District to see the film. Ultimately, we wanted to get the message out that domestic violence in the teen community should be taken seriously. I became so passionate about the issue of domestic violence that I signed up to take the 10-week State course to become a State Advocate for Victims of Domestic Violence. I figured if I was going to try to market the movie for the teen community I could add validity to my sales pitch if I was an Advocate. After considering various locations for the movie screening, we chose the Skirball Cultural Center. Even though it cost a pretty penny to rent the Skirball, we did not charge attendees to help us recoup the cost, however, we wanted the movie to count for something so we researched various organizations and asked for cash *donations* from attendees, so that we could donate all the proceeds to a selected organization. In keeping with the theme of the movie, the shelter we selected was a local Transitional Housing Shelter for Battered Women; the largest transitional housing shelter in California; W.A.V.E. (Women Advancing the Valley Through Education) founded by Corina Alarcon, the wife of a local politician; to be the recipient of the donations. The capacity of the auditorium at Skirball was 350 seats. I didn't know how the attendance would turn out but I did everything to ensure we had a packed house. After securing WAVE's support, and agreement to receive the donation, I drafted and sent out countless letters to school officials throughout the Los Angeles Unified School District, as well as private schools throughout all of Los Angeles County. I thought that the topic was sure to capture the attention of the Administrators, but I was wrong. I got no responses from any of the schools except for support from Cleveland High School where Natalia and the student filmmakers attended. Other schools were just not interested. The project didn't fall completely on deaf ears however, as my friend Myrna, who had retired from LAPD, was a full time family therapist and professor at two local Junior Colleges, and she opted to use the film as part of her curriculum, and the film was accepted into the Pan African Film Festival and was viewed by thousands of people. In spite of the lack of interest shown by the school district we packed the house at Skirball and raised thousands of dollars for the shelter. It was a worthwhile event, and a great celebration, and exhibit of the work done by the amazing teenagers and their dedicated teacher. That was the start of Natalia's filmmaking, directorial, and editing experience.

During that time I had no obvious health issues that I was worried about, but I could stand to lose a few pounds. I had started out 2005 by joining the Mission Area Transition Team; made it through the grand opening in May, and by August, had secured a new position at Internal Affairs, so I was on a roll. I worked hard and by late November 2005, my Assistant Officer In

Charge (OIC), a Detective III, decided to move on to another assignment after being in the unit for 6 years. His departure left me at the helm alone to run the unit, with a civilian Clerk Typist to assist me. It made for an increased workload for me as I inherited his work, which largely consisted of case management, case assignment, and case preparation for my final review. The workload was crazy for all of us because the investigators, who were in varying levels of skill set, were each carrying 15-20 criminal cases, and those cases needed to be completed within a one-year period from the time each complaint was reported to a Department Supervisor, so the Assistant OIC position was critical to the overall success and management of the unit. I didn't think the vacancy was a big deal at first because I figured the position would be filled within a few weeks, and I would have help in no time at all. Well, November and December came and went; and by early January 2006, I still had no Assistant Officer In Charge and I was starting to stress. Additionally our home was still not sold after being on the market for almost 4 months. I had *toooooooo muuuuuuuuch goiiiiiiing onnnnnn....*

Oooooh, I was groggy... It seemed like had been out for a while. The struggle was real...I had literally relived my *entire* life during the time that I was under. Oooooh... I was coming out of my biopsy-induced coma.

CHAPTER 13
"Wake Up"

~

I FELT LIKE MAMA WAS WITH ME WHEN I awakened from my biopsy-induced coma. I was confused when I saw Mama flying over my hospital bed still in the hospital gown that she died in, but I could not discern the expression on her pretty face.

"Mama? What's going on here?" I mouthed as I slowly opened my eyes peering up at PJ and Doctor Richter standing to the left of my bed. PJ was gently rubbing my left forearm as he pulled my crooked blue hospital bonnet straight. His smile was apologetic as Doctor Richter began to speak in a low and very generic tone.

"Welcome back Mrs. Morris." I was confused as my eyes flittered back and forth between PJ's face and Doctor Richter's lips.

"We removed your tumor. Unfortunately, there *was* cancer present, but I think we got it all. We cut about a one-inch margin around the tumor, and removed your Sentinel Node and two others, which showed no presence of cancer. The tissue has been sent out to pathology, so I will see you in a couple of weeks, and we will discuss your treatment options for your type of cancer."

My heart skipped a few beats as Richter spoke. It was bad news but I was drugged so at that moment it did not seem that bleak. I looked at PJ's handsome face as a tear ran down his cheek. I could not believe I was hearing that I had Breast Cancer. Mama's spirit still hovered above just long enough to comfort me as the doctor delivered the news then she drifted back off to heaven. I was in a fog. *Was this a curse or something?* I asked myself. *First Mama was stricken by the curse of breast cancer, then Aunt Laberta, and then me. Was my outcome attributed*

267

to family history, which my doctor spoke of for years? How would this family history affect my daughters? Would this curse be passed on to them? There were a million questions stirring around in my head. After receiving the news, I was whisked off to recovery for another 45 minutes or so, after which time I was sent home with post surgery instructions. I had a medium sized bandage covering the incision on my left breast, which was a reminder that I had breast cancer. The next few days were rough. *I have Breast Cancer* was becoming my mantra. I was very antsy wondering about my pathology report and what it would reveal. *What kind of treatment was I about to endure?* I could not focus on anything for too long. I had seen firsthand how chemotherapy and radiation mangled Mama's body, and it was ever present in my mind how Mama ultimately succumbed to her battle with breast cancer 9 years after being diagnosed. I was scared. I was really, really scared, but I put on a brave face because I didn't want my family to worry. PJ was supportive and encouraged by my positive disposition. On the other hand Brittany was a nervous wreck. She was in her senior year at the University and still under the constraints of the basketball scholarship mandates. She wanted nothing more than to be at home with me. She was dealt a double whammy with coach's diagnosis and then mine. Basketball and school instantly fell on her list of priorities. Natalia was living locally and was accustomed to coming home on the weekends when she wasn't otherwise engaged, so her lifestyle was not impacted as much by my diagnosis. I didn't want PJ or the girls to change their daily routines as long as I was able to do for myself, and I sure wasn't looking for a pity party. I was afraid my diagnosis was going to ruin the holidays and I couldn't imagine that since it was the first Christmas holiday in our new home. I wasn't in the mood to share my situation with my bosses or subordinates at work until I knew my prognosis. I think I was somewhat depressed but my mind was too full for me to succumb to a feeble state. I returned to work on the day following my biopsy and I needed to be around people but it was hard to keep my mind on work. Those two weeks following my biopsy were the longest two weeks ever. My left breast was still engorged but it was primarily due to post-operative swelling and fluid versus a growing tumor. I could actually hear the excess fluid sloshing around in there every time I moved. It was weird but normal during the healing process from the lumpectomy.

It was early December 2006, and time for me to return for my post op appointment with Doctor Richter. I was nervous and anxious to hear what was in store for me. I hoped and prayed that I did not have to undergo Chemotherapy. *Lord Jesus help me.* I prayed. That's all I was concerned with at that moment. I didn't have a problem cutting my hair if it was a style *choice* but I did not want to lose it due to Cancer treatment. *Was it shallow of me to think about losing my hair over and above everything else?* When Mama went through chemo I didn't focus on her hair loss because she often wore wigs so I thought that was just an opportunity for her to buy new wigs. Hair loss was just one superficial side affect of chemotherapy however, there were so many other side affects that were so much more serious than I ever imagined. Brittany's coach was going through Neo-adjuvant therapy for her breast cancer because she had a golf ball size tumor that needed to be shrunk prior to undergoing surgery to remove her tumor. I kept up with Coach's treatment as a way to forecast my impending treatment, even though Coach's situation was completely different than mine. She had felt a growing mass in her breast, which she failed to have checked out for months, versus my lump, which was detected via mammogram during a routine annual exam. How ironic was it that Brittany was affected so early in life by four women significant in her life; all challenged by Breast Cancer? Her memory at 7 was the death of Mama. It's no wonder she was devastated by the news of Coach's diagnosis, and then mine. I was happy Brittany was allowed to forego the remainder of her basketball season so that she could come home to be with me during this critical time in my life.

I left work early on the afternoon I was scheduled for my follow up visit with Dr. Richter. PJ met me at Richter's office. I hated waiting in exam rooms, and this day was exceptionally bothersome. I was anxious to hear about my fate. Finally after what seemed like an eternity Dr. Richter entered the room holding a computer printout in his hand. Richter began with the pleasantries, and then removed my stitches. I was prepared to learn my fate.

"How are you doing?"

"I'm good…" Blah blah blah, now please tell me about my prognosis. Let's get to it, *just the facts man.* I urged.

"Well I have good news and bad news." Richter went on to say after re-dressing my incision.

Oh wow! I thought to myself as my eyes stayed glued to the paper in Richter's hand. He was averting eye contact but not to the degree that I became mistrustful of his actions. Richter went on to say that the good news was that my tumor was small, less than 2 CM and that they cleared the margins, which meant they removed tissue around the cancerous mass. Richter noted that there was no further cancer detected in that tissue and furthermore none in my lymph nodes. I breathed a momentary sigh of relief until I remembered that he said there was also bad news.

"The bad news is that your tumor Mrs. Morris, was an aggressive type and it was identified as Hormone Receptor Negative, which means that your breast cancer can *not* be treated with hormone therapies in lieu of chemo-therapy." Richter said peering at me over his reading glasses. You could have knocked me over with a feather.

"Doctor… Ok you lost me," I mumbled. "I don't get what that means for me. How is that bad news?"

"Well, about 2 out of 3 breast cancers are hormone receptor positive, which can be treated with hormone therapies such as Tamoxifen and other pill form drugs, but that will not work for you." I heard what Richter was say-ing but I still did not get it. Now all of a sudden I didn't understand anything. *Was I stupid or what?*

"Mrs. Morris, hormone therapies can stop tumor growth in hormone receptor-positive cancers by preventing the cancer cells from getting the es-trogen they need to grow. They can do this in different ways. Some hormone therapies like Tamoxifen attach to hormone receptors inside the cancer cells and block estrogen from attaching to the receptors. Other therapies like in-hibitors lower the level of estrogen in the body so the cancer cells cannot get the estrogen they need to grow." Richter further explained.

"Ohhh." This retarded stupor I was in was starting to fade. I was starting to see the big picture but my understanding was still a little hazy.

"In a nutshell the only treatment for your type of cancer is chemotherapy followed by radiation. This treatment regimen is your only hope of keeping a recurrence at bay because hormone receptor-negative tumors such as yours also have a higher chance of breast cancer recurrence in the first five years after diagnosis versus hormone receptor positive tumors, but after five years there is no significant difference between the chance of recurrence for the two prognosis." Richter cocked his head to one side as if to say *you get it now?*

I felt like someone punched me in the gut. *Are you kidding me?* All I could focus on was that the only treatment for me was Chemotherapy. After hearing that, I faded to black. I was too numb to even cry. Richter ended our session by referring me to the Oncology Department. I could tell that PJ felt as bad for me as I felt for myself but we both tried to maintain our composure for each other's sake as we left Richter's office.

I went for a follow up visit with Doctor Nielsen a few days later before meeting with the Oncologist. It was my first time returning to his office after being officially diagnosed. The initial shock of my prognosis had worn off, so I didn't feel it was necessary for PJ to go with me to every follow up appointment with the various doctors. He was willing to go with me each and every time but I didn't want to cause a ripple in our normal routine so I put on my brave face and tried my best to deal with my inner turmoil by myself. The moment Doctor Nielsen walked into the room we locked eyes and his smile was tentative. I even mustered a smile in return but it was a fake smile. So what. Dr. Nielsen knew my family history as well as I did, and I read his facial expression like a blind girl reading braille. His expression said *I knew this was inevitable.* Dr. Nielsen was my primary physician, and we had discussed my family history for over 20 years. He explained to me how the process of chemotherapy worked. He was not an Oncologist therefore he spoke in generalities. The first thing he told me was that I would be subjected to countless blood tests throughout my cancer treatment, for various reasons. They would be checking for a series of things, some of which might interfere with my treatment. Primarily they needed to make sure that I was not anemic, otherwise my chemo treatments might be halted or changed in frequency. As a result of the frequent blood draws Dr. Nielsen recommended that I have a port catheter inserted in my chest for dispensing the chemo drugs. He felt it was a necessary option to accessing my veins every time, because otherwise, over time, my veins would probably collapse. The avalanche of information was too much for me to handle in such a short period of time. I was appalled at the thought of a contraption inserted in my chest. I recalled the round metal contraption inserted in Mama's chest, and I did not like it. I already had enough scars from various surgeries and the most recent scar from the lumpectomy was enough. I caught myself being a little vain at a time when I needed to lose all vanity and focus on saving my life. *Was I in denial?* I didn't think so, but obviously I was because I didn't get it. I was sinking further and further into this surreal cloud of confusion. My body was limp as I sat there looking like a lost puppy. With my head hanging low I peered up at Dr. Nielsen.

"What other option do I have to putting this thing in my chest?" I asked sheepishly.

"Well actually you can have it inserted in your forearm but I would not recommend it because you have to be really careful not to bang anything against it or impact it in any way." Nielsen replied in a bargaining tone.

I was happy to hear about that option and decided that I would explore the catheter in my arm versus my chest.

"Yeah, that will work." I said as tears welled up in my eyes. I didn't want to cry. I was too ornery at that moment and what good was crying going to do anyway?

I stayed in that mental space through the remainder of my visit with Dr. Nielsen. I left there in a daze but before I left I scheduled appointments to have the port catheter inserted, and an immediate appointment to meet with the Oncologist. In my haze I walked the short distance from Nielsen's office to the Oncology Department. The route from Nielsen's office to the Oncology Department was short but dreary. I didn't know the doctor I was meeting with and I did not know what to expect from him. It seemed like everything was in slow motion. The people all around me were operating in slow motion. The Oncology Department was right across from the Lab so my path was cluttered with people waiting for their names to be called for their blood draw; or for leaving a urine specimen. I squeezed through the crowded door of the Oncology Department excusing myself with every step. The receptionist who was handling patients at the window, and answering the phone greeted me. I watched and listened as the patients came and went ahead of me. It became pretty clear that I was just one of many on an assembly line of cancer patients. After speaking with the receptionist and exploring my options for treatment days and times I was given the grand tour of the infusion area and it was depressing. I would be seated amongst other cancer patients in oversized worn reclining chairs where my arm would be strapped to one of the arms of the chair to allow for a firm foundation for infusing my blood with poison. After explaining the routine to me I was ushered in to meet with the doctor. When I entered the doctor's office I was already in a funk. The doctor's office looked like a very crowded miniature library. The walls were lined with medical binders and books; and nestled amongst the clutter on the doctor's small desk was a big antiquated computer. Dr. Dedman was a Russian Ukrainian doctor, who was obviously a qualified medical professional, but his bedside manner was not just bad but rather devoid of any compassion. I didn't know him, and after meeting him I wish I hadn't met him. I was not in need of a doting doctor but would have welcomed one who expressed some care and/or concern, but instead I met with the cancer Nazi. He was all gloom and doom. Dedman was partially blocked by the big old antiquated computer monitor that was on his desk, so all I saw was one side of horn rimmed glasses and half of a mustache. He asked me a series of questions about my medical history; family history etc., and as I replied to the interrogatory he input my information into his computer. He never once looked at me. When he was done he read to me the results of his inquiry. Dedman started rattling off information as he read from his computer screen. He told me that based on my double negative tumor prognosis, coupled with my family history there was basically no hope for me, and he agreed that chemotherapy was the only treatment option for me. I swear, I thought that man had a death wish for me. Dedman said that chemotherapy may also be ineffective in my case because although there was no evidence of any cancer in my lymph nodes, the cancer could have bypassed my lymphatic system and gone directly to my blood. Lastly he told me that I had a 67 percent chance that the cancer would return prior to my 5-year mark. *Are you kidding me?* I became increasingly sad. I felt like I should just leave Dedman's office and go straight to Angelus Funeral Home and pick out my coffin. I was so appalled at Dedman's horrible bedside manner that I broke down right in front of him and cried uncontrollably and that was the last thing I wanted to do in front of that jerk. That was one time that I wished PJ was with me. But noooo I told him to go to work because I thought I had been given the worst news already. I was not crying because of my bleak prognosis but I was mad because Dedman treated me so poorly at such a difficult time in my life. I know... I know... Dedman was just doing his job, but man what an eye opener for me.

I sat up in that raggedy hospital chair in Dedman's office and I wiped the tears from my eyes; I gathered my things and I left without saying a word. I was not going back there for *any* kind of cancer treatment. Dedman's dismissive demeanor gave me permission to be brave. I vowed to show him what I was really made of. I left there feeling encouraged rather than defeated. I went home and I told PJ all about my dismal office visit and he felt bad that he hadn't gone with me. I would have been embarrassed at my display of weakness in front of PJ so I was glad he was not there. I couldn't sleep that night after my visit with Dedman. I was convinced that I needed to get a second opinion. I believed I was diagnosed properly, but I needed a second opinion about my treatment options. I was uncomfortable in the environment at Facey, and I could not fathom the bleak outlook Dedman provided for me. Deep down inside I was hoping that the second opinion would indicate that I didn't need chemotherapy after all.

In mid December 2006, my port catheter was placed inside my right forearm at Holy Cross Hospital. Whenever I thought of Cancer, the City of Hope was always at the forefront of my mind. It was a National Cancer Institute and was well equipped to treat any kind of cancer with traditional methods and/or clinical trials. That's where I needed to be so I told Dr. Nielsen I wanted him to refer me to City of Hope for a second opinion and he agreed. I made an appointment right away to see an Oncologist for my second opinion regarding treatment options. I looked forward to the second opinion at City of Hope because it was sure to help me determine what kind of treatment I would undergo, and where my treatment would be administered; Facey or City of Hope. I was blessed to have double medical coverage due to PJ and I both being employed by the City of LA. My cancer treatment was covered with no worries, so I just focused all of my attention on beating the disease. I made it through the holidays and was getting nervous about my impending treatment but I tried not to show it. The incision concealing the foreign object that pierced my vein was healing, but the bump felt weird on my forearm. When I arrived at City of Hope for my second opinion I was ushered into the lab for my blood draw before seeing the doctor. The waiting room was crowded with cancer patients and their family members ready to spend the day there. I kind of zoned out as I peered around the room, and across the hall at the pediatric ward where the babies played with their sick compadres, all wearing hospital masks. My heart was heavy for those babies. I was a 49 year-old woman who had lived a pretty full life, but those babies were innocent and devoid of life's experiences so how could I feel sorry for myself at that moment? I had drifted off into my thoughts while PJ flipped aimlessly through a magazine as we waited. I was brought back when they called my name.

"Mrs. Morris? Mrs. Morris?" The petite nurse walked out into the waiting room calling my name and looking around waiting for a response.

I stood up as soon as I heard my name and I waved my hand to get the nurse's attention. It was time to finally meet the doctor. The nurse checked my wristband to verify who I was. PJ closed his magazine and hurriedly followed me into the examining room. Between the two of us I was confident that we would ask all the right questions. Upon entering the examination room I was greeted by a nurse practitioner, Laura. We immediately hit it off. Laura was a sweetheart. She was from Massachusetts, and had all the class and sophistication of a young educated Bostonian. She was very personable, very compassionate, and highly inquisitive in general. I guess it came with the territory of conducting patient assessments. Laura was intrigued by my Police Lieutenant status. After her preliminary assessment, Doctor Selma entered the room. Doctor Giani Selma was a foreign gentleman, short in stature with a kind and gentle spirit, and kilowatt smile. Laura asked all of the preliminary questions and provided Selma with a verbal report before he conducted the physical examination. I felt comfortable with him. Unlike the *Debbie downer*, Dr. Dedman, who provided me with a bleak outcome, Selma and Laura were very encouraging. PJ and I felt at ease as they entertained our many questions. I knew then that City of Hope was where I needed to be for my cancer treatment. I had just been introduced to my new cancer management team. My visit was no longer for a mere second opinion. Dr. Selma confirmed that my only recourse was chemotherapy, and he described the various cocktails that would most effectively address my cancer. Selma indicated that I would need a *dense dose* of medication to attack my aggressive cancer. He described 3 different cocktails, and explained that each one had its very own side effects. My treatment was slated to span over a 16-week period, and would occur biweekly for a total of 8 treatments; followed by a shot of Neulasta on the day following each treatment. Neulasta, a man made form of a protein was designed to stimulate the growth of healthy white blood cells to help fight against infection but more specifically used to ward off certain white blood cells caused by receiving chemotherapy. Selma was very thorough in his assessment of my condition and determined just the right treatment for *me*.

"Doc, is my hair gonna fall out?" My question was superficial, but oh so valid considering that having hair was my norm, and like most people I didn't embrace change well at all. Doctor Selma didn't answer me right away as he smirked and continued to describe each cocktail he was prescribing for me.

"It sure is my dear. About 16 days after your first chemo treatment your hair will start to shed dramatically." Selma answered.

The reality was starting to set in. PJ looked at me with his eyebrows raised, as if to say *did you hear that? Your hair is about to fall out, all of it.* PJ had an incredible sense of humor and we often matched wits about a lot of things, so why should this situation be any different? I wasn't sure if I was really ready, but it really didn't matter because my path was chosen and being ready or not was a moot point. I was not in control of anything, but I decided I would cut my hair rather than see it fall out. Selma explained that the last cocktail towards the end of my treatment regimen included the drug Adriamycin, and *that* drug was problematic in that it was known to cause issues with your heart. Selma recommended that I undergo a Multi-gated Acquisition (MUGA) Scan, which was designed to create video images of the ventricles, the lower chambers of my heart that hold the blood, to check to see whether my ventricles were pumping blood properly. The test was commonly conducted before chemotherapy in order to identify preexisting heart conditions, or during or after cancer treatment to identify cancer related heart damage. It was prescribed for me prior to treatment in order to determine if my heart could withstand the combination of drugs contained in the cocktail. I notified Dr. Nielsen of the need for this test and he scheduled me to have the procedure performed at Holy Cross Hospital where my biopsy was performed. The results of the MUGA scan revealed my heart was strong enough to withstand the rigors of chemotherapy. Additionally, Selma referred me to a genetic counselor for genetic testing to see if I carried the BRCA gene so that I could make informed decisions relative to my chances of recurrence, and allow for prophylactic treatment options. The test used DNA analysis to identify harmful changes (mutations) in either one of the breast cancer susceptibility genes and would determine if the Cancer gene could be passed on to my daughters. I was not familiar with the genetic testing so I looked forward to meeting with the geneticist.

After returning home from my first appointment at City of Hope I was mentally exhausted. After relaxing for a bit I decided to go on line and research Doctor Selma. I was pleased to find out that he was a Professor of Medicine, and Director of Breast Oncology at City of Hope. I had cancer, and I had the worse case possible, so I felt I was in good hands. After reading about Selma I ventured off and started to research triple negative breast cancer. My research revealed that the five-year survival rates tended to be lower for triple-negative breast cancer, than any other form. A 2007 study of more than 50,000 women with all stages of breast cancer found that 77% of women with triple-negative breast cancer survived at least 5 years, versus 93% of women with other types of breast cancer. Another study of more than 1,600 women published in 2007 found that women with triple-negative breast cancer had a higher risk of death within 5 years of diagnosis. *Lord please let me live.* I prayed. I lived about 100 miles away from City of Hope but for my piece of mind I was willing to make that trip every two weeks, as well as the follow up trips after each treatment. City of Hope was the right choice for my journey. However, I had some decisions to make before my journey began. I thought about if I should continue working during my treatment period, and tried to determine *when* I would tell my staff about my medical situation? I didn't want to tell *anyone* about my cancer diagnosis because I knew that the moment I mentioned the "C" word people would treat me differently. Some would feel sorry for me; some who didn't like me, would be happy that I was sick, and some promotion seekers would be happy if I was too sick to continue working, because me being off would free up a Lieutenant position for the taking. Yes, that was the reality of life on the LAPD. I only had a couple of weeks before my treatments were scheduled to begin so I needed to notify my job. I had scheduled our annual office Holiday luncheon to take place the week before Christmas. We decided to do it up potluck style with all the trimmings straight from Costco. It wasn't traditional but we opted for Pizza and Cesar Salad, and we brought in all sorts of desserts, some store bought and some home made. It was a nice spread. Our luncheon also doubled as a squad meeting so I sat at the head of the u-shaped table in the conference room, and the investigators sat around the table. That was my second Christmas in that assignment so by then I had established a great rapport with most of the people in the unit. It was supposed to be a joyous time but I had no appetite, and besides I needed my mouth clear to talk. After everyone got their food and the idle chatter died down I started the meeting off with small talk about year-end stats and incidentals relative to closing out the year. I casually transitioned into my spiel about me.

"Well, everyone, I will be taking some time off because I have been diagnosed with Breast Cancer, so I will undergo Chemotherapy treatments real soon." There. I said it fast without taking a breath. I could hear the plastic forks drop as everyone's mouth fell open simultaneously and seventeen heads turned in my direction.

I wasn't emotional, nor did I feel sad delivering the news. I didn't know how any of them would respond, and frankly I didn't care, I just needed to account for my impending absence from command. I talked to Jay, to ensure that he was confident in leading the unit in my absence. I assured him that I was just going to be a phone call away. I then went to my office and called Jen to brief her. I had made up my mind that I would work if I felt up to it and I explained that I had a plan for having work brought to me. I needed to stay connected, and not dwell on my situation, and Jen was very supportive of me working from home. I could afford to take off during the 4 months of treatment because my primary medical benefits and supplemental insurance kept my salary at 100%, but I didn't know if my mind could stand the hiatus for that long, and besides I needed to be ever present for the upcoming Captains exam.

"I support whatever you want to do. You can work as little or as much as you want." Jen said.

"I really appreciate that. Thanks." Now the stage was set for me to focus on my treatment.

CHAPTER 14

"Going Through Treatment"

WHEN CHRISTMAS CAME I WAS not in the holiday spirit. Don't get me wrong, I was not depressed, but I was rather concerned about the huge obstacle that lay ahead of me. I was scheduled to start chemotherapy on Thursday January 4, 2007, and subsequent bi-weekly treatments were scheduled for January 18th, February 1st and 15th, March 1st, 15th and 29th and April 12th. I was concerned but not dismayed because Dr. Selma and Laura restored my hope that was diminished by Dedman. I hadn't seen or heard from my brothers but I wanted them to know about my cancer diagnosis. I loved my brothers in spite of their flaws but I had lost them to the ills of society. The last time I heard from Edris he was working in Long Beach, and living alone in a one-bedroom apartment close to his job. I was proud of him because he seemed to have bounced back after we put him out. It was about a week before I was due to start my cancer treatments when I got a call from Edris. He was calm and almost childlike in his tone.

"Hey T. I..I.. I... been arrested and I need you to go to my apartment and get my big screen TV and my clothes.

"*Whaaaat?* What are you talking about?"

"This crazy bitch I let stay with me called the police on me when we got into it, and they arrested *me* because she had a mark on her and if you don't get my things for me she is going to take my stuff."

"You are so stupid Edris. I don't even know where you live, and will not get mixed up in your mess. This is a vicious cycle and you will never learn. You are going to either kill someone or someone is going to kill you. I will not go to your apartment." I couldn't believe he was back in jail *again* for domestic violence. I was so annoyed by his call that I didn't bother to tell him about my cancer.

A few days later I started my treatments. I got up early on that cold winter morning and PJ and I made the 100-mile trek to City of Hope. I needed to get the show on the road. City of Hope was kind of mysterious, but comforting at the same time. There were patients there with varying stages of cancer, all kinds of cancer, and some of them looked like they were on their deathbed, but it was comfort in knowing that the best cancer treatment took place at City of Hope and I was ready for my blessing. I was warned that each visit would consume several hours of my day so I needed to come prepared with reading material and snacks and I was told to wear comfortable clothing that I could lounge in. After checking in that first time I was directed to the lab where my blood was drawn. I was then sent to another building to meet with Dr. Selma. That was my routine each and every time I visited City of Hope. I was amazed at how efficient the process was. The waiting room was overflowing with patients and their family members as PJ and I waited patiently for my turn in the Infusion Room. PJ went into the room with me and sat in the oversized recliner while I lay in the hospital bed for what seemed like an eternity with the pre-meds followed by the 3-4 hour infusion period. I worked from home Mondays thru Wednesdays; had my treatments on Thursdays; returned to City of Hope on Fridays for my Neulasta shot and then I rested on the weekends while the drugs infiltrated my body. During the weeks in between treatments if I felt like it, I went into the office. My office staff knew that my immune system was challenged so I oftentimes got calls telling me to stay home because someone in the office was sick. Dr. Selma also warned me about the possibility of cognitive impairment or dysfunction they referred to as "Chemo Brain," as well as unexplained hot flashes. I had already been having hot flashes for about 5 years before chemo due to my hysterectomy so I would not be able to discern between chemo related hot flashes or the menopausal hot flashes. I was also told to avoid drinking coffee so I would not become dehydrated. I felt completely overwhelmed by all the do's and don'ts but I managed.

The Captains Exam was coming up and I felt I was ready, but I had a huge boulder in my way. Being in law enforcement was stressful, and joining the ranks of the Command Staff added even more challenges. I asked PJ if I should continue on in the Captain's exam process since my focus in life had shifted due to my cancer diagnosis. I had been studying for months and was anxiously waiting to receive notification of my test date. The test was an 8-hour Assessment Center for managers.

"Just see how you feel on the morning of the test and if you feel up to it go, and if you don't feel like it don't go." PJ's advice was practical, and I agreed to do just that.

I handled my first treatment like a champ. I didn't get sick from the chemo or the Neulasta shot on the next day. Even though I had told Jen and my staff about my medical situation I had not told any of my close friends. I felt embarrassed, and I don't know why. I didn't want to be pitied or judged, and I knew some people didn't handle sickness well. One friend whom I had known for about twenty years, and worked with was the first person I told. During a brief conversation with her I *casually* mentioned that I had breast cancer.

"Oh, I thought nothing *ever* happened to the Morris's." She said laughing.

I couldn't believe my ears. That was exactly why I didn't want to tell anyone. That *friend* was an intelligent very accomplished woman. Her comment made me think that she was waiting for something bad to happen to me. I knew she liked me but maybe she didn't know how to respond appropriately to this type of news, and that was my fear of sharing this intimate detail about my life with my so-called *friends*. PJ felt that in spite of her insensitive comment I should still tell my closest friends. PJ occasionally asked if I had told anymore of my friends and I understood where he was coming from, but I told him that I would only talk about it if it came up in conversation when I talked to them. I knew that in short order everybody would know. Since I had told people at work it was sure to spread all over the Police Department because that's how things worked on the LAPD. Rumormongering and gossiping filled the hallways, squad rooms and squad cars on LAPD, whether the information was true or false. My closest friends knew that Mama died from breast cancer so they probably thought my fate would be the same. I had coworkers, male and female, who battled various types of cancer. Some prevailed and others did not, and that scared me just as it did when Mama fought her battle. I didn't feel like talking about it, and I sure was not going to make a call *just* to tell someone I had breast cancer. I eventually got around to telling them all.

By my second treatment I felt really good and had my chemo routine down. Brittany came home to be with me just in time for my second treatment. When I arrived at City of Hope that day my hair was still in tact. I had already cut it very short, so the fall out wouldn't be so drastic. Not only was my hair short, but by this time it was also dry and ashen. I had been dying my hair for years, since I started graying in my early 30's, so I thought maybe the hair dye was causing the dry brittle condition. It didn't dawn on me that my hair was literally *dying* from the chemo. Laura tugged on my hair and to her surprise it stayed put.

"Wow, I see you still have your hair and it looks pretty good too." Laura said as she examined my head.

"Well...Maybe my hair is *not* going to fall out after all." I exclaimed proudly.

"Chica, I'm here to tell you, your hair is going to fall out and soon. I'm sorry honey." Laura said as she pushed my head to one side playfully and looked at me sideways.

Then Dr. Selma chimed in with a cute little grin and a nod agreeing with what Laura said.

Before I headed off to the Infusion Room I discussed my upcoming Genetic testing with Dr. Selma and Laura, and all of the considerations should the test come back *positive*. Brittany and I were settling into the Infusion Room when I received a call from my friend Valerie. Our conversation started off normal but in short order I revealed that I was at City of Hope in treatment for Breast Cancer. Valerie started sobbing uncontrollably and no matter what I said she did not hear me. It might have been insensitive on my part by not telling *her* because she was really like a little sister to me. I guess I should have listened to PJ in that instance. I assured Valerie that I was ok but she was skeptical. I felt really bad because she took the news so hard, so I told her I would stop by her house on my way home from treatment that day. Brittany and I took turns taking naps during my treatment, and finally when it came time to leave I felt reenergized even though my veins were packed with poison.

**Top: Tia and Britt at City Of Hope/2nd Chemo
Treatment-Bottom: Valerie and Tia**

Before I left the doctor's office I called PJ and I told him to get the clippers ready so he could shave my head because I was not prepared to watch my hair fall out. Valerie lived about half way between City of Hope and my house, and she was anxiously awaiting my arrival. When I drove up she was standing in the doorway waiting for us to exit the car. Through Valerie's tears she saw that I still looked the same. Yes, my hair was a little ashy but I still looked pretty normal.

"Girl I've got Cancer... Now bye!" I said playfully as I embraced Valerie at the door.

You would have thought *she* had cancer, and I was consoling her. The visit was real quick because I was ready to go home. When Brittany and I arrived at home that day I received notification in the mail that my Captain's Exam date was February 8[th,] which was in between my 3rd and 4th treatments. I had already told Laura about my upcoming test and she was very optimistic for me. She thought because I did so well with my first two treatments, I would be ok to compete in the day long exam, just days after my 3rd treatment. Although they had cautioned me not to drink coffee, Laura *encouraged* me to drink a cup of coffee on the morning of the test to help me stay alert. PJ was waiting for me when I got home, with his clippers ready. He had set up shop in our bathroom. One of Brittany's friends from middle school; Brittany's boyfriend Mark, and Natalia were all there anxiously waiting to watch PJ shave my head. I wasn't quite ready to part with my little dry fro but I knew it was time. PJ draped me with a white plastic bag in preparation for the literal fall out. I was sitting on a stool facing away from the mirror when PJ steadied my shoulder with one hand, and with the other hand he attempted to shave the back of my head with the clippers. I got nervous as the clippers' vibration neared the nape of my neck so I pulled away from PJ's grasp. When he attempted to pull me back towards him, I kept moving forward away from him, and when he released his grasp, to my amazement, a hand full of my dry brittle hair was balled up in his fist. PJ reached around and showed me the brittle cluster of hair and I screeched.

"Oh nooooo!"

"Well then, sit back, and let me cut your hair." PJ scolded lovingly.

PJ pulled me back into my seat and shaved my head while Brittany video-taped and took photos. My photo shoot continued until I was clean-shaven. I put on a brave face throughout the party but clearly it was no celebration. I had mixed emotions. Shaving my head was the first step in gaining back some power from this grim situation.

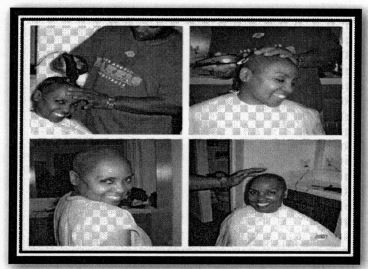

My Shaving Party 2007

After shaving my head I purchased a couple of cute wigs. I chose *short* wigs so that I could easily transition back into my pre-cancer treatment look. I bought scarves and hats, which I coordinated with my sweats and blue jeans for when I was not at work. I was not prepared to go out into the world bald, like I had seen some beautiful brave cancer warriors do. I wasn't even prepared to lay around the house bald, because it was all new to me, and I had not yet embraced my new look. When I went to the wig shop I found out that wigs could be considered as Prosthetics, and thus my wigs were covered by my Aflac Insurance policy. I was sure to sport one of my new wigs on the day of my upcoming exam.

My appointment with the Genetic Counselor was scheduled for late January 2007. The appointment needed to be timed just right in order to get the results back before I started Radiation treatments. That was important because if the results were positive I was going to have a double prophylactic mastectomy and breast reconstruction. That was long before Angelina Jolie opted for the same procedure. The thought was that I did not need to move forward with radiation treatments if I were to undergo the mastectomy, so timing was critical. When they called to confirm the appointment I was told I could have family members and friends join me so they could fully understand the importance of genetic testing. Josie and Rachel had family members affected by cancer so I invited them to come along with me to the appointment. They met me, PJ and Brittany at City of Hope.

Tia at Genetic testing consult at City of Hope March 2007

I felt good knowing that I could help my daughters make decisions about their future health care relative to their familial risk of breast cancer. I prayed that I didn't carry the gene so they couldn't inherit it. The meeting was very informative but it was stressful waiting several weeks to receive the results.

I needed to go in to work to check my personnel file before my Captain's test date. I needed to ensure that my personnel info was correct for my package review process. I was always good about checking my personnel file from time to time, to make sure the information contained within was accurate. Personnel workers were grossly over worked and underpaid so they sometimes filed erroneous information in personnel files. It was my responsibility to make sure that my file was accurate, and if not, to ensure that the erroneous information was removed. I was walking into the Personnel Division in the Police Administrative Building (PAB) when I ran into Katy, a female detective who had recently undergone a double mastectomy. Katy and I exchanged pleasantries and briefly chatted about our respective battles with breast cancer. I was going through treatment and she had already completed her treatment. Katy went on to tell me that she had just been awarded a favorable judgment against the City of Los Angeles for her breast cancer. I told her I had heard about the possibility of filing suit but I was going to wait for my BRCA1 genetic test results before I proceeded with a claim. I figured, if I had the genetic link, there was no way I would prevail against the City, however, Katy begged to differ. Katy told me that she inherited the gene, and she still prevailed against the City. She had a strong family history as her mother and sister had succumbed to breast cancer, so she referred me to her Attorney Alan Snitzer, a prominent Attorney in Pasadena, CA. Snitzer routinely represented police and fire officials in worker comp cases, and he was a leader amongst his peers in worker compensation claims. I gave Snitzer's office a call to file suit against the City pursuant to Labor Code Section 3212.1, which stated that cancer, including leukemia, was one of the presumptive illnesses for Law Enforcement personnel. Winning the claim resulted in the City picking up the tab for all of my cancer related medical care, and any resulting disabilities should any arise.

February 8th came all too fast. I felt pretty good but I was self-conscious about my appearance. For starters I looked bloated. Secondly, I wore one of my wigs, which I was not accustomed to, so I pulled and tugged at that thing all day. I wore a traditional navy skirt suit with a stark white starched blouse, navy panty hose and a pair of navy soft leather low heel pumps. Navy was always a great choice for me because I thought it was conservative and classy. I felt very alert that morning even when my Chemo Brain tried to sabotage my day. I arrived early at the Convention Center and received step-by-step instructions throughout the day. I was not in the mood for the interview games during the long process that day, but that's what I signed up for. My goal was to secure a good standing on the Captain's list, and ultimately make Captain. With my 27 years of vast experience I was hoping to score at the top of the promotional list. I had already decided not to disqualify any of the board members, I thought would not rate me fair, because that could be anyone of the LAPD Command Staff members. There were a couple of Chiefs on the panels and I couldn't stand either one of them. One Chief in particular, the highest-ranking African American member of the Command Staff, caused me great concern because he made it known that he did not care for me. He thought I was too *vocal* for a woman. He considered men who were *vocal*, were great leaders but women who were vocal needed to take a seat. I had great experience and an exemplary personnel package so I wasn't going to kiss his narrow derriere in order for him to like me. By the time the 8-hour day came to a close I was pretty much drained and my forehead throbbed from the tight little wig I wore. I studied and I did my absolute best so it was up to the powers to be to decide if I was worthy of a promotion. I exhaled slowly on the long walk back to my car. I couldn't wait to get home.

Over the next couple of months, my treatments continued on without concern. I had minimal side affects from the Chemo with the exception of my already gone hair, and discolored nail beds, and blackened fingernails, which I masked with dark nail polish or Band Aids wherever the nails had fallen off. I was a mess, but that was *my journey* and I had to go with it. I maintained my routine working from home, and only went in to work during my off treatment weeks. I was well into my treatment regimen before most of my friends found out about my cancer diagnosis. Many were stunned, and some started up with the pity crap, which I was not having. My friend Dede would always say, '*Girl you are not sick,'* and she was right. I was not *sick,* and I reminded everyone often that I was not sick; I was just *going through treatment* for a medical condition. Eventually everyone got the message that I was not having any pity parties and I was going to be ok. My friends were amazing. They sent me cards and well wishes on a regular basis, surprised me with church dates and pooled their funds and bought me beautiful gifts. They showed me they cared about what I was going through. I really enjoyed our Sunday church dates. Several of us would meet for 8AM service at FAME, where we fellowshipped for about 2 hours, and then headed over to the Pacific Dining Car for a very delicious overpriced breakfast. We laughed and talked for hours before heading out to our respective homes. We carried on this tradition month after month and coined our church group, the Sunday Divas. I loved those days getting my worship on with some of my best girlfriends.

Tia, Evangelyn, Carol, Dede and Brenda aka Sunday Divas after Church 2007

By late May the test results revealed that I did not carry the BRCA1 gene so I had the same risk for Breast Cancer as someone in the general population (1 in 8). That was uplifting news. My negative test results for the BRCA1 gene ruled out the need for a Prophylactic Mastectomy so I was back on course for Radiation Therapy. I continued on with my chemo treatments until April 12th when I had my last treatment. On April 13th when I returned for my Neulasta shot I received a Gold Medal (Distinguished Patient Award) for completing my chemo treatments. The medal came with lots of hugs from the nurses and I welcomed the love but I wasn't ready to leave their care. I was very happy that chemo was over with but I had to get prepared for the second half of my treatment regimen; 7 weeks of Radiation. Before leaving City of Hope that afternoon I was referred to and met with a Radiologist to discuss my radiation treatments. The Radiologist advised me that I would undergo radiation daily for a total of 31 zaps to my scarred chest. I was scheduled to start Radiation about 6 weeks after chemo ended to allow the chemo drugs to be completely out of my system. The six weeks was a welcome break, and a good time to go back to work full-time. On Monday April 23rd I returned to my post at Internal Affairs Division and I was happy to be back in my dusty office. It was early in the afternoon of my first day back when PJ told me that Asia, a Clerk Typist, who worked with him, was diagnosed with Breast Cancer. PJ told me that she wanted to talk to me about my treatment to help her make decisions about her treatment options. As soon as I got off the phone with Asia, one of my Detectives came into my office and closed the door. Marie went on to tell me that her brother was diagnosed with Leukemia. I remembered thinking, *what in the world is going on?* I wanted to scream. Marie was from a large very close-knit Hispanic family and although her brother had the most common kind of Leukemia, and his prognosis was favorable, she and her family were still thrown for a loop when he was diagnosed. Marie explained that her brother was going to be admitted into the Norris Cancer Center at County USC Medical Center where he would be an inpatient for several months of treatment. The problem was that Marie's family, including her brother all lived in Northern California, which meant her mom and brother's family had to travel to Southern California to be with him during his treatment period, and Marie was their sole transportation to and from the hospital. Not only was she one of the best investigators in my unit she was one of my biggest supporters, and had even come out to visit me at home when I was first diagnosed. I gave her major consideration in that I allowed her to go to the hospital daily for as long as she needed to sit with her brother, or to transport visiting family members to and from the hospital. I had not been back to work one day and here I was dealing with other people's cancer crisis.

I so enjoyed heading up the Criminal Investigative Unit. Soon after I returned to work, my Assistant OIC Jay landed another job assignment. I was a little bothered by his sudden departure because he had only been promoted into the assignment with me a few months before I went off. There was an unwritten rule when it came to commitment periods after transferring into assignments, especially when the job offered was a promotion. Jay was promoted to Detective 3, which was a lucrative 11% pay raise over his previous assignment. He got what he wanted, and it was time to jump ship. *Where was his loyalty?* Obviously it was all about self-gratification. He didn't owe me or anyone else anything. After all, I had abandoned him when I had the nerve to go off for my cancer treatment, so *where was my loyalty?* I'm being facetious because I mean, you really can't compare the two circumstances, but still the reality was that once again I had a very critical position to fill, and I was not looking forward to that whole selection process again. It wasn't long before I had a replacement for *Mr. Eye Candy*, and it was business as usual. A week after I returned to work I attended a Badge Ceremony for my friend Evangelyn who was promoted to Captain. Evangelyn was the fourth Black female to promote to Captain in the Department's 130-year history, and during the ceremony Chief Bratton presented each of the four black female Captains with a beautifully framed Newspaper article about their amazing accomplishment. I was so proud at that moment for my friend Evangelyn because she was one of the other two detectives, who were disqualified from the Lieutenant's process in 1994 with me, so like me she persevered. I was fresh off of my cancer treatment so I was not in uniform at her badge ceremony as I would like to have been, and I was still wearing that tight wig. During the ceremony, two young female Detectives approached me because they had heard about my battle with cancer, and were genuinely happy to see me. Although I didn't feel like I looked my best they said I looked like a *Dream Girl* with my short sporty wig. I hoped that maybe I was channeling one of the Supremes in my pixie wig but in actuality I was really channeling Effie the fat one in Dream Girls. I was puffy from all the steroids I ingested during chemo. The Detectives meant well and I appreciated their kindness.

In late May 2007, Brittany was back at school. Her basketball season was over and she was preparing for her graduation. She had done well by graduating in 4 years versus 5-6 years like most of her college athlete peers. Brittany was not sure about her career path after graduation but she knew she was coming home even though her boyfriend/fiancé was going to remain in school for at least another year. Brittany wasn't clear on how to make the long distance dating situation work but thought they would be able to manage some visits throughout the year as they continued on their respective paths toward adulthood. PJ always thought that Mark was not good enough for Brittany as most fathers think when sizing up their daughter's boyfriends. PJ always told Brittany '*You can't run from that DNA*' referring to Mark's dysfunctional lineage. Brittany always came to Mark's defense as she was in love. I was glad she had found love, and I genuinely liked Mark, so I wasn't as hard on him as PJ was. I thought he was a good kid.

Natalia was rounding out her sophomore year in college and was doing great. She didn't have a steady boyfriend that we knew of, but she was working part time at a Mall near the school, hanging out with friends, and engaging in normal college shenanigans. While on my six-week hiatus from cancer treatment PJ, Natalia and I drove up to San Jose for Brittany's graduation. We were heading into the Memorial Day Holiday weekend following the mid week ceremony. On our way home from the graduation we stopped to visit with Brittany's coach who was just slightly ahead of me in her breast cancer treatments. Coach Richard was packing up her home preparing to head out of town. She was not returning to San Jose University, but rather return-ing to her hometown of Louisiana where she would continue her battle with breast cancer amongst family and close friends. Coach Richard was waiting for movers when we drove up to her beautiful home in Morgan Hill, just outside of San Jose. She had just completed her Radiation treatments and she looked so beautiful. She had lost a considerable amount of weight and was sporting a beautiful short wig with blond highlights. I told her about my upcoming Radiation treatments and she showed me her battle scars. The skin on her chest around her affected breast was burned and peeling, and was very sensitive but she was still in great spirits. I was so happy to see her looking so fierce but I was scared of what was to come for me seeing her raw and scarred skin. I was not looking forward to the burn and skin irritation. We didn't stay long as we just wanted to say goodbye since she did not make it to Brittany's Commencement exercise. We said our goodbyes and headed south on the 101 Freeway towards Los Angeles. On that next Monday, May 29th I started my radiation treatments. I was scheduled for daily treatments so I thought I would go in to work at 6am, leave work at noon and drive to City of Hope for my 1PM appointment and then go home from there. I was told that I would experience a huge fatigue factor early on during the treatment but I had no idea I would experience the fatigue so suddenly, and after my first treatment. After the first week of Radiation I was literally too tired to go into work, drive to my treatments and then drive the 80 miles home. *What was I thinking?* I told Jen that I was going back to working from home until my Radiation treatments were done. Jen accommodated me because I was very productive whether I was at home or physically at work. From the start of my radiation treatments I used Aquaphor and Pure Aloe Gel on my breast after every treatment to minimize the burn to my skin. Trish, who battled breast cancer, a few years before I did told me how that regimen worked well for her. I didn't want my skin to be chaffed or burnt like Mama's or Coach Richard, and Trish's remedy worked wonders for me. By July 10th, when my radiation treatments ended I had minimal discoloration, and no burn what-soever so Trish was absolutely right about that amazing combination. After Radiation treatments ended I was ready to go back to the workplace fulltime. I was happy my treatments were over, however, I was apprehensive about my treatments ending. I had developed a false sense of security while at City of Hope because I believed that as long as I was undergoing treatment, any new cancer would be discovered in a timely manner, so I felt I was better off going through treatment, than back out on my own.

By the time I returned to work the Captain's list was published and I was in Band 4. I was disappointed at my mediocre ranking, because I didn't believe my standing on the list was indicative of my true abilities, however, I believed I was still in a position to *possibly* make it within the two-year period that the list was active. I had a stellar work history and a wide variety of supervisory and management experience, which had prepared me to effectively run a Command but I needed the powers to be to believe in me and that was a real crap shoot. I had no *sponsor* or friends in high places, and Jen, who I was working for, was a negative nelly. Prior to the test she expressed that I should come out pretty high on the list based on my experience however, when the list was published she took every opportunity to remind me that I would *never make Captain* from Band 4. I was fine with not making Captain because I had a good job as a Lieutenant, and there were so many other good jobs available at my rank if I didn't promote. But I didn't need to hear her negativity every time I saw her. I was so over it and her. In reviewing the list closely I realized there was one glimmer of hope that Jen failed to recognize. Chief Bratton's Aide was also in Band 4, so I knew the Chief would try his best to activate Band 4 for promotion before the list expired, which would also open the door for me. Guaranteed promotions were an unspoken right of passage for Aide's in high profile assignments, and the Chief's Aide was no different, so I was hopeful that they would give me the opportunity for promotion as well as the Chief's Aide.

I was getting back into the swing of things at work when I received a call from Captain Jackson of Robbery Homicide Division (RHD). I had known Captain Jackson for over 20 years and he was married to my girlfriend Alasea, but I never worked with him or for him. Jackson asked me if I was interested in a job heading up the Cold Case Homicide and Cold Case Sexual Assault Units. I was definitely interested in the opportunity because it was a permanent assignment versus the job at Internal Affairs, which was a 2 year limited tour assignment. Jackson went on to explain that earlier in the year, with the help of a $50 million grant from the state's Cold Hit Program, the Los Angeles Police Department was tasked with performing DNA analysis on more than 1,700 backlogged sex-crime cases. The Grant also enabled the Department to add more investigators to handle the increased workload generated by the anticipated DNA hits associated with homicide and sexual assault cases. As part of the increased workload and personnel, the Department felt the need to increase the level of oversight for the Unit from a Detective Supervisor to a Lieutenant, and that was the job Jackson recruited me for, and I was interested. There were two Homicide Sections; a Robbery Section; a Burglary Section, a Rape Section; a Cold Case Section and a couple of Task Forces, such as the Biggie Smalls Task Force and the Grimm Reaper Task Force, all under the umbrella of Robbery Homicide Division. I felt well equipped to handle the assignment however, the main reason I was being recruited was because Jackson, an African American Captain was tasked by Chief Bratton to add some diversity, minorities and women, to the Division so I appreciated that he thought of me. Male Lieutenants ran all of the sections, and task forces within RHD at that time; and the investigative staff was mostly comprised of male Detectives. Female Detectives in Homicide were scarce, especially at RHD, and Jackson was on a mission to change that. Regardless of the emphasis behind the recruitment process I was still excited for the opportunity to work RHD, so I agreed to make the move and two weeks after returning to work following my cancer treatment, I transferred into RHD as the new Officer In Charge of the Cold Case Special Section. I was the first African American female Lieutenant Officer In Charge of an investigative unit at the prestigious Robbery Homicide Division.

CHAPTER 15

"The Road to Recovery"

WHEN I STARTED WORKING RHD in late July 2007, my hair had barely started growing back, but everyday when I looked in the mirror I saw new growth. I felt like an oversized Chia Pet. My hair was growing in straight and peach fuzz adorned my face like a newborn baby. I had been sporting a wig for about 6 months, and I could not wait to wear my own hair again. Since I was changing jobs I figured it was the perfect time to stop wearing the wig, so on my first day at RHD I walked into the office with my short fine baby hair instead of a wig. I felt so liberated, and I was excited to experience my transition back to normalcy. Before my bout with Breast Cancer I loved getting my hair done at the salon, and I had a weekly standing appointment to keep my hair bouncing and behaving, however, after my hair grew back following chemo I was left with a much finer and curlier version of my former hair texture. As time went on I realized that my texture was never going to return to its former state so I wore it pulled back and slicked down, and creatively attached a faux braided bun to my short hair for a nice neat professional hairdo.

When I arrived in the office that first day the Cold Case Unit wasn't quite set up for me. The Cold Case Homicide Unit was located on the 5th floor at Police Headquarters; the Captain's office, regular Homicide; Robbery; Burglary and Rape Sections were all on the 3rd floor and the task forces and Cold Case Rape Unit were on the 8th floor. I walked around aimlessly from floor to floor for a couple of weeks chatting it up with investigators, some I knew and some I was meeting for the first time. I met with my peer Lieutenants, who were running other units, so I could become familiar with the lay of the land. The Rape Section was absent a Lieutenant at that time, so I was tasked with overseeing that Unit as well. I was intrigued by the high profile nature of the work being done in the various sections, but not so much by the personnel. Most of the investigators working RHD thought they were rock stars, when many of them were simply master manipulators, especially in the cold case unit. After a couple of weeks, another lieutenant was selected to head up the Rape Special Section, so I was able to finally focus on what I was hired to do, but there was only one problem, Detective Burt, who was in charge before I got there did not want to vacate my office. He was no longer in charge, and was not happy about it. I had been there for two weeks, and he still had not vacated my office. *Houston we have a problem*. I thought. Well no, *Burt* had a problem. Burt thought I should find a desk in the outer office with the working Detectives while he remained in the *bosses'* office. That was laughable. There I was a 27-year veteran with a ton of experience, and I still had to put up with that kind of disrespect. I was tired of being treated like a second-class citizen every time I changed assignments but it came with the territory of being a woman on the LAPD. After Burt finally relocated to the squad room, I was able to get into position, settle in and figure out what was going on in the unit. In addition to Burt's obstinate stance I was met with resistance right away by most of the investigators because there had been no protocol for managing the office, and they objected to me creating standards as directed by Captain Jackson, so I was in for an uphill battle.

My cancer treatments were done but my road to recovery was far from stable. I was on a three-month cycle for follow up treatments at City of Hope, at which times I underwent a variety of blood tests, mammograms, ultra sounds and breast MRI's. I had one of the worse breast cancer situations, being that I was *triple negative*, and that sucked. Every time I went in for my follow up appointments I literally held my breath wondering if they were going to find something new, so I was always stressed out. I worried about every ache and pain in my body regardless of where the pain emanated from, or how slight the pain was because in my mind the Cancer was back every time I felt *anything*. My ongoing Cancer follow-ups really toyed with my spirit. I could not wait to get to that 5-year mark to be considered cured from *that* left boob cancer, but I still had a long way to go. My body was slowly being restored; my missing nails started growing back and my chest discoloration started to disappear. My left breast was shrunken and pretty firm due to the radiation, but the doctor said the tissue would loosen up over time and eventually match my other breast in fluidity.

In the meantime, my Attorney called and told me that I had won my breast cancer case against the City. That was great news because the City became responsible for picking up the nearly $500,000 tab for all of my treatments at City of Hope, and was required to provide me with a monetary stipend for my pain and suffering.

It had been a couple of months since Brittany graduated from college. She was back home and actively looking for work but wasn't having too much luck. She had her degree in Mass Communications with an emphasis in Public Relations, but she didn't know quite what to do with it. She was glad to be out of school and happy to be home, however, she was unsure about her future with Mark, her boyfriend of 4 years, who was still at school trying to finish his degree. Brittany and Mark communicated often and she made a few trips up north to visit with him and friends, only to return home to idle time. After several trips up north and an exhaustive local job search, Brittany told PJ she knew what she wanted to do.

"Daddy, I think I'll be a Police Officer."

"Are you serious? Do you really want to do that?" PJ asked in a surprised tone.

"Yes, daddy, I think I want to do it. I was doing some research, and with my degree and my bilingual status they will start me at $62,000 a year."

"Ok. Ok. I see where you are coming from." PJ said pondering over the idea. "Let's see what your mom says about it."

PJ then told me that Brittany was considering employment with the Police Department and I was shocked to say the least because we had never discussed this option for Brittany's career path, and she had never expressed an interest.

"Are you *sure* you want to do that Brittany?" I asked, hoping she would change her mind.

"Mom, it was good enough for you."

"You are so right. You are a lot stronger, and smarter than I was at your age." I replied with a smile. I guess I came off a little apprehensive and that was exactly my intent. I had instant flashbacks from my rough patches over the years on the LAPD and that was not what I wanted for my baby.

Brittany wasted no time in applying once she told PJ, and me, about her plan. She started processing in August of 2007, and early on in the process she was disqualified. Personnel told Brittany she needed to lose 30 pounds before continuing on in the process. It was like déjà vu because I was similarly disqualified for my weight, when I was told I had to lose a measly 6 pounds before I was allowed to move on in the process 27 years prior. I was 5'4" and 123 pounds whereas Brittany on the other hand was 5'9" and 190 pounds. Brittany had just returned from playing 4 years of college basketball, and was firm and muscular, and I was all legs and skinny but the archaic pinch test indicated that we were both overweight. Brittany was discouraged, but PJ told her that he would whip her into shape in no time at all if she wanted it bad enough. Brittany was game, so PJ started her on a very strict diet resulting in consistent weight loss over a 6-week period. When weigh in day came in November of 2007, I drove Brittany to Medical Services Division where she weighed in at exactly 160 pounds, and she was approved to move on in the hiring process. Brittany had a clean background, and she passed the polygraph with no problem. She also passed the physical abilities test with flying colors, and was certified to start the December 2007 class. I had horrible memories of the Academy, so I was worried about whether Brittany could withstand the rigors of LAPD training that I had experienced and knew too well. I didn't worry long because she was confident she could handle it. By that time, Mark was tiring of school and was in need of a job. His Financial Aid had dried up, and he had no support from home to finish school, so PJ talked him into joining LAPD as well.

It was coming up on a year since I had my Port Catheter inserted in my arm, and since I had completed my cancer treatments Dr. Selma thought it was time to have the foreign object removed, so I returned to Holy Cross for that procedure and it was quick and painless.

By the beginning of 2008, I was making strides at work with managing DNA hits in the Cold Case Homicide and Sex Units. It was very exciting to see the cold cases come together with modern technology, and solving crimes that occurred up to 25 years prior. The staff, especially in the Cold Case Homicide

Section was upset that I had come in and set standards, and goals, as I was instructed to do by Captain Jackson. Some of them were not coming around to my style of leadership, and it had nothing to do with my sex or ethnicity. They liked the disorganized way of doing business because they couldn't be held accountable for the work. They wanted to go to 3-hour lunches with the likes of crime drama writer Michael Connelly, whom many of them had befriended over the years, and they wanted to come and go as they pleased without any interruption from management, and none of that was happening under my leadership. The Detectives in the unit were excellent investigators, and were very dedicated to their craft, but they fudged often and didn't want anyone, like me, telling them what to do.

I wanted desperately to have a cohesive team but there were some institutional terrorists amongst us, and one was a female detective who thought she was too valuable for us to live without her. She began to openly object to my direction, and thought that was ok. Olga was a beautiful Hispanic woman, slight in build and tall. She wore her hair in a jet-black shoulder length blunt cut bob, and always looked very professional. She was in the unit for about 6 years and she was very close to Detective Burt, who ran the unit before I took over. Olga, who was going through a divorce, was allowed to work around her child-care issues, which I didn't quite agree with. I was a mother too, and I worked out my child-care issues so that they never interfered with my work schedule whereas, Olga allowed her childcare issues to dictate when she came to work and at what time of the day. I wasn't worried about her working her required number of hours because quite honestly she was a diligent and hard worker and would have worked for free that's how passionate she was about working. Even still I needed structure in the unit and she and I needed to be on the same page. One day I noticed that Olga was scheduled to work but by 10AM she was not in, and had not called in to report that she would be late.

"Hey Burt, I thought Olga was working today."

"Yes Boss, she is coming in. She has child care issues so she will be in late." Burt replied rather nonchalantly.

"Ok, well tell her I need to see her when she comes in."

I could see the front door from my office, and at about 10:30 am, 2 hours after Olga's start time she came sauntering into the office in her usual cocky manner. Before she could get to her desk Burt told her that she needed to see "the Lieutenant." After getting settled in she finally came to my office.

"Yes Ma'am, you wanted to see me?" Olga asked as she poked her head into my office.

I motioned for her and Burt, who was seated outside my door ear hustling, to come *into* my office so we could have a conversation.

I needed Burt, who was my Assistant Officer In Charge to be present as a witness whenever I met with an employee about a personnel matter, which is why I summonsed him as well. Once Olga and Burt were in my office I started talking directly to Olga.

"Olga, I need you to complete an Employees Report 15.07, indicating what your child care hardship is, so that I can get the Captain to approve your start time deviation."

"Ma'am, I don't have a hardship. I have been allowed for the past 6 years to change my schedule to accommodate my child care." Olga was very dismissive.

"Well, it's an inappropriate start time regardless of *past practice*, and until the Captain has approved such a deviation, you are required to come in anytime between 6 AM and 8:30 AM."

Olga and I then became engaged in a verbal disagreement in my office that went back and forth for a few minutes, with Burt witnessing her blow up as I tried to reason with her.

"Enough Olga." I said rather sternly. "I am *directing* you to complete the 15.07." I said as Olga walked away from my office in a huff.

Burt was shocked at Olga's outburst, and ran to catch up to her to reason with her. I really didn't give a care if she cooperated or not because at that point I didn't want her working for me. She was disrespectful, and I needed to send a message loud and clear to the others that insubordination would not be tolerated in the paramilitary environment we worked in. After Olga and Burt left my office I got up from my desk, put on my jacket and walked into the outer office where I saw Burt standing over Olga's desk still trying to reason with her. I cut my eyes in their direction with no expression and then turned away towards the door and walked out. Captain Jackson was the nicest person you ever wanted to meet, but he was a no nonsense kind of guy when it came to *drama*. He reminded us often that he did not *do drama* so I reported Olga's *dramatic* breakdown to Jackson. Jackson conducted his due diligence, and met with Burt and others in the unit who independently verified that my assertion was correct about her inappropriate behavior. Burt, Olga's good friend, also confirmed my story as being most correct so Jackson asked if Olga apologized would I allow her to continue working for me. I agreed to that compromise because I was a forgiving boss. Jackson then met with Olga and discussed that ultimatum; either she apologize or find another job. Olga thought that because she was at RHD for 6 years, Jackson would side with her, and against me but during their meeting, Jackson told Olga that she owed me an apology, which she did not agree with. Jackson then asked Olga if she could work with me, and she said the magic word, "no" so she was out. Jackson told Olga to pack her things, and to look for a job at another Division. Olga was devastated but very quickly she found a Sergeant position in patrol at Van Nuys Division, and I was glad she was gone. After she left, the guys in the office who had put up with her crap for *6 years* expressed their delight that she was gone. A few months later Burt also accepted a job at Van Nuys so he could be close to his dear friend Olga. After Olga and Burt left RHD, others in the office slowly came around to my style of management primarily because they saw that I was just following the Captain's orders.

Mark took PJ's advice and successfully completed his processing for LAPD, and was scheduled to go into the April 2008 Academy class. Brittany still had 3 months to go in the Academy when Mark entered the Academy. Although Mark was from San Diego, he felt he had better job opportunities in Los Angeles, which is why he was easily persuaded to join the department in LA. PJ and I offered to let Mark stay with us temporarily until he completed the academy training, so he would have the support he needed. Up until this point Brittany and Mark thought they wanted to get married. They were not officially engaged but we took him in anyway. We had plenty of space so we set Mark up in one of the guest bedrooms.

On the morning of February 7, 2008, I was sitting at my desk when word got around that my classmate Officer Randy Simmons was shot and killed as he and other members of the SWAT Team made entry into a home in a community in the San Fernando Valley. It was approximately 12:30 am on that fateful morning when the SWAT team responded to the single-family home after a suspect inside called 911 claiming to have murdered three family members. As Randy's team entered the residence, the suspect opened fire, striking

Randy and a second officer. Many of us were devastated by the news because Randy was an amazing officer and person. The funeral procession and grave-side pomp and circumstance was so long that several officers, including Chief Kenny Garner, while standing at attention, locked out their legs, passed out and went down for the count as the bugle sounded in the distance. I could never get used to police funerals because they were so sad, and they reminded me just how tragic it was for officers killed in the line of duty.

Mark went into the Academy as planned but he didn't get past the first Physical Abilities test which resulted in his being deferred to the May 2008 class, giving him a second chance to get in better shape. Mark worked hard and reentered the Academy in May 2008. In July 2008, Brittany graduated from the Academy after 7 months, and she was assigned to West Los Angles Division where I had worked as a young officer with the likes of Martin Foster 24 years prior.

Like mother like daughter

I was actually relieved that Brittany was going to WLA because it was lo-cated in a great part of the City, so I didn't worry about her as much as I would have had she been assigned in South Los Angeles. The Captain at West Los Angeles at that time was Captain Gil Egan, who had worked with me when he was a young officer at Newton; and I was his Sergeant; and we worked together again when we were both Lieutenants at Internal Affairs right before he made Captain. Egan was still a genuinely caring person just as he was as a young officer. Egan assured me that Brittany was in good hands at his division, so I was one happy mama.

By July of 2008, it had been a year since I finished all of my cancer treatments so Dr. Selma scheduled me to have follow-up visits every six months at City of Hope, instead of every 3 months. I was happy that my follow up regimen had been relaxed so I could concentrate more on getting back to normal. That month 6 lieutenants were promoted to Captains, but clearly I wasn't one of them. At that point, I pretty much gave up on the idea of making Captain because I believed all of the vacancies had been filled, especially with the last batch of 6 recently being promoted. I could not believe I had studied and prepared for a whole year and I was not even being considered. I knew I wasn't the only qualified person being overlooked, but that didn't make me feel any better. *Oh well, it just wasn't meant to be.* I thought, so I decided to take my butt to New York and sulk in the Big Apple, and maybe do a little shopping. The National Organization of Black Law Enforcement Executives (NOBLE) was having their annual Conference in New York City that year so I took advantage of the all expense paid trip. I had been to New York many times on shopping sprees with Mama but never for work. Natalia was home for the summer and had no plans, so I had her join me since she had never been to New York. I booked our flights on Jet Blue, and when we arrived at the airport I realized that Chief Garner, who had passed out at the SWAT officer's funeral, was on our flight, and he was surprisingly pleasant. He could be a little arrogant at times so I was always a little intimidated by his bravado. Several of the newly appointed Captains were also on the trip, and one of those Captains was the Chief's Aide who was in Band 4 with me. Contrary to popular belief, they reached Band 4 just as I said they would. I congratulated them all for their recent promotions and I was sincere. I was not overjoyed about *their* promotions, but I was super excited about being in New York. We had first class accommodations at the Marquis Hotel in Times Square, in the heart of the Theatre District, which was right where I wanted to be. After my day long work sessions, Natalia and I dined late nights at Juniors Deli, and at Carmines Italian Restaurant right across the street from the hotel and next door to where the Lion King was playing. We went sight seeing in Harlem, where we dined at Sylvia's soul food Restaurant, and took pictures in front of the Apollo. One of my friends even made a late night taxi run to White Castle Hamburgers. I had not had a White Castle Burger since I left Detroit in 1970 so I was in seventh heaven. I had tried Krystal Burgers while in Atlanta but they just were not the same as White castle. The fun-filled mid week getaway came to an end after frolicking in New York City for a few days. It was time to go home, and get back to business as usual.

By August of 2008, I started to hear rumors that the Department was going to make a couple more Captains. The list was due to expire within a few months and I was not going through the process again because I didn't have the strength. There were many pros for me making Captain but the glaring con was that there was a high stress level inherent in the job and with my health issues I didn't need any added stress. I was still recovering following my battle with cancer, and I needed to work on rebuilding my overall health and strength. I had lost weight before my diagnosis, and during treatment my weight went back up and hovered around 167 pounds. I maintained that weight although Dr. Selma expected me to gain more weight due to the steroids I was given with my chemo. I was really burnt out from all the doctor's visits at City of Hope, but I still needed to have my annual physicals with my internist, Dr. Nielsen, as well as my annual eye exams. When I saw Dr. Nielsen for my physical that fall my weight was not an issue, but my glucose level was pushing me into the pre-diabetic range. I never thought I was a candidate for diabetes, because diabetes did not run in my family that I knew of; I was not obese, and I exercised regularly. Nielsen scheduled me to return in six months so he could see if my blood sugar had gone down. This new medical issue perplexed me but I was not overly concerned.

It was late August 2008, and I was sitting at my desk reviewing cold cases when I received a call from our new Captain as Captain Jackson had promoted to Commander and had changed commands. The new Captain called to tell me that I needed to prepare a report on the status of DNA Hits so that he and I could present our findings to Chief Bratton that afternoon. I was surprised by the sudden need for the report, but I went with it because I was a good soldier. I called in several resources and worked feverishly for a few hours to have the report ready for our 1PM meeting in the Chief's office. I was nervous because I hated presenting before the Chiefs. The good thing was that I was well versed in how we managed the DNA Hits and the issues inherent in the system, which inhibited ridding ourselves of the huge backlog. When I showed up at the meeting, the room was full of Command Staff officers including my new Captain, who rode in the elevator with me to the 6th floor. The whole meeting seemed a little strange but I walked in with copies of my Power Point presentation in hand.

"Here, let me pass those out for you." Captain Engles said as he grabbed the stack of papers from my hand.

"Oh, Ok Captain. Thanks." I said as I peered at Engles, a little surprised by his courteous gesture.

I took my seat at the conference table as the others took their respective seats. The meeting was called to order, and the Chief started to speak. It became very clear right away that the meeting was a hoax when Chief Bratton opened the meeting.

"Lieutenant Morris, you can dispense with those papers you brought here today because we won't need them. I am proud to announce that you are being promoted to Captain." They fooled me! I was shocked and excited, and felt like I was going to faint. "Your promotion will be effective on October 8th so it won't be announced just yet, which means you can't tell anyone, well except your family, and you will be assigned to Southwest Division."

Southwest Division was located in South Los Angeles right up the street from the Los Angeles Coliseum, and in the vicinity of the prestigious University of Southern California. I left the Chief's office that day, and couldn't dial the phone fast enough to tell PJ about my promotion. I walked around for the rest of the day on *Cloud 9* holding on to this wonderful secret. Within a few days of my meeting, my promotion was announced sooner than I expected so I was then able to openly acknowledge my joy. I remained at RHD until it came time for me to be sworn in, in early October. My elation quickly faded, as I was a ball of nerves because South Los Angeles was no joke. Southwest Division was home to the most notorious criminal gangs in the City of Los Angeles, and the thought of living amongst them for 10-12 hours a day was not my cup of tea. Gang members had no regard for human life, and there I was thrust into *their* environment heading up a police division in *their* territory.

CHAPTER 16

"So You Wanna Be
A Captain, Huh?"

THE NEW POLICE ADMINISTRATION BUILDING (PAB) in downtown Los Angeles was being built a short distance away from the soon to be closed down, dilapidated Police Headquarters aka Parker Center (Old PAB), so my badge ceremony was one of the last to take place in that auditorium. There were only two of us promoting to Captain at that time, and people came from all over the Department to wish us well. I was extremely happy that Brittany could partake in the once in a lifetime event, and the icing on the cake was that she proudly pinned my new badge on my chest, while donning a Los Angeles Police Officer badge herself. PJ, Brittany and I looked sharp in our uniforms that day, and it was a proud moment for all of us. Unfortunately, Natalia was unable to leave school to make it to the ceremony.

October 8th was a Sunday and my first day as a Patrol Commanding Officer at Southwest Division. Chief Kenny Garner was my boss, and Commander Jackson was working alongside Garner in South Bureau so they made sure that I was well prepared for my new role. I was still intimidated by Garner, but I truly believed he had my best interest at heart. I was also very fortunate to be teamed up at Southwest, with my academy classmate Captain James Craig. I met Craig in January of 1981, at the Los Angeles Police Academy. He was one of 690 Detroit police officers laid off from Detroit PD in the summer of 1980, due to a $135 million dollar budget deficit. Craig and several others from Detroit accepted the offer to join the ranks of the LAPD. Following our graduation from the Academy, Craig and I would run into each other over the years but we never worked together until we were assigned as partners at Southwest Division, as Captains. I felt good about being partnered up with Craig because we came up in the organization together, and we got along very well. Sundays were usually very quiet in most stations and my first Sunday was no different at Southwest. I was not scheduled to work that day but I was in the station painting and getting my office set up, so I arrived early and decided to attend Roll Call.

Captain Tia Morris October 2008

Brit, Tia and PJ at my Badge Ceremony October 2008

The first thing that caught my eye when I entered the back door, was a sign taped to the small dirty window, which warned of staph infections being a health concern at the station. I figured the signs just served to remind us to be more diligent about hygiene while in the workplace, rather than reporting an actual outbreak. Once inside, the signs were posted throughout the dirty cluttered facility. The place was a mess. Burn boxes and dusty police war bags lined the upstairs hallway leading to the roll call room, that was much of the same, a mess. I didn't know what was up with all the burn boxes but they were everywhere. Commanding Officers were encouraged to go to roll call in order to bond with the field officers who worked for them, so I thought I would start on my first day while I was there. Most officers respected the Command Staff, unless they were disgruntled employees, or just mean spirited. I was a happy person in general, and down to earth, so I thought I would be well received at Southwest. I walked into the dirty cluttered roll call room that morning where some officers, and some supervisors greeted me, as others looked right through me or past me. As a new Sergeant at Newton Division several years back, I had received poor treatment, but I always remained poised, and positive. The watch commander acknowledged me right away when I walked in, and he motioned for me to join him at the front of the room. I didn't want any fanfare; just wanted to say "Hi." I began telling the group of officers and supervisors about myself and hadn't gotten very far when an old grumpy male black patrol sergeant spoke up from a dark corner in the back of the room.

"Captain, what do you know about the south end? Because, according to you, you never worked down here so what can you possibly tell *us*?"

I couldn't believe he was actually talking to me in this challenging tone so I turned around to see if perhaps *another* Captain had entered the room because I just *knew* he wasn't talking to *me*. When I realized he was talking to *me* I scanned the room slowly until I spotted his angry face lurking in the corner of the room.

"Sergeant…"

"Sergeant Faulk, Ma'am." *Wait a minute. Did this asshole just cut me off?* I thought.

"Well, *Sergeant Faulk* (RIP 2014), first of all I don't think we have met so please allow me to introduce myself *again*. I am Captain Morris, I said, with an emphasis on *Captain*, and if you have any questions for me, that are not relevant to this roll call, you can talk with me in private *after* roll call. I don't think this is the right forum for a debate about my credentials, so you can see me after roll call ok?" I smirked at him and then turned my attention back to the masses.

There was a lot I wanted to say but I needed to keep it professional in the workplace. *Who did he think he was?* I finished what I had to say and returned to my office to finish setting up. I was shaking because I was so angry. The watch commander and a female sergeant followed me to my office; personally welcomed me to the Division, and offered an apology for Sergeant Faulk's rude outburst.

"Ma'am, he has issues. Everyone is afraid of him so he pretty much takes the liberty to say whatever he wants whenever he wants *and* he hates management."

"Oh, ok. Well, that's unfortunate for him but now I know, thank you very much. So, what's up with the Staph Infection signs?"

"Ma'am a few officers have come down with staph infections so we are trying to make sure we focus on hygiene by sanitizing our hands. As you can see the station is pretty filthy. Welcome to the south end Captain."

We talked a bit longer before they went on about their business as I began to paint my office. I needed to finish because I wanted to hit the ground running when I returned on Monday morning. I replayed the Sergeant's outburst in my head a few times thinking about how I should address the situation because I knew that I could not just let it be. It was too early for me to take any formal action against him because I didn't want my response to appear punitive or personal since I *just* got there. When I arrived for work that next morning, I told Craig about the Sergeant's outburst.

"You are shittin' me." Craig was pissed off.

"Nope, I'm serious as a heart attack." Then we both burst out into uncontrollable laughter.

"Whew, I already know I don't have to do nothin'. I'm gonna let you handle him." Craig said as we continued to laugh.

Within a couple of months, Sergeant Faulk had made enough dumb decisions to warrant a move to an assignment out of Patrol, and away from me. Craig and I discussed his antics at every turn and agreed to move him to our internal investigative section where he was tasked with conducting personnel complaint investigations that were not handled by Internal Affairs. He was not happy with his new assignment because he worked with peer supervisors and had no subordinates to boss around. I had quickly won that little battle. Craig and I worked well together and he often said that I was the best partner he ever had. If it was a lie, he told it, but I believed he was sincere. It was no secret that Craig was actively looking for Chief's jobs outside of LAPD because he made it clear to everyone that he was ready to leave the organization for various reasons. One such reason was because of the pressure he was getting from our bosses. Chief Garner, whose leadership style was *no nonsense*, and *in your face*, was largely responsible for Craig and I being assigned as partners, but I didn't understand why he was exceptionally hard on Craig when they were friends and Garner had a lot of respect for Craig.

Chief Garner (RIP March 2009) and Tia

Chief Garner thought I was a good fit for the division in that I could help resolve some major personnel and productivity issues that plagued the division, under the previous transient leadership in Patrol. Craig had been there for a while, but over the years he had several partners, which made it difficult for him to effectively run the division. Craig was very smart and capable, but he was on his way out so his heart wasn't there, and the turnover rate with partners made his job extremely tough. I immediately found ways to try to resolve some of the issues at the Division identified by Chief Garner and Craig. The most prevailing issue was the filth in the station and the accumulation of burn boxes, which were stored at the station way too long resulting in potential City code violations. Chief Garner was not happy about many of the issues at Southwest and openly chastised Craig and me for these issues not being resolved. I was off to a great start but I despised the consistently poor treatment directed at us by Garner. His aggression towards Craig and me was a little much in my opinion especially when he publicly humiliated us during staff meetings in front of our peers. After leaving those *beat down* meetings Garner would personally call me and privately apologize for his actions. He would then say that his aggression was directed at Craig as the primary leader at Southwest, but he did not want to be accused of singling Craig out so he had to include me in his rant. I thought his actions were pretty harsh but he was the Chief. Those calls really put me in a tough position because I didn't want to be in the middle of whatever was going on with Garner and Craig. I really liked my partner and I really respected Garner so I had to find a way to deal with those opposing factions. I stopped taking Garner's actions personal and just went along to get along and did not make any waves. Within a few months it became abundantly clear that Garner was under a lot of pressure from *his* boss, the evil Assistant Chief Patterson, so Garner passed his frustration on to me and Craig at the behest of Patterson so that's why we became Garner's punching bags.

Southwest was a very busy Division, which included venues such as USC, the Los Angeles Coliseum, Sports Arena, and the densely populated area of town called *the Jungle*. The Jungle was the area Mama had considered moving to when she first arrived in LA from Detroit in the 1970's but she settled on Ladera Heights instead. I knew Southwest Area like the back of my hand because I grew up in the vicinity, in Ladera.

I was driving 150 miles to and from work at Southwest so, once again I found myself burning the candle at both ends due to the busy workload. I started to feel the stress of everyday leadership, which was compounded by Garner and Patterson's ridiculous expectations, and the number of off-hour call outs due to the rampant gang violence, which oftentimes resulted in shootings with hits, and murders. Many days I would get home only to turn right back around and drive the 75 miles back to crime scenes and other unusual occurrences. Craig lived nearby in Ladera Heights, my old neck of the woods, and he was very accommodating. When there was a need for a Commanding Officer at a crime scene, Craig would respond to keep me from driving all the way back in, and I really appreciated him for that.

Brittany was still a probationary officer at WLA; Natalia was still in college; Mark was a probationary officer working 77th Division; and PJ was still a Homicide Coordinator at Northeast Division.

PJ and LAPD Northeast Division's Homicide Unit

Mark was doing well as a probationary officer, but by that time he and Brittany were not getting along. Brittany did not know what to make of Mark's gradual change towards her but she grew suspicious of his weekend trips to San Jose allegedly to hang out with *his boys* from college. Brittany was bothered by the frequent trips, but dealt with it as best she could without being overbearing. It was early in December of 2008, when Mark said he was planning to move out come January 2009. His notice caught Brittany totally by surprise because it just added to the unexplained rift they were experiencing. PJ and I were ok with him moving out because he was gainfully employed, and we had helped him make it through the Academy as we said we would, so it was time for him to go. It was hurtful to Brittany that Mark was acting so distant, and furthermore, declined her offer to assist him with looking for an apartment. Mark's mother, who had been very friendly whenever she came to visit, was also acting very strange when she came to visit Mark for the last time at our home that December, and by her actions she seemed to be spearheading Mark's move which was really strange. Mark moved out as planned in January 2009, and in February, right before Valentines Day, Mark and Brittany ended their relationship.

"Mom I don't know what is wrong with Mark. He is saying it's not me but he won't tell me why he is acting so weird."

"Girl, maybe he got someone else pregnant."

"No Mom, Mark is not like that. He would *never* do that mom." Brittany said angrily at the thought of that possibility.

"Well, nothing else makes any sense to me based on what you are telling me. He's acting like a guilty person, and that's all I can think of, *and* don't ever say what someone else won't do." About a week passed after they broke up when Mark contacted Brittany and asked if they could meet and talk.

"Mom, I'm meeting with Mark today. He's supposed to tell me what is going on with him."

"Ok, well I can't wait to hear what he has to say."

Later that day Brittany called and told me that in fact Mark had gotten a girl pregnant in San Jose before he left school. Although Mark said he had *just* found out a couple of months before, there was evidence to the contrary. He had slept with the girl and he *knew* all along that she was pregnant before he left San Jose, and his alleged trips to visit *his boys* were actually trips to visit his pregnant girlfriend. Before Mark left school in December 2007, he told the girl he didn't want to be with her and that he was marrying Brittany and was moving to LA. Mark lied to *all* of us, when in fact he was actually in San Jose when the baby was born in October 2008. Brittany was devastated, and PJ and I were disappointed, but mostly angry about his lying and deceit, and the nerve of his mother to acquiesce to his not being honest, while we had opened our home to him, and helped him when she wouldn't. PJ was right about his faulty DNA.

In March of 2009, Craig found a Chief's job across the Country in Maine, and he announced his retirement after 28 years with LAPD. I was happy for him but wondered who would replace him as my new partner. I was still in my one-year probationary period so I knew I would not be selected to assume Craig's position as the Commanding Officer in charge of the Area. When Craig was tying up some loose ends, in preparation for his retirement, I handled some Community meetings in his stead. Chief Garner called one evening and told me that I needed to attend one such community meeting on Wednesday, February 25th with him. I hated those late evening meetings because it made for a very long day for me but I met Garner at that 8PM meeting anyway. He seemed a little subdued, and it was kind of nice to actually see a hint of humility. He wasn't himself, but I chalked it up to him being tired because Patterson worked him like his name was Kunta Kinte. The community members were enamored with me. They were sweet people but those meetings were annoying most of the time because the same community members complained about the same stuff over and over and over again, and they wanted to occupy all of our time. I remember stepping up to the podium in the small neighborhood Church's community room. I started to discuss the state of the division, and crime stats etc. when Ms. Pat (RIP 2015) raised her hand.

"Yes Ms. Pat?" I asked.

"So how long you gonna be with us Captain Morris? Because they always changing these Captains so much we never get to know ya'll." Pat said with old lady attitude.

"Well, we are at the mercy of the Chief of Police, and can be moved at a moment's notice depending on the needs of the Department." That was always my politically correct answer.

"Captain Morris ain't going anywhere. She is gonna stay right here at Southwest." Chief Garner playfully yelled from where he was seated. His tone was down to earth and lighthearted. When I looked at him, he was grinning from ear to ear. I thought to myself *who is this man and what did he do with Chief Garner because Chief Garner don't smile and play like this.*

"Well alrighty then, I guess we gonna grow old together Ms. Pat." I retorted as laughter filled the room. It turned out to be a wonderful community meeting after all with our stakeholders hanging on my every word and Ms. Pat was the best community partner.

I was dead tired when I left work that Wednesday night but I was up bright and early on the next morning to report for duty all over again. From that night on Ms. Pat called me every night to make sure that I made it home safely. My first order of business the next morning was to call Chief Garner to report on a follow up issue from the meeting. He didn't answer his phone so I left a message. Chief Garner was very busy all the time but he *always* called me back even if it was to fuss at me about one thing or another. By the weekend I still had not heard from Chief but I didn't call him again because I did not want to get cussed out. On that Sunday morning March 1ˢᵗ, I was awakened by an early morning call from Evangelyn.

"Hey, did you hear what happened to Kenny?" When we were not in his presence we called the Chief by his first name. We had all come up on the Department in the same era but out of respect we referred to each other by rank while in the workplace.

"No. What happened to Kenny?" I thought maybe he had been arrested or injured in a traffic collision or something.

"Girl, Kenny died last night from a massive heart attack." Evangelyn said in a solemn voice.

"Oh no." My heart skipped a beat.

"Yeah apparently he was sick and had gone to the hospital on Thursday complaining of chest pains. They sent him home and Saturday he passed out at home and they couldn't revive him when paramedics arrived."

That's why he never called me back on Thursday. He was off sick. I thought. I knew that wasn't like him to not return my call. His death was a total shock to me. It was almost unimaginable. Chief Garner's death was the second high profile death of an African American on LAPD within a year, with the first being the murder of SWAT Officer Randy Simmons. Garner was a good man and awesome leader. He was known for improving minority relations in the community and helping diversify the police department. *I wondered if his passing out at Randy's funeral was a tell tale sign that his health was failing?* His death proved to be an incredible loss, especially for black officers on the Department. Within a couple of weeks following Craig's departure Captain Zimmerman was named as his replacement. Zimmerman was a very nice, rather intense guy who was an amazing taskmaster. He knew what he wanted for the division and knew how to achieve the goals he set. He and I immediately clicked and quickly became a good team. He stayed in his lane and trusted me to handle my business. Zimmerman thought

I was very skilled, especially for a newer Captain. I appreciated his confidence in my abilities but I had been around for many years and I too had great experience.

My hair was growing in beautifully, and it was shiny and wavy as it ascended into the fake bun I had started to wear. There was never a hair out of place and my baby hair was pretty awesome. However, absent the fake bun, when my hair was down, it was a wavy ball of cotton and I couldn't do anything with it. I was bored with always having to wear it up but I had no choice because I could not style the frizzy mess. I guess the stress of the long commute and long hours was getting to me because right about the time that Zimmerman joined me at Southwest I contracted a staph infection. Go figure. I saw the signs, and was always diligent with the use of my hand sanitizer, but the filthy station won out over my weakened immune system. The infection primarily affected my scalp, causing me to lose my pretty baby hair around my edges. When I combed through my hair in the shower, clumps of hair came out so I knew something was seriously wrong, but I didn't know what the extent of the staph infection was. I cut my then shoulder length ball of cotton to a short style but it was so thin around the edges I felt like a mangy dog. I finally gave in and drove down the street from the station to the Slauson Swap Meet and found me a cute little wig at Mr. Kim's Beauty Supply. So, there I was back in a wig again. The only difference was I was not bald underneath so it wasn't as bad because I could pin the wig to my hair and not have to pull it so tight around the perimeter of my big head. Zimmerman knew that I had recently undergone cancer treatment and expressed that he didn't want me to get sick again since he witnessed how the staph infection was affecting me. Unbeknownst to me, Zimmerman pleaded with Chief Patterson to move me to a Valley Division, which was a slower pace than Southwest, and it would put me much closer to home. On May 8th, 2009, before leaving the office for the weekend I received a call from Chief Albany, Garner's replacement.

"Hey Tia, I'm just calling to let you know we are making some command staff changes and you are one of them. We are moving you to Van Nuys."

I knew that Captains were moved at a moments notice, but I did not expect the move so soon after Garner's death and I had only been at Southwest Division 7 months. Ms. Pat was mad when she heard I was leaving so instead of checking on me that evening she called to fuss about my move. I promised her I would keep in touch.

"Ok Chief, when will the change take place?" I asked.

"This Sunday, May 10th."

"Ok, well I guess I'll be cleaning out my office this weekend." I chuckled. I was just getting in the swing of things at Southwest, but I did like the idea of being closer to home, and in a cleaner environment. Just as I hung up the phone Zimmerman's small frame appeared in my doorway.

"So, you're going to Van Nuys huh?"

"Yeah, so they told you first?" I asked.

"Well don't be mad at me, but I was in a meeting, and I told Patterson they needed to get you closer to home because you were working too much and I didn't want you sick again."

"Wow. Are you serious? What a sweetheart you are. I really appreciate you for that but I hope Chief Patterson doesn't think *I* put you up to this."

How could I be mad at someone who genuinely expressed care and concern for me? The last thing I needed was for Chief Patterson to think I was weak, and think I could not withstand the workload in the south end. Zimmerman quickly assured me that he made it clear to Patterson that it was *his* suggestion and not my expressed preference. Zimmerman said that Patterson commented, "Oh, I thought that Tia lived in the City." As usual, Patterson was as fake as a three-dollar bill because he knew everything about his Command Staff Officers, and he definitely knew where we lived. Patterson didn't like me, so my well being didn't matter to him. I knew that the distance was never brought up before because before Garner died he requested me to work in his Bureau and Patterson obliged without any other considerations.

On Monday May 11, 2009, when I showed up at Van Nuys Division I met with my new partner Gil Egan who had just returned to work after being off on medical leave for 3 months. Gil transferred into Van Nuys from West Los Angeles a couple of months earlier in late February 2009, however because of his medical leave, he never physically made it to Van Nuys until the same day I transferred into the division. It was so ironic that Gil and I were working together yet again. When I arrived at Van Nuys I was due to start my vacation right away. PJ and I had planned a trip to Cabo San Lucas the week of May 9th, and I was not changing my vacation plans just because *they* decided to move me to another division. We had started going to Cabo in 2008, when we took some friends up on an offer to join them at one of their time-share resorts. Glenn and Toni had been going to Cabo for many years, and had tried several times to get us to join them. Frankly, PJ and I were scared of Mexico because of the drug cartel issues we had heard about over the years but we finally relented and joined them, and we had a blast. We loved Cabo so much that we bought a timeshare while we were there. When we returned home after a beautiful week soaking up the sun on the Baja Peninsula we went directly from the airport to Cal State Northridge University just in time for Natalia's college graduation ceremony.

Natalia graduated from college with a B.A. in English/Education with an emphasis in writing, Natalia had no job prospects suitable for her locally so she accepted an offer to work at an elementary school in New Jersey. Clarice, Natalia's *bestie* from high school, and Clarice's mom Sherry had moved back to their hometown of New Jersey so they welcomed Natalia to stay with them. That was perfect for Natalia's transition to a new life across the Country. Since I was in a new assignment, I cut my month long vacation short and returned to work after only two weeks. I was happy to be working with Gil because he was such a nice guy. He was a big teddy bear. Gil stood about 6'3" and weighed in at about 300 pounds; he wasn't fat but he was just a really big guy. I was shocked to hear that Gil was going through a divorce because I had worked with his wife, who was a detective at another division. I had last seen Gil and his wife together in 2007, while I was going through my cancer treatment. They were in the midst of adopting two young boys from another Country, and they seemed happy, so I couldn't imagine what happened to change their lives so drastically and so quickly. It made good sense why Gil was so distracted from the beginning of our partnership. When I returned from vacation Gil and I sat down to discuss what was going on in the division. He explained that the Detectives in the Division *hated* him because his wife had worked there in the past and most of the detectives' allegiance was to *her*. Then *I* shared with Gil that one of his detectives, Olga, who I had worked with in the past at RHD hated me too, and she had turned other detectives in the unit against me, so our partnership was all bad as far as Detectives were concerned. It was crazy that I unexpectedly followed Olga *and* Burt to Van

Nuys. Burt and Olga had conducted a pretty good smear campaign and had thoroughly convinced their peers that I was the wicked witch of the west, so detectives were very biased against me from the start, and most of them didn't even know me. When I realized what was going on with their hate crusade I met with Burt and his Lieutenant to discuss the need for us to coexist in the workplace regardless of his personal feelings. I wasn't too affected by the rest of the Detectives' feelings for me, because they were a "*direct report*" to Gil, so I didn't have to deal with them too much, unless Gil was absent. Burt on the other hand was the Homicide Coordinator so I had to deal with him a great deal, which is the *only* reason I reached out to him. Burt pretended in front of his Lieutenant of course, that everything was *hunky dory* with me, and that he had no ill feelings, but he was not truthful. He was a coward.

From the start of our partnership at Van Nuys Gil was not a responsible partner. He had lost focus like a man going through a major mid life crisis. Gil spent more time off work with his new *girlfriend* than he did at work, so I inherited a lot of his duties in addition to mine. The more he flaunted his new life, and new woman, the more problematic his impending divorce became for him, and his adopted children. Gil eventually moved in with his girlfriend, who was a younger police officer, who had worked for him when he was a Captain at WLA. Their relationship was out in the open, and he acted like a love struck teenager. He regularly missed important meetings and events that eventually came to the attention of our bosses. Gil didn't care much about work but he was *very* happy about his new life. If he wasn't on a trip with his girlfriend, or off on extended sick leave, he was away at some training that he thought would help him make Commander. Yes, although he was derelict in his duties as a Captain, he was still vying for a promotion. He was an educated white man, and was loved by the Senior Command Staff, so he met the basic criteria for a promotion. I started to resent Gil, but I didn't go behind his back and talk about him. I repeatedly pointed out his neglectful ways and I told him directly to his face. Each time I discussed my issues with him, he acknowledged the error of his ways and apologized profusely, and then turned right back around and did the same thing over and over again. I was sick of his antics, but I still liked him as a person.

CHAPTER 17

"The New Family Business"

AT THE START OF 2010, Natalia expressed that she was going to finish the school year in Jersey and return home because she no longer wanted to work there. Natalia still had an overwhelming desire to hone her skills as a film director. Entertainment was her passion so she was serious about pursuing a career in the industry, on her own terms by starting her own Company. We had established Natalia's first company, Medium Entertainment, when she was 17 years old but she wanted to branch out and start a new company. Natalia's talents included song writing as well as writing screenplays and theatre plays. Natalia released her first album in 2006, called City in the Sky, and she was known in Los Angeles as a spoken word poet under the name Vintage Soul.

"Hey mom, before I come back home I want to start another company. I'm going to incorporate under Vintage City Entertainment. What you think?"

"Well you already have Medium Entertainment."

"Yeah mom but I have grown so much since then, and since I'm Vintage Soul I want to name my new Company Vintage City Entertainment (VCE)."

"Ok, well when you return home this summer we can talk about it with daddy and Brittany."

"Yeah but I want to incorporate now mom. I'm going to have all the Limited Liability Corporation (LLC) paperwork sent to the house ok because I want to hit the ground running when I get back. I want to do some stage plays and short films. It's going to be big. I'll be home in a couple of weeks for the weekend. I have an audition with Don B. Welch. He's a playwright in LA and he puts on *a lot* of plays."

"Ok girl, well send the LLC stuff and we will discuss it later."

Natalia did not receive a callback from Mr. Welch, after her audition so she returned to New Jersey but she continued to communicate with Don via Facebook. In January 2010, Vintage City Entertainment was incorporated. Natalia became the Chief Executive Officer; Brittany the President; PJ the Chief Operations Officer, and I was designated as the Chief Financial Officer.

**Doing Our Part to Find a Cure for Breast Cancer
(Revlon Run/Walk) Los Angeles**

Natalia adopted the pseudonym Tai French, and in July 2010, when she returned home from New Jersey she got to work immediately. Natalia enlisted Brittany's help with putting on her first stage production. PJ and I were busy working and hadn't given much thought to the new company.

"Brittany, I think I want to put on a play called Jesus on The Way. You know my friend Nina? Well, she belongs to a church in the Valley and she said we can put on the play there for free and I can get actors from the church."

Natalia didn't have a clue about running a business, so the church idea was her answer to putting up her production without an actual producer.

After getting the nod from Nina, Natalia started planning the logistics for Jesus On The Way using Nina's church actors. Everything started out well until the Church suggested a monetary compensation to host the play. Natalia saw that this *free* plan was not working. Natalia had already told me of her plan to have her production at Nina's church because it would be free. I told Natalia that was unrealistic because she was not a member of the church. I didn't mean to put a damper on Natalia's plans but I just didn't see that plan as viable.

"Natalia, nothing is free, let's just book a Theatre and do it the right way." Brittany said after the church plan started to unravel.

"Girl I ain't got no money for that."

"Well I have a job and I will produce the play for you."

Brittany and Natalia researched small theatres and came upon a little gem in Hollywood called the Complex Theatre, a 49-seat theatre. Brittany and Natalia worked throughout the summer of 2010 on the first stage play Jesus on The Way produced solely by Brittany. PJ and I were not involved in the production process but by the time the show was ready to open Brittany and Natalia needed help with props and furnishing the set.

"Mommy, I need help."

"With what?"

"I need you to help furnish the set for my play. Can we please use the brown couch in your office, and I need a Christmas tree and a bunch of small props." Natalia explained all the details of what was needed and additionally asked if I could bake some goodies to sell during intermission.

"Dang girl, you are asking a lot. Let me talk to daddy and see what we can do."

We had a truck to transport most of what the girls needed. What we didn't have at home we bought at the 99-Cent Store or Big Lots. In December 2010, Jesus on the Way debuted in Hollywood and sold out every weekend, for three weeks. PJ and I showed up on the first night not knowing what to expect and we were amazed at the outstanding quality of the show. We were *all in* after seeing the show, and we helped the girls fill the seats for the sold out performances. Don attended and enjoyed the show. PJ and I didn't know Don but Natalia was excited that someone of his status actually came out to support her very first show. He came and left immediately after the show so we didn't get a chance to talk to him. I didn't know what to make of him but clearly he was thoughtful enough to attend so I felt good about that considering we were new to the industry, and he was a veteran in the theatre arena, and a published author. It was a great beginning for Vintage City Entertainment, and the start of a wonderful relationship with Donald Welch who eventually became like family to us.

PJ and I were on the road to retirement so the start of a family business was perfect for our transition from law enforcement to a much happier place. As we approached our retirement years we had not had a pet in several years. I never liked dogs growing up but I changed over the years when the girls and PJ expressed their desire for a family dog. In March of 2010, PJ visited a local dog shelter to peruse the kennels when he crossed paths with a cute little brown dog, which started barking incessantly as PJ walked by. PJ turned to one of the workers and asked if he could take the female dog out on the yard to check her temperament. PJ enjoyed his time with the 6 month-old puppy and decided he wanted to bring her home.

"Ok thanks man. She's a cutie. I might come back, but I have to go talk to my wife."

"Well, sir we are going to have to put her down tomorrow at 9 AM because she's been here for a few weeks."

"What's her story?"

"She was found wandering the streets that's all."

"Ok. I may see you tomorrow."

The next morning we were out bright and early having breakfast when PJ told me all about the dog he had seen, and he made sure to tell me that the dog was going to be put down that morning.

"Oh gee whiz. I don't want another dog before we retire." I told PJ digging my heels in. I saw the look on PJ's face and I caved in. "Ok, go get the dog." I said sarcastically.

PJ swallowed the rest of his coffee and drove me home like a mad man. When we reached the house he slowed down just enough for me to jump out of the truck before he accelerated away towards the pound. About an hour later PJ returned and I anxiously greeted him in the driveway just in time to see the cutest dog emerge from the back seat of the truck. It was love at first sight. The beige mutt with a cropped tail stole my heart and instantly became my *road dog*. PJ loved Harley Davidson bikes so we thought it fitting to name her Harlee. Harlee always barked at Abel our gardener, and Tim our pool specialist but she liked them. She liked *everyone* except for Mark, Brittany's ex-boyfriend. She never growled at anyone in a mean spirited way until she met Mark. After Mark and Brittany broke up he came by the house to talk to PJ and get some advice about his messy life. When he entered the house Harlee growled and barked so much that PJ had to put her outside. Her instinct was incredible because Mark was in essence an enemy in the Morris household.

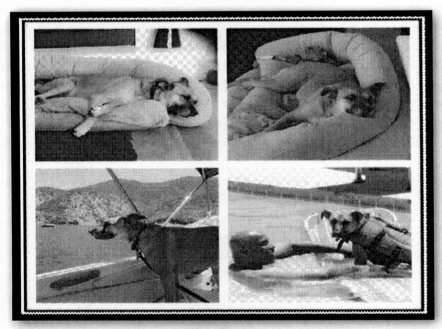

Miss Harlee

In the summer of 2011, Edris and Stefon were reunited. They were living and working together in the Valley near where I worked so they decided they would look me up. They called me at the station one day and I couldn't believe they were *working* together at a loan office and telemarketing call center, and they were living together in a condo allegedly owned by the company they worked for. I drove over to their office located in the West Valley area because I couldn't believe they were working together. Due to Stefon's age and criminal background his job options were limited but I was real suspect about any loan office that would hire an ex con to process loans for their company. Sure enough, when I arrived I noted that Stefon was gainfully employed by a home loan operation called Hi-Tech Lending, which was run by foreigners, who were probably crooks. I was happy to see my brothers, but it wasn't long before I realized they had not changed. Within a short period of time they were fighting and scheming against one another. Stefon swore that he was *clean* for about 10 years but he still smoked *weed*. Edris on the other hand was still an alcoholic and still involved in abusive relationships. I was a Captain of police and had no time for their tomfoolery, so I dealt with them from a distance after that first meet up. They called occasionally and tried to get me to loan them money but I could not bring myself to support their cigarette, alcohol and/or drug habits, so I kept my distance and just checked in by phone from time to time. Within a couple of months of them being reunited I started getting calls from LAPD Communications dispatch whenever officers were dispatched to Stefon and Edris's residence. These idiots mentioned my name whenever the police showed up, hoping that I would run interference for whatever mischief they were involved in. I couldn't take it. I was so embarrassed. They had been an embarrassment to me throughout my career in law enforcement, and enough was enough. After a couple such notifications I told Communications Division I did not want to be contacted when Stefon and/or Edris were detained. I was done with their foolishness.

That same year Mark transferred into my command at Van Nuys Division as a patrol officer. Of all the divisions in the City of Los Angeles they sent him to work for me. That was very awkward because of his recent split with Brittany, but I was able to remain fair in supervising him. Thankfully there were several levels of supervision between him and me so I didn't have to deal with him that much. At some point Mark talked to PJ and said he still wanted to be with Brittany but PJ firmly told him he needed to stay with his baby's mother and try to make it work for the baby's sake. Mark reluctantly agreed but a few weeks later Mark's baby's mother personally reached out to Brittany and appealed to her to give Mark another chance because according to her, Mark loved Brittany and not her. By that time Brittany's devastation had turned into scorn and although she initially agreed to give Mark another chance, after hearing from his baby's mother, after much consideration, she realized that she was not willing to allow Mark back in her life with all of his baggage. Mark and Brittany never reconciled.

It was three years since I ended my cancer treatment so I was considered to still be in remission rather than cured. During that three-year period, I had a couple of scares when shadows were mistaken for masses on my Breast MRI film. Each time I got those false positives I had to undergo Ultra Sounds and repeat mammograms. That was a worrisome routine that I had to deal with a few times. Dr. Selma was always of the opinion that he would rather be safe than sorry by performing these follow up tests considering my history, and I agreed with him. In addition to the false images, Dr. Selma was watching a lymph node located deep in my right armpit, which continued to grow slowly. When it got to about 3 CM, although Selma believed it was benign, he referred me to a surgeon at City of Hope to have it surgically removed. I met with Dr. Kramer who examined me and scheduled me for surgery to remove the lymph node. I wasn't looking forward to yet another surgery or another scar on my torso but at least it was under my arm. I already had the lumpectomy scar on my left breast, the scar under my left arm from removal of the Sentinel Node, and the scar on my right forearm resulting from my Port Catheter. All of these battle scars reminded me of my Cancer treatment. I went in on June 10th for the surgery and all went well. The node was removed and confirmed as benign. I immediately returned to work on the next day with duty restrictions. I was due to go on vacation in July, and Gil was scheduled for vacation in August. He was so selfish that he asked if I would cut my vacation short so that he could go to some sort of out of state training *prior* to the start of his long vacation. *Are you kidding me? How selfish can you be?*

As luck would have it, a couple of weeks after my surgery, before my vacation started, I developed a thickness around the incision in my armpit, and it was very sore. It was mid week, but I kept an eye on my surgical site, and by the weekend it was red, sore; and it was moist. PJ looked at it closely and pressed down around the incision when a stream of thick cloudy puss started oozing from one section of the incision, which had opened up. That's when I decided to call City of Hope for advice. After describing my situation to the on call doctor

I was told to come in. When I arrived at City of Hope that night the doctor said that I had an infection at the surgery site so she lanced my incision and drained it. That was the first time I had an infection that needed to be drained. Once she lanced it, the incision could not be stitched up again so the open incision had to be packed with gauze daily until it gradually closed up. PJ agreed to pack it for me so that I didn't have to return to City of Hope everyday and I was grateful for his loving touch and care. My Cancer business was becoming a never-ending saga, but I tried not to stress about it. I was placed off work for 6 weeks to allow for the incision to heal and close up, which meant that Gil *had* to work while I was off sick. After I was returned to work it was time for my scheduled vacation. Surprisingly enough the Chief *still* allowed Gil to go to his *out of state* training, while I was off on vacation, which he would never have allowed me to do. By the end of the summer of 2010, after I returned to work, Gil returned from his training just in time for *his* month long August vacation. It was about that time that Gil started to complain about throat pain, and his voice was very raspy. Gil was having trouble swallowing; and he had major acid reflux issues, which he had been treated for with previous surgeries. Gil was looking great because he had lost about 30 pounds and he was happy about the weight loss. Gil was having problems getting the City to approve his work comp doctor's visits in a timely manner to address the issues with his esophagus, and he did not want to use his private medical insurance, so he was in a state of limbo with his medical care during that time.

"Look Man," I told Gil. "You have good insurance so go to the doctor, and stop being jacked around by the City."

"You're right T, I'm going to make an appointment and go because I can't keep anything down."

"Gil, that's not good. You look amazing but I want you to *feel* amazing as well." I said staring across my desk at him sitting with his legs crossed as he stared back at me. I genuinely liked Gil but he was still a lousy partner.

I told Gil I was confident the City would eventually come through for him but he held off seeing a doctor for several weeks until he was finally approved to see a City doctor.

In August of 2010, Gil went on his 30-day long vacation with his girl-friend aka *home wrecker,* and he spent some time with his boys. Upon his return to work he planned yet another get-a-way for early November, to some exotic place for him and the *home wrecker,* during a time when his divorce issues were heating up. Gil claimed he looked forward to his divorce being finalized so that one day he could marry the *home wrecker* and start a family with her, but in reality he was dragging his feet because he didn't like the pressure he was getting from his little fire plug of a girlfriend. Gil had just turned 44 and *home wrecker* was in her 30's. Gil and his estranged wife were college sweethearts, and had been married for about 20 years before they split, so there were issues relative to division of property, and a one million dollar Insurance Policy that was a major source of contention for all parties involved. Gil took his time ending the marriage, and it was really frustrating *home wrecker.* When November rolled around and Gil was about to go on his exotic vacation, he wasn't feeling well. It was Tuesday November 9, 2010, PJ's birthday, and I was looking forward to leaving work a little early because we had a dinner date. I was packing my things and ready to leave the office when I got a call from *home wrecker.* She told me she and Gil were at the doctor's office, and as they were leaving the office Gil physically collapsed.

"What do you mean he collapsed?" *Home wrecke*r had my attention as I put my purse and keys down on my desk. I was worried about Gil because whatever was going on sounded like it was serious.

"Yes ma'am, he collapsed. Gil stood up in the doctor's office and was walking towards the door when he literally fell to the floor, so they are transporting him to UCLA Medical Center-Santa Monica."

"Oh wow, ok, well I will be right there. I'll meet you at the hospital."

I was truly concerned and needed to go to the hospital to check on Gil. I called PJ and told him what was going on, and he told me not to worry about dinner, and agreed that I needed to go check on Gil. When I told Brittany her favorite Captain was in the hospital she rode with me to the hospital so she could see him. When we arrived at the hospital, *home wrecker* was sitting by Gil's side as he sat up in the bed. He was very alert, and was determined to go on his trip, but his doctor said otherwise. They kept Gil in the hospital to run tests, and came up with a game plan to get him some nutrition. By the next morning Gil called and told me that he was diagnosed with Cancer of the esophagus. I was stunned that his condition went from acid reflux to cancer.

Then I thought back to the spittoon that he kept on his desk, and recalled the enormous amount of tobacco he chewed daily. Then I thought about how I might have contributed to his addiction when, for Christmas the year before, I gave him a nice decorative spittoon for his desk so I would not have to look at the disgusting brown drip on the side of his Styrofoam cup that he kept on his desk, or walked around with. Maybe I should have been encouraging him to stop chewing that crap instead. Within days, the word got out that Gil Egan had Cancer. Gil vowed to beat it, but he was Stage 4, as it had spread to multiple organs; and his cancer in his esophagus was inoperable. Gil was in and out of the hospital for weeks leading up to the Christmas holiday that was fast approaching. We had planned a Divisional Christmas Party that was to take place in early December, but because Gil's condition was touch-and-go, I cancelled the party. I could not fathom partying at work for the holidays when my partner and the figurehead of the Division was dying. That would have been insensitive, so instead we had a Christmas luncheon/fundraiser for Gil so that we could raise money for toys for his children. We raised a few thousand dollars and during the week leading up to the holiday, I met Gil and *home wrecker* at a restaurant near the station. I hadn't seen Gil in a couple of weeks, and when I walked into the restaurant he was seated at a table in the middle of the room. I totally did not recognize him. He was tall and gangly and pretty much emaciated. I put on a poker face and held back my tears at the same time. I couldn't believe how cancer had sucked the life right out of Gil in such a short period of time. My mind wandered back to the months that Gil and I had worked together, and I thought about how he was all over the place, and just not focused or concerned about work. The man was *dying, for goodness sakes,* so he was living out his last days, and neither of us knew it. At that moment I felt really bad that I was so hard on Gil. For weeks Gil was in the fight of his life, while I continued to run myself ragged running the Division. The holidays came and went and Gil's health continued to decline with Gil returning to the hospital where he remained on a respirator for a few weeks. Those last days at the hospital were like a scene right out of a Lana Turner movie. The *home wrecker* made sure that Gil gave her Power of Attorney before he lapsed into a coma. She even summonsed a Notary to the hospital so Gil could change this Will, and make her the sole beneficiary on all of his insurance policies. Gil was getting weaker by the day but before he lost all awareness he told *home wrecker* he did not want to die at the hospital, so it was arranged for Gil to be transported home in an ambulance with a police escort from Santa Monica Hospital to his home in Santa Clarita that he shared with *home wrecker*. On January 13, 2011, Gil Egan arrived at home and officers carried his limp, partially nude body, up a flight of stairs, to the bed he shared with *home wrecker*. A few minutes later Gil Egan died.

I had worked really hard my entire career and my time at Van Nuys was no different. Gil was gone, and it was time to bring in a new Commanding Officer to take Gil's place. Many thought I would be considered for the promotion, but there was one problem, Chief Patterson called the shots when it came to deployment of field resources, and he still *did not* like me so he emphatically denied me the promotion. I was disappointed but not surprised. I waited like everyone else, to see who was taking Gil's place. Some names were tossed around in the rumor mill, but many still held out hope that I would get the nod for the promotion. I was the Captain I *Patrol* Commanding Officer, responsible for the police officers, and supervisors assigned in the field, and Gil's position was the Captain III *Area* Commanding Officer responsible for the entire command, which included Patrol and all of the specialized units such as Vice, Community Relations, and Detectives. It was a huge responsibility, but I was up for the challenge, however, with all of the things going on, PJ and I thought it would be too stressful, and I didn't need that increased responsibility or stress because of my ongoing health issues. After the dust settled I found out that Patterson never considered me for the job, and in fact he removed my biggest supporter, Chief Albany from the decision making table because he knew Albany was pushing for me to be promoted. The Chief's Aide, who was in the same band as me on the Captain's list, was promoted and sent to Van Nuys as my new partner in early February of 2011. I had successfully run the division by myself for 4 months. When I was told about Patterson's shady ill intentions for me, I felt defeated and irrelevant, so I was *done* for once and for all with the LAPD. I had seen so much disparity in the workplace, and had gone through so much for over 30 years, that I was just plain tired, so I did what was expected of me at work and no more, and I focused my attention on the family business at home.

In August of 2011, we produced Natalia's second feature length film *The Molding Maverick Mason*. We hired a film crew and spent several months filming all over Los Angeles. Unlike Beast, this film was a fictional account of the life of a young man, 18 year-old Ricky Maverick Mason, who was a conflicted and tortured young man dealing with the stress of growing up in the projects. The film turned out to be a fascinating drama, which Natalia wrote, directed and edited however, the finished product was flawed due to wind noise in areas of the film, which could not be masked or corrected during post production. The flaws made the film impossible to submit the to festivals as we had hoped however, we still felt obliged to do something with it because of the time and money invested, so on September 8, 2011, we rented out the Laemmle Theatre in Santa Monica for a screening of the *rough cut* of the film. Over 250 guests filled the theatre, including actors from the film, and their families and friends. It was an amazing night but that's where it ended for the film until a few years later during a brainstorming session with Don. He suggested that Natalia make the movie into a Web Series, which was a brilliant idea so Natalia edited the film into 10 episodes, weeding out most of the parts with sound issues, and she posted it on the web, weekly, until all episodes were released. I liked the direction we were headed with the new company, and all the possibilities that could materialize from work that Natalia created.

The 30 years I spent on the LAPD had taken a toll on my mind, body and spirit. I felt renewed with the advent of the family business, and I really started to think seriously about retiring. I was scheduled to retire in late 2014 but I didn't know if I could hold on that long. I had several work comp injury claims that were in addition to my Breast Cancer claim, and they needed to be addressed before I retired. Attorney Snitzer was successful in filing and winning claims for both of my hands, my elbows, knees, and my cervical spine, all of which sustained cumulative trauma over the 30 plus years on the department.

I tried hard to stay out of my new partner's way when he showed up at Van Nuys. He and I had been friends for almost 20 years, but we had never worked together anywhere. Saul Panell was very smart, and capable, but he expressed very little regard for women in the workplace. Saul's way of doing business resulted in a divided camp within our administrative office, but in spite of our differences,

I worked diligently with him for the good of the division for about a year. By February 2012, I was scheduled to go off and have surgery on one hand to correct my Carpal Tunnel Syndrome. I wasn't happy about having surgery but I was happy to be away from work. Although I was off work recovering from my surgery, I still helped as much as I could with managing our family business on days I was not scheduled to work. I did not want any work comp fraud issues so I was letter of the law when it came to my activities while off on worker's comp. I remained off work until July 2012, and was recovering well following my surgery, but I kept having issues with skin rashes, and each time I sought medical attention from Dr. Nielsen, who eventually referred me to a dermatologist. During one of those visits with Dr. Nielsen, he indicated that my blood glucose level was still high, and he wanted me to see a Nutritionist to discuss *diabetes education*. I heard what he said but I didn't feel diabetes education was beneficial for me at that time because I thought my random sugar issue would pass. When I returned to work in late July I had planned on working for a few months before going back off for my second hand surgery. I had no feeling in my left hand and I had pain in my left shoulder due to the associated cubital tunnel. I needed surgery on my hand as well as my elbow to correct both ailments so I went back off to have my last two surgeries so I could retire and leave my toxic job situation.

I was coming up on the 5-year mark, at which time doctor's considered a patient cured from breast cancer when there was no recurrence. I wasn't ready for a celebration, because cancer is so uncertain, as to its origin, I could never rest easy in survivor mode. I returned to Nielsen's office for my follow up visit a few months later and at that time, my blood tests indicated that my glucose level had crossed the threshold into Type II Diabetic territory. I was devastated because I had no family history of diabetes, and I had no reason to believe I would ever become diabetic. I think I was more shocked about the Diabetes than I was the Breast Cancer.

"Doctor, I noticed that my blood sugar became uncontrollable *after* Chemotherapy."

"It's funny you say that because I know that your chemo involved steroids and I have seen patients who are given steroids for a variety of ailments, not just cancer, and they develop Type II Diabetes as well. So there may be some truth to what you are saying." Nielsen responded.

Dr. Nielsen prescribed me a low dose of medication and once again sent me to the Education Department to discuss my Diabetes. The Nutritionist provided me with a blood testing kit, and showed me how to check my blood sugar. I did my research about Diabetes, and I noted that unexplained skin rashes were oftentimes the first signs of diabetes, and I had experienced several unexplained rashes prior to my diagnosis, so it was all making sense.

By late 2012, I had not seen or heard from Junior in about 9 years, so I decided to look him up on Facebook. I figured as a teenager he would definitely have a page, and indeed he did. When I found his page I in-boxed him.

"Hi Edris, I am trying to contact my nephew (DOB January 29th named after my younger brother Edris Pugh; and his mother's name is Shelly). I have not seen my nephew since he was about 6. If you are my nephew, whom we called Junior, please let me know. Thanks

"Yea this is me. Hi aunt Tia, I haven't heard from you in a while. Call my mom when you get a chance. Please call my mom; she will be excited to hear from you. I'll send you her number."

I was happy to have found Junior thanks to Facebook. He was 15, and attending a private school in West Los Angeles. I called Shelly, and we talked for a bit, after which time we met. Shelly was still living in the duplex over Frank; Frank's mother and father had since passed away; Shelly was still running her childcare business, and Shelly and Frank were enemies. Obviously her plan to seduce, and marry Frank, in order to secure her future did not work. Shelly had been living over Frank for 18 years, and he desperately wanted her to move out so that he could increase the rent. Shelly had fought Frank over the years, whenever he threatened to go up on her rent. She would in turn threaten to report him for violating some rent control measure. PJ, the girls and I were all happy to see Junior, and it was haunting to see just how much he looked like my brother. I thought Shelly had done a great job of raising Junior by herself as he was a classically trained pianist, an exceptional football player, and was very smart academically. As a single parent working from home, Shelly chose to home school Junior until he was 15. Junior was mysteriously quiet and withdrawn but regardless of his weird personality I was happy we reconnected with him.

CHAPTER 18

"I'm Done KMA 367"

By January 2013, I was still off work and preparing for my final surgery. On one morning a few weeks before my scheduled surgery I woke up with a small bump on my left forearm. That area on my arm later turned red, and was warm to the touch. Right away, I thought I might have another darn staph infection. I marked the area around the redness, with a black marker and eventually the redness extended beyond the markings. I went to Urgent Care at Facey and was given some antibiotics. A few weeks later, after that infection was remedied a similar bump and redness appeared on my right rear shoulder and it was so painful that I returned to Urgent Care where the doctor lanced it and tested the fluid for staph. The results revealed that I had MRSA (Methicillin Resistant Staphylococcus Aureus). In discussing my staph history with the Urgent Care doctor he believed that all of the infections I had from the time I was at Southwest Division were MRSA infections. Once again I contacted Attorney Snitzer and filed, and won my final claim against the City of LA for MRSA.

In June of 2013, Junior graduated from high school with high marks on his SAT. He wanted to play football in college, but his size prohibited him from getting many offers from most Division I and Division II Universities, so Shelly had him enroll in Santa Monica City College where he could play, and hopefully, later get a scholarship to play at UCLA. It was widely known that Santa Monica City College was a feeder school for UCLA. Summer had just ended when I received a call from Shelly.

"Hi Tia, I need your help." Shelly sounded bewildered.

"What's going on?"

"The State just shut me down." Shelly started crying uncontrollably.

"They shut your daycare business down? Why?"

"Well… well…a baby died in my care yesterday. I went out to run some errands and I left a lady working here by herself. She was not certified to be alone with an infant, so I'm under investigation now because of that. The problem is that I have no income if my business is shut down, so Frank said I *have* to move by September, which is next week since I can't pay my rent. I have no savings so I'm going to stay with my brother in Anaheim, but I have no way to get Junior to school in Santa Monica, with me living that far out."

My heart went out to Shelly and Junior, as this was devastating news. They had been in a stable environment for 19 years, and now they were being uprooted because of an unfortunate incident. Literally their lives changed over night. I quickly briefed PJ about what was going on and we were on the same page with how we could help Junior.

"Don't worry Shelly, we will come and get Junior and take care of him. We will take care of all of his needs, and make sure he finishes college. You just worry about *you* right now." PJ told Shelly.

"Ok. Thank you guys so much. I'm packing his things right now because we have to be out of here in a few days and my brother is coming to move my things into storage."

"Ok, we are on our way to get Junior now."

After all that I had been through with Shelly over the years, I still went to her aid without hesitation. PJ and I were living alone with plenty of room to spare, but we lived quite a ways from Santa Monica College. Brittany on the other hand owned a two-bedroom condominium in Los Angeles and Natalia was living with her. They didn't have room for Junior; however, they agreed to allow him to stay with them during the week so he could commute from there to school. PJ and I picked Junior up on Fridays and he stayed with us on the weekends to give Brittany's couch a break and we would then take him to school on Mondays. That plan worked for about 4 months until Shelly's inappropriate meddling, and misuse of Junior's financial aid funds severely impacted our agreement to help him. It didn't help matters that Junior was depressed and withdrawn being away from his mother so, Shelly decided to have Junior live with *his* best friend's family, in their old neighborhood. After relocating, we rarely heard from Shelly or Junior again.

Living with all of the residual effects of cancer treatment could have been depressing but I did not let it get the best of me, or take over my life. I had too much to live for. I could not stand the thought of going back to work because I was mentally drained, so on September 30, 2013 I was honorably retired from the Los Angeles Police Department, after 33 years of dedicated service. I planned my Retirement celebration, and was looking forward to my life in the free world. It was Labor Day weekend 2013, and I was thinking about Mama because she died on Labor Day weekend 20 years prior. That year, Natalia went on a weekend trip to San Diego with her college roommate for the holiday weekend, where she met up with another college friend, Michael Edwards, an amazing singer, who went by the name *Mike Eddie*. It had been about 8 years since Natalia and Michael last saw each other in person, but they followed each other on Instagram. When Natalia and her girlfriend arrived in San Diego and met up with Mike, Natalia took one look at him, and told him he was going to be her husband.

"I'm flattered." Mike responded grinning from ear to ear. Mike told Natalia he always liked her when they were in college, but she didn't give him the time of day. When Natalia returned home from her weekend trip she couldn't wait to tell me all about her meet up with Michael.

"Mom, I think I met my husband."

"Girl what are you talking about?"

"I'm going to text you a picture." Within a few seconds I received the photo of Michael. "He's handsome huh mommy?"

"Yes, he's very handsome. What's wrong with him?"

"Mom! Nothing is wrong with him. I told him that Daddy will like him but you will love him.

"Well, I can't wait to meet him."

"He's coming to LA next weekend. So you will meet him then."

Sure enough, that next weekend the whole family was introduced to Mike Eddie when he attended one of our stage plays in Hollywood.

On October 25, 2013, I hosted my retirement gala. It was a red carpet event and celebration for my 55th birthday *and* perfect transition into my civilian life as Chief Financial Officer for Vintage City Entertainment. My family, and over two hundred friends, coworkers, and community members attended the gala, which was a beautiful event sending me off in style.

Life on LAPD Comes To an End

In February of 2014, Michael and Natalia became engaged after dating for a year, and on December 13, 2014, they were married in a beautiful ceremony officiated by Mama's mentor and community icon Reverend Cecil "Chip" Murray.

PJ, Tia, Natalia, Michael, Christine and Rev Cecil "Chip" Murray 12/13/14

In late December of 2014, I received a reminder call about my upcoming mammogram appointment at City of Hope scheduled for December 30th. It had been 4 years since I last saw Dr. Selma, my original doctor at City of Hope because I had been under the care of Dr. Kramer from 2010, following my lymph node removal surgery. It was a beautiful sunny day when I arrived at City of Hope for my mammogram. After my exam that day I was told that my film appeared to be "normal," so I was directed to see Dr. Kramer to complete my visit.

"I see that your test results are *normal* once again. You know we love you, but we are tired of seeing ya! Kramer said playfully. "It's been 8 years now, and we have checked you and re-checked you, and poked and pried, and I do believe that you have been healed from this bout of breast cancer my dear, so I'm officially kicking you out and sending you back into the community."

I didn't quite know what to make of that eviction, but I was happy at what I considered to be good news. I was happy to go back to my routine of annual check ups. I got dressed and after I left the location I later posted a brief message about my healing on Facebook. As soon as I posted, I received a message in my inbox from Dr. Selma, who was my friend on Facebook. Dr. Selma was surprised that I was released from City of Hope so he urged me to make an appointment to see *him*, as he wanted to continue to follow me and monitor my health. It then dawned on me that Dr. Selma was still my primary doctor, and that Dr. Kramer was just releasing me from *her* care, so I called Selma's office as he suggested, and I made an appointment for my 2015 mammogram. In addition to all of my visits at City of Hope, I still had my routine physicals with Dr. Nielsen and it was time for my annual physical that year.

"Mrs. Morris, it's been 8 years since your cancer diagnosis, so there is less than a 5% chance that you will have a recurrence of *that* cancer." Nielsen said proudly.

"Ok, well I will never boast about being *cancer free* doctor, because I have been bitten once already, so what's to say it won't happen again?" I hated sounding pessimistic, but I didn't want to be overly optimistic either.

"I notice that your AC1 blood tests for diabetes have consistently been more towards the normal end of the spectrum than the diabetes end, so keep up the great work. I wish all of my diabetes patients were like you, in controlling their diabetes."

I was starting to feel like a hypochondriac with all of the doctor's visits and medical issues I had inherited over the years following my cancer diagnosis. I was surprised that I had the energy to do anything, but I suppose I had a strong *will*, which kept me forging ahead rather than pitying myself. On December 28, 2015, it was time for my annual mammogram again. It was cold and raining on that winter morning when I walked into City of Hope.

Outside of the main entrance were signs warning patients with influenza, that they would not be allowed to remain in the facility, due to patients with compromised immune systems. I had already had my flu shot and was not ill, so I continued to walk in alongside many who adorned masks covering half their faces. I was a little thrown off as I walked through the reception area when I observed the long line that extended down a long hallway. The more I walked the longer the line became until it ended at some 50 people back. Sadness overtook my spirit, as it became abundantly clear that, although strides were being made to find a cure for cancer, cancer was alive and well, more than ever before. After checking in, I tried to shake the feeling I had as I walked to the 3rd floor for my visit with Dr. Selma. By this time Laura had been long gone from City of hope for a few years. She and her husband returned to the east coast, and started a family, so doctor Selma came into the room alone.

"Good morning Mrs. Morris. How are you feeling? You look amazing." Dr. Selma was smiling from ear to ear. I tried to keep my gown closed but it was a futile effort because I had to disrobe anyway for him to conduct my breast exam.

"Hi doctor. I'm doing well. Thanks for not allowing me to get away. I guess I was thinking Dr. Kramer *replaced* you, so when she said adios, I thought I was kicked out for good." I responded playfully.

"No way. I want to monitor you, especially since you are triple negative, but everything looks fine. You know it's very funny that you mention Dr. Kramer, because just this morning, I received an email from her. She asked about you, and told me to tell you '*Hi*' the next time I see you. I chuckled, and told her, as a matter of fact, you were coming in today."

"Aww how sweet. Maybe I will see her when I go across to the Women's Center for my mammogram." I smiled at the thought of Kramer asking about me. She was my buddy.

I finished my visit with Dr. Selma and walked across the campus to the Women's Center. After finishing my mammogram, the radiologist reviewed my film and determined my images appeared *normal* so I was relieved. I got dressed, and went to the reception area to schedule my next year's mammogram.

"Is Dr. Kramer working today?" I asked the receptionist

"Yes, I believe she might be with a patient, but I will check."

Just as the receptionist got up to peer into Kramer's office, Kramer came out like gang-busters, and rushed towards me with her arms opened wide. We squealed like two teenaged girls, and hugged like two long lost friends.

"I wasn't supposed to be here today but I needed to come in just to see a couple of patients." Kramer said with a big Kool-Aid grin on her face.

"Of course you came in, because that's the kind of awesome doctor you are. Happy New Year, doctor." I said as I walked away.

"Happy New Year." Kramer said as she walked backwards, back into her office blowing kisses at me.

Only God knows what is in store for me, but I can say for certain I am a survivor in so many ways. I now live with MRSA, and I'm told I have diabetes. I have more energy than I did at 30; I eat and drink what I want in moderation; and I run at least three miles a day with Miss Harlee, panting by my side. My life was forever changed by my cancer diagnosis, but my life was also enriched by the experience. I am not invincible, but neither am I weakened. I am not fearful but rather fearless. It has been a long daunting journey of struggle and survival in every aspect of my life, but God spared me for a reason.

Mama's Curse embodied so many societal woes. It contained single-motherhood, familial dysfunction, domestic violence, drug and alcohol abuse, and the seemingly ominous breast cancer. My brothers were unfortunate victims of the curse; Stefon, a genius, failed to successfully cope with Mama's realistic but, ultimately, lofty expectations of him becoming a doctor. Instead, the monster of drug addiction, and all of the residue from that lifestyle devoured him. Edris too, fell short of escaping the generational trap of the visions of seeing his mother attacked and nearly killed by one of her husbands; by drowning his sorrows in alcohol, and resorting to using his wife and girlfriends as punching bags; and he abandoned his children in his wake. My poor brothers destroyed themselves. *But what about me?* I thought. Did I become another casualty of a demented inheritance? Did I become one of the negative statistics scribbled in the margins of Black and Latino history books? Did I succumb to the trials and tribulations of an oversold cliché of a welfare generation?

The short answer: I don't think so. I was definitely affected by Mama's curse, there's no doubt about that. I suffered by first watching Mama slowly disappear before my eyes; I saw her whittle away, eaten up by a disease that feeds on the warmth, tenderness, and nurturing spirit of a mother's love. Then, I witnessed the destruction of my brothers. The men I loved, who could've become kings, were reduced to adult wards of the state. I suffered through the infamous racism, sexism, and other sadistic forms of jealousies on the LAPD; I suffered through my own battle with breast cancer, which replayed in my mind like an eerie brand of deja vu. I suffered, and yet, I survived. I overcame the hardships passed down from a strong and beautiful mother, who did the best she could with what she had. It has always been my belief that God saves the toughest battles for His strongest warriors, and that the night is darkest just before the dawn. So, I took what I saw and experienced, and rose above it. I learned to be diligent about life. I take nothing for granted, and I pray for consistent and continued strength and favor. I scheduled annual cancer screenings, outworked my peers on the job, and I loved and fought for my family hard. I survived; and I am so thankful to God that I did, because He showed me, as only He can, that Mama's Curse was actually a blessing. KMA-367

Acknowledgements

GOD PLACED WONDERFUL PEOPLE IN my life for a reason. **Wanda Noah-Wimbley** I thank God for bringing us back together, and I look forward to our continued sisterhood and travels, as we continue to check things and places off of our bucket list. You are truly my sister and I love you. **Shirlye Brox**, whew…we been through it, but God saw fit to bring your beautiful spirit back into my life, and at just the right time. I love you with all my heart and soul. You mean the world to me. **Valerie Howard** thanks for loving me. You will always be my little sister and I love you much. To my God daughters **Azur De** and **Courtney Brox**, my Godson **Victor Taylor,** and my nieces **Miya Blue, Camille Brox, Calynne Brox, Stacie Carrier, Katherine and Alisha** I love you more than you will ever know. Stay true to yourselves; know your family history and don't be afraid to share your story, you just might help someone else. **Glen Younger**, my brother, and **Antoinette Younger,** my sister, I love you guys so much. Thanks for your many years of love and friendship, and for introducing us to Cabo San Lucas! Two for one all day baby!!! To all of my Sisters-In-Law Enforcement **Evangelyn Nathan**, **Alasea Jackson, Chris Waters, Rachel Agnew, Carol Mitchell, Stephany Powell, Stephanie Sims-Banks, and Brenda Hayes**, I can't thank you ladies enough for always being there for me, and for persevering against all odds. We stayed the course, and made it through some tough times on the job that God chose for us. I thank you for your love. I love you and will truly cherish our friendship and sisterhood for as long as I live. **Cheryl Nalls** thanks for having my back *a few* times during our time together on the force. I am so grateful for you and **Tracey**

Benjamin for being shining examples of true cancer warriors. Your beauty and grace gave me hope, and helped me fight this disease.

Cheryl, Tia and Tracey; Survivors

DEDE "PRICELESS" PRICE THANK YOU for always being there for me. You have been very supportive, and a beautiful spirit. I love you more than you know. You will always be my *cutie patootie.* **Donald Welch** thanks for opening your arms, and accepting me as your sister and "us" as your family. You have inspired me, and I look forward to seeing what God has in store for our next ventures. **Malika Blessing,** you have been a blessing to me as my bonus daughter. Thanks for loving me. Lastly, I want to thank my Aunt **Linda Jackson** for embracing Mama as your big sister, confidant and prayer partner. She loved you so very much, that it was fitting for you to be there when she took her last breath. I love you. **Special Thanks** to my fur baby **Harlee** for enriching my life with unconditional love. Even though PJ is your master, I'm always going to be Mama.

On May 23rd, 2016, my dear friend Josie Mapson died following a long uphill battle with Cancer. She fought a brave fight. I'm going to miss you sister.

RIP Josephine Mapson May 23, 2016

On June 11, 2016, my dear friend Kim Jones-Harris died following a long brave battle with Cancer. She fought a brave fight and wanted nothing more than to see her babies grow up. They are in good hands with your beautiful family, so I hope you are resting in heaven my sister with that beautiful smile of yours.

RIP Kim Jones-Harris June 11, 2016

Special Acknowledgement

PJ THANK YOU FOR YOUR consistent encouragement, and support in telling our story. Thank you for allowing me to share *our* life with the world. I thank God for you each and every day. You are my rock and my protector, my father, my healer and the best "hood doctor." You are an amazing partner, and my handsome hero. I know for certain that you love me because you say it, but most importantly you have shown it consistently for over 30 years. Trust me, I take nothing for granted. Thank you for loving me, always and forever, and thank you for believing in me and always inspiring me to press forward in every aspect of my life. With you, and God, I can do anything. I love you.

Brittany Alese Morris you are my angel here on earth. I thank you for your love and adoration. You are intelligent, and driven like no other. Your unconditional love is the wind beneath my wings, so because of you I soar. Living with you in my life is easy, but most importantly you give me a reason to thrive. If we reach for the moon and miss we will still be amongst the stars! I am forever indebted to you for your expert advice and your patience with me. You truly know how much it meant to me to get this story told, and you made me feel secure throughout the process. I love you more than life itself.

Natalia Edwards your talent amazes me and your storytelling is brilliant. You are and will forever be that beautiful baby girl lying on my chest, like my external heartbeat. Thank you for creating Vintage City Entertainment for it has allowed me to utilize my creativity, and allowed me to escape to a happy place in this world right beside you. Thank you for all of the challenges you presented us while growing up, because you made *me* a better parent and person. Continue to embrace your independence. The sky is the limit for you doll, and I'm going with you all the way up. I love you more than life itself.

Michael Edwards welcome to the family, and thanks for loving and caring for my baby. Your voice is angelic and your talent is boundless. I can't wait to see how God uses you and your amazing gift. I love you son.

Wilkerson Johnson Jr. I can't thank you enough for sharing some amazing family history with me. This is OUR story cousin. I love you to the moon and back.

I dedicate this book to PJ, Brittany, Natalia, my brothers S.P. Pugh and E.E. Pugh, and my Mama, Carmen Rose May Pugh Vaughn Ely Speights.

PJ and Tia 2014 (Photo Courtesy of Ron T Young Photography)

About the Author

TM MORRIS IS A BREAST cancer survivor who was diagnosed with an aggressive form of the disease in 2006 long after her mother passed away from metastatic breast cancer. TM was inspired to write this personal memoir while undergoing treatment and contemplating her family history. She also has served as a police officer, detective, sergeant, lieutenant, and captain for the Los Angeles Police Department. She was state advocate for victims of domestic violence, and was the first African American woman to serve as lieutenant in the LAPD's Robbery Homicide Division. After retiring in 2013, TM joined the family business—Vintage City Entertainment—founded by her youngest daughter. TM lives in Quartz Hill, California, with her husband.

CPSIA information can be obtained
at www.ICGtesting.com
Printed in the USA
FSOW02n0528241217
42691FS